Examining the Relationship Between Economics and Philosophy

Ilkben Akansel
University of Bartin, Turkey

A volume in the Advances in Finance, Accounting, and Economics (AFAE) Book Series

IGI Global
DISSEMINATOR OF KNOWLEDGE

Published in the United States of America by
IGI Global
Business Science Reference (an imprint of IGI Global)
701 E. Chocolate Avenue
Hershey PA, USA 17033
Tel: 717-533-8845
Fax: 717-533-8661
E-mail: cust@igi-global.com
Web site: http://www.igi-global.com

Library of Congress Cataloging-in-Publication Data

Names: Akansel, Ilkben, 1978- editor.
Title: Examining the relationship between economics and philosophy / Ilkben Akansel.
Description: Hershey, PA : Business Science Reference, [2020] | Includes bibliographical references and index. | Summary: "This book examines the relationship between philosophy and economics"-- Provided by publisher.
Identifiers: LCCN 2019023694 (print) | LCCN 2019023695 (ebook) | ISBN 9781799810377 (hardcover) | ISBN 9781799810384 (paperback) | ISBN 9781799810391 (ebook)
Subjects: LCSH: Economics--Moral and ethical aspects. | Philosophy--Economic aspects.
Classification: LCC HB72 .E89 2020 (print) | LCC HB72 (ebook) | DDC 330.01--dc23
LC record available at https://lccn.loc.gov/2019023694
LC ebook record available at https://lccn.loc.gov/2019023695

This book is published in the IGI Global book series Advances in Finance, Accounting, and Economics (AFAE) (ISSN: 2327-5677; eISSN: 2327-5685)

British Cataloguing in Publication Data
A Cataloguing in Publication record for this book is available from the British Library.

Advances in Finance, Accounting, and Economics (AFAE) Book Series

ISSN:2327-5677
EISSN:2327-5685

Editor-in-Chief: Ahmed Driouchi, Al Akhawayn University, Morocco

MISSION

In our changing economic and business environment, it is important to consider the financial changes occurring internationally as well as within individual organizations and business environments. Understanding these changes as well as the factors that influence them is crucial in preparing for our financial future and ensuring economic sustainability and growth.

The **Advances in Finance, Accounting, and Economics (AFAE)** book series aims to publish comprehensive and informative titles in all areas of economics and economic theory, finance, and accounting to assist in advancing the available knowledge and providing for further research development in these dynamic fields.

COVERAGE

- E-Accounting
- Microeconomics
- Applied Accounting
- Economic Policy
- Wages and Employment
- Internet Banking
- Interest Rates and Annuities
- Economics Geography
- Finance
- Economics of Natural and Environmental Resources

IGI Global is currently accepting manuscripts for publication within this series. To submit a proposal for a volume in this series, please contact our Acquisition Editors at Acquisitions@igi-global.com or visit: http://www.igi-global.com/publish/.

The Advances in Finance, Accounting, and Economics (AFAE) Book Series (ISSN 2327-5677) is published by IGI Global, 701 E. Chocolate Avenue, Hershey, PA 17033-1240, USA, www.igi-global.com. This series is composed of titles available for purchase individually; each title is edited to be contextually exclusive from any other title within the series. For pricing and ordering information please visit http://www.igi-global.com/book-series/advances-finance-accounting-economics/73685. Postmaster: Send all address changes to above address.

Titles in this Series

For a list of additional titles in this series, please visit:
https://www.igi-global.com/book-series/advances-finance-accounting-economics/73685

Migration and Urbanization Local Solutions for Global Economic Challenges
Denis Ushakov (Suan Sunandha Rajabhat University, Thailand)
Business Science Reference • ©2020 • 365pp • H/C (ISBN: 9781799801115) • US $245.00

Financial Technology and Disruptive Innovation in ASEAN
Muhammad Anshari (Universiti Brunei Darussalam, Brunei) Mohammad Nabil Almunawar (Universiti Brunei Darussalam, Brunei) and Masairol Masri (Universiti Brunei Darussalam, Brunei)
Business Science Reference • ©2020 • 331pp • H/C (ISBN: 9781522591832) • US $195.00

International Trade Policies in the Era of Globalization
Ahu Coşkun Özer (Marmara University, Turkey)
Business Science Reference • ©2020 • 363pp • H/C (ISBN: 9781522595663) • US $205.00

Management Accounting Standards for Sustainable Business Practices
Ionica Oncioiu (Titu Maiorescu University, Romania) Gary Cokins (Analytics-Based Performance Management LLC, USA) Sorinel Căpuşneanu (Titu Maiorescu University, Romania) and Dan Ioan Topor (1 Decembrie 1918 University, Romania)
Business Science Reference • ©2020 • 360pp • H/C (ISBN: 9781799801788) • US $215.00

Handbook of Research on Economic and Political Implications of Green Trading and Energy Use
Ramesh Chandra Das (Vidyasagar University, India)
Business Science Reference • ©2019 • 421pp • H/C (ISBN: 9781522585473) • US $225.00

Emerging Research on Monetary Policy, Banking, and Financial Markets
Cristi Spulbar (University of Craiova, Romania) and Ramona Birau (Constantin Brâncuşi University of Targu Jiu, Romania)
Business Science Reference • ©2019 • 322pp • H/C (ISBN: 9781522592693) • US $195.00

For an entire list of titles in this series, please visit:
https://www.igi-global.com/book-series/advances-finance-accounting-economics/73685

IGI Global
DISSEMINATOR OF KNOWLEDGE

701 East Chocolate Avenue, Hershey, PA 17033, USA
Tel: 717-533-8845 x100 • Fax: 717-533-8661
E-Mail: cust@igi-global.com • www.igi-global.com

Editorial Advisory Board

List of Reviewers

Itir Ozer-Imer, *Hacettepe University, Turkey*
Orhan Simsek, *Artvin Coruh University, Turkey*
Pinar Yardimci, *Selcuk University, Turkey*
Emek Yildirim-Sahin, *Artvin Coruh University, Turkey*
Gloria Zúñiga y Postigo, *Ashford University, USA*

Table of Contents

Preface xv

Chapter 1
The Relationship Between Old Institutional Economics (OIE) and Feminist Economics: An Essay on Veblen and Feminist Economics 1
Ilkben Akansel, University of Bartin, Turkey

Chapter 2
The Significance of Public Goods in Market Failure Debates: The Role of Public Goods on Market Failure From the Perspective of Schools of Economic Thought 27
Kubra Onder, Burdur Mehmet Akif Ersoy University, Turkey
Muhammet Sahin, Gumushane University, Turkey

Chapter 3
Neoliberalism, Self-Identity, and Consumer Culture in the UAE 48
Başak Özoral, Istanbul Commerce University, Turkey
İlke Civelekoğlu, Istanbul Commerce University, Turkey

Chapter 4
Critical Theory: The Human Being Takes the Stage Again 66
Derya Guler Aydin, Hacettepe University, Turkey
Itir Ozer-Imer, Hacettepe University, Turkey

Chapter 5
Complexity Economics and Innovation Systems: Mersin Regional Innovation Strategy (RIS) Plus Project From Perspective of Complexity Science 84
Pınar Yardımcı, Selcuk University, Turkey

Chapter 6
Irregular Migration and Economic Nationalism in EU 127
Tugba Aydin Halisoglu, Artvin Coruh University, Turkey

Chapter 7
Positive Economics From the Perspective of Kant's Thought 146
Ertuğrul İbrahim Kızılkaya, Istanbul University, Turkey

Chapter 8
An Analysis on Turkey's Urbanization Process in the Context of Urban Development Paradigms 161
Aygül Kılınç, Gaziantep University, Turkey

Chapter 9
A Challenge to Homo Economicus: Behavioral Economics 182
Hatice Isıl Alkan, Ondokuz Mayıs University, Turkey

Chapter 10
The Narh Prices of Various Comestibles in the First Half of the 19th Century..202
Ramazan Arslan, Bartın University, Turkey

Chapter 11
What Economics Can Learn From Ontology: Toward an Interdisciplinary Reconciliation 218
Gloria Zúñiga y Postigo, Ashford University, USA

Chapter 12
Challenges of Developing Countries in Imitating Technological Progress 240
Ikbal Maulana, Indonesian Institute of Sciences (LIPI), Indonesia

Compilation of References 266

Related References 301

About the Contributors 332

Index 336

Detailed Table of Contents

Preface xv

Chapter 1
The Relationship Between Old Institutional Economics (OIE) and Feminist Economics: An Essay on Veblen and Feminist Economics 1
Ilkben Akansel, University of Bartin, Turkey

Economics and philosophy has a deep connection. It sometimes intertwined with each other whether economics needs philosophy or not. Philosophy of economics is a neccessity in order to understand the circumstances behind the economics events. Comprehension of such a neccessity can be complicated on certain occasions because of neoclassical economics thought. Neoclassical economics is also described as mainstream economics. This has long been a debate that critisizes mainstream economics. All followers critisizing mainstream economics are characterized as heterodox economics. Two of the fundemantal heterodox economics concepts are institutional economics and feminist economics. This study will therefore scrutinize mainstream economics in terms of the idea of old institutional economics and feminist economics.

Chapter 2
The Significance of Public Goods in Market Failure Debates: The Role of Public Goods on Market Failure From the Perspective of Schools of Economic Thought 27
Kubra Onder, Burdur Mehmet Akif Ersoy University, Turkey
Muhammet Sahin, Gumushane University, Turkey

Before the emergence of the neoclassical economic approach, the idea that market instabilities are temporary and markets are spontaneously able to reach equilibrium was prevalent. However, with the neoclassical economic thought the idea that market economy alone is far from attaining equilibrium and there is a need for public economy. This is also known as market failure theory. There are many reasons of market failure. One of them is public goods. Public goods are generally regarded as an example of market failure and seen as a problem requiring government intervention. However, when main stream public goods theories are analyzed in-depth, it is seen that there is no agreement on the properties of public goods which may create a reason to the government presentation and public presentation is not approved in general. Therefore, the aim of this study is to make a comparative analysis of the approaches of different economics schools of thought which have contributions to the subject of public goods.

Chapter 3
Neoliberalism, Self-Identity, and Consumer Culture in the UAE........................48
Başak Özoral, Istanbul Commerce University, Turkey
İlke Civelekoğlu, Istanbul Commerce University, Turkey

Over the last half-century, modern societies have been experiencing a drastic social, cultural, and economic transformation. The change in the behaviors and habits of consumers under the strong impact of neoliberalism demonstrates the close relationship between economy and social psychology. Globalized neo-liberalization has become an unavoidable, powerful force that impacts all elements of social, cultural, and economic life and defines people's identities and their consumption preferences. This chapter addresses the link between neoliberalism and consumer behavior, with a focus on non-Western societies. It examines if there is a contradiction between the features of consumer culture and the prevailing domestic culture in these societies. Many scholars associate consumer culture with Western societies, but the authors argue that consumer culture has become a significant phenomenon even in the most religiously conservative, non-Western societies. By taking Dubai in the UAE as the case study, this chapter demonstrates how consumer culture helps redefine culture and self-identity. The chapter concludes by arguing that since individual behavior is not rational, individuals' needs are defined by the dictates of consumer culture across the globe in neoliberal times.

Chapter 4
Critical Theory: The Human Being Takes the Stage Again 66
Derya Guler Aydin, Hacettepe University, Turkey
Itir Ozer-Imer, Hacettepe University, Turkey

Based on the historical developments in the philosophy of science, it can be claimed that the method of social sciences is mainly dominated by the method of the natural sciences. Social sciences, especially, economics have been affected by the method of physics. From a critical viewpoint, this study aims to scrutinize the method of social sciences by taking into account the concept of devaluation of human beings. The study puts forward that mainstream economics devalue human being at the level of its methodology by excluding the real creator of value from the analyses and by disregarding social and historical factors. The study demonstrates that by taking into consideration the neglected cultural, political and historical factors in addition to the economic ones, the critical theory includes human being and his/her values in the analyses, and hence, it unifies scientific knowledge with human behavior, which is the intentional behavior behind all economic decisions.

Chapter 5
Complexity Economics and Innovation Systems: Mersin Regional Innovation Strategy (RIS) Plus Project From Perspective of Complexity Science................84
Pınar Yardımcı, Selcuk University, Turkey

Knowledge determines the relationship between regional development and innovation in a knowledge-based economy. The Mersin Regional Innovation Strategy (RIS) Plus Project is based on the European Union's new regional innovation strategy referred to as 'smart specialization' that is related with industrialization and economic development. This approach is an indicator of the change and transformation in the regional development paradigm in terms of knowledge generation and innovation processes. These developments also reflect the impact of complexity in the philosophy and understanding of the 21st century. Complexity Science and Complexity Economics have increasingly become determinants in the formation of institutional structures and policies within the global economic system. This chapter aims to evaluate the basic characteristics of Mersin RIS Plus Project within the framework of complexity science. This study discusses the development potentials of Mersin and TR62 regions in accordance with the scientific and theoretical basis of the project, and policy proposals are suggested.

Chapter 6
Irregular Migration and Economic Nationalism in EU 127
Tugba Aydin Halisoglu, Artvin Coruh University, Turkey

Nationalism is one of the controversial issues in political science studies. Nationalism includes rational approaches as well as emotional ones, both strong support and intense criticism. This chapter will apply the primordial approach of nationalism, considering its roots from before the French Revolution and as a result of human psychology. So, the sense of belonging, is the main argument of the primordial approach in nationalism studies, will be examined with its effect on the migration economy. The main focus of the chapter will be the European Union facing huge refugee flows from Syria, the economic impact of refugees by the effect of migration, and citizen reaction to immigrants and the economy.

Chapter 7
Positive Economics From the Perspective of Kant's Thought............................146
Ertuğrul İbrahim Kızılkaya, Istanbul University, Turkey

Departing from Kant's thought, we could argue that the portrait of homo economicus drawn by positive economics corresponds to a homo phainomenon as a heteronomous person of concrete economic reality. In addition, we could try to show that economics could not get rid of naturalism, materialism, and fatalism, justifying Kant's concerns. We could also emphasize that, while in the beginning the aim of being a positive science to be able to produce synthetic a posteriori propositions, positive economics tried to continue its way by the method of synthetic a priori. Finally, we must also point out the possibility for an autonomous or free homo noumenon to establish an original ethos by setting goals for itself.

Chapter 8
An Analysis on Turkey's Urbanization Process in the Context of Urban Development Paradigms 161
Aygül Kılınç, Gaziantep University, Turkey

The ideological, economic, and technological phenomena experienced in the history of the world have surprisingly affected the social order. These phenomena have transformed the social order and have been effective in their reshaping. Since the first quarter of the 20th century, this has led to the emergence of three new paradigms of urban development. The first paradigm includes the period from the Second World War to the end of the 1970s, and this paradigm is defined as the state-based urban development period. The period from the 1980s to the mid-1990s was named as the market-centered urban development period. Last, the period that continued since the mid-1990s was named as the governance period, or the third way.

Chapter 9
A Challenge to Homo Economicus: Behavioral Economics 182
Hatice Isıl Alkan, Ondokuz Mayıs University, Turkey

Neoclassical economics is the mainstream economic paradigm of the present era and has certain assumptions such as rationality, perfect knowledge and unique equilibrium. In this regard, homo economicus, namely rational economic man is the main agent of mainstream economics. However, this main agent has aspects that are inconsistent with reality. In other words, decision units are likely to be irrational in the real word because individuals are emotional and social beings. Considering that this conception of rationality contradicts with the instability of economies and crises that have happened, it seems that the dominant economic view cannot exactly explain current events. This chapter questions the concept of homo economicus, the compatibility of homo economicus with homo sapiens and attempts to reveal the shortcomings of the dominant view. It substantially tries to explore why behavioral economics is necessary and how behavioral economics can make up for the shortcomings of the mainstream economic paradigm by the help of its branches; experimental economics and neuroeconomics.

Chapter 10
The Narh Prices of Various Comestibles in the First Half of the 19th Century...202
Ramazan Arslan, Bartın University, Turkey

Since the food prices are the essential needs of people, they have usually been a topical issue in every period. Therefore, this issue mobilized the administrators of aforementioned period, and necessitated to take measures on this issue. Perhaps one of the most significant measures were the narh (price fixing) system. In this study, narh prices of various comestibles have been approached according to dated 1241-1826 and numbered 09264 in the book of senior accountant (Başmuhasebe Kalemi Defteri). The purpose of study is to prove the given importance of the stability of food prices by Ottoman administration comparatively and to contribute to the studies that have been conducted or will be conducted. The documents in the Ottoman Archives of Turkish Presidency (COA in Turkish) have been used as a study method and other works have been used as well in terms of integrity of the topic. As a result of the study, it is found that Ottoman Empire prioritized the price stability in the comestibles, especially to the benefit of her people.

Chapter 11
What Economics Can Learn From Ontology: Toward an Interdisciplinary Reconciliation...218
Gloria Zúñiga y Postigo, Ashford University, USA

This chapter will present the argument that the tools of ontology offer a means for teaching the philosophical foundations of economic value and for engaging interdisciplinarily the examinations of economics. Ontology is the branch of philosophy that is concerned with the description of existing domains in the world, the objects in such domains, and their relations. It does not attempt to explain or interpret, only to describe, and it is in this sense that ontology is reconcilable with the scientific methods of economics. Additionally, it is capable of describing the complex structures, relations, and emergence of economic objects in human economic activity. This chapter will address three insights from ontology that shed light on the implications of the notion of subjectivity in the theory of subjective economic value, the differences between economic value and other kinds of value, and the role that subjectivity and economic value have in the emergence of the social object we know as money.

Chapter 12
Challenges of Developing Countries in Imitating Technological Progress 240
Ikbal Maulana, Indonesian Institute of Sciences (LIPI), Indonesia

Technological progress has become an important characteristics of economic progress. The most economically developed nations are also the most technologically advanced ones, that is, the ones that not only make a proper and innovative utilization of technology, but also develop it on their own. Newly developed countries, such as South Korea and China, have economically surpassed many Western countries, because they can catch up and surpass the technological capability of the latter. However, the technological progress of one country cannot be just imitated by another. Technological development is much more than just allocating a large budget for research and development. It involves and transform a heterogeneous network of actors, and hence requires a complex set of institutions and governance that enable the network to upgrade their collective capabilities.

Compilation of References 266

Related References 301

About the Contributors 332

Index 336

Preface

Economics is one of the most intricate sciences as it merges several disciplines in the same pot. It is infamous that economics is fundamentally divided into two parts: Microeconomics and macroeconomics. Microeconomics mostly considers individuals and firms. Concerns like rational decision, supply and demand efficiency, etc., are the main themes of microanalyses. On the other hand, macroeconomics mostly concerned with geographical region. This region may include a country or sometimes it can cover a continent. In any case, the main concerns of macroeconomics are foreign trade, governmental fiscal and monetary policy, unemployment rates, the level of inflation, etc. Briefly, the total amount of largescale indicators is inclusive of macroeconomics.

Economics is a science of human actions given the economics is generally divided into two main bodies as mentioned. Those human actions are related with decisions, supply-demand, GDP, inflation, which are directly related to economics. However, being a creation of intelligence of human mind, the frame of mind is philosophy. Especially, after the revolution of marginalism, many economists relinquished the bound between philosophy and economics, because they think that solely mathematics suffices to solve the economic problems. However, one major situation is ignored: economics is the action, so it has a philosophy by thought per se apparently. That is why; all economic actions are the reflection of humans' decisions and behaviors. In that way, it is truly said:

Economics needs philosophy very desperately to learn how to analyze and explain paradoxical realities. A paradox defies intuition: it is the opposite of what seems to be the truth.

Here are some of the paradoxes:

1. The perfect money is the perfect fit with no intrinsic value, and indeed no physical existence at all. A money that is not even printed on a piece of paper nonetheless is a perfect payment for any real good.

2. Natural resource has a negative correlation with growth of income, as nations with abundant natural resources (like Congo) grow more slowly than nations with little natural resource (like Singapore or Taiwan). (Quora, n.d.).

In that case, for instance money, which is very important for both microeconomics and macroeconomics, is actually a piece of paper. Nevertheless, the role of money in economics policy is greater than its physical existence. All individual's/firm's decisions are determined by their budget based on their accounts. Monetary policy, which has a critical power for a country's inflation rates, unemployment, growth etc., is directly affected by the amount of money. Ironically, a piece of paper that has no power for any real good. It has however a great power to determine all economic actions.

Another example is natural resources. It is so peculiar that geographically located, almost all developed countries have fewer natural resources. Normally, the expectation is, they would have gained less economic power given the lack of natural resources. Albeit, in reality they are wealthy. That is why; they have found a way to exploit all natural resources and turning them to useful products. They have an ability to sell all of the products in which case they grow faster than the other nations who have abundant natural resources.

At that point, one can ask how economics are related to philosophy. It is rather a good question. Because two different disciplines, that seem highly unrelated, have many common points. First, economics is a part of human social organization. Philosophy suggests bringing balance to competing principles. More specifically, philosophy starts with a number of questions: What is truth; How do I know; Should I believe; etc.?

From a broader sense, philosophy is the way to know better and to get more out of it. Explicitly, "philosophy is a well-coordinated and systematized attempt at evaluating life and the universe as a whole, with reference to the first principles that underlie all things as their causes and are implicit in all experience… Philosophy investigates the very possibility and conditions of knowledge, its extent, nature and value" (Swami Krishnananda, n.d.).

The method of science or the method of economics are the most complex part of the relationship between economics and philosophy. The truth is, this complexity lies down under realizing the system of economics. Economics is rather close to natural sciences and rather close to philosophy. This circumstance is caused by the procedure of implementation of economics. Some scientists do agree with the opinion to prove their assumptions on paper. When assumptions are proved mathematically, they think that the economics proceeds. However, in reality it does not work like that. For example, a very conflicting assumption is rationality. Presumably, rational decision works, but the economics accepts this notion as stationary, so a new notion have been found: "bounded rationality." Some others have highly deep relationship between its philosophical modes.

Of course, all these systems have a mentality at the background: "Some economists insist that economic theory is purely descriptive or 'positive': its purpose is to predict human behavior, and nothing more. On this view, rational-choice theory describes certain regularities in human behavior. If the theory works - that is, if it generates predictions that are generally in accord with our observations - then this provides us with all the justification we need for accepting its assumptions as working hypotheses. Conversely, if the theory's predictions fail to accord with our observations, then we must look for a better theory. We may be entitled to be more skeptical of animal spirits than of well-behaved preference orderings, but only on grounds of parsimony, or because (and if) we have more experience of successfully predicting human behavior in terms of preference orderings" (Sugden, 1991, p. 751).

In this path, one of the most important relationship between economics and philosophy is the methodology.

The issues with which the philosophy of science has been concerned that are most relevant to economics can be divided into five groups:

1. Goals What are the goals of science and scientific theorizing? Is science primarily a practical activity that aims to discover useful generalizations or should science seek explanations and truth?
2. Explanation What is science explanation?
3. Theories What are theories, models, and laws? How are they related to one another? How are they discovered or constructed?
4. Testing, induction and demarcation How does one test and confirm or disconfirm scientific theories, models and laws? What are the differences between the attitudes and practices of scientists and those of members of other disciplines?
5. Are the answers to these four questions the same for all sciences at all times? Can human actions and institutions be studied in the same way that one studies nature? (Hausman, 2008, p. 5).

The first question rises whether economics must be descriptive or positive. Generally, most of the economists all around the world tend to be positive. They do not use mathematics or econometrics techniques in order to suggest a good theory rather than using these methods to prove their assumptions. Of course, using mathematics as a tool is a good method to prove a theory. Nevertheless, the debate here is whether these methods will solve the actual economics methods or not. At that point, the relationship between economics and philosophy may be an answer. Because, almost all economics historians or economics thought expertise are seen as second-class economists mostly. Here, the economists, who are fond of mathematics or econometrics models, are considered as if the economics historians could see the economics problems incomplete. In reality, history of economics investigations merged with philosophy rather than positive economics. Admittedly, they have a broader sense theorizing economics literature.

Almost all economics theories are related to each other. That is why, when one theory has suggested its ideas, law, discoveries etc., time has changed; new inventions discovered. It means that human's economic actions change. In other words, necessities change, preferences change, the aspect of looking to World changes. It means that philosophy of economics is changed. For example, there had been no social media twenty years ago.

Today, almost all people share their ideas, their lives etc. via social media. By that way, the firms' marketing tactics slides into social media as it has never been before. One other important point is in today's World; all scientists are connected to each other. For social sciences, this embeddedness merges their terms, their approaches more than it used to be. So, does economics. Different kinds of heterodox economics schools such as neuro-economics, behavioral economics etc. used other sciences' terms and theories. Actually, they are trying to find out inclusive economics science in order to reach better solutions to economics theories/issues.

Most philosophers have argued that science proceeds by the discovery of theories and laws, but economists are comfortable talking about models than about laws and theories. (Hausman, 2008, p. 9)

In editor's view, this maybe the most influential conflict of the relationship between economics and philosophy. In economics, laws are sometimes used, for instance law of demand. However, the term "law" here is used for describing an action of piece mechanism, and it is derived from a model. The laws of philosophy have sense and emotion deeper than economics.

Merging economics and philosophy is a very complex process. Briefly, philosophy is to understand the World with querying the circumstances, trying to discover what all events have existed. On the contrary, to this discipline, economics has certain boundaries. Using positive methods rewards the economics more accurate communication skills. However, this method does not allow the economics to completely understand the human's economics actions. Human is a complex creature. Her/his appraisal about all events can change time to time. At the perspective of the editor, whenever economics actions, preferences, habits are changed by the mediation of technology or any other new events, economics feels to discuss the big picture of the society in terms of philosophy. More explicitly, economics needs to have philosophy to see what kind of changes occur in economies. As a very powerful tool of discussing the circumstances, philosophy helps economics to see its deficiencies. Philosophy helps the humankind to see the economics events within a broader sense. Consequently, economics and philosophy are embedded. This embeddedness still needs more investigation.

The aim of this book is to scrutinize the relationship between economics and philosophy. Actually, I dare to prepare such a book, because I have experienced difficulties by not suggesting mathematical methods in my publications. I always try to understand how economics actions can be seen gathering information from other disciplines. Philosophy was one of them. Whenever I have been criticized by "scientists" who are fond of econometrics, they accused these kinds of attempts were unnecessary.

This book is especially dedicated to scholars, colleagues and students who have a curiosity on heterodox approaches. The editor of this book aims to combine different chapters from different disciplines. Because, this situation will comply with the spirit of the book's name. As philosophy examines to get involved in different kinds of sciences, powerful relationships among sciences will be seen. This situation gains more importance when talking about economics. That is why; the most important contributors of economics science are philosophers. Thinking this action suggests importance and the aim of this attempt as entrepreneurship.

This book is also for both economists and philosophers, but not only for them. All social scientists can find a relationship between the chapters and their specialization fields. I hope all readers can find knowledge, intelligence and joy while reading.

ORGANIZATION OF THE BOOK

The book is organized into twelve chapters. A brief description of each of the chapters follows:

Chapter 1 identifies the deep relationship between economics and philosophy by the mediation of two of the most important heterodox schools. Heterodox schools have better relations with philosophy, because they are opponent to mainstream economics' methodology, assumptions etc. One of most eminent schools of heterodox economics – Old Institutional Economics has a very broad sense with feminist economics ideas. For suggesting the idea, the mutual opinions can be scrutinized by both Veblen and feminist economics. The author tries to make a philosophical connection between these two schools.

Chapter 2 establishes the philosophy of market failure. Neoclassical economics presumes that whenever no public goods are served by state, the market will be more balanced. Contrary to this idea, different kinds of schools suggest different opinions than neoclassical school did. The authors scrutinize these differences among the schools of thoughts.

Chapter 3 handles the importance of the institutions. One of the most important institution of capitalism is property rights. Property rights have a great philosophical background. In addition, it is the most prominent notion of New Institutional Economics (NIE). The authors scrutinized the bridge of NIE and political economy.

Chapter 4 reviews the method of social sciences that is almost dominated by the method of the natural sciences. A critical viewpoint is that the method of social sciences is by considering the concept of devaluation of human beings. The most important reason of devaluating human beings is the mainstream economics' disregard of social and historical factors. The authors aim to show how these method neglects cultural, political and historical factors.

Chapter 5 reviews how knowledge determines the relationship between regional development and innovation. The example of this study is the Mersin Regional Innovation Strategy (RIS) Plus Project. RIS has a very strong relationship with EU's new regional programme related to industrialization and economic development. This is a strategy that recognizes the new complexity in the philosophy of the 21st century. This kind of philosophy is predominantly important while complex economics has increasingly been becoming dominant factor.

Chapter 6 presents the philosophy of the nationalism. In 21st century, nationalism is one of the most debatable notions. Because wars, economic crisis all around the World pushed the peoples to pursuit new countries. Of course, the residents of immigrant accepting countries do have opposing ideas, solutions to those immigrants. Naturally, this rising nationalism wind has been a great and deep historical and philosophical mind since the French Revolution until today.

Chapter 7 addresses the *homo economicus* drawn by positive economics. The author examines today's economic view that has still use the naturalism, materialism and fatalism notions. The main concern of this chapter is to emphasize how positive science is able to produce synthetic a posteriori propositions. At the last point of the chapter how an autonomous homo noumenon establishes for an original ethos.

Chapter 8 analyses three new paradigms of urban development. Indeed, economic progress has caused to urban progress. This mutual progress has actually caused by a philosophical change. From the early beginning of the 19th century, urban development was parallel to the development of the economics. Therefore, this chapter recognizes how these three new paradigms have aroused and defined from the end of the Second World War until 1990s. The paradigm that totally changed by philosophy of economics affected the urban development.

Chapter 9 reviews *homo economicus* concept or neoclassical economics. *Homo economicus* is far away from the reality. It is criticized by different school of thoughts and different ways. A rising school, behavioral economics criticizes *homo economicus* notion with a point of view of successive experiments suggesting its homo sapiens way. It is very new and important point of view to scrutinize how an individual cannot be described by *homo economicus*. This chapter tries to understand this evolution.

Chapter 10 discusses narh (price fixing) system. The food prices have always been the essential focus point of economics. Historically scrutinizing this kind of system will shed the light on today's view. This chapter tries to explain how Ottoman Empire could have achieved this implementation.

Chapter 11 presents the connection with ontology and economics objects in human economic activity. Ontology is very important for making a relationship between economics and philosophy. Because, the main concern of ontology is whether existing domains are available or not. So, the chapter discusses three insights: the differences between economic value and the other kinds of value, subjective economic value, and money.

Chapter 12 concludes how technology is important for a country. It is well known that technology is the booster of the developed countries. Of course, technological progress has a philosophical sentiment as well. The indicator of this conclusion is new developed countries have surpassed the Western developed countries. On the contrary, of this situation this chapter reviews that how allocating large budgets to technological development and heterogeneous networks are important for the technological development. In addition, it states the relationship of these factors with governance and institutional process.

Ilkben Akansel
University of Bartin, Turkey

REFERENCES

Hausman, D. M. (2008). Introduction. In D. M. Hausman (Ed.), *The Philosophy of Economics An Anthology*. Cambridge: Cambridge University Press.

Quora. (n.d.). Role of Philosophy. Retrieved from https://www.quora.com/What-is-the-role-of-philosophy-in-economics

Sugden, R. (1991). Rational Choice: A Survey of Contributions from Economics and Philosophy. *Economic Journal (London)*, *101*(407), 751–785. doi:10.2307/2233854

Swami Krishnananda. (n.d.). Philosophy. Retrieved from https://www.swami-krishnananda.org/phil/phil_01.html

Chapter 1
The Relationship Between Old Institutional Economics (OIE) and Feminist Economics:
An Essay on Veblen and Feminist Economics

Ilkben Akansel
https://orcid.org/0000-0001-8167-7416
University of Bartin, Turkey

ABSTRACT

Economics and philosophy has a deep connection. It sometimes intertwined with each other whether economics needs philosophy or not. Philosophy of economics is a neccessity in order to understand the circumstances behind the economics events. Comprehension of such a neccessity can be complicated on certain occasions because of neoclassical economics thought. Neoclassical economics is also described as mainstream economics. This has long been a debate that critisizes mainstream economics. All followers critisizing mainstream economics are characterized as heterodox economics. Two of the fundemantal heterodox economics concepts are institutional economics and feminist economics. This study will therefore scrutinize mainstream economics in terms of the idea of old institutional economics and feminist economics.

DOI: 10.4018/978-1-7998-1037-7.ch001

INTRODUCTION

Economics is actually embedded in philosophy, whereas, the philosophy of economics rather excludes this aspect. Since mathematics, statistics and mostly econometrics were merged into economics, the philosophy of economics lapsed from grace of many academicians. At that point, combined with too much mathematics brought another approach to economics, and neo-classical economics. From the early beginning of the twentieth century till twentyfirst century, economics world met several new economics approaches came to the scene that affected by neoclassical economics. There is curiously not one quite definition of what neoclassical economics is or how to describe it accurately (Bénicourt & Guerrien, 2017); one major definition of neoclassical economics comes from the orthodox or mainstream economics. Today, we define all markets, all working modalities, all economics actions in terms of neclassical economics. It is therefore atrributed to mainstream economics. In any case, this dominant thought brings an opposition with it. It is generally called as heterodox economics. The economics world today have different kinds of heterodox economics views like, behavioral economics, Marxist economics, ecological economics, neuro economics, etc. Most of them are new cogitations, but several of them date back to the late 19th Century and to the early 20th Century like institutional economics or post-1960s feminist economics. Albeit these two economics approaches – institutional and feminist economics – seem to have distinctive features per se, they accomodate deeply several common points as well.

The most prominent common point of institutional economics and feminist economics, aside being a part of heterodox economics, is that they both pose an opposition to neoclasscial econonomics whilst having distinctive aspects that critisizes neoclassical economics.

Institutional economics, which has an outstanding historical background, must be discussed explicitly. Originated from the USA at the early beginning of the 20th Century, institutional economics is accepted as a non-Marxist modality that critisizes mainstream economics. It was introduced by Thorstein Veblen. He was a prominent figure in terms of institutional economics thought. Because if Veblen was to be removed from institutional economics history, institutional economics would not transpire as it is realized today. Thorstein Veblen's opinions will be therefore a preliminary concern of this study.

On the other hand, feminist economics was introduced later, but its effects marked a new epoch in economics. Gender is the main issue in feminist economics. It determines almost every economic action. Mainstream economics has initially a masculine cognition in every economic action. This is a phenomenon that mostly experienced in employment conditions. Naturally, having a job and the type of the job directly affects human's life.

Feminist economics inquires the gender roles and their consequences that occur in economics field. Intriguingly, fed by different vains, both institutional economics and feminist economics has a common point on criticising mainstream economics. Although, at the first glance it may seem as if they have different opinions about women, several common points can however be found about women and economics.

This study will focus on what contemplations can be found generally in institutional economics, exclusively in Thorstein Veblen's thoughts, about women and economics. Similarly, feminist economics will be scrutinized in similar means. This study will start with gender and its definition, later a comparison between Veblen's opinions about the subject and feminist economics. Lastly, the author will assess the topic in light of all figures.

BACKGROUND

Several publications about institutional economics and feminist economics can be found in the literature. There are however a few publications focusing on both topics at the same time. The nature of those schools gets to be ignored every so often. Nevertheless, there would be a precise common point between two schools, women and their institutional feature. Naturally, feminist economics focuses on how women's conditions are affected by economics. There are several notions to describe the circumtances. The very renowned aspects are discrimination and segregation. Then again, institutional economics focuses on how institutions are determined by economics. At this point, defining the ownership of property is very important. Because, even women are seen a part of ownership model. The institutional economics seeks for answers to institutions' evolution and how much effect they have on individual's behavior. So, as a matter of fact, both institutional economic and feminist economic has an inquisitiveness on women's working conditions.

CAN OLD INSTITUTIONAL ECONOMICS (OIE) BE ACKNOWLEDGED AS A PRECURSOR OF FEMINIST ECONOMICS (FE)?

The Connection Between OIE and Feminist Economics (FE)

There is not much philosopher than Thorstein Veblen (1857-1929) whose ideas about women must be analyzed. Thorstein Veblen, who is intriguingly the greatest scientist of institutional economics, deserves to be analyzed in terms of emancipation of women. He was a great philosopher who is not only played a huge role contrubuting the institutional economics, but also he suggested very challenging ideas that are ahead of his time. Thus, there has been an early link with the institutional economics and the feminist economics. Essentially, it is no surprise that there can be link to understand subjugating position of women in terms of economics.

Feminists have had long-standing engagement with institutional theory, querying at times the assumed ahistorical nature of institutions, insisting that "the family" be recognized as a social institution (as opposed to a natural and incontestable one), and challenging assumptions about the "abstract individuals" taken to inhabit institutions. Feminist scholarship, both in international relations and in political theory, has opened up for questioning the meaning and nature of "the state", an assumed institution in mainstream international and comparative politics. Destabilizing "institutions"—querying their "facticity"—is a well established feminist political intervention. (Bacchi & Rönnblom, 2014, p. 171).

Although feminist economics can be dissolved into several entities peculiarly like Marxist, Post-Keynesian, Radical, Liberal, etc. However, the actual connection between the feminist economics and institutional economics can be assembled into institutional feminist economics. As seen in notion it covers both institutional approach and feminist approach for the topic. This study will also be an examination of institutional feminist economics approach.

What's feminist about feminist economics? Does it imply the use of methodological approaches that have been argued to be important for feminist praxis? Does it reflect the concerns and adopt the proposals of feminists writing on economic methodology? Or is it about 'seeing' women instead of assuming economic subjects are neutral and studying topics considered relevant for feminist politics? (Tejani, 2019, p. 101).

Feminist economics is a rethinking of the discipline of economics for the purpose of improving women's economic condition. ... Feminist economics is hardly monolithic. Its practitioners come from multiple 'schools' within economics, mainstream, institutional, and Marxist, to name a few (Strober, 2001, p. 144, 145).

Feminist economics especially focuses on gender. Gender is a very important term for feminist economics given almost every form of feminist economics are fashioned by gender and its roles on division of labor. Feminist economics uses gender to describe how bodily sexual diffference affects working life. Honestly, gender is beyond working life. It is the most central entity of feminist economics.

To refer to the cognitive patterning a culture constructs on the base of actual or perceived differences between males and females. Gender is the metaphorical connection of non-biological phenomena with a bodily experience of biological differentiation. ... The dominant conception of gender is as a hierarchical dualism. ... That is, masculinity and femininity are construed of largely as opposites, with masculinity claiming the high status side of the line. Rough "tomboy" girls are socially acceptable and even praised, but woe to the gentle boy who is labeled a "sissy." A woman may wear pants but a man may not wear a skirt. Seen in this way, sexism is a cultural and even a cognitive habit, not just an isolated personal trait (Nelson, 1996, p. 5, 7).

A society's economic and social actions are determined by these cultural and cognitive habits. For instance, women are employed in 'the woman works' or women cannot go out late at night without surveillance. Women, who are not employed or do not need to work by themselves, has to live along other surveillance methods of the society. They are pushed to be deprived of employement, instead they have rich husbands or other male relatives. Sociologically, women who have to work to afford their lives are seen inferior. Interestingly, this is the mutual presumption both shared by Veblen and FE. Veblen sees this reality by the mediation of the leisure classes' life, whereas FE sees this reality as a conclusion of gender. It is the most intriguing part of these two different schools; Veblen could have seen 'gender' as a conclusion of pecuniary life of people in USA in the 20th century, on the contrary of Veblen, FE could have seen this notion as a conclusion of discriminative applications to women on economics and social life.

Gender is constructed by sociologically. It is a part of economics. According to Oxford Dictionary gender is either of the two sexes (male and female), especially when considered with reference to social and cultural differences rather than biological ones. The term is also used more broadly to denote a range of identities that do not correspond to established ideas of male and female (Hopkins et al., 2001).

In almost every tradition, women are told what they can or cannot do. As a part of economical conditions women are also told which job they can work or which job they cannot work. All behaviors of women are determined by hiearchical dualism. This kind of dualism must be relevant to a historical context. This context is directly affected by its economical phenomenon, and ownership of property. The ownership of property discussed by Veblen geniously in order to explain how women become inferior class. Interestingly, Veblen was the first philosopher who put forward the gender roles and its reflections to economics before feminist economics has first said something about it.

Institutionalists first recognized gender norms as important institutions in the economy. Thorstein Veblen recognized gender norms as exemplary for how historical and cultural patterns influence the economic process of provisioning. He stressed the fact that pecuniary activities, those of buying and selling, were not synonymous with provisioning (Mayhew 1999, 480). Feminist economists have also found the notion of an institution useful for the analysis of the relationship between gender and economy. Institutional economics begins its analysis by looking at cultural processes rather than isolated individual (Mazurkiewicz-Zachorowska, 2015, p. 407, 408).

Interestingly, both institutional economics and feminist economics raise their ideas as cultural process. Rather than using mathematical formulas, complex equations etc. constructing cultural manners help both schools to see how women's situation have changed historically. This glance allows them to see it both economically and sociologically. Economics and sociology are embedded. At that point as a secondary class or as an institution without no property, women's subordination must be scrutinized remarkably. There has always been a woman issue in economics science. The structure of capitalism has no sense about women, but not as much regard as on men. Historically, the development of capitalist process felt at most. "The 1930s brought the Depression, the 40s the war, during the 50s there was there was a general period of affluence and rising expectations along with the ideal family life syndrome." (Ryan, 1982, p. 32).

According to Peterson, Veblen's views on "women's social and economic status were an integral part of both his critique of American society and mainstream economic thought (Peterson, 1988)." (Peterson, 2012, p. 278). As a great observer of American society Veblen himself made a fabulous criticism on both ideas. American society was possibly the first society that took care of property more than it has to be. There would be no surprise at that point. The industry has first arisen to change the capital accumulation in the USA, naturally it would change the society's life condition. Briefly, it can be said that gender role is the first common point of both institutional economics and FE as discussed above.

One other very important common point of institutional economics and FE, they both agree that Great Recession is also a man-made recession.

Discussions of the "gender gap" in unemployment rates, and predictions of women taking over the work force, gained wide attention through their association with a narrative that labeled the "Great Recession" the Great Mancession" (or "Mancession" or "He-cession"). The introduction and popularization of the term "Mancession" is often attributed to Mark Perry (University of Michigan—Flint and the American Enterprise Institute) who, in a December 9, 2008 post to his blog, Carpe Diem (Peterson, 2012, p. 278, 279).

In the Great Recession period, although women are employed, they could have been disposable in terms of employment. Inasmuch as, due to the gender roles, their employment would have been seen as a gift for them. These gender roles are accepted by neoclassical economics, namely, Gary Becker who is the leading representative of combining neoclassical economics and its important premises of women's working as the priliminary reason of excluding women from work-force. However, understanding this manner of neoclassical economics is highly related with the idea of Veblen about ownership of property. For Veblen, since women became owners of property, this started to extend towards inclusion of industry products, thus both people and things became as property (Veblen, 2015, p. 28). Since the beginning of women's seizure as slaves or war plunders, the women's roles have been changed. Patronizing women would start by accepting domestic roles. So, neoclassical economics claims that women were not able to be allowed to find a proper job in the labor market because of the gender roles undertaken. Besides if they find a proper job, it is just a reflection of the jobs that are similar to house works. This one of the main assumption of feminist economics. Also, it is very interesting that Veblen claimed this situation reluctantly in the early beginning of the 20th Century. For sure, Veblen's aim didn't emphasize this modus. On the other hand, seeing women's seizure in this way made him to define the women's situation as an institution. Feminist economics do not have the same idea as being an institution, excluding institutional feminist economics.

By reason of the bizarre structure of capitalism, classes are so important. As a very old method, capitalism rules by dividing. One of the most important separation of capitalism is dividing sexes as men and women. Thanks to Veblen's genious, this division of labor was elaborated at the early of the 20th Century. This situation caused to be seen as the odd circumtances by the latter schools like feminist economics.

Discrimination is one of the most important point what feminist economics concerns. For institutional economists, discrimination is embedded in cultural process, it must be eliminated. Because gender based discriminiation is one of the most egregious nondemocratic practice in economics which causes an unbalanced situation for a country. This is the most common point that shared by both institutional economics and feminist economics. "The institutional paradigm, on the ther hand, shows promise of providing a body of theory, through which a more intellectually satisfying feminist economics may be developed." (Waddoups & Tilman, p. 182). At that point, Veblen with his eminent genious has introduced several publications. In those publications, Veblen tries to suggest the tenacious bond between economics and sociology. Naturally, Veblen tries to connect almost all social sciences, but not only economics, from antropology to psychology to sociology that are the main concern of his philosophy. That's the main reason why there must be a connection between Veblen'n thoughts and Feminist Economics (FE). Because, "Feminist economists seek to the better by questioning implicit assumptions about traditional gender roles and about appropriate race, class, ethnicity and national hierarchies thus revealing the biases and distortions in masculinist view of economics." (Serdaroglu, 2008, p. 1). Veblen made a brilliant connection between women and ownership of property. Also, there is a great connection of those extention in all of them with the term *conspicious consumption* he proposed. So, Veblen suggested the first steps of FE.

The most significant publication of Veblen is *The Theory of the Leisure Class* (1899). He takes into consideration the origins of private property. Institutional feminist economics can search for initial connections between institutional economics and FE by taking this piece. According to Veblen, the origin of property "had begun with the ownership of persons, particularly females. [...] The incentives to acquiring such property have apparently been, 1) a propensity for dominance and coercion; 2) the utility of these persons as evidence of the prowess of their owner 3) the utility of their services." (Waddoups & Tilman, p. 183, 184).

Those three properties are seen in different levels of the society at any time. The most observed is about gender roles and its reflections to the job division. Dividing jobs is the most anticipated issue of feminist economics. Naturally, the time when Veblen's discussions appeared is far beyond what feminist economics foresees. However with the time, evolution of savage property to the modern business cycles is the only assumption to have changed the slavery. Of course, the shape of slavery has changed by women.

As Veblen demonstrated in his Theory of the Leisure Class, capitalism evolved from predominantly male activities of hunting and warfare, with successful individuals consolidating their power through the booty gained in battle. Women were confined to the camp, preparing food and clothing and bearing burdens. As western civilisation evolved, the range of occupations open to the "leisure class," were rigidly defined. Debarred from all industrial occupations, they were limited to government, warfare, religious observances, and sports. Women and "inferior" men, consigned to menial work, supported and esteemed the leisured class precisely because they did not create the real wealth of basic necessities or, indeed, any wealth at all (Hutchinson & Burkitt, 1997, p. 321).

Implicitly, Veblen can be called as the early harbinger of feminist economics. He lived in the USA as a child of a Norwegian immigrant family. He was able to see how capitalism works or how capitalism destroys every shape of work life. All the unfair situation of capitalism is embedded on the social structure. All discriminations aligned above, make the women's position in the working life worse. Veblen, who lived in the time of wild capitalism, has foreseen how capitalism uses sociological merger to divide men and women. So, he behaved like a precursor of feminist economics.

Gender roles could not be occured abruptly. There are historical reasons why it has first evolved. Veblen was possibly the first scientists who had shown this circumstances at first. Of course, he had no intention to construct a FE, but Veblen's ideas were so clear and effective that he can be named as the first academic father of gender roles. Gender roles are so disputable. Many FE scientists try to develop an idea why these roles are segregated. Of course, every FE suggest different reasons why it has emerged. Veblen tries to indicate the equiality of men and women before archaic societies. Considering the population of the world in that epoch, it is no surprise. Notion of property was very scarce and the sources were quite sufficient enough for people's demands. So, there was an equality. However, once the world population has raised gradually and the demand for sources started to raise; the warfares for ownership of property was raised. This also brought women to be seen as sources/properties as well. Women were pushed to be back by men. According to this situation women started to seen the creatures to do only allegedly inferior jobs like, motherhood, cooking etc. Of course, these jobs are appropriate to inferior class women, but not the women in the leisure class. Their positions developed in another way. Veblen's thoughts about this situation is directly related with consumer society.

More interesting than any other suggestion is what Veblen thinks about consumer society. Sociologically, because of the reason that women are of an instrumental or utilitarian sort, they are tend to be gathered in a part of consumer society. Because, in a consumer society women tend to spend more money than men. It means that women make their consumption by overseeing their utility and instrumentality. Consumer society is proceeded by different shapes, but the most significant sign of a member of a consuming society is related with fashion and dress. Veblen gives utmost importance to this situation.

According to Veblen's "analysis this meanes that clothing must be 1) fashionable 2) expensive 3) cumbersome, that is today, provide visible evidence that its wearer cannot perform socially useful labor." (Waddoups & Tilman, p. 186).

What Veblen did see in his time about fashion is still valid for both fashion and sports, social media, etc. all areas releated with this process. Because, social media is now a stage for women's social and economic positions in contemporary society. It is for everyone especially working-class women who are victims of this stage severly. How Veblen's time fashion oppressed working-class women severely by the mediation of conspicuous consumption, today social media coerce such women. Women want to be seen, want to be realized. Social media provides a medium to fulfill these desires. But at the same time, it exploits them. Realizing more than anything women may do conspicuous consumption like how fashion oppressed working-class women in Veblen's era.

With respect to gender relations, a differentiation is made between sex as biological gender and gender as socially constructed gender. Persons with female (reproductive) body parts are considered to be 'feminine', i.e. emotional, altruistic and dependent. Persons with male (reproductive) body parts are considered to be 'masculine', i.e. rational, egoistic and independent. Such socially constructed characteristics can be more stable than material relations in the economy and society if, for example, conceptions of the working father and the caring mother are maintained in language and imagination even if other family constellations are possible (Bauhardt, 2016, p. 3).

This makes women to be seen in a dualistic way. At that point it must be remembered that there is a relationship between institutional feminism and Veblenian social theory. This dichotomy sometimes is called as 'double-dualism', sometimes "economy/state dichotomy".

Veblen gave a great importance to the division between pecuniary and industrial occupations. At this point Veblen is very important in terms of feminist economics. Because he had a common sense between Veblenian institutional theory and feminist theory. They have an approach to see why this occupation has occurred related to gender roles.

Thorstein Veblen was an economist and sociologist who regularly incorpated antrophology, philosophy and psychology into his numerous written works on American society during the early 1900s. As a scientist who gathered different kinds of social science like sociology, economics and politics, Veblen's topics included capitalism, bureaucratization, occupations, education, sex differentiation, government policy, economics structures and class divisions (Ryan, 1982, p. 29).

Veblen sees gender as an institution. Gender makes a huge role in distribution of entities in economics. Gender plays a role both determining the behavior and distributing an inefficient effect in economy. As an institution, gender makes the other economics institutions to be seen like pecuniary and predatory relations in the ecnomics. What Veblen told about predatory and pecuniary elements are embedded into society. They are visible hands of discrimination against women. Unlike feminist economics, institutional economics makes a far more debatable philosophical basis.

Conspicuous consumption focuses primarily on "luxury" goods-commodities that serve no useful purpose in sustaining life, but instead show the superior wealth of the consumer and his or her concomitant ability to engage in wasteful, i.e., nonuseful, consumption. Because of the generally competitive and opulent nature of contemporary society, no one, not even the most abject, escapes the process of inherently wasteful conspicuous consumption; no one is so poor that they can not engage in the essentially upper-class game of consumption for display. What sets people apart socially, therefore, is the quantity and quality of conspicuous con sumption they engage in, the more waste, the more honor. Veblen described as "barbarian" communities that organized their consumption around such "invidious" forms of social dis play, thereby implying that they were the opposite of progressive and enlightened" (Gilman, 1999, p. 692).

Conspicuous consumption has a far important point in Veblen's idea. It has a great insight in terms of what feminist economics might be ignoring. Conspicuous consumption is the life style of opulent class. At that point, women from the high rich class tended to waste more conspicuos consumption. It is the way to show their spouse's pecuniary revenue. Since the mass communication tools evolved, low-level income class women are pushed to make conspicuous consumption as well. Especially today, majority of women tend to make their consumption more extravagantly as it is developing with social media. The more they consume, the more they are acknowledged by the society. This display of expenditure is originated from 'barbarian' process. But of course, consuming too much is just for the women in upper-class. Mostly, male display the power by using conspicuous consumption on women. Because conspicuous consumption is the exhibition of male wealth. Women are mostly to be seen as a tool of sustenance. Patriarchal values believe that women are the primary consumers of sustenance. Today, women are still restricted by the patriarchal rules. Nevertheless, especially social media women tend to consume conspiciuously. They don't actually pay more money than men to conspicuous consumption, developing technology on social media serve them to exhibit their pecuniary or at least their husband's pecuniary prowess. Feminist economics, on the contrary, does not see women who are imposed by conspicuous consumption via social media or any other channel.

Historically and sociologically women have been a secondry class. It is historically, because all jobs are served by men, all duties to make money are seen as men's duty. Women are excluded by making money. It is sociologically, because men and women have been discriminated by historical manners. This is obviously has caused by division of labor which is the main concern of feminist economics. Nevertheless what Veblen makes so important in terms of feminist economics is to foresee the division of labor. This division of labor is divided by into two sections, firstly, discriminiation; secondly segregation.

Veblen saw the discrimination, because women are discriminated by some jobs just as they are women. This is one of the main assumption that feminist economics suggested. Women are excluded by some jobs, because some jobs are seen as pecuniary and predatory functions. It means that historically men work unlike women . Veblen saw segragation, because jobs are divided as man's jobs and woman's job. It means that women can make money too, but only for the woman's jobs like nursing, baby sitting, teaching (prefably not in academia) etc.

Domination in order to gain prestige. This theme is found most clearly with regard to the divisions between the sexes, and between pecuniary and industrial occupations. Veblen devoted most of his work to these divisions; however, only the latter, along with his economic theory, has been promoted and utilized in the social sciences. His theory of the relation between the sexes has largely been obscured or ignored, even though he clearly asserted this as the first division from which all other class distinctions followed (Ryan, 1982, p. 30).

Nevertheless, this kind of division or dichotomy makes Veblen's ideas to predict the division of labor in terms of women and men. His famous dichotomy is 'enterprise' and 'industry'. According to Veblen 'industry' is a physical term which is close to a productional engineering. On the other hand, enterprise is an organization that aims to make profit. In that sense, for Veblen, the enterprise subdues the industry in order to make its profit maximized (Özveren, 2007, p. 26).

Initially, it may seem that there is no relationship between Veblen's dichotomy and what feminist economics argues, but reversly there is, indeed. As it is known that Veblen gives much important to pecuniary and predatory. So, being a dichotomy between industry and enterprise pushes the enterprise to make discrimination on women and men. Because, literally women are seen weak and gained less profit than men. It means that there is a two-fold dichotomy proceeds with Veblen's ideas and feminist economics. Sex differences makes the first dichotomy between men and women uses. Industry-enterprise dichotomy makes the second dichotomy serves as the maximization of profit. Because women and men are accepted to have different roles to get pecuniary jobs.

It is an important point that rules defining the society are not universal, instead rather gender specific. Gender rules determine every form of economy. It determines sometimes working styles, working hours etc. Expectations from gender roles are defined by women oriented roles. Staying at home is the most expected behavior. As a part of division of labor women can only have what their male family members give them. Feminist economics argues this circumstance, as a matter of fact, over sexual division of labor. FE's objection to neoclassical assumption of this kind of allocation provides the marriage of gaining growth. Naturally, FE believes that this kind of division of labor only provides men's economic growth. Because, they tend to pay extra money to be assisted in housework rather than a women staying at home. Also, one important point of view is shared by institutional economics is how Veblen's approach to women's occasion. Institutional economics of Veblen is seen that this kind of unpossesion of women as a consequence of their seizure by men. Of course, an institution who pushed stay at home or step one aside, women have no capcity to reach their economics maximization. According to Veblen there was no voice for a habit of expropriation to property before seizing on women. Almost all archaic societies both women and men in the society can seize the property without being owner of that property. In barbaric societies women started to get to be seized in order to reflect as a memory of victory (Veblen, 2015, p. 28).

Unwittingly, when feminist economics creates the gender roles or division of labor is covertly embedded on social factors. Feminist economics sees that situation from the approach of sex differences and its reflections to gender roles. However feminist economists do not look at this division in terms of institutional way. Their approach is a bit close to sociological perspective.

Women continue to occupy a different position in the economy to that occupied by men. They generally comprise a lower proportion of the [paid] workforce, have lower incomes, work in highly segmented, and lower status, occupational and industry groupings, and undertake a far greater share of the unpaid economic activities carried out in the home. Many of the differences between men's and women's economic status are due to the different amount of involvement that men and women have in the direct care of children. Caring for children and other dependents is still largely a female. [...] task, whether paid or unpaid. In most countries, child care is a very poorly paid occupation. Women's continuing responsibility for the direct care of their children (and the associated domestic work) is arguably one of the major sources of women's continuing economic disadvantage relative to men (Donath, 2000, p. 115).

For Veblen, when a culture proceeds, it is gradually changes. Within the era of cultural sequence emerging of idle class and ownership of property has appeared at the same time. These two institutions are the same consequence of economic power. What make difference between idle class and working class is getting an ownership of property of women by the most powerful men in the society. (Veblen, 2015, p. 15, 27). This is what FE's primary concerns. Because, historically defined, the situation of women will cause to be determined economically as well. Also, it creates the determination of division of labor. One other common point of institutional economics and FE is about feminist economists' the division of labor in terms of gender roles. Gender roles is reflected to the job satisfaction as discrimination and segregation of occupations emerge.

In other words, fashion victimized working-class women most severely. Thus, we can see that Veblen's idea of conspicuous consumption emerged out of a dual critique of women's social and economic positions in contemporary society (Gilman, 1999, p. 695).

Market processes, far from alleviating the inequality problem, can exacerbate it. Gender norms are embedded in labor markets, and fostering competition can perpetuate gender inequality. For example, when women enter the labor market, they are often paid less than men on the assumption that they are dependent on men. Assigning men the role of breadwinner also provides a rationale for hiring men into jobs with upward mobility. Women, in turn, are slotted into low-wage, insecure jobs considered to be fitting for their assumed role as secondary wage earner (Berik, Rodger&Seguino, 2009, p. 5).

This situation is directly related about discrimination and segregation. Discrimination is the highest point of property ownership in terms of institutional economics, for sure it can be seen as to be paid inequal wages for equal jobs, but it can also be seen as working at different levels with equal productivity. As a reflection of gender roles, women are seen as inequal payment owners. Discrimination arises due to the fact that the institutional role of women accompanying with feminist approach. Put it differently, discrimination proceeds as an institution; for FE the way of excluding women from the labor market. Besides both horizontal segregation and vertical segregation are ways of discrimination as same as it could be. Horizantal segregation is separating jobs as women jobs' and men jobs'. Vertical segration is hierarchical separation in the institution.

As stated by Akansel (2004) women are not equal in working life conditions. This can be caused by institutional ways or feminist ways. However, according to the author either way it is institutional. All barriers constructed in front of women are institutional. Because, all barriers are embedded sociologically. When people think that 'a women cannot wear a short, a women cannot go to outside at the late of midnight' etc. stereotypes are constructed sociologically. Excluding women from labor market one way or another is economically, however it takes its power from sociological level.

From OIE-FE to Institutional Feminist Economics (IFE)

As it is well-kown that Veblen was the first scientist who gave the name of 'neoclassical economics'. He has insistly given this name in order to be distinguished from classical economics. In other words, Veblen did see the first scientist what was happening on the economy of the late nineteenth century and early twentieth centuries. "In the twenty-first century makes several points, but perhaps the key one is this, the literature on economic restructuring and globalization has paid far too little attention to womens issues." (Brown, 1999, p. 1035, 1036).

One can asks this question, 'If there is a link between Veblenian thought and feminist economics, why would feminist economics became to the thought of economics earlier than it has first arose?' There are several explanations to evaluate this process. *At the time Veblen wrote, feminists were concerned about women's equality in a much narrower sense. The other reason why feminist economists want to exclude Veblen's though from their vision is his vicious reputation by women. He is called as 'womanizer.' Although, he acted to deserve his bad reputation, it doesn't mean that he wasn't the first one who called a great link between the false position of women souced by historical/antrophological situation. Because 1) the question of the validity of Veblen's assumptions about early societal relations; and 2) the relevance of a comparison between the strictly defined role assignments of that time period with the sex role expectations of today* (Ryan, 1982, p. 33, 34).

At this point the reason why women and men are divided by gender role for certain occupations is mainly releated with the evolutionary approach of Veblen. As it is known Veblen declares that economics must be an 'institutional political economics.' This is caused by considering the economics as an evolutionary approach. Otherwise, economics must be considered as just consisting of the market. If the market is accepted as a legitimate medium of economics, the discrimination must be seen naturally. Because the market represents the division of labor at the same time. If the market is natural, the division of occupations are gender based. This composition of the economics is the most reverse position to both institutional economics and feminist economics demand. The reason is it makes the gender gaps neutralized. However, the more evolutionary economics becomes clear, the less discrimination becomes clear. Of course, the division of labor has a great tie with pecuniary manner. It helps to distinguish the leisure class from the industrious class. For Veblen, the enterprise owner is kind of a barbarian and naturally, he can be a representative of leisure class. Unlike those men, industrial class can be representative of the savage and these are females.

"Feminist economists incorporate considerations of class, race-ethnicity, and other factors into their research, recognizing the limits of theorizing 'women' as a homogenous category." (Power, 2008, p. 5). So, all classes accepted by capitalism like gender, color, caste and class are the main concern of feminist economics. More specifically feminist economics search for an answer to the reason why women face with discriminatory situations particularly economically by means of race, gender and other. While doing this, historical aspect is guide for FE. One common point between Veblen's institutionalism and FE is to find out why women are discriminated historically. As Veblen, women are seen institutional features of property rights, it is no surprise that they are discriminated.

What FE does question is the concept of "independence," because life is always life in common, people need each other and need care at all stages of their lives, and especially at certain moments of the life cycle. This takes us to a fundamental critique of homo economicus, defined as a self-sufficient, selfish, and rational individual, who is active, has perfectly defined preferences, is not influenced by society, and interacts on the basis of self-interest in an ideal market where prices are the only necessary means of communication (Calderon-Agenjo & Munoz-Galvez, 2019, p. 144).

As it is very well-known that Veblen did totally oppose to *homo economicus*. For Veblen, ownership of property causes emulation of lower classes. Emulation is the first step of being in an ownership. Also, having ownership of property is going one step further to idleness. When having idleness, one cannot react as rational. Just as having 'that ownership of property' like the stimulation of individual. So, here having a property is not a choice determined by a rational mind, but conspicuous consumption. It can be accepted by a methodological simulation between FE and Veblen.

One of the biggest feminist economists, Julie Nelson tells us about rational choice that it would rather be used by many economists, or any social behavior (Nelson, 1996, p. 6). "In this framework, consumption, prosuction, and distributional questions define each other and are linked in ways that go beyond individuals interacting in markets." (Peterson, 1995, p. 571).

Feminist economics argues that more women's experiences must be added to economics issues. For institutional economics, women experiences are more releated to predatory functions. Because in accordance with rational theory, there are no experiences in economy. Put it differently, the common point shared by institutional economics and feminist economics in terms of opposing to rational choice is about women experience. Feminist economics opposes to rational choice by skipping many norms and customs including women's experience. Institutional economics has a larger point in terms of women's experiences. It considers that all these norms and customs, which push the women away from the market, is all about pecuniary jobs. In other words, women historically are accepted to be owned and this way they have predatory occupation experiences. Thus, if economics accepts rational choice to be really rational in terms of all humans, there will not be place to predatory occupations, especially for women. These kinds of experiences are ignored by economics. Ignoring especially women's experiences – and to some degree men's experiences – leads to believing in rationality.

Women's interest are disadvantaged by the centrality in economic theory of the concepts of scarcity, selfishness, and competition. The feminist rethinking of these concepts benefits not only women, but also economic theory and policy (Strober, 1994, p. 145).

For FE, women's experiences must be added to economics more. In that way, it will allow to widen economics both politically and theoretically. More important than that, it will give a chance to women to be known as subjects (İşler, 2010, p. 117).

Being women as a subject to be known is the implicit methodological desire of Veblen. Inasmuch as, Veblen tries to clarify women's situation historically, Veblen also states that the theoretical shape of neoclassical economics lacks one of the gender.

One must be notified that all systematic differences are sourced by society, and, the society is constructed by norms and preferences. These norms and preferences are determined by the institutions of this society. If these institutions are defined more accurately and value-laden, the society may have more options to women. It means that the societies, which have eased off the discrimination between men and women and its reflection to the job occupation, namely, segregation, will benefit from all human's experiences in economics. In that way, rational choices will turn to be bounded by rationality.

"Neoclassical accounts tend to pay too little attention (1) to systematic differences in the options available to men and women and (2) to the socially constructed nature of the 'preferences' guiding choices. "Institutional economist have been advancing similar criticisms for decades." (Seiz, 1995, p. 609). At that point, Veblen enlightens how women's situation have been altered by the ownership of property and women have no equal or similar preferences as much as the same by men. More oddly, only the idle class women can have elite preferences like their men or more than their men have. Because, this is the only way to survive in that class for them.

Another common point methodological of Veblen and FE is the rejection of too much formularisation. Actually this is the most common method observed in mainstream economics. This is a tool to prove their assumptions with mathematical formulas and to be believed by people that as if it is the sole reality. The reality is definitely both political and economical. Put it differently, it is politics economics. This politics economics cannot be completely suggested or proved by mathematics. The issues are embedded in the society. So, the most expected method of institutional economics and FE is qualitative methods.

What Veblen told in his time is still valid for women's situation in the twenty-first century. Because, especially globalisation makes the women to be pushed outward of the market more than men. Nevertheless, in the globalization, women are seen as consumers than being employers. This is mostly about conspicuous consumption. Veblen allows us to see this process.

"Preferences for action are formed outside the context of economic activity-for example, that some women prefer to be homemakers because they indepently value that role, not because their labor market experiences have been limited, discriminatory, or incompatible with child rearing. The notion that that people have decontextualized preferences for producing and consuming certain products and services is fundamentally incompatible with feminist conseptions of the soial production of gender, race and class (including the alleged preferences of individuals occupying these categories)." (Glass, 1996, p. 500).

There is not any doubt that some women would prefer rearing, staying at home. Yet, it doesn't mean that if they would have the choices or preferences other than staying at home, majority of them would choose to find a proper job to afford their lives. Thus, the institutionalism of the society compels women to stay at home. According to feminist economists it can be called as discriminiation of women from the market, but for institutional system of a society. Because, historically women must be supported by pecuniary occupations which have undertaken by men.

Institutional economics is grounded in a very different definition of economics, a definition that explicitly rejects the notion that economics is cultural notion of 'scarcity.' Institutional economics recognizes that both 'human rights' and 'resources' are largely socially defined and created. Thus, economists becomes a study of 'social provisioning'-how societies organize themselves to secure the material goods and services necessary to maintain and reproduce themselves.... For example, consumption decisions are viewed in the context of economic class, social norms, and corporate power; production decisions are viewed in the context of the legal/institutional environment, social rules, and market power; the disrtubution of income is analyzed in terms social custom, bargaining power, race and gender discrimination (Peterson, 1995, p. 570).

In other words, one important point shared by both institutional economics and feminist economics is rejecting rational choices. It has two reasons, firstly, rational choices focus on micro-level of economics. Secondly, it is really depending on 'scarcity.' The reasons like 'human demands' and 'resources' are mostly socially made up definitions that puts the institutional economics to an opposing position against rational choice. Because people do not act rational. Most of the decisions people make are emotional. Although, neoclassical economics surpasses this issue with 'bounded rationality' notion, 'human demands' and 'scarcity' is still valid in mainstream economics. For feminist economics, this is a little bit different than institutional economics' position. Feminist economics tend to see the economics events on a more macro-level. All these 'human demands' and 'scarcity' issues are considered as the way to compel women away from the working life. Secondly, all economics activities like resource allocation and income distribution decisions are interrelated with the economics.

Economics is the field that investigates economics events in two main sections, micro-level and macro-level. In micro-level, economics focuses on human behavior that strives to understand with rational choice. After exploration of Thorstein Veblen, institutionalism was a great curiosity among scientists. Of course, this curiosity has led to create different levels of institutionalism. Those are sociological institutionalism associated with organizational theory and concerned with criticizing the institutions and process of Weberian bureaucracy, discursive institutionalism combines with historical institutonalism and discourse analysis and finally historical institutionalism.

Feminist economics to a certain degree can be accepted by a part of socio-economics school. Firstly, what is socio-economics? Although feminist economics claims that women and women's expriences are embedded into economy, it cannot be called as a part of the society. Put it differently, according to socio-economics, feminist economics may not be a part of socio-economics. However, the real effect why feminist economics cannot be seen a part of socio-economics, focuses on the unbalanced and unfair power dominance of the economics. It says that unequal gender roles of the society cause unbalanced economics distrubution. Nevertheless, socio-economics recognizes gender as a part of labor economics, household economics or welfare economics, it does not see intrinsic divison of roles in those economics. According to socio-economics, these economics thought makes the division of roles natural.

Interestingly, one of the important components of socio-economics, institutional economics explored by Veblen focuses on the role of the institutions in the economy and their evolution. Because:

Veblen regularly referred to patriarchal norms as an example of the disruptive role that instutions aften play in the economy, leading not only to inequalities but also to ineffieciences. ... Indeed, institutions are the object of study in institutional economics and gender is reconized to be a major instituion affecting economic behaviour and in turn influenced by economic process. Examples are labour market segmentation into typical masculine and femine jobs, or an open, more communicative managerial style often attributed to female leaders (Staveren, 2010, p. 4).

Consequently, Veblen's institutional ideas and FE have many common points like methodology, notions etc. Although, when Veblen declared his ideas, he didn't think that he would able to create a new economical school like FE. Nevertheless, FE have no intention to construct their own ideas over Veblen. On the other hand, considering only eminent philosophers like Veblen, unintentionally suggested the ideas combining with FE, and FE – sometimes intentionally sometimes not – uses Veblen's ideas in order to create a robust theoretical approach.

SOLUTIONS AND RECOMMENDATIONS

"Since capitalism has first arisen in the 18th Century, it has debatbale process for all economic classes." (Akansel, 2017, p. 225). This brought some falls and rises not only for classes, but also for sexes. It pushed men and women using gender roles. This has caused to an economic loss for all economies. Because, there is no doubt half of an economic power is working while the other part of the economy staying at home, doesn't bring a progress to any economy. Although, excluding women's economic power all around the world is still continuing, it doesn't mean that there has not been a progress to solve this problem. Especially, western world has surpassed this meaningless implementation on a large scale. Of course, it doesn't mean that their conditions are perfect, however it has a quite good enough look in terms of women labour. This is also a sign to read and implicate with heterodox economics. Intrinsically, economies who read the different sounds of heterodox economics have been developed. Institutional economics and FE ideology may be a root for all economics to solve working conditions of women . They may help to solve gender issues as well.

FUTURE RESEARCH DIRECTIONS

Solution to gender roles in working life will be by the help of institutional economics and feminist economics methods. If any country wants to surpass gender roles issues, it needs to follow especially the examples of western countries who have already mostly surmounted gender issues. If gender issues may be surmounted by increasing women employment, it can decrease conspicuous consumption. Also, it may change the appearance of the women's economics role in the economy.

CONCLUSION

Institutional economics and FE are very important for heterodox economics flows. Naturally, institutional economics dates back early. The main influencer of it is Thorstein Veblen (1857-1929). Veblen's thoughts, that were suggested at the beginning of the 20th Century, has a similar way with FE. The philosophy of FE serves the economics by dealing with gender issues. Gender is different than sex. Gender is a moral definition. Because seperating sexes as men and women reflects itself in society. Women and men having different roles in economics is originated from being segregated in economics. Albeit, being the leader of institutional economics, Veblen thinks that the reason women are dismissed from working life is related with 'barbarian' age. He makes a comparison of such ages economics; the richer man is, the more women they can have. In any case, the upper class women do not neccessary to work, but the lower class women does need to serve as servants. Here conspicuous consumption has an important role in women working conditions. Because, upper-class women use it to display their spouses wealth; lower-class women use it to display how good enough they emulate the upper-classes. Consequently, both Veblen and FE related with women's conditions in working life. Veblen serves his ideas using the term conspicuous consumption and the effect of how this term makes women worse; FE gender terms and its effects on women's inferior conditions in working life.

REFERENCES

Akansel, I. (2004). *The Situation Of Woman Labourforce in the Art Sector, An Investigation on Ankara State Opera and Ballet (ASOB).* Unpublished MSc dissertation, University of Gazi, Ankara, Turkey.

Akansel, I. (2017). Reading the Relationship between Public Relations and Economics by the Mediation of Thorstein Veblen. *Proceedings of the 3rd International Annual Meeting of SosyoEkonomi Society* (pp. 145-150). Academic Press.

Bacchi, C., & Rönnblom, M. (2014). Feminist Discursive Institutionalism-A Poststructural Alternative. *NORA*, *22*(3), 170–186. doi:10.1080/08038740.2013.864701

Bénicourt, E., & Guerrien, B. (2017). Neoklasik İkisat Teorisi [The Theory of Neoclassical Economics]. Istanbul: The Publishing House of Kabalci.

Berik, G., Rodgers, Y., & Seguino, S. (2009). Feminist Economics of Inequality, Development, and Growth. *Feminist Economics*, *15*(3), 1–33. doi:10.1080/13545700903093524

Brown, W. S. (1999).. . *Thorstein Veblen in the Twenty-First Century.*, *33*(4), 1035–1037.

Calderon-Agenjo, A., & Munoz-Galvez, L. (2019). Feminist Economics, Theoretical and Political Dimensions. *American Journal of Economics and Sociology*, *78*(1), 137–166. doi:10.1111/ajes.12264

Cohen, J. (2018). What's "Radical" about [Feminist] Radical Political Economy? *The Review of Radical Political Economics*, *50*(4), 716–726. doi:10.1177/0486613418789704

Dolfsma, W., & Hoppe, H. (1996). The Challenges of Feminist Economics. *Freiburger FrauenStudien*, *2*, 59–72.

Dolfsma, W., & Hoppe, H. (2003). On Feminist Economics. *Feminist Review*, *73*, 1–17.

Donath, S. (2000). The Other Economy, A Suggestion for a Distinctively Feminist Economics. *Feminist Economics*, *6*(1), 115–123. doi:10.1080/135457000337723

Findlay, T. (2012). Feminist Institutionalism and Feminist Political Economy, A Dialogue on Gender, the State and Representation. *Proceeding of the Annual Meeting of the Canadian Political Science Association*. Academic Press.

Gilman, N. (1999). Thorstein Veblen's Neglected Feminism. *Journal of Economic Issues*, *33*(3), 689–711. doi:10.1080/00213624.1999.11506193

Glass, J. (1996). Review, Beyond Economic Man, Feminist Theory and Economics, Marianne A.Ferber and Julie A. Nelson; The Economic Status of Women under Capitalism, Institutional Economics and Feminist Theory, Janice Peterson and Doug Brown; Unequal Burden, Economic Crises, Persistent Poverty and Women's Work, Lourdes Beneria and Shelley Feldman. *Signs*, *21*(2), 499–502. doi:10.1086/495084

Hopkins, B. E., & Duggan, L. (2001). A Feminist Comparative Economic Systems. *Feminist Economics*, *17*(3), 35–69. doi:10.1080/13545701.2011.582847

Hutchinson, F., & Burkitt, B. (1997, March). An economic silence: Women and social credit. *Women's Studies International Forum*, *20*(2), 321–327.

İşler, R. (2010). Feminist İktisadın Geleneksel İktisada Metedolojik Açıdan Getirdiği Eleştiriler [The Methodological Criticism of Feminist Economics to the mainstream economics]. *Ekonomi Bilimleri Dergisi [The Journal of Economics Science]*, *2*(1), 115–122.

Lexico. (n.d.). Gender. Retrieved from www.lexico.com/en/definition/gender

Mazurkiewicz-Zachorowska, A. (2015). The Concept of Care in Institutional and Feminist Economics and Its Impact on Public Policy. *Journal of Economic Issues*, *49*(2), 405–413. doi:10.1080/00213624.2015.1042747

Nelson, J. (1996). Feminism, Objectivity and Economics. New York: Routledge.

Nelson, J. (1996). What is Feminist Economics All About? *Challenge*, *39*(2), 4–8.

Peterson, J. (1995). For Whom? Institutional Economics and Distributional Issuses in the Economics Classroom. *Journal of Economic Issues*, *29*(2), 567–574. doi:10.1080/00213624.1995.11505693

Peterson, J. (2012). The Great Crisis and the Significance of Gender in the U.S. Economy. *Journal of Economic Issues*, *46*(2), 277–290. doi:10.2753/JEI0021-3624460203

Power, M. (2004). Social Provisioning as a Starting Point for Feminist Economics. *Feminist Economics*, *10*(3), 3–19. doi:10.1080/1354570042000267608

Ryan, B. E. (1982). Thorstein Veblen, A New Perspective. *Mid-American Review of Sociology*, *7*(2), 29–47.

Seiz, J. (1995). Bargaining Models, Feminism and Institutionalism. *Journal of Economic Issues*, *29*(2), 609–618. doi:10.1080/00213624.1995.11505698

Serdaroglu, U. (2008). Feminist İktisat Bilimi Sorguluyor [Feminist Economics queries Science] *Ekonomik Yaklşaşım [Ekonomik Yaklaşım Association]*, *19*(66), 1–28. doi:10.5455/ey.10658

Staveren, I. V. (2010). Post-Keynesianism meets feminist economics. *Cambridge Journal of Economics*, *34*(6), 1123–1144.

Strober, M. H. (1994). Can Feminist Thought Improve Economics Rethinking Economics Through a Feminist Lens. *AEA Papers and Proceedings*, *84*(2), 143–147.

Tejani, S. (2019). What's feminist about feminist economics? *Journal of Economic Methodology*, *26*(2), 99–117. doi:10.1080/1350178X.2018.1556799

van Straven, I. (2005). Feminist Economics, Settiong out the Parametres. In C. Bauhardt & G. Caglar (Eds.), Feministiche Kritik der politischen Ökonomie (pp. 18-48). Wiesbaden: VS Verlag für Sozialwissenschaften.

Veblen, T. B. (2015). Aylak Sınıfın Teorisi Kurumların İktisadi İncelemesi [The Theory of Leisure Class An Economic Study of Institutions]. Ankara: Heretik Yayınları.

Waddoups, J., & Tilman, R. (1992). Thorstein Veblen and Feminism of Institutional Economics. *International Review of Sociology*, *3*(3), 182–204. doi:10.1080/0390 6701.1992.9971127

Woolley, F. (2005). The Citation Impact of Feminist Economics. *Feminist Economics*, *11*(3), 85–106. doi:10.1080/13545700500301312

KEY TERM AND DEFINITIONS

Discrimination: A treatment or making a distinction in favor or against between sexes. It can be seen at the same job or emerging different payment conditions.

Feminist Economics: A heteredox economics branch which focuses on how women's work and economics can be gathered.

Gender: Either of the two sexes (male and female), especially when considered with reference to social and cultural differences rather than biological ones. The term is also used more broadly to denote a range of identities that do not correspond to established ideas of male and female.

Horizontal Segregation: It arises when men and women do different type of Works like if woman works as secretary or a nurse.

Institutional Economics: A heterodox economics branch how institutions are effective on economics.

Segregation: It can emerge the jobs divided as men's job and women's job.

Vertical Segregation: The situation when people do not getting jobs above a particular rank in their jobs because of their especially sexes.

Chapter 2
The Significance of Public Goods in Market Failure Debates:
The Role of Public Goods on Market Failure From the Perspective of Schools of Economic Thought

Kubra Onder
Burdur Mehmet Akif Ersoy University, Turkey

Muhammet Sahin
Gumushane University, Turkey

ABSTRACT

Before the emergence of the neoclassical economic approach, the idea that market instabilities are temporary and markets are spontaneously able to reach equilibrium was prevalent. However, with the neoclassical economic thought the idea that market economy alone is far from attaining equilibrium and there is a need for public economy. This is also known as market failure theory. There are many reasons of market failure. One of them is public goods. Public goods are generally regarded as an example of market failure and seen as a problem requiring government intervention. However, when main stream public goods theories are analyzed in-depth, it is seen that there is no agreement on the properties of public goods which may create a reason to the government presentation and public presentation is not approved in general. Therefore, the aim of this study is to make a comparative analysis of the approaches of different economics schools of thought which have contributions to the subject of public goods.

DOI: 10.4018/978-1-7998-1037-7.ch002

INTRODUCTION

Individuals always seek for utility maximization and as a result of this effectiveness and efficiency of the competitive capitalist system increase. This economic approach had been dominant until the first half of the 19th century, however beginning from this period it paved the way for a new economic thought as it couldn't find solutions to social problems. This economic thought which is called as the neoclassical economic thought is based on the concepts of rationality and maximum utility in which consumers are in a struggle for utility maximization and producers are in a struggle for profit maximization (Menard & Shirley, 2005). Besides, unlike classical economic thought, neoclassical economic thought proposes that the market is not always in equilibrium and may deviate from equilibrium, in other words market may fail. Market resource allocation may fail or may be inadequate to fulfill its functions in this approach which is expressed as the market failure (Le Grand, 1991). There are some factors disrupting optimal resource allocation of the market. These are imperfect competition markets, public goods, externalities, natural monopolies and asymmetric information. Economic schools of thought have different approaches on the factors disrupting resource allocation of the market. Particularly, there are various approaches on the theory of public goods. There are many questions to be answered on the theory of public goods by the schools of economic thought. However, this has been a much debated topic in theory due to some unanswered questions or some of the answers to this questions were not clear enough.

Despite the theory of public goods is a long standing issue, it came to the fore systematically for the first time with an article (1954, 1955) written by Samuelson in the mid-50's These are the years corresponding to a period in which Keynesian policies are adapted both in national and international level, unemployment levels were highly decreased, growth rates increased rapidly, welfare state implementations became widespread due to cold war, developing countries realized development initiatives. Neoclassical synthesis which combines Keynesian macroeconomics (widely accepted in the academic world between the years 1945 and 1970) and Marshallian microeconomics was concretized in the studies of P. Samuelson and R. Musgrave. This is a period in which public goods are considered as market failure and there are theories on the necessity of production of goods and services by the benevolent government in order to eliminate this market failure. With this period, the function of the government was started to be criticized along with the issue of public goods. Hence, economic crises at the end of 1960's, political and social chaos encountered with the high inflation and unemployment broke the confidence on the effectiveness of Keynesian policies and government intervention. In this period, government was considered as the source of the problems and from 1970's, the role of government was started to be discussed by Austria and Chicago schools. Crisis emerging in 1980's, instability in unemployment and economics didn't break the confidence on neoliberal approach, however led to different regulations (Kayıran, 2013, pp. 149-151). This constituted a basic area for the studies of R. Coase (one of the representatives of Chicago School) based on property rights, transaction costs and special market solutions. As well as R. Coase, this subject was also included in the studies of new theoretical economists such as A. Alchian, H. Demsetz, D. North and E. Ostrom.

The theory on public goods has been a subject discussed by economists since the first time expressed by Samuelson but the focal point of the theory was changed along with the historical and corporate developments encountered. The approach on the role of the government under the framework firstly put forward in the subject of public goods underwent a change from market failure towards government failure and governing state. Therefore, the aim of this study is to evaluate the role of public goods in market failure and the success and failure of the theories on public goods under the framework of different schools of economic thought from a critical point of view.

MARKET FAILURE

The basic argument of the classical economics which forms the basis of the economics is "natural order" and "utilitarian philosophy". Classical economists base their assumptions on the smallest decision making units of the economy. According to the classical economical thought, the core issue is the benefits of this decision-making units. Under the assumption of rationalization, decision-making units make their decisions under the principle of maximization. While the producers try to maximize their profits and the consumers try to maximize their profits in the event that there is no intervention to the market and perfect competition conditions are prevalent, they unawerely maximize the benefits of the society with the principle of invisible hand. In other words, under perfect competition conditions, total welfare level is increased through reallocation of scarce resources to alternative activity areas. According to the classical economists who support that the market will reach equilibrium of supply and demand spontaneously, the government has two main duties. These are defense, justice and education. Therefore, the government should not interfere into the economy and it should only offer services with high costs and having externalities. (Hayek, 2004, pp. 53). Briefly, the idea that the market economy will alone provide optimization of social welfare and there is no need for government intervention into the economy is prevalent in classical economic thought.

Despite the classical economic thought was considered to be reliable until the first half of the 19th century as a prevalent theory, beginning from this period it slowly paved the way for a new theory as it couldn't find solutions to social problems. By the 1870's, all theories of classical economics except for theory of rent were highly criticized. In this period, liberalism and the future of the classical theory were among the most discussed topics along with the role of the government in the economy. While on one hand these kinds of developments were experienced, on the other hand, marginalist development started to emerge and as of the end of 19th century economic paradigm had encountered a fundamental change. With the neo-classical economic approach emerging in this century, the concept of "efficient use of scarce resources and maximum utility" was contributed to the literature of economics. Rationality and maximum utility are the underlying concepts of neo-classical economic thought. Starting point of this economic approach is the rationally behaving individuals. Producers struggle for profit maximization whereas consumers struggle for utility maximization (Hutchison, 1984, pp. 23-24; Parsons, 1967, pp. 60; Ostrom, 2000, pp. 137-158).

Unlike classical economic thought, neo-classics adapted the view that the market may deviate from equilibrium, may fail and move away from optimization of social welfare due to some factors. This view is expressed as the "Failure of Market Economy" in the literature of economics. According to the neo-classical economic view, the market is far from providing optimum alone and therefore public economy is required. Again, apart from classical economists, they defend the idea that government intervention into the economy is required, however this intervention should be limited (Etzioni, 1999; Razeen, 2002, pp. 16-18).

Market failure is the failure or insufficiency of market economics in fulfilling its function of resource allocation (Le Grand, 1991). The resource allocation expressed here is the pareto optimal resource allocation. Therefore, the market economy cannot fulfill its function of optimal resource allocation under the framework of the principle of "laissez faire laissez passer" due to the influence of various factors (Perloff, 2007, pp. 278)). These factors are discussed under two main topics as static and dynamic factors (Table 1) (Benáček, 1992, pp. 5-7).

Although market failure is discussed under two main topics as static and dynamic, here imperfect (incomplete) competition, economies of scale (natural monopolies), asymmetric information, externalities and public goods among static market failure factors which leads market economy failure will be discussed.

Table 1. Reasons of market failure

Static Market Failure	Dynamic Market Failure
• Imperfect competition. • Existence of public goods. • Externalities (positive or negative). • Existence of resources subject to joint ownership. • Existence of natural monopolies • Unavailability of some goods markets. • Inequality in income distribution. • High cost of acquisition of information and asymmetry of information. • Social moral weakness.	• Not attaining a reasonable growth rate. • Macro imbalances or conjuncture movements. • Skewness in the factor endowment of economics and halt of production due inadequacy of some factor supplies. • Myopia of time or existence of tendency to discount future at a high rate. • Inhibiting finance of industrialization due to lack of money and capital markets.

Reference: (Benáček, 1992, pp. 5-7)

Imperfect (Incomplete) Competition Markets

One of the elements that may lead to pareto efficient distribution of market mechanism is the existence of perfect competition market conditions. Imperfect competition market is valid in case these assumption does not function partially or in full. Discrimination between perfect and imperfect competition is mostly made in accordance to the multiplicity requirement which is the most important element of perfect competition conditions. That is to say, price in imperfect competition market is determined or changed by the buyer and/or one or more of the sellers. In the case of imperfect competition, “perfect information” assumption which is one of the assumptions of perfect competition is violated. Therefore, firms in imperfect competition markets are the price makers in other words they have the power to determine the price. In case competition conditions does not function in the market and competitive behaviors are disregarded by the economic units, the price of all goods and services are not determined by the competition phenomenon in the economic system and the price is not equal to marginal cost. Firms operating in imperfect competition market have a certain control over the economic parameters such as price, supply, production and amount of distribution (Benáček, 1992). This causes the price to be greater than the marginal cost, inefficient production or consumption and the market cannot attain the expected equilibrium. The situation that the price is greater than the marginal cost is the inefficient use of resources in terms of social welfare, welfare loss and as a result emergence of market imperfection. (Perloff, 2007, pp. 278).

Externalities

One of the most important factors of market failure is the externality. In case perfect competition conditions are fully satisfied, marginal rate of transformation is equal to marginal rate of substitution and decisions taken by consumer and producer don't have any positive or negative impact on producers or consumers. Nonetheless, it is possible that any decision taken by a producer or consumer in economic life may have an impact on another producer or consumer. Therefore, externality in the broadest sense is a cost burden or utility on third parties other than buyers and sellers as a result of consumption and production of any good and this impact cannot be priced by the market mechanism. In other words, externality is the negative or positive effect of production and/or consumption of an economic unit's activity on utility functions of other economic units. (Buchanan and Stubblebine, 1962, pp. 138-139). Benefits and losses arising due to externalities cannot be priced in the market. Therefore, market prices do not reflect real prices. For this reason, in case of existence of externalities, prices have a disrupting impact on resource allocation and they lead more and less production than required. As well as a decision taken by any of the economic decision-making units, on condition that it should be both in production and consumption, may not only have a positive impact on the other decision making unit, but also may have a negative impact. Negative externalities lead production of goods or services more than social optimum whereas positive externalities lead less production. In the economies of negative externalities, the producer does not consider costs undertaken by the society and may have the tendency for excessive production. In the economies of positive externalities, the producer who is disregarding the utility produced by the society has no motivation to make production at the optimum level and the producer has the tendency to make production below this level.

Several recommendations were made in order to increase economic efficiency and compensate externalities. Taxation practice developed by A. C. Pigou (1912) is one of them. In the negative resource utilization which is defined as Pigouvian taxation in the literature, decision making unit which causes negative externality in order to eliminate inefficiency is subject to a tax at an amount equal to the loss incurred. According to Pigou, it is possible to reach resource distribution efficiency as a result of internalization of externalities through tax practice as much as the loss incurred as a result of negative externality. In cases of positives externality, marginal social utility is realized at a lower rate than marginal specific utility and the firm produces less than the optimum production amount. In such a case, the loss incurred due to externalities is subsidized (internalized) and optimum production level is attained. In other words, positive externalities are internalized by Pigouvian subsidy method (Pigou, 1920, pp. 117-18; Caldari and Masini, 2011, pp. 716-718).

The theory of Pigou on internalization of externalities by public taxation and subsidization was criticized by Ronal Coase (1960). R. Coase asserted that it was not possible to internalize externalities by government intervention as in Pigouvian approach and instead of this resource utilization efficiency could be sustained under certain conditions in which there is no intervention to the market. Although Coase has a very different perspective on the problem of externalities, his assumptions on the economy are not much different than Pigou's. Coase also assumes that conditions required for the operation of the competitive market mechanism are satisfied. In the context of the problem tackled, what should be underlined is that operation costs are at a negligible level (close to zero). The second assumption of Coase is that property rights are precisely determined. Coase states that, when these conditions are satisfied, the parties will reach a settlement through bargaining and the result will be Pareto efficient (Aslanbeigui and Medema, 1998, pp. 603).

Asymmetric (Imperfect) Information

According to the assumption of perfect information or openness there is symmetric information among all sellers and buyers in the market. However, in practice the condition that buyers and sellers have perfect information cannot usually be satisfied. In other words, there is a possibility that one of the parties may have less information than the other about the operation created in the market. This case in which some economic units in the markets has more or less information compared to others is called asymmetric information (Mankiw, 2001, pp. 599). In case of asymmetric information, the party having more information compared to the other party has an advantage for making the right decision. Information level of the decision-making units effects their behaviors (Auronen, 2003, pp. 4). Level of information on investment, production, consumption and saving decisions is crucial for economic decision-making units who wants to optimize their profits or utility. Therefore, asymmetric information in the market come into question and the market moves away from efficiency, if one of the parties has information and the other doesn't have or one of the parties has more information compared to the other. The concept of asymmetric information was expressed first time in the study of George A. Akerlof titled "Quality Uncertainty and the Market Mechanism" in 1970. G. Akerlof (1970) explained information asymmetry and resulting adverse selection problem discussing the case of used car market (Auronen, 2003, pp. 7). This problem is also called as lemons problem. In this case it is stated that buyer and sellers do not have same level information on the quality of the traded goods, this situation causes deterioration in the market and results transaction of lower quality goods in the market (Huffman, 2009, pp. 2).

Another situation that arises as a result of asymmetric information is moral hazard or moral risk. Adverse selection problem is a situation arising before the transaction between the buyers and the sellers whereas moral hazard arises after the realization of the transaction. In other words, moral hazard is also expressed as giving harm to the other party by misusing the rights arising from a set of agreements due to asymmetric information after the mutual agreement of the parties. As well in adverse selection, moral hazard also leads to the problem of inefficient of resources (Mirrless, 1999, pp. 6-8).

Natural Monopolies (Economies of Scale)

Monopoly refers to a market situation in which there is a single producer and seller of goods which have no close substitutes. In order to sustain the strength of the monopolistic market there should be barriers for other firms' entry into the market. There are some factors preventing other firms' entry into the market. One of them is scale economies.

Decrease in production costs as the scale of production increases causes firms to move away from the competitive environment and assume a monopolistic structure. As time passes by, monopolistic structure becomes insufficient and a new structure which is also expressed as natural monopoly arises. This is a result of the firms having a greater capacity compared to their competitors or realizing production with a lower cost per unit production as their capacities increases by the time. Decrease in long-run average cost depending on the production capacity of the firm may lead the firm to remain as the single company in the market. This development in favor of the firm arises a situation to the detriment of other firms. In other words, monopolistic firm with a specific scale of production prevents small scale companies' entrance into market due to the scale economies advantage it has. Therefore, scale economies effect allocation distribution and moves market economy away from efficiency (Sharkey, 1983, pp. 13-24).

Inequality in Income Distribution

Income distribution is not exactly an economic phenomenon. It is a result and an indicator of the social and economic policies implemented. Income distribution mostly reminds personal and functional income distribution. Income distribution, either personal or functional is one of the most crucial problems of both developed and less developed countries. Some economists, particularly Keynesian economists, advocate that the government should not intervene into the economy justifying that income distribution problem cannot come up with a solution spontaneously within the market economy. In other words, a fair income distribution is accepted among the duties of the government. According to the Keynesians, the government should put into practice a mechanism called redistribution policy and should undertake the role of realizing a fair income and wealth distribution. Redistribution can be defined as retransferring some part of national income in a country to the society through taxes and other forced saving tools. In the redistribution policy which is called as the secondary distribution in the literature, some tools are utilized in order to realize a fair income distribution. Some of these tools are classified under the main framework of income policy (fiscal policy), social policy and monetary & credit policy. The most efficient one of these distribution policy tools is the fiscal policy. Fiscal policy has three different tools as tax, public spending and public credit in order to eliminate the inequality in fiscal policy income and welfare distribution. The government intervenes into the market while conducting its duty to ensure a fair income distribution. Therefore, intervention of government into the market leads market failure (Cornia, 1999, pp. 11-17).

LITERATURE REVIEW

Public Goods: Classifications and Basic Properties

Public goods have a very important place in fiscal literature. These goods and services encountered almost in every area of daily life are necessary for satisfying social requirements and they cover a wide range from defense to justice, from education to health, from infrastructure to public order. Studies of US economist Paul A. Samuelson are accepted as the pioneer in defining public goods and approaching them differently from private goods. In one of his articles Samuelson (1954) made a comparison of private (individual) consumption goods and collective (common) consumption good. In this article, he stated that private consumptions goods are goods which are subject to separate consumption of each individual and therefore as a result of consumption of an individual other individuals' consumption will be restricted. Nevertheless, for public goods collective consumption is in question and thus consumption of an individual does not hinder consumption of other individuals. Samuelson cited bread and defense goods as an example of the subject. Each slice of bread which is a special product which can be consumed by one person only. If an individual consumes more than one slice, one of the other individuals will be out of consumption. However, for the defense services which bear the characteristics of public goods, all the individuals may utilize service equally and none of the individuals will be out of defense umbrella provided by the army.

Indication of the difference between private and public goods in this way is related with the properties of the aforementioned goods related with being subject to competition or not and being deprived or not. (Hyman, 2010, pp. 145-149; Gruber, 2016, pp. 192-193). Private goods and services are subject to competition in terms of their nature. These kinds of goods have the characteristics of divisibility, pricing, marketing and being subject to competition. Consumption of a limited amount of goods through individual usage may lead to competition among those who want to consume the goods. However, public goods do not have the characteristics of divisibility, pricing, marketing and being subject to competition. Therefore, as a result of collective consumption, competition among individuals does not arise.

Lack of competition causes lack of exclusion. Individuals who do not pay the price of private goods may be deprived of the consumption of the goods. Likewise, consumption of the goods in this kind of goods and services purchased and sold in the market (supply & demand) conditions depends on paying the price at a determined price level. Individuals may utilize public goods and services including goods and services out of the market mechanism even they do not pay the price for them since their production are realized in line with the political decision-making processes. This second property of public goods causes a situation called free rider problem in fiscal literature (Hillman, 2009, pp. 143-144; Ulbrich, 2011, pp. 95-97). In this case, although all citizens may equally utilize public goods, some of them are included in financing public goods by paying taxes whereas some other does not fulfill their tax obligations.

The second important step in grouping public goods was taken by Richard A. Musgrave. Musgrave (1959, pp. 43-44), made a dual discrimination of public goods; public goods which must absolutely be produced by the government and publics goods which may also be produced by the public sector, but more appropriate to be produced by the government. Thus, in the terminology of Musgrave, public goods were fundamentally related with the authority supplying them. In his classification; first group of goods (goods which must absolutely be produced by the government) include defense and justice services. For the second group of goods education services provided an example. Essentially, this kind of goods and services may be also be produced by private sector. However according to Musgrave, it will be more beneficial to provide educational services by the public sector in terms of sustaining social harmony and creating cultural codes.

This classification form of Musgrave indicates the status of public goods either fully public or semi-public in one dimension. Defense and justice are accepted as public goods as they are absolutely produced by the government. On the other hand, education is a service which may be provided by the government due to external utilities it provides although it may also be provided by the private sector. Educational services are accepted to have economic and non-economic positive externalities such as adaption to technological innovations, development of democratic corporations, decreasing the rate of crime, providing market efficiency, decreasing welfare and healthcare costs and eliminating disorders in capital markets. (McMahon, 1987, pp. 133-134). Existence of this and similar social added values gives a public dimension to education which is actually a private service.

James M. Buchanan (1999, pp. 164-167), one of the most prominent figures of Public Choices School, made a classification based on the number of people using the good and degree of divisibility of the good and created a quinary scale providing transition from private goods to public goods. Here, the good acquires a public quality as the number of utilizing people increases and degree of divisibility decreases and on the contrary (number of utilizing people decrease and divisibility increases) the good approximate a private good. In other words, in Buchanan's approach, being a private or public good depends on the inverse relation between the number of utilizing people and degree of divisibility. In the classification number (1) is the perfect private good. Likewise, the number of utilizing persons is one and the divisibility degree of the good is at a maximum level. Number (5) is perfect public good and it is accepted this good which is utilized by the entire society has a divisibility level of zero. In addition to this, number (2) and (3), respectively, denotes semi-private and semi-public goods and number (4) denotes club goods.

Today, a new goods group is added to the public goods. The emergence of this group is basically related with the process of globalization. After the 1973 oil crisis, the impacts of globalization process emerging in a manner to form integrity with the paradigm change observed in economic thought also continues for today. Globalization carries national one to the international scale and spreads many economic and non-economic domestic factors almost everywhere on earth. The reflection of this paradigm change encountered is the emergence of a new public good type which called global public good. Global public goods which provide the utility of a public good to overflow abroad (Kaul et al., 1999) includes a wide range such as economic stability, ecological balance, preventing epidemics, developments in information and communication technologies and development of democracy and basic human rights. In parallel with this, public goods are not only examined with their national dimensions but also with their international dimensions.

Optimum Level of Production in Public Goods

Public goods are considered as one of the basic reasons of market failure in the literature of economics (Bator, 1958, pp. 369-371; Stiglitz, 2000, pp. 79-80; Winston, 2006, pp. 2). Neoclassical economists, while putting forward the concept of market failure, take into consideration public goods as well as the factors such as externalities, internal economies, imperfect competition and monopoly. These are such goods that their production makes the existence of public authority an obligation. Likewise, production of these in market conditions will lead to inefficiency depending on over or under production. Today, defense services (perfect public goods) are absolutely provided by the government and there is no private sector production in question. Although training and health (semi-public goods) can be provided by the private sector, they can also be provided by the government due to positive externality and social utility yielded. Goods providing utility (virtuous goods) to the society such as preventing epidemics and nursing homes and goods giving harm to the society (unvirtuous goods) should be regulated by the public authority through incentives in virtuous goods and deterrence in unvirtuous goods (Seidman, 2009, pp. 27-28; Greene, 2012, pp. 15-18). In addition to these, the existence of an argument (Hardin, 1968) defending the protection of the goods for the common use of the society such as the tragedy of the partners and environment, by the public authority makes the role of the government in social and economic life inevitable.

Thus, public goods include goods and services which are mainly inappropriate to be produced under market conditions, in other words goods and services that should be produced by the government. However, the basic problem of the public goods is that if they are produced at an optimum level or not. Theoretical explanations related with this depend on Pareto approach in essence. Pareto optimality includes three conditions; equilibrium in production, equilibrium in consumption and simultaneous equilibrium of production and consumption. Equilibrium in production indicates that it is possible to make an additional one unit production of a good under full employment condition is possible by trading-off at least one unit of the other good. Equilibrium in consumption includes that in a society which realized welfare maximization, the condition of an individual to consume more means less consumption of at least one of the other individuals. Thus, simultaneous equilibrium expresses that simultaneous equivalency of the marginal transformation rate indicating equilibrium in production condition and marginal rate of substitution indicating equilibrium in consumption condition (Pindyck and Rubinfeld, 2018, pp. 615-632; Varian, 2010, pp. 596-604).

In sustaining optimality condition in public goods, equality condition of not only one individual's but all individuals' (society's) total marginal rate of substitution and total marginal rate of transformation is searched and the amount of private goods that the individuals are willing to give up against one unit of additional public good is tried to be determined. For example, a good such as bread (private good) that each is individual is willing to give up in order to get one additional unit of defense service (public good) will be different for each individual. According to the Pareto optimality, to receive an additional unit of defense service is possible by giving up one unit of bread. If trade-off preference of the individuals in the society between the private goods and public goods creates equivalence, then Pareto optimality is sustained in the production of public goods. On the contrary, is there is no such equivalence it is not possible to talk about the existence of Pareto optimality.

Another explanation of optimality condition is based on equalization of social marginal cost and social marginal utility level of the individual starting from marginal cost and marginal utility levels. Accordingly, in case of equivalence of the additional utility of the society received from public good and the additional cost incurred for its production (taxes paid by individuals as a whole) it is accepted that optimal equilibrium condition is realized for public goods. As it is known, it is assumed that the individual gets utility as much as the individual pays for it within the market mechanism. In public economics, under the assumption of a tax system with increasing rates, while the amount of tax paid according to the income is different the utility obtained as a result of collective consumption of public goods is the same. In parallel with this, since same utility level for each individual but variable cost (tax) amount according to income is in question, a balance (optimality) condition should be realized for all society not for each individual separately (Hyman, 2010, pp. 58-62).

Various models have been developed for the optimal production of public goods. Samuelson model (1995) is one of them and in the essence of this model Pareto optimality is taken as a basis and an optimality condition starting from basic assumptions is tried to be put forward. In other words, globalization means the situation in which the national one exceeds beyond domestic borders and spreads to other countries. The model is based on the assumption of an economy with two goods and two persons. Essentially, the condition that marginal substitution limit is equal to marginal transformation limit is also valid for Samuelson model. Since the public goods are indivisible in Samuelson's approach and they are consumed together, optimality condition is not attained by taking into consideration the marginal rates of substitutions of individuals separately, but it is attained by the addition of marginal rates of substitution of all individuals. Besides in the model, just like in Pareto optimality, it is assumed that to make someone better-off is only possible by making others worse-off. Thus, in his model of ideal society consisting of two people, under Pareto optimality conditions, an increase in the welfare level of the first individual (here since public goods are in question, consumption of more public goods) is possible with a decrease in the welfare level of the second individual (consumption of less public goods).

Another model is the Lindahl's model (1958) of the Swedish economist Erik Lindahl. This model can be interpreted as adaptation of market price-quantity and supply-demand relations to public goods. Lindhal, starting from the assumption of an economy with two individuals preferred the way of using demand law which creates one of the basic cornerstones of market mechanism for the optimal production level of public goods. In accordance with the law of demand, there is price that each individual is willing to pay for a good and if this price decreases the amount demanded will increases and on the contrary if the price increases demand will decrease. In the Lindhal model taxes are taken as the basis of the price of the public goods. The government realizes public good supply at a certain amount. The individuals request these goods according to the amount of tax they paid. If high price (high tax rate) is in question public good supply will stay higher than the demand, in other words excess supply (or lack of demand) problem will arise. In such a case optimal production level of public goods will not be realized. Starting from this point, it can be said that utility-cost analysis is taken as the basis in Lindhal model in contradistinction to Pareto optimality approach. The relation between the utility received from consumption of public goods and taxes used for their financing that is cost to the individual constitutes the essence of Lindhal model's optimality condition.

Knut Wicsell, a fellow citizen who lived almost at the same era with Erik Lindhal, developed a pioneering model to Lindhal's model. Wicksell's (1958) model is based on identifying utility obtained from public goods and based on utility approach with the money paid for their finance (taxes). As Wick sell model is the pioneer of Lindhal's model, it has brought the condition of optimality depending on the equivalence of utility obtained from public goods and services as in the Lindhal model and taxes paid for them. In this sense, Wicksell's model and Lindhal's model are parallel to each other. In his approach, trade-off between taxes and public goods are realized according to the will of an individual (voluntary trade-off desire). Thus, the individual may establish a relation between the utility received from public goods and the taxes paid as their price. Moreover, according to him majority of votes is not sufficient for collecting taxes and making public spending, but all the individuals are required make decision in common.

An important model included in public finance literature was put forward by US economist Howard. R. Bowen. Optimality condition in Bowel's model (1943) differs from the approaches in the models of Samuelson, Lindhal or Wicksell. Samuelson relates optimality to Pareto optimality in his model. However, Lindshal and Wicksell searched for cost-utility equality in their models. Bowen model is based on the equivalency of supply and demand. His optimality condition is created as a result of intersection of the supply curve including public good production of the government and total demand curve obtained as a result of vertical addition of demand curves of the individuals who wishes to utilize a specified public good (here dual member market assumption is valid.) Thus, Bowen model tried to determine public goods optimality condition starting from the basis of equality of horizontal sum of individual requests for private goods.

SOLUTIONS AND RECOMMENDATIONS

Offering public goods which are accepted as one of the reasons of market failure at an optimum production level is important in terms of social utility maximization. Not only public economy policy-makers but also scientists have responsibilities for the optimum production of these goods which cannot be produced within the market mechanism due to their spesific characteristics. In this sense, it will be beneficial for the solution to increase quantity and quality of theoeratical and emprical studies for the development of approaches related with the subject, application of these studies to economic and fiscal areas by the public authorities on a scientific basis and while doing all this, to take the opinions of stakeholders covering all segments of society.

FUTURE RESEARCH DIRECTIONS

The aim of this study is to discuss public goods which are one of the basic reasons of market failure theoretically and to study ideas on ideal supply levels of the public goods. In this direction; after presenting the basic approaches within the framework of public goods theory, theories on the ideal optimum production level of public goods is explained. Researchers who are interested in this topic should follow a path which combines theoretical and emprical findings in order to contribute to the theory of public goods.

CONCLUSION

The topic of market failure has a very important place in economic literature. Neoclassical economists developed various theories in order to remove the deficiencies of liberal-classical school and thus to provide sustainability by giving answers to the criticisms againist capitalist economy in the nineteenth century. One of them is about the reasons of market failure. According to them, the first reason of market failure is imperfect (incomplete) competition conditions. Homogeneity (the uniformity of goods in the market), atomicity (the existence of so many buyers and sellers that no one can determine prices), mobility (uninterrupted entry and exit to the market) and perfect information (cost-free and completely free access to information) are the *sine qua non* conditions of a perfect competition market. If any of these conditions are missing than imperfect competition conditions prevail instead of perfect competition conditions. However, in real life as well as the goods are not exactly the same, there are neither many sellers and buyers nor a perfectly costless and unimpeded acces to the information with exit and entry into the market. In that case, since perfect competition conditions are not valid, the existence of imperfect competition requires government intervention to the economy.

Secondly, economic activities may lead to positive or negative externalities. An activity realized by an economic unit may have positive or negative impacts on other economic units by increasing or decreasing their costs. This prevents formation of fair competition conditions. For instance, a factory polluting environment is a source of a great negative externality for the society and a serious cost for the national economy as a whole. Therefore, implementations to regulate externalities are required to be adopted by the public authority.

According to the neoclassical economists, other factors which necessitate government intervention into the economy are asymettric information, monopolies and public goods. Among them, assymettric information includes a situation in which buyers and sellers in the market have different information on a good. Market failure is inevitable since the parties have different data on the economic value subject to trade. Likewise, a monopoly has a structure contrary to the spirit of market mechanism (competitive conditions) due to their monopolistic characteristics. Thus, public practice and policies should be implemented in these two aforementioned areas.

Public goods—particularly perfect public goods—discussed in this study include goods and services which are not suitable to supply within the market conditions since they should be produced by the government. Among these, defense and security services are absolutely produced by the government since they are accepted as perfect public goods. Perfect public goods and services are utilized collectively and competition and exclusion is out of the question since they cannot be marketed (subject to sale) as they cannot be priced out because of indivisibility. And also, this makes existence of government in economic life compulsory although there is a free-rider problem. Training and health services which are included in semi-public goods and services can both be produced private sector and by the government due to social utility (positive externality) provided. In addition to this, the existence of tragedy of commons argument which expresses that the social utility of regulation of virtuous and non-virtuous public goods and club goods and goods for common use by the public authority reveals supply of public goods and services.

As it is seen, according to the market failure argument of neoclassical thought, perfectly operating markets are not always possible and sometimes public policies and implementations are also required. Here, since the existence of public goods and sometimes production of these in market conditions is not appropriate or possible, the existence of public sector in economic and soical life becomes a necessity. On the other hand, compulsory existence of these goods and services and being subject to a production process out of market operation revives discussions about the level of ideal production. The models based on Pareto optimum approach by Samuelson, based on cost-benefit relation between taxes and public goods by Lindhal and Wicksell, based on supply-demand equilibrium of public goods and services by Bowen were developed for this purpose. Throughout the historical development of economic thought, these models constitute a significant theoretical basis on the optimality conditions of public goods and services which are required to be produced by the government.

REFERENCES

Akerlof, G. A. (1970). The market for "lemons": Quality uncertainty and the market mechanism. *The Quarterly Journal of Economics, 84*(3), 488–500. doi:10.2307/1879431

Aslanbeigui, N., & Medema, S. G. (1998). Beyond the dark clouds: Pigou and Coase on social cost. *History of Political Economy, 30*(4), 601–625. doi:10.1215/00182702-30-4-601

Auronen, L. (2003, May). Asymmetric information: Theory and applications. *Proceedings of the Seminar in Strategy and International Business*. Academic Press.

Bator, F. M. (1958). The anatomy of market failure. *The Quarterly Journal of Economics, 72*(3), 351–379. doi:10.2307/1882231

Benáček, V. (1992). Market failure versus government failure - The optıons of the emerging market economies. Retrieved from ww1.ceses.cuni.cz/benacek/FAILURE.pdf

Bowen, H. R. (1943). The interpretation of voting in the allocation of economic resources. *The Quarterly Journal of Economics, 58*(1), 27–48. doi:10.2307/1885754

Buchanan, J. M. (1999). *The collected works of James M. Buchanan (Volume-5): The Demand and Supply of Public Goods*. Indianapolis: Liberty Fund. (Original work published 1968)

Buchanan, J. M., & Stubblebine, W. C. (1962). Externality. In Classic papers in natural resource economics (pp. 138-154). London: Palgrave Macmillan.

Caldari, K., & Masini, F. (2011). Pigouvian versus Marshallian tax: Market failure, public intervention and the problem of externalities. *European Journal of the History of Economic Thought, 18*(5), 715–732. doi:10.1080/09672567.2011.629300

Coase, R. H. (1960). The problem of social cost. *The Journal of Law & Economics, 3*(October), 1–44. doi:10.1086/466560

Cornia, G. A. (1999). *Liberalization, globalization and ıncome distribution, UNU World Institute for Development Economics Research*. UNU/WIDER.

Etzioni, A. (1999). *Essays in socio-economics*. New York: Springer. doi:10.1007/978-3-662-03900-7

Greene, J. E. (2012). *Public finance: An international perspective*. Singapore: World Scientific Publishing.

Gruber, J. (2016). *Public finance and public policy* (5th ed.). New York: Worth Publishers.

Hardin, G. (1968). The tragedy of the commons. *Science, 162*(3859), 1243–1248. doi:10.1126cience.162.3859.1243 PMID:5699198

Hayek, F. A. (2004). *The road to serfdom, Caldwell, B*. Westminster: The Institute of Economic Affairs.

Hillman, A. L. (2009). *Public finance and public policy: responsibilities and limitations of government* (2nd ed.). Cambridge: Cambridge University Press. doi:10.1017/CBO9780511813788

Huffman, W. E. (2009). Does information change behaviour? *Proceedings of the OECD World Forum, Statistics, Knowledge and Policy*, Buson, Korea, October 27-30. Academic Press.

Hutchison, T. W. (1984). Institutionalist economics old and new. *Journal of Institutional and Theoretical Economics, 140*(1), 20–29.

Hyman, D. N. (2010). *Public finance: A contemporary application of theory to policy* (10th ed.). Ohio: South-Westen Cengage Learning.

Kaul, I., Grunberg, I., & Stern, M. A. (1999). *Global public goods: Concepts, policies and strategies, Kaul, I., Grunberg, I., & Stern, M. A: Global Public Goods: International Cooperation in the 21st Century*. New York: Oxford University Press.

Kayıran, M. (2013). Kamu malları: Piyasa başarısızlığı mı teorilerin başarısızlığı mı? [Public Goods: Market Failure or the Failure of the Theories?]. *Ankara Universty SBF Juornal, 68*(4), 147–184.

Le Grand, J. (1991). The theory of government failure. *British Journal of Political Science, 21*(4), 423–442. doi:10.1017/S0007123400006244

Lindahl, E. (1958). *Just taxation – A positive solution, Musgrave, R. A. & Peacock, A. T.: Classics in the Theory of Public Finance*. London: The Macmillan Press. (Original work published 1919)

Mankiw, N. G. (2001). *Principles of economics* (2nd ed.). USA: Harcourt.

McMahon, W. W. (1987). *Externalities in education, Psacharopoulos, G.:Economics of Education, Research and Studies* (pp. 133–137). Oxford: Pergamon.

Menard, C., & Mary, M. S. (2005). *Handbook of new institutional economics*. Netherlands: Springer. doi:10.1007/b106770

Mirrlees, J. A. (1999). The theory of moral hazard and unobservable behaviour: Part I. *The Review of Economic Studies*, *66*(1), 3–21. doi:10.1111/1467-937X.00075

Musgrave, R. A. (1959). *The theory of public finance: A study in pubic economy*. Bombay: Tata-McGraw Hill.

Ostrom, E. (2000). Collective action and the evolution of social norms. *The Journal of Economic Perspectives*, *14*(3), 137–158. doi:10.1257/jep.14.3.137

Parsons, T. (1967). *The structure of social action*. New York: Free Press.

Perloff, J. M. (2007). *Microeconomics* (4th ed.). USA: Pearson Addison Wesley.

Pigou, A. C. (1912). *Wealth and welfare*. London: Macmillan.

Pigou, A. C. (1920). *Welfare economics, Londra*. Macmillan.

Pindyck, R. S., & Rubinfeld, D. L. (2018). *Microeconomics* (9th ed.). Edinburgh: Pearson.

Razeen, S. (2002). *Classical liberalism and ınternational economic order*. New York: Routledge.

Samuelson, P. A. (1954). The pure theory of public expenditure. *The Review of Economics and Statistics*, *36*(4), 387–389. doi:10.2307/1925895

Samuelson, P. A. (1955). Diagrammatic exposition of a theory of public expenditure. *The Review of Economics and Statistics*, *37*(4), 350–356. doi:10.2307/1925849

Seidman, L. S. (2009). *Public finance*. NewYork: McGraw Hill/Irwin.

Sharkey, W. W. (1983). *The theory of natural monopoly, Cambridge Books*. Cambridge University Press.

Stiglitz, J. E. (2000). Economics of the public sector (3rd ed.). New York: W.W. Norton & Company.

Ulbrich, H. H. (2011). *Public finance in theory and practice* (*2nd ed.*). London: Routledge.

Varian, H. R. (2010). *Intermediate microeconomics: A modern approach* (*8th ed.*). New York: W. W. Norton & Company.

Wicksell, K. (1958). *A new principle of just taxation. In R.A. Musgrave & A.T. Peacock (Eds.), Classics in the theory of public finance* (pp. 72–118). London: The Macmillan Press. (Original work published 1896)

Winston, C. (2006). *Government failure versus market failure: microeconomics policy research and government performance*. Washington, D.C.: AEI-Brookings.

KEY TERMS AND DEFINITIONS

Asymmetric Information: This is a situation where there is imperfect knowledge.

Externality: Externality is situations when the effect of production or consumption of goods and services imposes costs or benefits on others.

Incomplete Competition Market: Imperfect competition is not a competitive market situation.

Market Failure: The economic situation defined by an inefficient distribution of goods and services in the free market.

Neoclassical Economics: It is an approach to economics that relates supply and demand to an individual's rationality and his ability to maximize utility or profit.

Paul Anthony Samuelson: He became a groundbreaking economist through his use of mathematical principles.

Public Goods: A commodity or service that is provided without profit to all members of a society, either by the government or by a private individual or organization.

Scale Economics: It is cost advantages reaped by companies when production becomes efficient.

Chapter 3

Neoliberalism, Self-Identity, and Consumer Culture in the UAE

Başak Özoral
https://orcid.org/0000-0003-3075-6362
Istanbul Commerce University, Turkey

İlke Civelekoğlu
https://orcid.org/0000-0001-8892-0802
Istanbul Commerce University, Turkey

ABSTRACT

Over the last half-century, modern societies have been experiencing a drastic social, cultural, and economic transformation. The change in the behaviors and habits of consumers under the strong impact of neoliberalism demonstrates the close relationship between economy and social psychology. Globalized neo-liberalization has become an unavoidable, powerful force that impacts all elements of social, cultural, and economic life and defines people's identities and their consumption preferences. This chapter addresses the link between neoliberalism and consumer behavior, with a focus on non-Western societies. It examines if there is a contradiction between the features of consumer culture and the prevailing domestic culture in these societies. Many scholars associate consumer culture with Western societies, but the authors argue that consumer culture has become a significant phenomenon even in the most religiously conservative, non-Western societies. By taking Dubai in the UAE as the case study, this chapter demonstrates how consumer culture helps redefine culture and self-identity. The chapter concludes by arguing that since individual behavior is not rational, individuals' needs are defined by the dictates of consumer culture across the globe in neoliberal times.

DOI: 10.4018/978-1-7998-1037-7.ch003

INTRODUCTION

How the citizens of the UAE have redefined their behavior, values and identity under consumerism help us understand the influences of globalized neoliberalism in non-Western societies. In order to understand the dynamic processes of acculturation on identity in a setting where cultural pressures are obvious, this study was undertaken in a religiously conservative city of the UAE. The data was collected in Dubai, a city with a liberal economic environment in which a very big expatriate population contributes to its economy (Malecki & Ewers, 2007).

With the welcoming liberal environment it offers, Dubai is an important cosmopolitan hub in the Gulf. The increase in foreign investments and job opportunities has made the expat population significant within the total population of Dubai and thus, multiculturalism has become the central feature of the Emirati culture. The multicultural and the multinational environment in the city has produced cross-cultural communication and cultural exchange.

Not only this multicultural population but also multinational companies, hotels, investments and schools have changed the social and cultural structure of the Emirati society. With the strong penetration of foreign western brands such as Armani, Chanel, Sony and Mercedes, luxury consumption has penetrated into the city. As Shukla and Purani (2012:1417) indicate, the symbolic value attached to consumer goods may be '*highly influential among all cultures and countries. However, their degree of influence may differ dramatically.*' Similarly Al-Mutaaw (2013) points out that this influence is more related with cultures, where differences are more significant. According to Marciniak and Mohsen (June, 2014) consumers in the Gulf are almost obsessed with brands that have highly recognizable logos such as Louis Vuitton, Tiffany and Dior. This chapter argues that the choices of consumers in Dubai represent a homogeneous attitude when it comes to consumption of luxury products and famous Western brands with flashy decoration. The consumers in Dubai have economic power to engage in luxury consumption. Also, they are extremely interested in consuming Western life style. In contrast to traditional Emirati life that was very simple and modest, the Emiratis today have an interest in integrating themselves into a globalized world. In this context luxury consumption has become not only a consumer behavior but a matter of identity, prestige and power in the UAE society.

This chapter aims to understand the main motivation of Emirati consumers in consuming luxury goods and redefining their identities at the age of globalization. In doing so, the purposes of the research are: to understand how Emiratis perceive luxury, modernization and materialism; to define the greatest personal motivation for the consumption of luxury goods among the people of the UAE. This chapter also highlights the increasingly important position of shopping malls in Dubai nowadays. Today, shopping malls with their restaurants, bars, cafes or even hairdressers, beauty salons, gyms, cinemas and entertainment parks have become the centers of consumer culture. Since the biggest and most impressive shopping malls were founded in Dubai, analyzing their influence on consuming behavior helps address how globalization has deeply penetrated into the cultural and social life of Emiratis and led to significant changes in the daily practices and preferences.

With its interdisciplinary approach, the chapter aims to make a contribution to the model of rational economic man in economics by bringing in the psychological approach to unpack the consumer behavior in traditional local cultures. Put differently, it aims to bring together social psychology and economics to better understand the contemporary cultural, economic and other factors affecting societies of hyper-consumption. Most significantly, this chapter addresses how the personal choices and actions of consumers reflect a wider pro-market paradigm that encourages certain values, habits and practices across the globe. Thus, the study aims to contribute to the growing literature on the intersection of economics and psychology, in general, and to the literature of the sub-discipline of consumer behavior, in particular.

CONSUMERISM, NEOLIBERALISM, AND THE HOMOGENIZATION OF CULTURES ACROSS THE WORLD

Over the last half-century modern societies have been experiencing a drastic social, cultural and economic transformation. The change in behaviors and habits of consumers under the strong impact of neoliberalism demonstrates the close relationship between economy and social psychology. Today, globalized neo-liberalization has become unavoidably powerful with its impact on social, cultural and economic life in a society, and with its ability to define individuals' consumption preferences.

Before proceeding, it is important to define what consumer culture means. Consumer culture refers to a culture organized around the consumption of goods and leisure rather than the production of materials and services (Marshall, 1998:112-113) and it has become a significant phenomenon both in Western and non-Western societies under neoliberalism. In order to understand consumer culture and how it became a global phenomenon, it is critical to unpack the link between consumerism and neoliberalism. With the onset of neoliberalism in the early 1980s, citizens were encouraged to pursue their self-interest through economic freedoms conferred upon them by the market. The almost religious-like faith of neoliberalism in the powers of the unregulated market to generate economic growth and prosperity stems from the assumption that as people and businesses compete freely at the marketplace, the market itself organizes these activities into an optimal economic order that benefits everyone (Hayek, 1944).

Free markets while effectively distributing resources based on individual needs and desires also lead to an increase in marketplace choice and thus, seek to empower the consumer. Freedom, therefore, takes on a very specific meaning in the neoliberal universe as it is synonymous with the liberty to compete freely as well as having choice as a consumer (Perez & Esposito: 2010: 93). In neoliberal universe, human nature is depicted as naturally competitive and self-serving. Thus, individuals are assumed to act in ways that serve their best interests and bring them the most happiness- which is associated with a natural human longing to possess things and/or attain recognition from others (Perez & Esposito: 2010: 93).

This is why neoliberalism encourages individuals for an unrestrained appetite for personal and material satisfaction and thus, makes consumption the primary ritual of modern society (ibid: 85). The hyper-materialistic mode of life- what Veblen (1965) called the conspicuous consumption- became the dominant ethos associated with neoliberalism and expanded virtually to all corners of the globe. As individualism and empowerment of consumers were steadily encouraged under neoliberalism, consumer items have become symbols of self-identity, impression management and associations with others in the social milieu (Bourdieu, 1982; Lury, 1996). Consequently, consumption has become an indicator of a person's worth and status. As McDonald et al. (2017: 368) argues, gaining membership to social categories now became dependent on the level of discretionary spending and the knowledge and ability to manipulate the signs and symbols of consumer products: the clothes that people wear, the type of food that they eat, home decorations and travel/holiday destinations they choose help signal or mark a person's status and position within a social and cultural hierarchy. Moreover, the social context, including social relations and value systems, in which individuals act started to reflect the neoliberal notion that all people are driven to compete and consume excessively. At the individual level, as citizens were re-constituted as consumers, and became subject to market based logic through various discourses and policies; "commodification of self-identity", meaning looking and being desirable for the visual consumption of others became a reality in market-dominated societies (McDonald et al., 2017). Put differently, neoliberalism created a specific cultural context, where personality began to be associated with ability to be attractive and unique, to stand out in the crowd, to be distinctive and noticed by others (Schroer, 2014). From cosmetic surgery to fitness industry consumer choices started to reflect the impacts of neoliberal ethos on self-identity (self-esteem and self-enhancement) and exemplified how market took over social life. At the societal and even global level excessive consumerism became promoted under market-driven values as neoliberalism successfully associated human nature with competition; freedom with consumer choice; and success and desirability with material wealth.

The above discussion indicates that the assumption of "rational economic man" does not hold in neoliberal era as individuals are turned into consumers, who purchase products for their symbolic value rather than for the utilitarian purposes. After all, in consumer culture, many of purchased consumer items are non-necessary for survival. However, they represent important symbols regarding the formation of self-identity. This is why the intersection between consumerism, neoliberal political economy and social psychology needs to be explored.

As this chapter claims, in the context of consumer behavior and neoliberalism, the authors see homogenization of cultures as an inevitable trend across the world. In this sense developing countries might treat advanced Western economies as reference nations not only in the domain of economic development, but also in the realm of cultural restructuring (Chiu et. al., 2011: 667). With the spread of neoliberalism, we can talk of a global culture that privileges consumerism, individualism and competition. Even people in developing countries living in poverty are subject to the same market-driven forces that advance a culture of conspicuous consumption, making it a global phenomenon promoted by neoliberal ethos. Hence, one can argue for the hegemonic influence of neoliberalism on local cultures as it creates similar lifestyles, tastes and consumer choices. In line with Perez and Esposito (2010), this chapter claims that a paradigmatic shift from the current neoliberal approach is necessary to break this cycle.

The worldwide trade and investment opportunities presented by neoliberalism enabled multinational companies to move some of their factories and companies from their home countries to different parts of the world to reduce costs (labor and raw materials) or find new markets, or both (Al-Yousif, 2004). Thus, it is becoming increasingly hard to identify a product with a given nationality. However, as the biggest and most popular international companies that produce and sell goods in the global market are Western companies, their products represent Western technology and culture. When we look at the impact of this process on the culture of non-Western developing countries, we see that the increase in consumption tends to bring homogenization of culture among traditional societies and of local people along the lines of consumerism and individualism. Since consumer goods represent cultural belongings, consuming practices of imported goods can result in a sense of cultural change. This neoliberal globalization process is more obvious in the non-Western societies than elsewhere in the world, where it is seen as a process of "Westernization". This phenomenon has grown after the 1990s. The concepts of 'consumerism' and 'modern consumer society' came to symbolize a particular western version of modern consumption in the current debate.

THE RISE OF CONSUMER CULTURE IN THE GULF

As Heron (2012) argues, neoliberal globalization process has contributed to changes in traditional societies and cultures across the globe. Over the last three decades the Gulf region has witnessed this process intensively as it experienced a growing integration into the global economy. Although Arabs in the Gulf welcome globalization, they recognize that globalization process delivers challenges as well as opportunities. The Gulf countries have similar cultural characteristics, such as Arabic language, Islamic religion, Bedouin heritage and identity (Ahmed, 1998). As Meltcalfe says globalization has led to unexpected economic opportunities between countries, within countries and among individuals (Meltcalfe, November, 2008). A developing capital market with e-commerce, free trade zones and worldwide production companies have begun to emerge especially in the Gulf region by creating job opportunities for locals and outsiders (Moghadam, 2003, 2005). This very rapid economic development created an unexpected change in the Gulf societies, especially on their cultural practices. Social life in these societies has changed significantly with the rise of globalization in the region.

Dubai, along with its neighbor states of the Gulf region, has emerged as a significant geographic location that demonstrates the social and cultural effects of globalization (Hvidt, May, 2015). Dubai's amazing economic development makes this Emirate the most attractive city for foreign investors, international companies, visitors, expats and migrant workers. This is why in this chapter Dubai is taken as an example to discuss the great impact of globalization on the social and cultural aspects of non-western societies, and on the consumer choices of individuals living in these societies. The transformation of Dubai since 1990s is unique because, similar to other Gulf societies, Dubai also has a very strict local tradition and an Islamic heritage in its social and cultural life. This Emirate, however, also enjoys all benefits of modern global economy. In this sense Dubai represents an interesting mixture of old and modern in its culture. Besides, Emiratis' increasing income and their engagement in the global economy led to extensive acceptance of Western cultural practices and a great interest in obtaining material goods through consumer culture. So, documenting and analyzing Dubai's development path helps us better understand how ascendancy of neoliberalism could take place within the political and cultural territory of the Middle East in general.

RESEARCH METHODS

The data of this chapter comes from both written sources and conducted interviews. The research was made in Dubai in 2016 throughout a period of five months. Thirty-five interviews with 15 males and 20 females, aged between 20-45 years, from different industries were conducted. Three semi-structured interviews took place with the participants. Fifteen interview questions (see Appendix) were designed to investigate participants' perceptions of globalization and its influence on Emirati culture. Qualitative data analysis techniques were used to analyze participants' responses.

This chapter asks three questions. First, how globalization and neoliberal economic development have influenced identity, culture and values in social life of Emiratis? Second, what are the main motivations of consumers in Dubai? Third, what is the impact of globalization on local cultures?

DUBAI

Over the last three decades Dubai, one of the Emirates of the UAE, has become the main center of trade, finance, tourism and construction in the Gulf. In the 1970s Dubai was an insignificant, poor settlement of 30,000. Its population reached to 1.4 million people over time and the city has become the center of high-profile investments and purchases. The GDP per capita has increased to $ 41449.68 in April 2019 as a result of a booming economy[1]. The population of Dubai has increased very rapidly in last 40 years and reached to 2 million in 2015. (Elessawy, April 2017). The city has a heterogeneous population: Indians, Indonesians, Philippines, Africans immigrant workers coexist with European, American and Middle Eastern expats that have risen in number very dramatically over the years. This multicultural, multi-religious and multinational environment has affected the changes on the local culture and lifestyle in the region.

Until the 1980s traditional markets, the "Souqs", were the only centers of trade and shopping in the region. The first super mall, Al Ghurair Mall, was opened in Dubai in 1981. Today Dubai is famous with its supermalls, shopping festivals and luxury hotels. The biggest shopping mall, Dubai Mall, has become one of the most visited shopping malls in the world as it was visited by 65 million visitors in 2012 (Duncan, 2013). There are currently 96 shopping malls in the city. Each of them was designed on the basis of a different concept and they all have cultural activities, zoos, concept parks, exhibitions, playgrounds, beauty salons, bookstores, theaters and branches of well-known restaurants from all over the world.

Dubai is also famous for its ultramodern architecture and a lively nightlife scene. Burj Khalifa, an 830m-tall tower, dominates the skyscraper-filled skyline. There is Dubai Fountain, with jets and lights choreographed to music in Dubai Mall. Artificial islands of Dubai, Atlantis and The Palm, have luxury resort with water and marine-animal parks. Not only tourists but also local people come and spend time in these shopping malls. Hence, Dubai, with its shopping festivals, gigantic luxury hotels and super malls stand out as the center of consumerism in the Gulf.

Local Culture in Dubai

In all societies cultural identity is important as it reflects how an individual defines the self and its role in a community. Emirati culture has a Bedouin root which is a traditional heritage in the Arabian Peninsula. Obviously, many Arab customs are very different from those in the west. The UAE seeks to preserve its language, history and heritage as its cultural identity for many generations to come. Very briefly the features of the culture in Dubai can be summarized as follows:

1. The main characteristic of the Emirati society is close family relations as blood relationship is very important for Emiratis. Extended families have many members and respect for elders in the family and society is a rule. In extended families all family members used to live together in the same house including grandparents, parents, children, and perhaps aunts and uncles.
2. It is a patriarchal society; men are the decision makers and bread earners in the family. Women do not participate very actively in social and economic life. Their main responsibility is taking care of the family. Traditionally, women do not go outside or travel alone.
3. Hospitality is very important part of Emirati culture as Emiratis socialize by gathering together at their homes and sharing their meal as the most important event for Fridays and festivities. Women and men stay separate in their meetings and celebrations. Men occasionally come together to talk about various subjects and listen to elders for advice. These traditional meetings are called "*majlis.*" Poor and wealthy people, children and adults gather in these meetings. Marriage decisions or business contracts can be the subject of these gatherings. Traditional Arab houses have a central courtyard (housh) and a veranda (*liwan*) and the majlis are still an essential part of every Emirati household in Dubai (Shoufani, 2014).
4. Camels are very crucial part of the Emirati heritage and life in the desert. Traditionally, they were used for transportation, and they served as an important source of nourishment. Camels are extremely important for Emirati people as having a camel is very prestigious for them. So are falcons. They were part of

the desert life and falcons were often trained to hunt to supplement the family meals. Today, falcons are still trained in the traditional way. Camel race and falconry are still popular among the local people.

5. Men in the Dubai wear the traditional *kandoora* which is a white dress that covers the body. Depending on the season the kandoora can be in different colors such as blue, grey, black, and brown. The *ghutra* is also another traditional male wearing, it combines a white cloth to cover the head and the *agal*, a black cord, wrapped around twice to keep the ghutra on the head. The young Emirati nowadays also wears a red and white ghutra which they tie around their head. The traditional clothing for women is an *abaya* which is a black outfit and the *shaila*, a black scarf that covers the hair. Old ladies also wear *burga* which covers part of their face. Wearing the shaila and abaya today is still popular for women as signs of their culture and Emirati identity (Shoufani, 2014).
6. Life in Dubai was simple and humble in old days. Architecture and daily objects that Emirati people were using tended to be very modest. Emiratis have lived in tents in the desert and even today most of the Emiratis enjoy spending their spare time in desert by camping.
7. Islam is an integral part and perhaps the most important element that has shaped Emirati culture. Islam highlights the importance of modesty, prudence, non-worldly devotion, spiritualism and communitarianism. Given these features of Islam, one can say that consumerism is inherently incompatible with Islam and current cultural environment in Dubai.

Economic Development, Super Malls, and The Influence of Globalization in Dubai

Since the UAE gained its independency in 1971, it has maintained political stability. The country has rich oil reserves and a good portion of oil revenues are distributed to Emirati people in the form of social and economic benefits. Government provides excellent social services, such as free education and health services for its citizens. Over time, high income levels have raised the standard of living for Emirati citizens and contributed to political and social peace and stability in the society.

The UAE is an active member of many regional and international associations such as the Arab League, the United Nations, the Non-Aligned Movement, the Arab Gulf Cooperation Council, and the Organization of the Islamic Conference. International relations of the UAE with the Western world and many other countries have been good. Over the last thirty years especially tourism, construction, finance and energy industries have developed tremendously in the UAE. Urbanization has led to the development of the most important city of the UAE, Dubai, which has become the center of attraction in the Middle East with its infrastructure, trade centers and technologic investments. The most drastic transformation in cultural and social life in the Gulf Cooperation Council (GCC) countries has appeared in the UAE. As a result of the increasing prosperity, westernization and consumerism have penetrated into the society (Sampler & Eigner, 2008). The cultural, social and demographic change in the UAE is a mixture of religiously conservative, traditional social structure, and a consumer culture that was brought by globalization.

Since Dubai has very attractive and big shopping malls in the Gulf region, one can suggest a clear relationship between the rise of consuming culture and these super shopping malls. With modern times is no longer possible to observe an active social life on the main streets of old towns as shopping centers have replaced the old by fulfilling all needs under one roof (Frączkiewicz, 2013). Hence shopping malls have penetrated into the daily life of the people in Dubai. As people of different nationality and age prefer to spend their time in these malls, they began to play an important role in transforming social relations and contributing to new consuming behaviors. Consequently, Dubai's famous shopping festivals and huge malls helped generate the rise of consumerism in the city.

Findings, Discussion, and Conclusion

Participants in the survey mentioned that they usually spend their time by going to movies, restaurants, coffee shops or by doing window and real shopping in the malls of Dubai. Most of the participants stated that they are going to super malls to socialize or to involve in cultural activities. Some participants said there are ice-skating rinks or artificial lakes in super malls and these are very new for Emiratis. Nowadays Emiratis can take hockey courses or take a boat tour in the middle of the desert. This opportunity is an excellent example which demonstrates how cultural differences in different geographic locations could be mitigated by globalization. In Emirati culture women do not go outside alone. However, shopping malls provide an opportunity to change this traditional practice. Currently Emirati women are able to participate in social life mostly by doing shopping in super malls. Women can also go to movies, stores and restaurants with their families or friends, where they get a chance to see the products of other cultures. Dubai stores, restaurants and coffee shops offer goods representative of American or European lifestyle. Participants stated that they like to celebrate birthdays and other important days in these restaurants with their families.

The 80 per cent of the participants mentioned that they wear local clothes. However, participants also said that they like to buy and wear western clothes, especially famous Western brands' bags and shoes. Using designer bags is an important sign of economic power and prestige in the society for Emirati ladies. Similarly, Emirati men say having an expensive watch and a luxury car is highly valued in their social environment. These goods are not even accepted as luxury items but just necessities in the UAE. In support of this materialist view, the interviews uncovered how luxury was usually perceived by the wealthy. One young participate (31 years old, woman, married) stated "If you are coming from a well-known family or if you have a good job, you have to show it. And people want to see this". Although fashion is a foreign concept in traditional Emirati and Islamic culture, at present days Emiratis follow fashion trends very closely. The exhibitions, fashion shows and well-known designers' boutiques are very popular in Dubai. They all encourage people to consume more. For instance, Emirati young girls have begun to wear jeans and many of the participants say they prefer to wear western style clothes even at home. The spread of western style clothes among Emirati people is an example of how consumer culture changes behavior of Emiratis.

Especially younger participants said that they like to spend their time in Western style cafes and tea shops where they like to drink green tea or Western type of coffee, instead of sitting at traditional Arabic cafés. So now they have new habits and behaviors in eating and drinking. Participants mentioned that they feel "lucky" to have international brands, Western or Asian famous restaurants, hotels and coffee shops in Dubai. One participant (29 years old, single, man) said "Eating beef in a Texas restaurant then having a cup of green tea in a Japanese tea house and watching an American movie in the same mall is a bless and very exciting, I feel myself as a world citizen". Many of the participants mentioned that when they consume the goods of these international brands they feel "modern" and believe that all these opportunities have come to the region with the spread of globalization.

Participants also mentioned that new stores have brought new behaviors for Emiratis, such as the biggest bookstore of the Dubai, *Kinokuniya* Bookstore, which is one of the most visited stores in the city. People can read newspapers and magazines, see the bestsellers and find publications in different languages there. There is also a very rich book collection for kids. Women participants said they like to read fashion magazines while men mostly read sports and cars magazines and economy journals. In *Virjin*, a music store, the latest music albums from all over the world, the newest high technology, new computer games, concert tickets and music books are available for Emiratis. Traditionally, going to concerts or reading magazines is not a very popular activity in Emirati culture but these stores have changed the habits in the society. Emiratis have integrated themselves into the global world by encountering other cultures and using their various intellectual products with the help of these stores.

Participants said they prefer to consume foreign well-known products because they trust their quality and also these products give them more satisfaction. Furthermore, more than %70 of the participants said they frequently buy goods which they do not really need. Most of the participants also mentioned that shopping itself has become a joyful activity, especially after the opening up of super malls in Dubai. They believe there is no association between consumption and necessities as participants mentioned that the consumer culture is not about consuming for necessary goods, but it is consuming especially luxury goods for social status, prestige and power in the society. What Coco Chanel said as "Luxury is the necessity that begins where necessity ends" (Husic and Cicic 2008: p. 235) really fits the life style and attitude of consumers in Dubai.

Recently some of the Western cultural celebrations, such as *Halloween, Valentine Day* or *Christmas* have begun to be celebrated with western music and figures in stores and malls in Dubai. One could see many exhibitions and special markets during the season especially on beaches and in shopping malls. Horror costumes, pumpkin cakes, red heart shaped balloons or Santa Figures have entered the life of Emiratis through the festivals and celebration seasons. Participants said they like celebrations and they enjoy shopping in these markets and seeing very different cultural events. Actually, there are no such celebrations in local culture as these celebrations contradict with Islamic values and traditions. Interestingly they are more and more welcomed by Emiratis.

The responses of participants signal that not only the Emiratis' choices of clothes, food and beverages, but also their home style and furniture preferences have started to change. Traditionally Emirati families used to live as extended family members in big houses. Today families are much smaller and Emiratis gather together in apartments and small flats. Western style luxury furniture also entered into the life of Emiratis. Instead of traditional carpets, divan and cushions, Emiratis have begun to use table, western type of coaches, kitchen staff, televisions, air conditionings and other technological goods. The changes regarding their home designs and living environments are another striking example of new consuming behavior among Emiratis.

Emirati women participants indicated that since it is now easy to find frozen food in supermarkets and restaurants, they prefer to buy such meals for their families. Thus, the routine of Emirati women has also changed as they now show interest in hobbies as many of them have begun to spend their time in new yoga saloons and swimming pools. Being a member of expensive sport clubs and showing interest in different sports is a completely new habit but it is definitely the new trend for Emirati society nowadays. As many participants said Western beauty trends have become extremely popular in Emirati society: while men prefer to have hair plant operations, women like to have aesthetical operations to change their facial features.

In the traditional Emirati society, status and power of the individuals were determined by their family reputation, tribal relations, personal success and capabilities. As the findings of this research demonstrates the social status of individuals in modern globalized world is now determined by their consumer preferences regarding cars, houses, clothes and life style they choose to have.

CONCLUSION

With the ascendancy of neoliberalism and the establishment of super malls in Dubai, one could see the rise of consumer culture that stem from people's experience with new consumer practices and, more broadly, from the impact of cultural globalization (Jamala et al., 2006). This chapter argues that there are changes in the patterns of behavior and the daily lives of a group of participants in Dubai: family eating habits have changed as many families prefer ready meals at home or going to restaurants at the supermall to cooking at home. Social and family relationships have also changed as visiting families at their homes has become less common, and individuals now spend their time at supermalls, doing shopping, watching movies, and engaging in Western activities, such as exhibitions and shows. This study suggests that Emiratis have experienced changes in their social relations and behaviors, when it comes to consumption of goods, such as cars, clothes and eating habits. The reconstruction of cultural identity via the impact of globalization and consumerism took place in Dubai. In Emirates we observe a globalization process in social life that involves Western attitudes and behaviors. The rapid change in social life has created a gap between old and young generations as younger generations are largely pleased with the shifts in types of daily life, consumer behaviors, and new forms of entertainment. The strong influence of globalization on consuming behavior of Emirati people can be accepted as rebuilding of a new collective identity in the UAE. The choices of individuals make them a member of consuming society while their integration in modern global life has resulted in detachment from traditional values.

The findings of this study show the depth of the social and cultural changes experienced by a religiously conservative Emirati society under the influence of globalization. The rise of a consumer culture has changed the daily routine of Emiratis dramatically. We conclude that many aspects of cultural diversity and cultural identity are threatened by globalized consumerism, because they could slowly replace the symbols and values that define the traditional Emirati culture.

This chapter is an attempt to enlarge our understanding of the influences of globalization and consumer culture as drivers of the social and cultural changes in the UAE's traditional society, and in similar cultural configurations in the Gulf, as well as the changes in non-Western countries' cultural diversity. This research demonstrates that individualism and empowerment of consumers were steadily encouraged under neoliberalism as consumer items have become symbols of self-identity, impression management and association with others in the social life even in religiously conservative and traditional societies. Thus, consumption has become an indicator of a person's prestige and status in western and in non-Western societies at the age of globalization. The changing consuming habits in the UAE demonstrate us that there is a strong link between social psychology and economics even in a religiously conservative society.

REFERENCES

Ahmed, A. S. (1998). *Islam Today*. London, UK: Tauris Publishers, I. B.

Al-Yousif, Y. K. (2004, September). Oil economies and globalization: The case of the GCC countries. *Middle Eastern and African Economies*, *6*(2), 167–176.

Bourdieu, P. (1982). *Distinction: A social critique of the judgment of taste*. Cambridge, MA: Harvard University Press.

Chiu, C., Gries, P., Torelli, C., & Cheng, S. Y. Y. (2011). Toward a social psychology of globalization. *The Journal of Social Issues*, *67*(4), 663–676. doi:10.1111/j.1540-4560.2011.01721.x

Cohen, L. (2003). *A Consumers' Republic*. New York, NY: Random House.

Duncan, G. (2013, November). The evolution of UAE retail: From corner shops to mega malls. Retrieved from https://www.thenational.ae/business/the-evolution-of-uae-retail-from-corner-shops-to-mega-malls-1.652113

Elessawy, F. (2015, July). *Dubai City, A study in geography of beauty.* Conference Paper (PDF available) Conference: The Annual International Conference of Geography Dept. Alexandria University, at Alexandria

Elessawy, F. (2017). The boom: Population and urban growth of Dubai City. Retrieved from https://www.researchgate.net/publication/317564338_The_Boom_Population_and_Urban_Growth_of_Dubai_City

Frączkiewicz, M. (2013). The cultural role of the malls. *Prace Etnograficzne.*, *41*(4), 335–342.

Hamilton, C. & Dennis, R. (2205). *Affluenza: When Too Much Is Never Enough.* Crows Nest; Allen & Unwin.

Hayek, F. (1944). *The road to serfdom*. London, UK: Routledge.

Heron, T. (2008). Globalization, neoliberalism and the exercise of human agency. *International Journal of Politics Culture and Society*, *28*(1-4), 85–101. doi:10.100710767-007-9019-z

Hovland, R., & Wolburg, J. (2015). *Advertising, Society, and Consumer Culture.* London, UK: Taylor and Francis.

Husic, M., & Cicic, M. (2009). Luxury consumption factors. *Journal of Fashion Marketing and Management*, *13*(2), 231–245. doi:10.1108/13612020910957734

Hvidt, M. (2009, August). The Dubai model: An outline of key development-process elements in Dubai. *International Journal of Middle East Studies*, *41*(3), 397–418. doi:10.1017/S0020743809091120

Jamala, A., Daviesa, F., Chudryb, F., & Al-Marric, M. (2006). Profiling consumers: A study of Qatari consumers shopping motivations. *Journal of Retailing and Consumer Services*, *13*(1), 67–80. doi:10.1016/j.jretconser.2005.08.002

Khan, T. M., Clear, F., Al-Kaabi, A., & Pezeshki, V. (2010). An exploratory study of the effects of diversity dimensions and intervening variables on attitudes to diversity. *Team Performance Management*, *16*(5/6), 289-308.

Lury, C. (1996). *Consumer culture.* Cambridge, UK: Polity Press.

Malecki, E. J. & Ewers, M. C. (2007). Labor migration to World cities: With a research agenda for the Arab Gulf. *Progress in Human Geography*, *31*(4), 467-484.

Marciniak, R.; Mohsen, M. G. (n.d.). Homogeneity in luxury fashion consumption: An exploration of Arab women. *The Business & Management Review*, *5*(1), pp. 32-41.

Marshall, G. (1998). Oxford dictionary of sociology (2nded.). Oxford, UK: Oxford University Press

McDonald, M., Gough, B., Wearing, S., & Deville, A. (2017). Social psychology, consumer culture and neoliberal political economy. *Journal for the Theory of Social Behaviour*, *47*(3), 363–379. doi:10.1111/jtsb.12135

Metcafe, B. D. (2008, November). Women, management and globalization in the Middle East, *Journal of Business Ethics*, *83*(1), pp. 85-100.

Mogdaham, V. (Ed.). (2003). *Modernizing women: Gender and social change in the Middle East. Boulder*, CO: Lyne Reiner Publications.

Moghadam, V. M. (2005). *Women's economic participation in the Middle East. Journal of Middle East Women's Studies*, *1*(1), 110–146.

Molavi, A. (2007). Sudden city: A feverish dream for the future springs from the sands in Dubai. *National Geographic*, *211*(1), 96–113.

Perez, F., & Esposito, L. (2010). The global addiction and human rights: Insatiable consumerism, neoliberalism, and harm reduction. *Perspectives on Global Development and Technology*, *9*(1-2), 84–100. doi:10.1163/156914910X487933

Sampler, J. & Eigner, S. (2008). Sand To silicon going global. Dubai, UAE: Motivate Publishing.

Schroer, M. (2014). Visual culture and the fight for visibility. *Journal for the Theory of Social Behaviour*, *44*(2), 206–228. doi:10.1111/jtsb.12038

Shoufani, H. (2014). *Uncommon: Dubai*. Dubai, UAE: Uncommon Ltd.

Shukla, P., & Purani, K. (2012). Comparing the importance of luxury value perceptions in cross national contexts. *Journal of Business Research*, *65*(10), 1417–1424. doi:10.1016/j.jbusres.2011.10.007

Veblen, T. (1965). *The theory of the leisure class*. New York, NY: A. M. Kelley Bookseller.

ADDITIONAL READING

Davidson, C. (2009). *Dubai: The Vulnerability of Success*. Oxford: Oxford University.

Gökarıksel, B.,McLarney, E.(Fall, 2010). Muslim Women, Consumer Capitalism, and the Islamic Culture Industry. *Journal of Middle East Women's Studies*, Vol 6, 3.1 18.

Krane, J. (2010). *City of Gold: Dubai and the Dream of Capitalism*. UK: Picador.

Parahoo, S. K., & Harvey, H. L. 2014. Consumer behavior in Gulfcountries: Are traditional satisfactionmodelsvalid?". In: Edward, M. andZakariya, K.A. (Ed), Marketing dynamics in emerging market, CochinUniversity of Science and Technology, Kerala, India, pp 163-173.

Rehman, A. A. (2007). *Dubai &Co.:Global Strategies for Doing Business in the Gulf States*. UK: McGraw - Hill Education.

Trentmann, F. (2004). Beyond Consumerism: New Historical Perspectives on Consumption. *Journal of Contemporary History*, *39*(3), 373–401. doi:10.1177/0022009404044446

KEY TERMS AND DEFINITIONS

Consumer: A consumer is someone who buys products or services just for personal use. During the decision making process this individual can be influenced by marketing and advertisement strategies. Any time someone goes to a store and decides to purchase something, let it be a car, jean, food, or anything else, he is making that decision as a consumer.

Consumer Culture: A culture organized around the consumption of goods and leisure. The items consumed are non-necessary but they represent important symbols related to the formation of self-identity.

Consumerism: Consumerism is a social and economic order that inspires the buying of goods and services in large amounts. In economics, consumerism refers to economic policies which emphasize consumption. Consumerism is also defined as the trap of material goods. It would be helpful to know that the theoretical debate about consumption in the last two decades has mainly been driven by a philosophical engagement with 'modernity'.

Consumer Society: It is a society that associates personal success, happiness and well-being with the purchasing of material possessions.

Cultural Capital: A marker of one's status and position within a social and cultural hierarchy. It enables an individual to gain membership to social categories.

Dubai: Dubai is the largest and most populated city of the United Arab Emirates. It is the most liberal and developed city and has become a role model for many other Gulf cities. Dubai is known for luxury shopping, ultramodern architecture and a lively nightlife.

The United Arab Emirates (UAE): The UAE is composed of seven Emirates, namely Abu Dhabi, Ajman, Al Fujayrah, Ash Shariqah, Dubai, Umm al Qaywayn and Ra's al Khaymah. Emirates got its independence in 1971. Oil and global finance are the most important economic activities the UAE. The UAE in recent years has played a significant role in regional affairs.

ENDNOTE

1 https://tradingeconomics.com/united-arab-emirates/gdp-per-capita

APPENDIX

Interview Questions

1. How many times in a week do you go for shopping?
2. Where do you go for shopping?
3. How do you spend your time in shopping malls?
4. Which brands do you prefer when you buy your clothes?
5. What items do you buy the most?
6. Are you member of a sport club?
7. Do you prefer to buy from local stores or from global chains?
8. Do you ever buy goods even if you do not need them?
9. What is the most prestigious and wanted item for Emirati women/men?
10. What has changed in your daily routine after the establishment of super malls in Dubai?
11. How many times do you go out for dining in a week?
12. Do you prefer to eat local or other cultures' cousin?
13. Do you think that having luxury items is important? If the answer is yes, why?
14. Do you think that there is a relationship between your material choices and your reputation in the society?
15. Do you see any contradiction between Islamic and traditional values, and consumerism?

Chapter 4
Critical Theory:
The Human Being Takes the Stage Again

Derya Guler Aydin
Hacettepe University, Turkey

Itir Ozer-Imer
Hacettepe University, Turkey

ABSTRACT

Based on the historical developments in the philosophy of science, it can be claimed that the method of social sciences is mainly dominated by the method of the natural sciences. Social sciences, especially, economics have been affected by the method of physics. From a critical viewpoint, this study aims to scrutinize the method of social sciences by taking into account the concept of devaluation of human beings. The study puts forward that mainstream economics devalue human being at the level of its methodology by excluding the real creator of value from the analyses and by disregarding social and historical factors. The study demonstrates that by taking into consideration the neglected cultural, political and historical factors in addition to the economic ones, the critical theory includes human being and his/her values in the analyses, and hence, it unifies scientific knowledge with human behavior, which is the intentional behavior behind all economic decisions.

DOI: 10.4018/978-1-7998-1037-7.ch004

INTRODUCTION

Epistemology, within the framework of its own criteria, deals with the demarcation between science and non-science. According to the positivist approach, philosophy is an unscientific task since it contains relative knowledge, and the aim of science is to achieve objective results. Within this context, positivist theory of knowledge argues that reality can only be produced through sense experiences. Therefore, as suggested above, positivism considers metaphysical factors as unscientific. With modernity, the God-centered universe has been transformed to the human-centered universe, and reason and science have come to the fore. Scientific progress has continued its development in the rationalist and empiricist line, which is appreciated as the source of knowledge. Empiricism, which comprises sense, perception, observation, and experiment, has gotten ahead of rationalism with the prominence of the criteria of reality and universality in the theory of knowledge. Accordingly, scientific propositions should be verifiable (Hollis & Nell, 1975). In this context, positivism has, in fact, influenced social scientists as a theory of knowledge that includes both naturalism and empiricism.

The development of the social sciences in the modern period has been to imitate the method of the natural sciences, in other words, to maintain a framework based on experimentation, observation and confirmation like in the natural sciences. With Auguste Comte (1798-1857), who is accepted as the founder of sociology, positivism was thought to be the only method of natural and social sciences, and developments in the philosophy of science proceeded from the line of methodological monism. According to positivism, sciences may differ according to their fields; for example, a physicist investigates the matter, a biologist examines the plant, while a social scientist scrutinizes topics based on the human being. Although the research subjects are different, scientific knowledge can be produced by a single method.

Social sciences, which take the human being as the basis, are aware of the abstract value of the human being. However, for the social scientists, who adopted the positivist method, the application of methodological monism has been in the form of explaining the human being's abstract, immeasurable values within the framework of the concrete, physical and biological existence, and they have even proceeded by reducing these values to a concept such as social physics. A similar concept called social engineering, which is used in sociology, and the atomistic individual, who represents the individual of the neoclassic school are the concepts adopted within this context. According to the positivists, social sciences should produce knowledge by experiment and observation, while taking into account the phenomenon like in the natural sciences, and this process should be independent of metaphysical factors. Because, in the case of metaphysical factors, one cannot mention scientific inquiry. Values and meanings are the subject field of philosophy, not of science, and according to the positivist social scientists, the main purpose of social science is not to find a meaningful link between concrete events as in natural sciences, but is to find the causal link. In other words, positivism is the theory of knowledge that adopts observation and human causality understanding. The existence of a causal link between events refers to the explanation of regularities and continuities regarding social reality. It is unscientific to go beyond this explanation, that is, to go beyond the realities perceived by sense experiences. Hence, according to the positivist understanding of scientific knowledge, the outside world can be perceived through our senses.

From the viewpoint of the social sciences, however, an important problem arises since their research subject is the human being. Experiences of human beings cannot be shaped independent of their values /value judgements and thoughts. In this context, thoughts come into prominence rather than the phenomena. The adoption of positivism by social scientists refers to the exclusion of subjectivity, values, in other words, the human being, who is a social entity. For this reason, as mentioned above, in their analyses, social sciences have used concepts that are specific to natural sciences and have preferred to investigate the human being as an abstract entity, who is independent of his/her values. In this way, the human beings have been regarded as the passive actors of the physical world, who are devoid of any subjective and personal differences (Bhaskar, 1978).

Such an examination of human beings refers to ignoring his/her social aspect. Thereby, the society, in fact, is a static and mechanical structure, in which historical, cultural, institutional, teological factors are solely taken into consideration as phenomena, while the emergence of such factors are neglected. In such an understanding of the society, the individual is the smallest part of the society, with a function similar to the function of matter in the physical world. In the positivist approach, the individual, on the one hand, is considered as the basic unit of the society, and social problems, on the other hand, are tried to be understood through a passive, uniform and mechanical human model.

For example, neoclassical economists, as known, take into consideration solely the concrete problems. They ground their analysis, particularly, on exchange relations, while neglecting the production domain of the economy. Hence, they ignore the real creator of value (human being) in their analysis. Besides, they atomize both the human being and society by paying no attention to social and historical dynamics.

In order to overcome this unrealistic and mechanical world, one needs to embed the ethical side in economic problems. Both preferences and the vision of the researcher has a crucial role on knowledge in the critical approach, while such a relationship does not exist in the positivist approach. Therefore, it is possible to claim that discontinuity occurs in the production of scientific knowledge in the latter. According to Kuhn (1962), there are differences between these two paradigms with regard to the progress of knowledge. In social sciences, including economics, economic reality is essentially associated with the thoughts of the scientist. Positivist approach stresses the objectivity of scientific knowledge, and according to this approach, value judgments should not be included in theory (Buğra, 1989). Nevertheless, in social sciences, the scientist is not only influenced from the values that he/she is surrounded by, but he/she also affects them.

The main starting point of this study is the contradiction arising from the fact that positivist science understanding, on the one hand, emphasizes the individual but it, on the other hand, analyzes the human being with the concepts of the physical world, and hence, breaks it from the bond of meaning. As a result of this contradiction, human being is not a social entity, and ontologically, the individual is analyzed as objects of the physical world, not of the society. In this way, while the individual becomes passive, while he/she is separated from his/her values and from the differences that have occurred during the historical process. Regarding the human being as a passive transfer mechanism is to ignore the fact that the individual is a social being. This not only dismantles the ontological unity of the individual, but it also means to detach human beings from science, which is a social activity and societal, and which is, to a great extent, dependent on the human being (Bhaskar, 1978, p. 34).

The aim of this study is to scrutinize the methodology underlying critical theory, which we believe is a superior alternative to positivism. Since positivism imprisons social reality in the Newton's mechanical reality in social sciences, in general, and in economics, in particular, this study aims to discuss the critical theory, which does not neglect issues on human beings, human values, ideas and his/her active aspects in its methodological approach. For this purpose, the first part of the study examines the general characteristics of the positivist methodology and its understanding of human being, and the second part analyzes the critical theory, which is considered to be a better alternative to the human being approach in the process of positivist knowledge production. After such a scrutinization, this study puts forward that mainstream economics devalue human being at the level of its methodology and that it is necessary to take into consideration the methodological framework underlying the critical theory in order to reestablish the crucial relationship between the economic and social structure.

GENERAL FRAMEWORK OF POSITIVISM AND HUMAN UNDERSTANDING

The positivism is a methodological approach, which attaches importance to the criteria of objective science, and believes that the most important factor of science is to obtain common universal results. Positivism has created a sort of domination by means of methodological monism, and by leaving out alternative methods, which are especially important from the viewpoint of social sciences. Diffusion and exclusion, which can be defined as methodological imperialism, confine the mind to certain limits. The subject of social sciences is the human being. Social sciences examine various matters regarding the human being within the framework of different fields. For example, in economics, whose subject theme is the human needs, production, distribution and exchange relations cannot be considered as independent of what is better, more peaceful and livable. That is, the social sciences and the scientific knowledge production process carry a moral dimension. However, since the positivist science understanding regards factual reality as the basic criterion of science, it accepts all the moral factors, other values, different ideas, cultural and historical dynamics as unscientific. Knowledge, which takes into account the benefits of human beings, and which is produced only for the sake of being scientific, leads scientists to a dangerous point known as "scienticism". Scienticism is a view, which advocates that one should depend solely on science and the scientific method when obtaining knowledge on the human being and society (Elliot, 1919: 138). It was F.A. Hayek, who disseminated the concept of scienticism, and he defined is as the "slavish imitation of the method and language of science" (Hayek, 1942: 267-291). Karl Popper defines scienticism as "the aping of what is widely mistaken for the method of science" (Popper, 1979: 185). On the other hand, positivism has become a common methodology adopted by both natural and social scientists in the production of scientific knowledge, and has remained valid until today as a theory of knowledge that includes empiricism with naturalism. The positivist method, which asserts that obtaining common universal results is the main criterion of science, seeks causality between social phenomena with its functionality, and its propositions are based on experiment and observation. The main aim of positivism is to explain the regularities in societal reality through factual realities and to produce laws as in nature. This aspect, especially, has been very attractive to scientists.

Logical positivism has originated in Austria and Germany in the 1920s and is considered as one of the key constituents of the fabric of the 20th century philosophy. It was introduced by the Berlin School and popularized by Ayer's (1952) book entitled *Language, Truth and Logic*. Carnap (1937), Fiegl (1931), Hempel (1966) and Reihenbach (1951) provided the pioneering studies in the positivist approach. These thinkers are essentially "analytical philosophers". Many are physicists and mathematicians, and search for the source of reliable knowledge.

Logical positivists believe that merely two kinds of statements are meaningful. Those are the statements regarding the truths of logic, mathematics and ordinary language, and empirical propositions about the world around us. According to the logical positivists, meaning depends, essentially, and basically, on sense experiences. The verifiability principle is the most well-known principle of logical positivism. The verifiability principle asserts that whether a proposition is valid and meaningful depends on its verification. If a statement cannot be verified, then it becomes automatically invalid and meaningless. Metaphysical statements can be given as an example.

The verifiability principle served as a basis for logical positivists in their line of attack to metaphysics and religion since both make various statements that are not verifiable. Within this context, the basic rules of positivism are as follows. Positivists believe that all meaningful statements are analytical or synthetic (Friedman, 1953). That is, all meaningful statements that are not involved are easily acknowledged, however, a secondary importance is attached to this "expressive" surplus in terms of the alleged "cognitive" meaning and discountability in science (Carnap, 1937, 1966). Schlick (1996) also accuses metaphysics for falsely trying to explain what the logically structured cognition is but in fact, the qualitative content of experience is inexpressible. In his book entitled *the Philosophical Foundations of Physics*, Carnap (1966) recommends a somewhat different approach to the distinction between observation and theory. Here, one should start from the difference between empirical and theoretical laws. While an empirical law can be directly confirmed, it is possible to test a theoretical law simply through the empirical laws, which remain among the consequences of those theoretical laws. Furthermore, whereas an empirical law elucidates facts, a theoretical law illuminates empirical laws. Hence, it is possible to state three levels:

1. Empirical facts.
2. Generalizations that are simple and can be directly tested, i.e. empirical laws. These generalizations clarify facts and are used to forecast facts.
3. Principles that are general and can be used to elucidate empirical laws, i.e. theoretical laws.

Empirical laws comprise observational terms, while theoretical terms find their place in theoretical laws (Murzi, 2007). Basic characteristics of logical positivism can be enumerated as follows:

1. Schlick (1996) takes into consideration all meaningful statements, and a logical procedure of verification is possible for these statements. In addition, Schlick is interested solely in constructed languages. On the other hand, Carnap (1937) regards only those meaningful statements, for which a nomological procedure of confirmation or disconfirmation is possible. According to positivists, meaningful statements can be exclusively divided into analytic and synthetic, and these statements strictly match with apriori and aposteriori premises. In other words, logical positivism depends on the analytic and synthetic distinction. The method of Carnap enlightens the meaning of theoretical terms and reveals their relationship with observational notions, provides a method for making a distinction between synthetic and analytic sentences, and for distinguishing theoretical axioms from the rules of correspondence (Hill, 1968).
2. Logical positivists state that a scientific theory is an axiomatic system. It acquires an empirical interpretation merely through appropriate statements that are named as the rules of correspondence, and it builds a relationship between real objects/processes and the abstract concepts of the theory. Without these types of statements, a physical interpretation is absent in theory, and hence, it is not possible to verify the theory. However, this is an abstract formal system, and the requirement is simply the consistency of axioms. The language of a theory comprises three forms of terms. First of these are the logical terms that contain all mathematical terms. Second form are observational terms, which indicate objects or properties that are directly observable or measurable. And the final form are theoretical terms, which represent objects or properties that cannot be observed or measured but can only be deduced from direct observations (Murzi, 2007).
3. Logical positivists follow inductive reasoning, and propose two different theories regarding probability. The first is the frequency interpretation, where probability is the limit of a frequency, while the second is the logical interpretation, where probability is considered as the degree of confirmation of a statement from a given set of other statements.
4. Other crucial elements of logical positivism are reductionism and the unity of science. Carnap proposes a systematic explanation regarding the reformulation of propositions stated in terms of one field, for example, reduction of

propositions in biology into equivalent propositions in terms of another, for example, physics. Despite the fact that it is possible to reduce the propositions of physics to those of biology along with the other way, in fact, the assumption was that the eventual aim of all reductions would be physics: "The thesis of physicalism maintains that the physical language is a universal language of science — that is to say, that every language of any sub-domain of science can be equipollently translated into the physical language. From this it follows that science is unitary system within which there are no fundamentally diverse object-domains, and consequently no gulf, for example, between natural and psychological sciences. This is the thesis of the unity of science" (Carnap, 1937, p. 320).

5. Ethics is the final and the most crucial tenet from the viewpoint of this study. One of the results of the verifiability principle is that statements regarding ethical principles can be considered as neither true nor false; they are more of feeling expressions. Hence, it is not possible to set forth a theory of ethics. Schlick (1996) is among the logical positivists, who is mostly concerned with ethics. He tries to provide a detailed explanation of ethics that is compliant with logical positivist philosophy. Schlick believes that ethics can be regarded as a descriptive scientific theory. It can be seen in a society that an altruistic action is more useful than a solely egoistic one.

The logical positivist movement has already begun to disintegrate by the 1930s. Even though this constituted the path towards the end, the movement lasted for a number of more years, and its influence still persists in many fields in terms of its approaches and methods. The reasons for the demise of logical positivism can be classified as its internal weaknesses and external criticisms.

The positivist methodology gives importance to sense experiences and factual reality, and explains the individual and societal events within the framework of apostreriori propositions (experimental data). Apriori propositions (before the experiment) are considered as unscientific because they are metaphysical. The source of knowledge is the experiment and observation as mentioned before. Comte mentions the law of three states in social sciences; the logical period, metaphysical period and the positive period. In this context, the method of the positive period is experiment, observation and reasoning. Reasoning is the theorization of experiments and observations through mind. Within this context, the mind, in fact, has no constituent function in the process of producing scientific knowledge. The only function of the mind, in this process, is to reach the result by systematizing the data obtained through experiment and observation. Therefore, the source of knowledge is, actually, empiricism but not rationalism. The positivist methodology defines science as finding the real law of events and phenomena through reasoning and observation, and as finding out the regularities in social events. In the positivist methodology, science is related to factual reality, and the aim of science is to create rules, theories and laws in social life like in nature. In this way, all metaphysical factors are left out of science. This characteristic of positivism is, on the one hand, an advance in the history of epistemology in the sense of elimination of many dogmatic, belief-based factors. However, the same characteristic means that irrational values, which are part of the essential integrity of the human being, are also considered as unscientific. This situation has led positivism to reduce social reality to a static, mechanical and measurable reality and to open the door to another dogmatism. In other words, with the positivist methodology, the human being is examined by reduction to a mechanical entity, who is independent of value judgments, thoughts, and who is apart from his/her social entity. The war against dogmatism, on the other hand, has led to another dogmatism in the social sciences, in which the concrete reality expresses the truth. Yet, the social reality is complex, continuous and is subject to change. The dynamics behind the realities that bring about the social structure often involve irregularities and uncertainties. Therefore, it is not possible to obtain general laws in the social sphere, in which human beings are the central research unit. Social scientists can point to trends, produce average results and make predictions. This is the result of the reality in the nature of social life that is continuously changing. For this reason, the social scientist should be open to relative results, and move away from a mechanical understanding of human being for the sake of producing laws.

CRITICAL THEORY: A CRITIQUE OF POSITIVISM

Critical theory rests on the ideas of German philosophers and the social theorists of Marxism and is named as the Frankfurt school. Critical theory searches for human liberation, and it aims "to liberate human beings from the circumstances that enslave them" (Horkheimer, 1982: 244). The major goal of the critical theory is to elucidate and change all the conditions that enslave human beings. Briefly, the critical theory offers the descriptive and normative foundations for social investigation and increases freedom in its all forms (Bohman, 2005).

The works of critical theorists are concrete and ethical rather than being instrumental. They, therefore, pursue an interdisciplinary approach in their studies. Critical theory is often considered narrowly as referring to the Frankfurt School.

It begins with the works of Horkheimer and Adorno, and reaches out to Marcuse and Habermas. According to the definition of Horkheimer (1982), there are three criteria that a critical theory needs to fulfill: It should be explanatory, practical, and normative. As the Director of the Institute for Social Research of the Frankfurt School, Horkheimer, in addition, puts forward that it "has as its object human beings as producers of their own historical form of life" (Horkheimer, 1982, p. 21). Horkheimer also considers it as an alternative for the present social and political philosophy (Horkheimer, 1982: 203). Habermas (1993), and Giddens (1979), who are the members of the second generation of critical theory, has principally introduced this extent of normative political theory.

Methodologically, critical theory is based on the "Hegelian Dialectic." There are three dialectical stages of the Hegelian dialectic; thesis, which gives rise to its reaction, antithesis, which contradicts thesis, and synthesis, which solves the tension between thesis and antithesis. The real comprises contradictions and these contradictions are at the heart of change in the dialectical method. In this respect, the philosophical foundations of critical theory are based on Marx. Even before Marx, utopian socialists such as Robert Owen (1771-1858), Pierre Joseph Proudhon (1809-1865) had contributed to the development of this approach. Marx's philosophy is ontologically and epistemologically materialist, and the dialectic process operates on this materialist basis.

"In the social production of their existence, men inevitably enter into definite relations, which are independent of their will, namely relations of production appropriate to a given stage in the development of their material forces of production. The totality of these relations of production constitutes the economic structure of society, the real foundation, on which arises a legal and political superstructure and to which correspond definite forms of social consciousness. The mode of production of material life conditions the general process of social, political and intellectual life. It is not the consciousness of men that determines their existence, but their social existence that determines their consciousness. At a certain stage of development, the material productive forces of society come into conflict with the existing relations of production or – this merely expresses the same thing in legal terms – with the property relations within the framework of which they have operated hitherto. From forms of development of the productive forces these relations turn into their fetters. Then begins an era of social revolution. The changes in the economic foundation lead sooner or later to the transformation of the whole immense superstructure" (Marx, 1970: 20-21). This approach also refers to values as a reflection of the impact of the infrastructure, which is known as production relations, on the superstructure. In Marx, material production relations are a fundamental factor that determines the values of the society – morals, law, religion, ideology, and the impact of the scientific knowledge production process should also be taken into account.

The superstructure of societies is determined by their mode of production (Marx, 1970). In light of the above discussions, it is possible to assert that the source of historical change is productive forces and production relations in Marx. The history understanding of Marx underlies the establishment of its own historical preconditions by capital, whereas his examination of capitalism asserts processes of dehumanization and alienation of the individual. Although it is possible that the essence of human beings does not change within different historical periods, material conditions determine its existence (Güler Aydın, 2010).

As discussed above, the materialist philosophy, and accordingly, the alienation that emerges within capitalism constitute the starting point of the critical approach to the human being, and at the same time, they are the basis of the criticism of the positivist method.

As previously emphasized, the positivist method emphasizes the verification of observable knowledge. Logical validation is the main tool of the positivist method and this way of verification for natural sciences is more possible than social sciences. Because determinism in nature is possible since nature is essentially more static than social sciences, but the fact that social sciences exhibit changes in accordance with its nature indicates that the causal relationship between variables is not so possible. More importantly, human behavior is very complex, and it is difficult to determine the direction of these behaviors since they depend on many other factors. Therefore, in social sciences, rather than determinism, there is interrelation between variables, there is even “overdeterminism” as Althusser (1965) uses. The multidimensional relationship between variables means that social reality alone would not be explained by logical validation.

The scientific subject, that is the scientist himself, begins the research with a certain value judgment before the study. As Schumpeter argues, the pre-analytical vision of the scientist appears to be another subjective factor that influences the research during the course of the scientific activity. In other words, there is a fuzzy relationship between the subject and the object of science from the viewpoint of prejudgement, and observation depends on what the scientist sees, knows, experiences, and the theories he/she believes (Hanson, 1965). If the object of research in science is also changing as the socio-economic structure, then, in this case, scientific activity, on the one hand, should take into account this changing socio-economic structure, and, it, on the other hand, should consider human behavior within this structure and should conduct the analysis without disregarding the effects of the socio-economic structure on the individual. In this context, Marx and the concept of alienation were effective in the emergence of critical approach.

Economic and Philosophic Manuscripts of 1844 of Marx emphasizes two different forms of alienation that is delineated as the dehumanization of the individual. The first form of alienation is the alienation of the human being, which isolates him/her from nature and creates a new nature for himself/herself in the cultural-social domain. In this way, the human being frees from the nature, and this can be regarded as positive alienation from the viewpoint of the human being's existence and development. The second form is the alienation, which already exists within the capitalist system. Hence, the human being is distant from his/her own nature, labor and product. That is, the human being alienates himself/herself from not only his/her labor but also from his/her social relations, world and life. Although the reason for alienation stems from the private property relations of the means of production, especially, under the capitalist system, this issue becomes more severe since the power of labor is considered as a commodity. In capitalism, when the worker is distanced from the means of production, the capital owner buys him/her as a commodity in the market. After the production process is complete, the capital owner captures the surplus value that the worker produces, while the worker gets only the sufficient amount to reproduce himself/herself. It can be claimed that the surplus value, on the one hand, is a result of private ownership, and it, on the other hand, arises because of alienation and the alienated labor himself/herself. In this respect, there is a continuous reproduction of the relationship between alienation and private ownership, hence, labor is cut off from human values and he/she becomes a commodity (Güler Aydın, 2010). In this context, critical theory mainly criticizes the socio-political aspect of the capitalist system, based on Marx's concept of alienation. It should be noted, however, that the critical school is mostly influenced by the works of Young Marx, and the effect in all of them is different and not in line with Marx.

We pointed out that in the emergence of the Frankfurt school and the critical approach, Marx's philosophical views, especially, the materialist worldview and dialectics, were influential. In relation to this, we emphasized that the concept of alienation is also effective in the critical approach. At this point, what should be understood from the concept of historical materialism, to what extent the critical approach is affected by Marx and at what point it differs from Marx should be clearly revealed. Historical materialism comes into prominence in two of Marx's major works. The first of these is *The German Ideology* (1970), with Engels, and the other is *A Contribution to the Critique of Political Economy* (1970). In the preface of this study, Marx suggests that the infrastructure determines the superstructure (Marx, 1970: 20). Marx, however, puts forward that in a certain stage of development, the material productive forces of society / the existing production relations go into conflict with the property relations that they have hitherto operated (Marx, 1970: 21). It should be noted, however, that historical materialism is not the definitive laws and canons that explain human history (Krieger, 1962: 375). As Marx stated in the Grundrisse, some identifications belong to all periods, while some to a few (Marx, 1979: 143). In this context, Marx's general methodological approach takes into account the peculiar age-specific conditions, rather than the universal factors that involve the whole human history. It should be noted that in Marx, the effect of the infrastructure on the superstructure is emphasized and a dynamic and interactive relationship is considered. Although there are different interpretations of Marx regarding this issue, the basis of the critical approach is based on the interaction between the infrastructure and the superstructure. If interpreted from the viewpoint of the dialectical process, matter and spirit turned to the determinism of the spirit in Hegel (1977), while it turned to the determinism of matter in Marx, and according to the Frankfurt school, the reciprocal determinism between the matter and the spirit came to the fore.

In its approach that takes into account the importance of the socio-cultural structure, the critical approach highlights not only the production relations but also the historical, cultural, religious and legal factors behind these. In this respect, the metaphysical factors that are left out by the positivist method are taken into consideration in the scientific research process by the critical theory. The criticisms initiated at the *Center for Social Studies* was first advanced through criticisms against capitalism (Kızılçelik, 2008: 25), and then positivism has been the subject of criticism because of its mechanization of the human being and the human mind. With the mechanization in capitalism and the culture embedded in the industry (Habermas, 2001), the society became mechanic, and this process led to a mechanical life style, which resulted in the fragmentation of the human being and his consciousness. According to Horkheiemer, modern life, and consequently, rationality detach individuals from their personal characteristics by engraving them into certain patterns. The culture industry brought about by this structure alienates man (Horkheimer, 1986: 78). Marcuse (1964) in his work entitled *One Dimensional Man: Studies in the Ideology of Advanced Industrial Society* criticizes cultural degeneration in the capitalist society. Adorno and Horkheimer (2010) also criticize the culture industry.

The essence of the criticisms of the Frankfurt school can be summarized as follows: Popular culture is driven by large capital and this artificial and degenerate culture is fed through the tools of mass media. The consumption society created, on the one hand, provides material gains, it, on the other hand, objectifies the individual. In this context, it is the subject of knowledge that is important in the social sciences and the cultural environment, in which this subject lives. The Frankfurt school, together with Eric Fromm, emphasizes the diversity of the superstructure factors by highlighting the psychological factors. The Frankfurt school, which presents a different framework of methodology in this respect, has shown that unlike the positivists, the methodology of the social sciences should be different because of the differences in the subject and object of research. This is because the social sphere is shaped by the human will and vice versa. Human being is not passive but rather, he/she shapes the society and is shaped by it through his/her active will. For this reason, not only irrational but also the rational values are the research theme of the social sciences. Different processes, and the processes of institutionalization cannot be explained by experiment and observation alone. Within this framework, criticisms of the critical approach to positivism can be gathered under the following headings.

1. **Critique of Instrumentalist Reasoning:** Critical theorists argue against the notion of absolutism since knowledge and the mind occur as a result of historical and social processes. They favor "open-ended reasoning" instead of the instrumentalist reasoning. Hence, in their analysis of the society, critical theorists propose the dialectical method. In this way, human being as well as his/her problems can be included in the scientific inquiries.
2. **Traditional and Critical Theory:** All disciplines accept positivism as the standard. In positivism, the scientific inquiries do not take into consideration the nature of knowledge, and human values and norms. Self-reflexivity is suggested by Horkheimer, Adorno and Marcuse in order to create a Marxist historical materialist theory. Different than the traditional theory, critical theory is developed from Marx's critique of political economy. Horkheimer argues that it is not possible to scrutinize social reality by induction. An ideological form of the capitalist society is instrumental rationalism. Traditional theory does not include communication, dialogue and debate in this process. Hence, human values are excluded.
3. **Critique of Empiricism:** Adorno & Horkheimer (2010) are inclined to generalize subjective reality of the individuals as well as their social entity. These realities cannot be dealt with adequately by the traditional theory. While positivism uses empirical studies as an instrument of critical analysis of the society, critical theorists believe that such a reasoning devalues the human being.
4. **Comprehending the Society and Social Phenomena:** The capitalist mode of production is based on the product of labor. During the production process, it alienates itself. Critical theory argues that conscious human behavior plays

a crucial role in the unjust nature of social life, and takes into consideration historical and social factors in the analysis. Historical reality is created by the society, which comprises human beings and their values. In short, critical theory does not construct a new reality but it is a reality of human values. Herein, the critical theory unifies scientific knowledge and human behavior, and attaches importance to the sphere of human behavior. Different than the positivist approach, there are ideological and political features in critical theories.

CONCLUSION

While social reality is a crucial factor in the critical theory, factors such as human beings, society, and historical processes are not scrutinized in the traditional theory. Positivists believe in the objectivity of knowledge, whereas critical theorists argue that positivism atomizes human beings. For example, the neoclassical economists are concerned only with the concrete problems. They ignore the production sphere, while basing their analysis, principally, on exchange relations. Therefore, the human being, who is, in fact, the real creator of value, does not take his/her place in their analysis. In addition, the neoclassical economists attach no importance to social and historical aspects, and the human being and society are atomized in this respect. It is necessary that the ethical dimension is included in economic problems so that such an unrealistic and mechanical world understanding can be eliminated. In the critical approach, preferences and the vision of the researcher play an important role on knowledge, whereas there is no such a relationship between the researcher and knowledge in the positivist approach.

According to the positivist methodology, the human being is a mechanical entity, hence, his/her value judgments, thoughts, and social entity have no role in the analysis. During its war against dogmatism, positivism has led to another dogmatism in the social sciences, in which the concrete reality expresses the truth. However, it would be more appropriate to consider the social reality as complex, continuous and subject to change. There are irregularities and uncertainties in the social structure, which are brought about by the dynamics behind the realities. Hence, it is crucial to accept the fact that one cannot reach to general laws in the social domain. It is also essential that the role of the human beings, as the central research unit, should be appreciated. Rather than embracing a universal path, the social scientist can emphasize trends, reach average results and make predictions. This is a natural outcome since the nature of social life, which is subject to continuous change, lies behind reality. That's why, the social scientist should welcome relative results, and give up his/her mechanical understanding of human being in order to produce laws.

From this point of view, the critical theory stresses the prominence of not only economic factors but also takes into consideration the human being as well as the cultural, political and historical factors. Exclusion of history and society in a scientific research refers to devaluing the human being and his/her values. Within this framework, the critical theory principally reconsiders the socio-political characteristic of the capitalist system, and grounds its analysis on Marx's dialectic reasoning and the concept of alienation. Accordingy, human being should not be regarded as passive since he/she not only shapes the society but is also shaped by it through his/her active will. Hence, the research subject of social sciences should comprise not only irrational but also the rational values. Finally, experiment and observation alone cannot illuminate different processes, and the processes of institutionalization as the positivist approach claims.

REFERENCES

Adorno, T. W., & Horkheimer, M. (2010). *Aydınlanmanın diyalektiği*. Kabalcı Yayınevi.

Althusser, L. (1965). *For Marx*. The Penguin Press.

Ayer, A. J. (1952). *Language, truth, and logic* (2nd ed.). Dover Publications. (Original work published 1936)

Bhaskar, R. (1978). *A realist theory f science*. Great Britain: Harvester Wheatsheaf.

Bohman, J. (2005). *Critical theory*. Stanford. Retrieved from http://plato.stanford.edu/entries/critical-theory

Buğra, A. (1989). *İktisatçılar ve insanlar*. İstanbul: İletişim Yayınları.

Carnap, R. (1937). *Logical syntax of language*. New York: Harcourt, Brace and Company.

Carnap, R. (1966). The philosophical foundations of physics (M. Gardner, Ed.). Basic Books.

Feigl, H., & Blumberg, A. E. (1931). Logical positivism. *The Journal of Philosophy*, *28*(3), 281–296.

Friedman, M. (1953). The methodology of positive economics. In *Essays in positive economics*. University of Chicago Press.

Gidens, A. (1979). *Central problems in social theory*. California: University of California Press. doi:10.1007/978-1-349-16161-4

Güler Aydın, D. (2010). Kapitalist sistemde bireyin sorgulanması: Yabancılaşma ve demir kafes. *Amme Idaresi Dergisi*, *43*(2), 17–32.

Habermas, J. (1993). *İdeoloji olarak teknik ve bilim* (M. Tüzel, Trans.). İstanbul: Yapıkredi Yayınları.

Habermas, J. (2001). *İletişimsel eylem kuramı* (M. Tüzel, Trans.). İstanbul.

Hanson, N. R. (1965). *Patterns of discovery*. Cambridge: Cambridge University Press.

Hayek, F. A. (1942). Scientism and the study of society. Part I. *Economica*, *9*(35), 267–291. doi:10.2307/2549540

Hegel, F. (1977). *The phenomenology of spirit*. Oxford: Clarendon Press.

Hempel, C. (1966). *Philosophy of natural science*. Oxford, England: Prentice-Hall.

Hill, E. L. (1968). A critique of positive economics. *American Journal of Economics and Sociology*, *27*(3), 259–266. doi:10.1111/j.1536-7150.1968.tb01047.x

Hollis, M., & Nell, E. J. (1975). *Rational economic man: A Philosophical critique of neo-classical economics*. Cambridge University Press. doi:10.1017/CBO9780511554551

Horkhemier, M. (1982). *Critical theory*. New York: The Continiuum Publishing Company.

Horkhemier, M. (1986). *Akıl Tutulması*. İstanbul: Metis Yayınları.

Hugh, E. (1919). *Modern science and materialism*. London: Longmans Green and Co.

Kızılçelik, S. (2008). *Frankfurt okulu*. Ankara: Anı Yayıncılık.

Krieger, L. (1962). The uses of Marx for history. *Political Science Quarterly*, *75*(3), 355–378. doi:10.2307/2146388

Kuhn, T. (1962). *The structure of scientific revolutions*. University of California Press.

Marcuse, H. (1964). *One-dimensional man: Studies in the ideology of advanced industrial society*. Boston: Beacon.

Marx, K. (1970). *A contribution to the critique of political economy*. New York: International Publishers.

Marx, K. (1979). *Grundrisse*. Birilim Yayıncılık.

Marx, K. (2007). *Economic and philosophic manuscripts of 1844*. Dover Publications.

Marx, K., & Engels, F. (1970). *The German ideology*. London: Lawrence & Wishart.

Murzi, M. (2007) *Logical positivism*. Retrieved from http://www.murzim.net/Articles/Positivism.pdf

Popper, K. R. (1979). Objective knowledge: An evolutionary approach (rev. ed.). Oxford: Clarendon Press.

Reihenbech, H. (1951). *The rise of scientific philosophy*. University of California Press.

Schlick, M. (1996). *The emergence of logical empiricism*. Garland Publishing Inc.

Chapter 5
Complexity Economics and Innovation Systems:
Mersin Regional Innovation Strategy (RIS) Plus Project From Perspective of Complexity Science

Pınar Yardımcı
Selcuk University, Turkey

ABSTRACT

Knowledge determines the relationship between regional development and innovation in a knowledge-based economy. The Mersin Regional Innovation Strategy (RIS) Plus Project is based on the European Union's new regional innovation strategy referred to as 'smart specialization' that is related with industrialization and economic development. This approach is an indicator of the change and transformation in the regional development paradigm in terms of knowledge generation and innovation processes. These developments also reflect the impact of complexity in the philosophy and understanding of the 21st century. Complexity Science and Complexity Economics have increasingly become determinants in the formation of institutional structures and policies within the global economic system. This chapter aims to evaluate the basic characteristics of Mersin RIS Plus Project within the framework of complexity science. This study discusses the development potentials of Mersin and TR62 regions in accordance with the scientific and theoretical basis of the project, and policy proposals are suggested.

DOI: 10.4018/978-1-7998-1037-7.ch005

INTRODUCTION

The national and regional innovation system approach was adopted as an innovation strategy by institutions, such as OECD, the European Commission, UNCTAD, World Bank and IMF, after the 1980s and began to be included in policy texts (Lundvall et al., 2002, p. 214). Although this approach, implementation and period of globalization does not seem to be compatible with the process of change, the changing structure of technological knowledge, innovation, and especially the OECD's studies related to the evaluation of technological development and economic analysis, have been developments requiring systemic thinking. The system approach can be used on a local, national, international and global scale or as a methodology that can be applied on a sectoral and project basis. The 1960s and 1970s were the years in which the differences in growth and development among the countries increased, and the search for policies to address this issue involved great effort. Until the 1980s, innovations were concentrated in the industrial sector, technology and R&D-based, and able to be carried out by large companies that obtained patents, but later they transformed to be incremental, non-industrial, independent of R&D, and have a patent-free structure (Martin, 2013, p. 171). A new method of technological development, called 'innovation', which requires knowledge based on interaction, plays an important role in the formation of complexity science and complexity economics. Innovation economics, where tacit knowledge enters the production and consumption process as both input and output, is referred to as the 'knowledge-based economy'. Therefore, there is a close relationship between the knowledge-based economy, complexity economics and the innovation system approach.

The RIS Mersin Project is the first regional innovation system application that the European Union supported within the framework of regional innovation strategies in Turkey in 2005. This study evaluates RIS Mersin and its follow-up, Mersin RIS Plus projects, by taking into consideration the system approach that forms the basis of the innovation systems and the complexity science developed from the end of the 20th century. First, the contributions made to complexity science and system theory are discussed along with the changes in the philosophy of science. Next, the impact of these changes on the regional development paradigm are discussed within the framework of the knowledge-based economy, followed by an explanation of the evolution of regional innovation systems in Europe and the basic characteristics of the smart specialization strategy. Lastly, the innovation systems approaches taken as a model in the Mersin RIS Plus projects in the scale of the TR62 region are evaluated, and policies are suggested within the framework of the digital transformation of the knowledge-based economy, its global economic order dimension and the developments that emerged based on complexity science.

COMPLEXITY SCIENCE AND EVOLUTION OF SYSTEMS THEORY

Complexity science refers to a new multidisciplinary scientific approach based on developments in nature and the social sciences that serves to facilitate the examination of complex systems in explaining universal reality and change. The term, complexity science, started to be used at the end of the 20th century; however, the origins of complexity and system concepts, which are the sources of complexity science, date back to ancient times, in terms of the philosophy of science. From the 17th century onwards, which covers the period of the Renaissance and the Industrial Revolution, technological developments in the natural sciences resulted in the emergence of the Cartesian thought system and the Newtonian mechanistic universe in Europe, both of which gave rise to the understanding that the perceived world was a simple, stable, static and closed system (Hester & Adams, 2014, p. 42; Hammond, 2005, p. 21). In this hypothetical deductive structure, the idea of reductionism was dominant in terms of the relationship between the part and the whole. Reductionism represents methodological individualism in the social sciences (Hodgson, 2000, p. 72). Accordingly, when examined analytically, the behavior of the part explains the behavior of the whole system, meaning that it is possible to have knowledge about the structure and operation of the part and system, or in other words, the structure of the whole to which the part belongs; but the system itself (the behavior of the whole) cannot be understood (Ackoff, 1979, p. 96). This understanding is related to the fact that there is no interaction between the parts. Therefore, the cause-effect relationship can be demonstrated linearly in the analysis, and the reality obtained has universal validity independent of time and space. The world order of that period was shaped according to this idea.

The spread of the industrial revolution and the emergent shortcomings of the capitalist system were clearly felt with the economic crisis and wars that took place at the end of the 19th century and the beginning of the 20th century. The United States (USA) became the dominant actor in the governing of the capitalist system in North America after the two world wars. Those years were a chaotic period, one marked by an increasing complexity of the Western world, wherein reductionist scientific methods were insufficient in establishing new systems and solving social, economic, political and military problems. Both the technological discoveries that the defense industry needs and the related scientific innovations led to a growth in knowledge, and synthetic-expansionist systemic thinking was replaced by an analytical-reductionist approach. The adoption of the system concept increased the importance of the science of biology, which is used as a model and as a metaphor by different disciplines. Therefore, it can be argued that the modern West abandoned the mechanistic approach starting from the beginning of the 20th century and had recourse to the system concept in order to maintain its economic and political power, as well as to manage the growing complexity of the world.

Systems Theory and System Thinking in Economics

The concept of a system, as based on biological modeling and analogy, resulted in significant changes and transformations, especially in the understanding of economics and the economic system. The concept of a biology-based organism, which is used as a metaphor against the notion of a mechanism – a physics-based idea in the discipline of economics – represents the concept of a system. Systems theory gained scientific validity as a result of a research program called "organismic biology" (Lewis, 2016, p. 127; Drack, 2015, p. 80). According to this system, economies are handled as social organisms, and the concept of a system determines the formation of order in the organismic sense. Aristotle, the earliest- known advocate of this idea, stated that the whole is greater than the sum of its parts. Immanuel Kant noted three criteria that determine the organism: *i*- The shapes and relationships of the parts are determined by the whole, *ii*- The parts identify one another mutually, and *iii*- The organic whole reproduces itself within its wholeness. According to Ludwig von Bertalanffy a living organism is an open and dynamic system, consisting of a large number of different parts that interact with one another and that are in a hierarchical order to protect the existing structure against external influences. German historical school of thought representatives, such as Friedrich List, adopted the organismic approach as a metaphor (Hutter, 1994, pp. 289-291; Drack, 2015, pp. 79-84; Bertalanffy, 1972, p. 410). Apart from the organismic biological analogy and metaphor approach informing the concept of system, some economists, such as Joseph Schumpeter, Friedrich Hayek (Austrian school) and Thorstein Veblen (old institutionalist economics), used Darwinian biological evolution (evolutionary biology) as a model. These approaches, referred to as 'economic evolution', view the economy as a social organism. However, the Darwinian organismic approach assumes that there is no inter-part interaction, and therefore a mechanistic thought, that is, methodological individualism, which does not regard the living organism as a system, applies. The change is largely explained by the external chance factor. On the other hand, Alfred Marshall, known as the founder of mechanistic neo-classical economics, argued that the adoption of a biological analogy for describing the economy is a more rational approach (Hart, 2013, p. 14).

The combination of different disciplines adopting distinct conceptual approaches related to the concept of system led to the formation of systems theory. The prevailing idea governing the systems theory is the General System Theory (GST), developed by the theoretical biologist Ludwig von Bertalanffy. The studies that formed the Society for General Systems Research, which was founded by Bertalanffy, together with Kenneth Boulding, Anatol Rapoport and Ralph Gerard in 1954, is known as the beginning of GST (Hester & Adams, 2014, p. 51). The idea of the organismic system that Bertalanffy started to develop from the 1930s onwards led to the emergence of a unifying and comprehensive systems science as a result of this group's studies. The isomorphic characteristics of GST allow the idea of system to be presented as a holistic unifying science. There are many new applications that support this development and that are discussed with the system approach. Innovations such as cybernetics (based on feedback cycles), information theory (based on negative entropy), game and decision theories (based on rational competition and preference), network theory, and factor analysis have emerged as key developments in this field. GST, in a narrow context, has been applied in studies to investigate the behavior of systems that have the characteristics of 'organized complexity' and that have interactions between their parts (Bertalanffy, 1969, pp. 90-91; Weaver, 1948, p. 537). Although there are similarities between cybernetics and GST, system behavior for GST is more comprehensive. Goal-seeking behavior is seen in cybernetics as a result of information and negative feedback, whereas in GST, equifinality is observed as a result of an open system fed by negative entropy (Oliva, 2015, p. 32). Instead of feedback cycle behavior, GST focuses on dynamic behavior that is emergent and self-organizing in terms of inter-component and system environment interactions. This open system characterizing GST has an important place for the complex dynamic structure. The existence of an open system that exchanges information with the environment has been recognized not only in biology but also in the physics of non-living beings by Ilya Prigogine (Bertalanffy, 1950, p. 23; Prigogine & Stengers, 1984, p. 298). Thermodynamics, general relativity, quantum mechanics and chaos theory have also made significant contributions to systems science (Mirowski, 1991, p. 389).

By combining system theory with the theory of evolution, economist Kenneth Boulding pioneered the ecosystem approach (Dopfer, 1994, p. 1202; Valentinov, 2015, p. 72). Ecologically, in a closed system, the forces of entropy (the arrow of time, according to the second law of thermodynamics), which creates an effect similar to the equilibrium mechanism and the economic law of decreasing returns resulting from negative feedback, will result in the inevitable destruction of the world. The system approach, which is known as 'system dynamics' and is the basis of the limits to growth, is based on this scenario. For this reason, Boulding (1956) pointed out that excessive specialization hinders scientific development by limiting knowledge generation, and further reported that a general framework of systems science can provide interdisciplinary connections to ensure co-development and sustainability of organic and non-organic life. For example, the development of system knowledge that is related to growth behavior would allow this knowledge to be used in different disciplines in a similar way and thereby facilitate interdisciplinary knowledge exchange. According to Boulding, biological evolution can resolve the paradox of entropy, insofar as it can lead to an increase in diversity as well as enable the exchange of knowledge and thus function as negative entropy (Rosser, 2011, p. 116; Boulding, 1997, p. 120). In line with the goal of maintaining the existence of organisms in biological evolution and continuing their growth, these relations will result in the creation of new energy fields that will enable the establishment of new orders through the differentiating, complex and self-organizing processes of the evolutionary process, as well as through the advantages and mutations that accidentally arise from the traits acquired through irreversible natural selection. The combination of Darwinian evolution and system approaches has been very influential in the formation of the economic models used to explain the dynamic economic growth and development processes in social systems like the economy. In addition, the existence of system knowledge that is bound to inter-part and environmental interactions reflects the spatial and tacit dimension of knowledge.

Complexity Science, Complexity Economics and System Thinking

Complexity science, which addresses the concept of complexity, was originally based on system thinking. For example, the world in which Newtonian mechanical laws are valid and related to linear, reversible, predictable processes is in fact just related to simple systems. In this sense, classical science sought to explain even the complex phenomena in human activities, such as complex biological processes, the economy and urban planning, in simple ways. However, the new understanding of science supported by technological developments proposes to use the philosophy and methodology related to a complex system in the face of evolutionary development, differentiation, and imbalances, all of which are irreversible (Prigogine, 1987, p. 97). Thus, system thinking requires the complexity to be resolved, while complexity science examines the behavior of complex systems. Determining the properties of complex systems provides insight into the ontological and epistemological dimensions of complexity science. Simon, who coined the concept, 'limited rationality' — one of the important foundations of complexity— described the complex system as follows: (Simon, 1962, p. 468).

Roughly, by a complex system I mean one made up of a large number of parts that interact in a non-simple way. In such systems, the whole is more than the sum of the parts, not in an ultimate, metaphysical sense, but in the important pragmatic sense that, given the properties of the parts and the laws of their interaction, it is not a trivial matter to infer the properties of the whole. In the face of complexity, an in-principle reductionist may be at the same time a pragmatic holist.

Complex systems consist of sub-systems (in a hierarchical structure) that interact with one another (Holt et al., 2011, p. 359). Self-organizing through a dynamic evolutionary process, the system produces new emergences. Emergence refers to the system adapting itself to external influences (adaptation) and maintaining the internal balance (homeostasis); in other words, the emergence of the new order (Simon, 2018, p. 5; Cilliers, 2000, p. 23; Noell, 2007, p. 233). In cases where complexity science is applied both to metaphor and to economics as a model, the economics of complexity emerges (Öğüt & Sunal, 2017, p. 44; Martin & Sunley, 2007, p. 578). Complexity economics structurally changes the features of neo-classical economics. Table 1 shows the features that are associated with the development of complexity science.

Table 1. Complexity science: evolving dynamics

Complexity Science Features				
Behavior of system	Complex systems	Complexity economics	Complexity research methodologies	Complexity policy
Self-organization, emergence and creating new order	Non-linear dynamics, adaptive behavior, connectivity co-evolving, decentralization, uncertainty hierarchy, path-dependence, local interactions, open systems, cumulative causation	Bounded rationality, heterogeneous agents, non-equilibrium, increasing returns, imperfect information, externalities, complementarities, learning	Network science, chaos theory econophysics, game theory, cybernetics, agent-based models, simulations	Bottom-up strategies, holism, resilience, reflectivity, agility,

Complexity Science and Economics Approaches	
Europe (Brussel School)	USA (Santa Fe School)
Physics-based: Dissipative open systems and quantum economics	Biology-based: Evolutionary open systems and agent-based computational economics

Source: Author's compilation

Complexity science is mainly concerned with the mechanisms of creating order in complexity (Mckelvey, 2004, pp. 315-318; Mckelvey, 2001, p. 137). Accordingly, while a system adapts itself to the changes in the environment through decentralization to maintain its existence, it also continually co-evaluates with other systems in the ecosystem where it exists. The process of creating order is nonlinear, path-dependent, stochastic and incomplete, and it is defined as holistic self-organization (Mitleton-Kelly, 2003, pp. 29-30). Studies on complexity investigate the mechanism of this change using different methods.

Approaches to complex systems centered around two different views after the 1980s: Europe-based views and US-based views. In the European approach, Ilya Prigogine's new order is based on what he called 'dissipative structures'. In the US approach, studies at the Santa Fe Institute have focused on modeling the behavior of complex systems arising from the interaction between different agents on the basis of chaotic and evolutionary developments. Research programs led by scientists from different disciplines, such as Brian Arthur, Stuart Kauffman and Kenneth Arrow, laid the foundations for complexity economics. The economy is an evolving and adaptive complex system. The complexity of this system can be in the forms of computation, interconnection and dynamism (Fontana, 2010; Arthur, 2010; Comim, 2000; Eren, 2018). Although both approaches have similar dynamics specific to complex systems, they emerged from different disciplines, as shown in Table 1. In addition, while Prigogine's approach explores the behavior of real systems that encounter an energy input, the Santa Fe approach investigates the algorithmic logic of a system taken as a model (White et al., 2015, p. 15).

Complexity economics has addressed the increasing returns caused by positive feedback, which is referred to as 'self-reinforcing processes', in the field of cybernetics from the 1980s onwards. These processes lead to the initial conditions bound to time and space that will serve as the determinants (lock-in) in economic development through externalities and complementarities. The views claiming multiple equilibrium, uncertainty, road dependence, or history matters are important, which were expressed in different contexts by the representatives of critical discourses for mainstream economics, such as the historian school, institutional economics, the post-Keynesian and Austrian school, have begun to fall within the scope of complexity science. Thus, the internal determination of technological development in economic growth and development, and the relationship between technological knowledge, learning and innovation in the production processes have started to be expressed more. Internal economic growth models, behavioral models and economic geography theories are the areas from which neo-classical economics first started to be affected. Evolutionist approaches, on the other hand, have adjusted these developments in the form of neo-Darwinian and Neo-Schumpeterian models. The trend that has been apparent since the 1990s suggests that all these approaches be discussed under complexity science and complexity economics (Martin & Sunley, 2010). Globalization processes increase complexity as a result of the growth in connectivity, and these processes are affected by the ecological system. Local, national and global systems interact with each other due to technological developments. Therefore, system thinking and the complex and dynamic system discourse came to the forefront in the discipline of economics, especially in the 21st century.

REGIONAL DEVELOPMENT, INNOVATION SYSTEMS AND COMPLEXITY SCIENCE

Issues of economic development and improvement are related to the concepts of backwardness and catch-up. The relation between development and the concept of complexity is that the structures (countries) under different conditions encounter different results through different processes. Development is a dynamic process. For the science of classical economics, which was shaped according to the Newtonian world view after the 18th century, development was a linear process, proceeding independently of the initial conditions of the countries. Due to the capitalist space that geographically expanded on the basis of the growth of the industrial revolution and ongoing technological developments as well as the policies required by the world trade system, problems in the market mechanism began to manifest themselves beginning in the mid-19th century. Friedrich List addressed economic liberalism in line with the holistic approach in examining the capitalist system in the 19th century and developed a thesis that considered historical differences in the industrialization of underdeveloped countries, and he advocated for government intervention. The suggested approach for Germany, which lagged behind Britain in the first phase of the industrial revolution, to narrow the gap in terms of development, served as the basis for the German history school of thought in Europe and later, the institutional school of thought in the USA (Kazgan, 2016, p. 180). Lists' approach was termed 'economic nationalism' nationwide and became a basis for certain applications, like a protective foreign trade policy, the infant industry argument, a customs union and an import substitution industrialization strategy (Archibugi & Michie, 1997, p. 126). List's thesis defending national policy and political economy revealed that technological development and the economic development based on it should be addressed institutionally and systemically.

The international development agenda, which involved the nation states that had gained their independence during and after the world wars, has been at the fore since the beginning of the 20th century (Dulupçu & Okçu, 2000, p. 40). As part of this agenda, first, Alfred Marshall put forward regional agglomeration economies and counterfeiting externalities in industrialization. Although Marshallian externalities and the industrial regions model are within the framework of neo-classical partial equilibrium theory and economies of scale, they have a systemic institutional structure since they address local and regional interactions (Antonelli, 2011, p. 10). Thus, the increasing returns resulting from internal and external advantages within the market mechanism could be used to explain the underdevelopment. Schumpeter, in the evolutionary development model, was influenced by Marshall's approach on industrial areas based on local interactions and externalities. In this approach, which considers the roles of entrepreneurs and their externalities, the fundamentals of innovation emerged, but systemic relationships became obscure.

Nelson & Winter's (1982) evolutionary neo-Schumpeterian model similarly addressed the innovations based on bounded rationality and externalities (Antonelli, 2018, p. 59). Generally speaking, the importance of technological development in national and regional development increasingly grew up to the 1980s, and the issues related to complexity were explained with alternative evolutionary models. It can be argued that throughout this century, when neo-classical economics prevailed, holistic systemic thought lost ground, and development issues were more commonly investigated on the micro basis in firms and sectors. However, since Neo-Schumpeterian evolutionary models have a common ontological foundation with complexity economics, they have formed an important transitional form for the approach of complexity economics and the innovation system (Robert et al., 2017, p. 768). For example, the competition among companies, self organization process and emergence of innovation materialized. The systemic structure of innovation and the role of interactions correspond to the innovation system in the process of learning and innovation. Habits and routines of the firms show the knowledge generated by the system collectively and the state of learning and adaptation of the organization.

Innovation Systems, Knowledge-Based Economy and Complexity Economics: Theoretical Aspects

Some important studies that led to the development of national innovation system approaches were carried out after the 1980s. These studies were based on the research programs and projects carried out starting from the 1950s in Europe by Christopher

Freeman at the Science Policy Research Unit (SPRU) and in the OECD; and in the USA, by Kenneth Arrow, Richard Nelson and Sidney Winter at RAND Corporation, which provided research support to US military institutions (Fagerberg et al., 2013, pp. 2-3). This enormous effort largely resulted from the fact that Europe had caught up with the USA in science and technology, and that the USA needed to maintain its power and sovereignty in the post-World War II era. On the other hand, adopting models different from traditional technological development models, Japan, and later South Korea, made a breakthrough in technology and achieved development goals in the 1950s and 1960s. The investigation of these development models also served as the basis for the innovation system. Without making investments in R & D, these countries were able to develop new products and designs by using methods like reverse engineering, imitation and counterfeiting. The studies mentioned above included processes outside of the technological knowledge development methodology (Kim & Nelson, 2000, p. 3; Freeman, 1995, p. 11). For example, there are differences in the place and structure of knowledge in the production process, as well as in the features, such as the act of learning during counterfeiting, adaptation, local interaction, experience, uncertainty and institutional organization. Emergence of knowledge is not as linear and predictable as it is in the R & D process. These features were marked by the emergence of a new method of technological development with systemic knowledge, in what came to be termed innovation. Thus, an innovation systems approach entered into the policy area as a kind of theoretical innovation developed with the application of system thinking on the innovation process.

Two important books on innovation in Europe and America were published in the 1990s, namely, *National Systems of Innovation: Towards a Theory of Innovation and Interactive Learning* by Bengt-Ake Lundvall (1992) and *National Systems of Innovation* by Richard Nelson (1993), both of which served to form the institutional infrastructure of system thinking in accordance with the evolutionary structure of innovation. (Edquist, 2005, pp. 3-4). Nelson's approach focused on the institutional structure of innovation, while Lundvall, emphasized the conceptual aspect of knowledge and the learning process. Theoretical and conceptual contributions, such as learning-by-doing and tacit knowledge, by Kenneth Arrow and Karl Polanyi are seen to be included in Lundall's innovation system. Therefore, systemic approaches known as 'learning economics' and 'knowledge-based economy' emerged out of Lundvall's system of innovation. In addition, Lundvall served as the head of the Directorate for Science, Technology and Industry (DSTI) in the OECD between 1992 and 1995 (Godin, 2007; Godin, 2006, p. 20; OECD, 1997). OECD seems to have officially adopted the national innovation system and systemic approach policies during this term. Lundvall stated that traditional economics proved inadequate to explain the difference between information and knowledge, which are important for the development process.

The understanding has been further developed using the basic distinctions between information and knowledge, between ''knowing about the world'' and ''knowing how to change the world'' and between knowledge that is explicit and codified versus knowledge that remains implicit and tacit. These distinctions are especially helpful when it comes to contrasting the theoretical micro-foundations of innovation systems with those of standard economics. (Lundvall, 2007, p. 108)

Innovation, in a knowledge-based economy, is a dynamic, complex process, one based on interaction that involves recombination, diffusion and use. Therefore, innovation is a complex adaptive system (Katz, 2016, pp. 1-2; Katz, 2006, p. 907). Innovation is achieved through adaptation and learning. A complex adaptive system has the same characteristics as the mechanism that Friedrich Hayek described as spontaneous order (Camplin & Elliot, 2014, p. 186). In addition, the adaptive capability of the innovation system is important for increasing returns. Learning occurs with a bottom-up strategy, but local networks and proximities have a determining role in the emergence of dynamic local interactions (Turkcan, 2014, p. 1430; Antonelli, 2009, p. 632). Knowledge dissemination and learning capacity indicate the local characteristics of knowledge generation. In complexity economics, dynamic local systems that continuously move from one equilibrium to another are regarded as regional innovation systems.

The regional innovation strategy referred to as the regional innovation system (RIS) was developed out of the effort to address innovation systems at the regional level. This new strategy was first proposed by Cook (1992), who analyzed the success of some technology regions in Europe and their competitiveness. The new understanding of regional development and innovation strategy are based on the use of systemic innovation potential in the evolutionary development of the region (Cook et al., 1998, p. 1578). Regionalism can be used to express the conditions enabling economically lagging regions to be more successful through their interactive and dynamic use of socio-economic resources, and when used as such, the idea of regionalism is compatible with the innovation system approach. Regional, national and global connectivity and inter-institutional interactions in the process of globalization has led to the global innovation of systems (Fig.1). Regions, cities etc. can benefit from the knowledge flows created by these networks, independently of the national scale, and thereby increase their innovation capacity and become a center of attraction (Asheim & Coenen, 2006, p. 171). The most valuable regional resource is talented people with embedded knowledge in the knowledge-based economy.

The innovation process has an evolutionary and path-dependent structure, and the innovation system must be self-organized without central planning. While the innovation of systems approach has already emerged in developed countries and

Figure 1. The Relationship between global, national, regional, sectoral and technological systems of innovation
Source: Frenz&Oughton, 2005 and Asheim et al., 2011, p. 884.

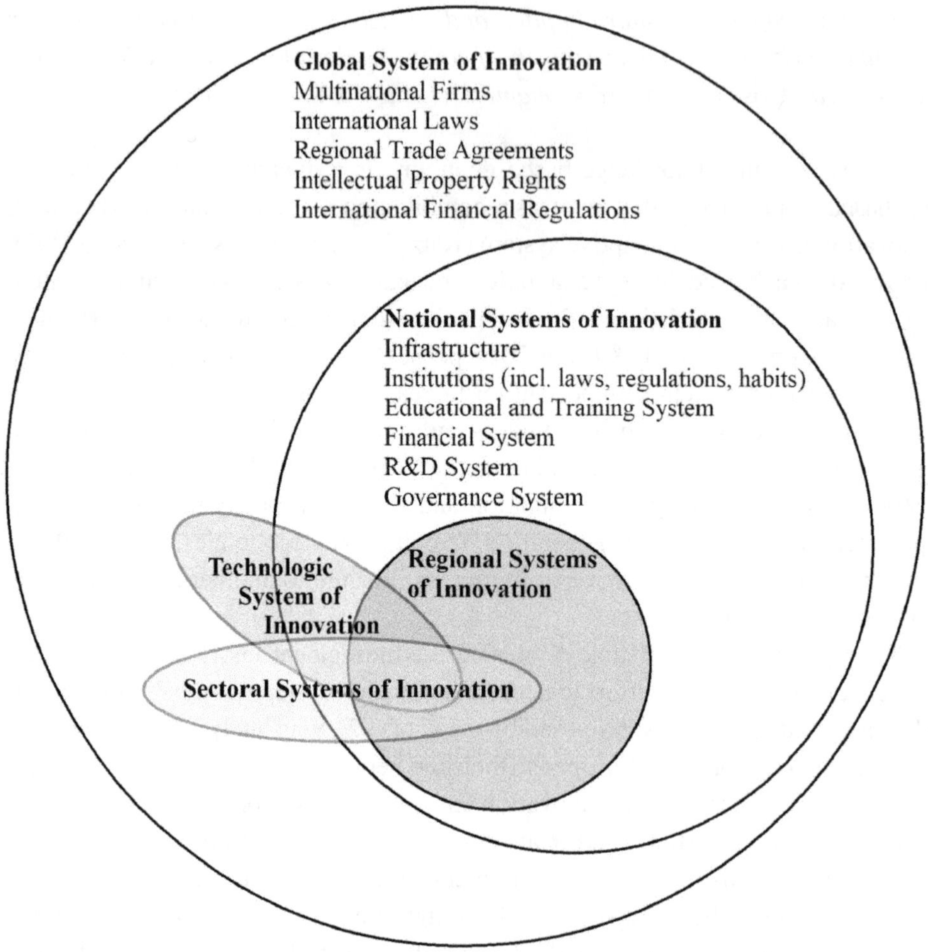

has been adopted as a model in developing countries, it needs to be adapted to take structural differences into consideration. The innovation system should consider local and global interactions as well as connectivity. Innovation systems that are focused on economic growth should undergo changes to include more of the development phenomena. Particularly, interaction-based learning and innovation processes affect the implementation results of the system (Johnson et al., 2003). Lundwall emphasized that during the 1990s when the innovation system approach was introduced, the limits of the system were determined nationally, but it needs to be adapted to the 21st century by considering the globalization processes. Accordingly, national innovation systems are open and heterogeneous systems. Innovation processes go beyond national boundaries and sometimes occur locally rather than nationally (Lundvall, 2016, p. 89). These developments lead to an enlargement of the common areas that the theory of innovation and the theory of evolutionary economic geography will unify (Coenen et al., 2017, p. 612). As a result, the contribution of complexity economics to understanding the dynamics of regional innovation system is increasing.

Regional Development and Innovation Policy in Global Economics and Paradigm Shift

Developments in the global economy have increased the importance of complexity science in the analysis of economic growth and development at both the national and regional scale. The fact that the source of economic growth and development became increasingly dependent on technology led to the introduction of technology on the agenda of development after the 1950s. Especially during the globalization process, which was spearheaded by production and trade networks that were based on micro-electronics before 1980, growth rates were different, and national and global economic institutions and structures in the political and economic order served to increase inequalities between regions (Freeman, 1995, p. 14). On the other hand, the role of technological development was highlighted in overcoming the 1970s stagflation crisis and in explaining the growth differences. The views arguing that innovation is a more powerful instrument than wage-based market competition in mobilizing the economy were discussed in detail in a report put out by the OECD (1980) titled 'Technical Change and Economic Policy' (Mytelka & Smiths, 2002, p. 1473; Wyckoff, 2017, p. 80). Thus, the increase in the share of electronic technology as an input in the manufacturing industry led to the development of technical development and innovation within the field of economy policy. This has also brought about a policy initiative that opposes the neoclassical economic growth approach, which regards technological development as an external variable.

In 1963, the sectors that included R&D activities, in which technological knowledge was produced for the first time by the OECD, were referred to as research-intensive industries and statistics began to be published in the Frascati Guide. The term high-technology was also used after the mid-1980s (Godin, 2004, p. 12). The argument that innovation be discussed within the framework systems approach was published in a report issued by the OECD (1992) titled *Technology and Economics: Key Relationships*, and the Oslo Guidelines were prepared to evaluate innovation processes. These developments have shown that the stages of the production of knowledge has become increasingly complex and show system behavior; therefore, the structures organized as innovation systems on the national or local scale have entered policy (DeBresson & Hu, 1999, p. 27). The innovation system is clearly defined as a complex adaptive system in the third edition of the Oslo Guidelines (2005, p. 28). The innovation system described according to Schumpeter's creative destruction and evolutionist approach highlights the relationships and adaptation mechanisms among the system elements.

Inadequacy of regional development policies and instruments produced by the system based on the established economic theory was also put on the global development agenda. With the acceleration of globalization, new technologies have been developed, and these new technologies need to link developed and underdeveloped regions and be integrated into place-based policies. According to the World Bank (2009), developing countries are entering a new agglomeration space, wherein service-oriented industrial production has increased, yet the scale effect has decreased. In this process, the share of agriculture is expected to decrease while the pace of urbanization is expected to increase. Spatial proximity is important for accessing service markets as well as for obtaining views and knowledge. Intercity infrastructure links will be useful for complementarity and agglomeration. In this period, when firms are expected to need more economies of agglomeration, it is necessary to strengthen regional administrations. Thus, institutions and infrastructure should co-evolve and adapt to changes. In order to diminish social and economic differences, interventions unique to spaces should be made within the boundaries of the cities after they are made for infrastructure and institutions (The World Bank, 2009, pp. xxiii-128-132;206-212).

The increase in the sensitivity of the regions to external shocks as a result of globalization has caused the requirements related to stability and durability in regional development to be politically prioritized. The increase in global and local interactions and connections because of the changes in regional development approaches after the 1980s requires that more comprehensive interventions be made in economy policies. The main titles of the OECD (2010a) regarding the paradigm shift in Table 2 points to a significant transformation in terms of the economic system. The old approach focuses on the redistribution of economic resources in order to promote selected economic units in underdeveloped regions in a relatively stationary process. The new paradigm, on the other hand, aims to regard local differences

Table 2. Shift of regional development policy

	Old Paradigm	New Paradigm
Problem Recognition	Regional disparities in income, infrastructure stock, and employment	Lack of regional competitiveness, underused regional potential
Objectives	Equity through balanced regional development	Competitiveness and equity
General Policy Framework	Compensating temporally for location disadvantages of underdeveloped regions, responding to shocks (e.g. industrial decline) (reactive to problems)	Tapping underutilized regional potential through regional programming (proactive for potential)
- Theme Coverage	Sectoral approach with a limited set of sectors	Integrated and comprehensive development projects with wider policy area coverage
- Spatial Orientation	Targeted at underdeveloped regions	All region focus
- Unit for policy intervention	Administrative areas	Functional areas
- Time dimension	Short term	Long term
- Approach	One-size-fits-all approach	Context-specific approach (place-based approach)
- Focus	Exogenous investments and transfers	Endogenous local assets and knowledge
Instruments	Subsidies and State aid (often to individual firms)	Mixed investment for soft and hard capital (business environment, labor market, infrastructure)
Actors	Central Government	Different levels of government, various stakeholders (public, private, NGOs)

Source: OECD, 2010a, p. 13.

as an economic resource on the basis of policy or market failures, and to use this potential for economic growth (Ferry & McMaster, 2013: p. 1509). The incentives necessary for the development of the regions emerge from the implementation of strategies that stimulate the internal dynamics of the region. Intensity of interaction between agents internalizes the contribution of diversity to knowledge generation in the development process.

The differences in local development in Europe have affected both the deepening process of the European Union and regional development policies. After the 1990s, the Single Market process increased the importance of Cohesion policies and brought forth the need for new local development approaches that would involve complex technologies and knowledge production mechanisms (McCann & Ortega-Argiles, 2013, p. 406). Differences in development and the failure of the 'one size-fits-all' development policies have been ascribed to the specific structure of the problems in underdeveloped regions. Internal variables and external parameters have cumulative and path dependent behavior on the local scale. This means that place-based policies should be addressed in a complex system (Barca, 2009, p. 108). Another development contributing to complexity is the need for regional policies to adapt to globalization. Generating and sharing knowledge can be realized simultaneously through networks, regardless of location, thanks to communication technology. As the borders are opened, the competitive superiority of a region due to innovative production becomes dependent on external sources (OECD, 2009, p. 15). In this way, based on the institutional infrastructure and adaptation capacity of local actors, internal dynamics can provide continuous regeneration and learning and develop faster through the creation of a center of attraction.

Innovation Policy and System Innovation

The innovation concept that the transition from a resource-based economy to a knowledge-based economy has created has been felt in the science and technology policies in the OECD area and Europe and has thus led to the inadequacy of traditional economics to be understood. Traditional economics defines the problems related to technological development as market failure, encourages R&D in regional clusters or techno-parks in basic science and research fields, and suggests mission-oriented policies in the new period. However, the complexity economics encompassing system and evolutionary approaches focuses on dynamic and system-oriented holistic policies in the innovation systems approach (Edler & Fagerberg, 2017, p. 8). For this reason, innovation policy should be designed in a way to consider systemic failures as well as market failure in the innovation systems approach. When the solution to systemic problems involves top-down market regulations, the innovation systems strategy is designed incompletely from the beginning. Theoretically, the theory of market failure has been developed for market disruptions of a neo-classical economics understanding, and the policy tools are compatible with the theory. However, the theory of innovation is explained by complex and evolutionary mechanisms and does not comply with the theoretical structure of neo-classical economics (Dodgson et al., 2010; Edquist, 2011, p. 1725; Bleda & del Rio, 2013, p. 1039). Systemic thinking, therefore, requires an economic and political transformation in terms of the global world order.

Globalization and regionalization increase complexity. Innovation policies now cover not only economic but also social targets due to bottom-up strategies. The interaction between the elements of the system requires the consideration and coordination of all parties contributing to the production of knowledge. Along with the adoption of systemic approaches, the OECD put systemic failures on its policy agenda as of the end of the 1990s (OECD, 1998, p. 132). However, these practices are mostly eclectic, in the sense that the state undertakes new tasks for systemic failures.

For the most part, governments address current challenges with administrative structures and policy instruments that have been shaped by responses to past problems. Traditionally, they have intervened in the technology arena to address market failures. They should also address systemic failures that block the functioning of innovation systems, hinder the flow of knowledge and technology and, consequently, reduce the overall efficiency of R&D efforts. Such systemic failures can emerge from mismatches between the different components of an innovation system, such as conflicting incentives for market and non-market institutions (e.g. enterprises and the public research sector), or from institutional rigidities based on narrow specialization, asymmetric information and communication gaps, and lack of networking or mobility of personnel. (OECD, 1999, p. 10)

Innovation policies became more important in the face of rapidly changing conditions during the 2000s. General equilibrium and stability, two of the main ideas of neo-classical economics, has been replaced by imbalance and instability in the real world, where complexity prevails. Therefore, innovation policies are emphasized as being more comprehensive and the coordination function is given priority (OECDb, 2010, pp. 192-194). Innovation capacity, institutional structure, network connectivity and the proactive applications to be implemented for any systemic failures that can occur in the regulations regarding social and cultural infrastructure positively affect the resilience and adaptability of the system in innovation system management.

Considered based on complexity science, the global economy is becoming a complex, adaptive system as a result of its increasing connectivity. A new approach, called 'system innovation', which involves systemic thinking and increasingly decentralized dynamic processes, has been proposed by the OECD in recent years. Accordingly, a system needs to adapt and transform itself in the face of new developments in order to fulfill its functions. The failures met in the innovation system are referred to as 'structural systemic failures', while the problems faced in system innovation are referred to as 'transformational system failures'. The main factors governing system transformation are the determination of direction of change, articulation of demand changes, policy coordination, and reflexivity. System innovation requires a successful transformation of the system, complexity terminology, self-organization and the emergence of a new system, and capacity to use both local and global impulses. This is an issue related to system design and is included in the system theory, as defended by Donella Meadow's "system dynamics approach", the correct design of the system at the beginning is a more effective method compared to detecting system failures and then intervening in the system.

According to the OECD (2015), system innovation is a political project that prioritizes cooperation rather than competition in such a way as to include not only the winners but also the losers. Regulations for the negative externalities regarding failure in competition and market failure in science and technology policies are faced with political resistance from the winners in the market. Therefore, public sector policy making is gaining importance in the orientation, preparation, coordination, evaluation and reflexivity of the policies. As a result, the need to apply the system innovation approach in the application of innovation systems arises as a regional development strategy as the first quarter of the 21st century approaches.

REGIONAL INNOVATION SYSTEMS (RIS) AND THE SMART SPECIALIZATION (RIS3) POLICY IN THE EUROPEAN UNION

Technological development and economic growth in Europe have been shaped by the economic policies of the European Union (EU). While the years 1950-1973 are referred to as the golden years of growth, from the 1980s onwards, Europe has fallen behind the USA and Japan (Gordon, 2004; Temin, 2002). The policy choices of the EU in the enlargement and deepening processes and the efforts to adapt to the changes in the world economy have been carried out in accordance with both evolutionary and systemic approaches. As stated above, while traditional mechanical economic policy has been the dominant paradigm in economic political discourse and in areas of application, it is observed that complexity science and complexity economics have been employed to determine technology and innovation strategies. Studies on the innovation systems in Europe and on the comprehensive support programs for technology development began in the 1980s. The first technological research and development framework program was implemented in 1984 (Reillon, 2017). With the expansion of the EU after this period, the fact that countries with different development levels became members of the Union prioritized the goal of eliminating inter-regional development differences for the success of the integration (Landabaso, 1997, p. 3; Kaufmann & Wagner, 2005, p. 582). These differences further increased the importance of developing regional policies and cohesion policies aimed at addressing these differences. Thus, innovation system implementations have started to take on the function of making the region more competitive, both at the local, national and Union level, and of reducing the differences in intra-regional social and economic statuses.

Regional innovation system implementations, which can be considered as laying the groundwork for the smart specialization strategy in Europe, started to be supported with the Fourth Framework Programme in the 1990s . Supports like the Regional Innovation Strategies (RIS) and the Regional Innovation and Technology Transfer Strategies (RITTS) were among the important applications of the system approach until the mid-2000s (Charles et al., 2012, p. 3; De Bruijn & Lagendijk, 2005, p. 1155; Cooke, 1996, p. 161). More recently, the need to adopt a knowledge-based economy that involved complex system mechanisms has started to appear in the Union's policy texts.

The economic impact of technological progress on growth and employment depends on the innovation process, which has become interactive. The linear model innovation, with the innovative act being isolated, has in today's world been replaced by complex mechanisms: innovation requires constant and organized interdependence between the upstream phases linked to technology, and the downstream phases linked to the market. (EC, 1993, p. 93)

The area of complexity has been limited to economic processes, since the evolution of technological knowledge has largely influenced industrialization policies. Along with the innovation period that became evident starting in the 1990s, the reality of complexity began to enter the policy area in such a way as to include ecological, social, cultural and political disciplines. The regional advantages obtained based on knowledge differentiation have replaced the hitherto comparative and competitive advantages (Asheim et al., 2011, p. 896; Cook & Leydesdorff, 2006, p. 5). As a matter of fact, the EU announced in 2000 that the Union adopted a knowledge-based economy through the Lisbon Strategy, and the research strategy for the new strategy was planned by the European Research Area (ERA) (Eur Council, 2000; EC, 2000). Following the 2008 crisis, which aggravated economic growth and employment problems, the union formed a working group called the 'Knowledge-Based Economy Expert Group' to address systemic problems in the innovation policy. In its report, the group suggested that the innovation system should be more open to knowledge flows (open innovation) (EC, 2009; EC, 2010). Traditionally, in agglomeration economies, while it was necessary for knowledge to be accumulated in a specific region for specialization, in an interaction-based process it had to be mobile. Thus, the concept of smart growth that was used in knowledge-based growth was replaced by smart specialization.

The *smart specialization for research and innovation strategy* (RIS3), which serves as evidence of the change in the industrialization strategy of the EU, is seen as the emergence of a new innovation system approach that can be adapted to the open innovation model at the regional and national level. This change was put into practice upon the EU's 2020 Strategy and Innovation Union policy decisions in 2010 (Foray, 2012, p. 2; Foray et al., 2009, p. 20; EC, 2010; EC, 2010a). RIS3 was adopted as a regional policy tool that would contribute to sustainable growth in line with the *EU 2020* strategy of the same year (EC, 2010b). Unlike previous RIS models in terms of systemic approach, RIS3 emphasizes more dynamic and open system features. RIS was designed as a closed system, like cluster, that aims at increasing efficiency-productivity through learning effects based on inter-domain interaction, and scale economies. Therefore, it is compatible with the spatially-blind *One Size Fits All* approach, which was standard and proposed for all regions (Pellegrin, 2007, p. 212; Chorafakis & Pontikakis, 2011, p. 133).

On the other hand, the place-based innovation system approach, along with RIS3, is on its way to becoming a more resilient, dynamic and open system that is less centralized, continuously self-organizing and generating formation and that can use horizontal and vertical connections to produce new growth paths (Uyarra et al., 2014, p. 7). Designing a system that can be used to generate knowledge and produce product(s) specific to the region will create region-specific competitiveness. Thus, each region will gain the capacity of dynamic specialization, and regions will not compete for the same resources in cases where they specialize in the same fields. The process of entrepreneurial discovery in RIS3 has an important place. In this process, innovative firms, universities, local government agencies, non-governmental organizations, or individuals identify priority areas of interference by using horizontal and vertical connections. These priorities constantly change. The discoveries enable the region as a whole to experience structural transformative growth (Foray & Goenega, 2013, p. 2). Smart specialization strategy also suggests public policy due to its lack of coordination and market failures. However, incentive mechanisms are not used for sectors but rather, for firms or enterprises. In addition, both bottom-up and top-down methods can be used in policy preferences (Foray, 2014, p. 499). According to the RIS3 model, the practical steps that should be followed to design an innovation system at the national and regional level are as follows (EC, 2012, p. 5; Foray&Rainoldi, 2013, p. 2):

1. The analysis of the national/regional context and potential for innovation
2. The set-up of a sound and inclusive governance structure
3. The production of a shared vision about the future of the country/region
4. THE selection of a limited number of priorities for national/regional development
5. the establishment of suitable policy mixes
6. The integration of monitoring and evaluation mechanisms

Lack of interaction is one of the major problems in RIS3 applications (Gianella et al., 2016, p. 84). Fragmentation of regional and national innovation systems means that there is no knowledge flow between the regions where the knowledge is accumulated, and that therefore, the externalities resulting from the spillovers and complementarities do not occur. The entrepreneurial discovery process mechanism of an intelligent specialization strategy can provide a link between the open innovation model and different innovation systems and global value chains (EC, 2017a). When the innovation system is robust, learning effects to be obtained from the knowledge flows result in an increase in its capacity to absorb (EC, 2017b, p. 26). As seen in Figure 2, the S3 process requires feedback loops among different system elements. Each system is surrounded by higher system layers that reflect local, regional, national, and international levels. The emergence of feedback loops through horizontal and vertical interactions indicates the reflexivity of the system. Reflexivity is related to the system being in harmony and organized; in other words, it is related to the learning process. For this reason, the performance of open innovation eco-systems that interact with cross-border links and networks, such as value chains or platforms, depends on the combination of capacity expansion and reflexivity.

Complex processes, such as adapting rapidly to changes in RIS3, establishing networks, inter-regional collaborations, taking advantage of the synergies created by complementary resources, and selecting the right policy priorities, lead to positive feedback loops and increased returns to scale. As RIS3 considers the demand dimension in the innovation process, innovation users, as well as firms, public institutions and universities are included in the system. This approach is called the *quadruple helix* model. In addition, mission-based policies come to the forefront, since all these changes will result in social transformations (Foray et al., 2018, p. 3). When these characteristics are discussed in terms of regional development and innovation policies, it appears that RIS3 has shifted from the traditional positive economic theory and has taken on a more normative character, as it includes different economic views and disciplines. In addition, unpredictable complex structures, such as the learning ability of the elements of the region, determine the performance of the innovation

Figure 2. S3 implementation as a continuous learning process
Source: Mariussen et al., 2016, p.13

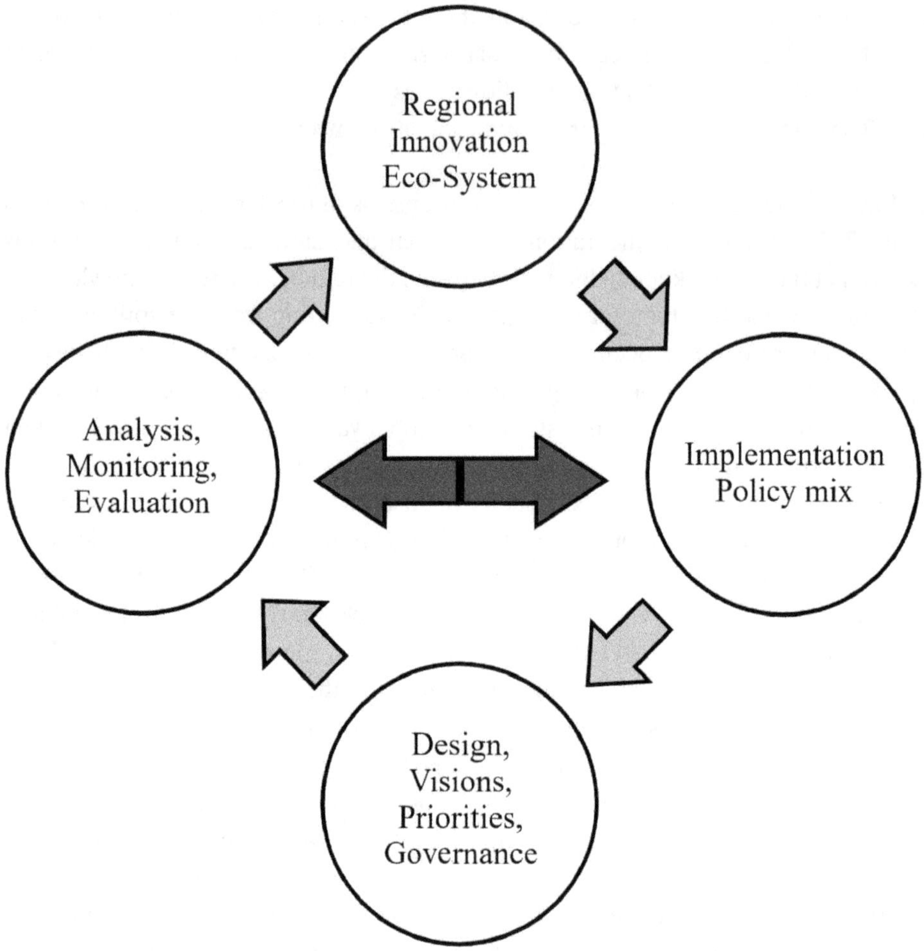

system to a great extent (Morgan, 2013, p. 104). RIS3, which is currently under trial phase, can be regarded as an important step in the transition to a dynamic adaptive, complex system setup in regional innovation system applications. Hence, in 2016, the EU declared that it adopted a complex system approach in innovation policy (Madelin & Ringrose, 2016, p. 18).

Considering RIS3 within the framework of complexity science has important implications for development policies. Transformative development, rather than sustainable development, comes to the fore in the complex system. The system constantly undergoes interdependent, unpredictable and destructive changes in complex dynamic processes. For example, due to globalization, extreme volatility at the global and regional level, like economic fluctuations, political crises, technological developments, climate change and increased uncertainties, make the management of these developments difficult. Because sustainability requires only that the existing system is protected, the public policies made to achieve this have the potential to fail. In order for the system to function in line with the development objectives in such an environment, it is necessary to continue with a transformational strategy in order to change priorities and redistribute and reorganize resources, rather than resist change (Eraydın, 2016, p. 611). Only in this way can the resilience of the institutions, projects and policies be secured, in the sense of permanence and sustainability (Castaneda & Guerrero, 2018, pp. 2-3). Policy makers must adapt to innovations in the face of changing developments without deviating from the project objectives of the innovation system projects, and said projects should have formal administrative flexibility . Thus, learning mechanisms should be given importance to improve the adaptation capacities of the leaders and stakeholders.

MERSIN RIS PLUS PROJECT AND SMART SYSTEM DESIGNING

Among the OECD countries, Turkey is among those that follow the process of technology and innovation, but it lags behind their counterparts in terms of level of development. Based on the data obtained for the 2002-2012 period, Turkey's manufacturing industry exports mainly consist of low and medium-low-tech products. In comparing different cities of Turkey, the volume of technological products in the export of manufacturing industries is low in the city of Mersin (ÇKA & TKA, 2014, p. 244). The technology policy approach and national innovation systems have an important place in enhancing Turkey's competitiveness on the national scale. In 2014, the ratio of R&D expenditures to GDP exceeded the critical value of 1%. This means that the R&D, innovation and entrepreneurship eco-system haves matured at the national level in Turkey. Turkey ranked fourth after China, Egypt and Indonesia, in terms of the rate of R&D spending growth between the years 2005-2015 (Ergin, 2016). The technology and innovation system practices of Turkey at a regional level are weak, or not at a satisfactory level, compared to those of the EU. Until the 2000s, regional development had been addressed mainly under the 5-Year Development Plans. The process that began with the Lisbon Strategy in Europe has also affected

Turkey. First, a 3-stage system that complied with the European Union Regional Statistical System based on the Nomenclature of Territorial Units for Statistics (NUTS) was established in 2002. Turkey was divided into 26 regions according to the Level 2 classification, and 26 development agencies were established accordingly. The Cukurova Development Agency (CDA) (Turkish: Çukurova Kalkınma Ajansı - ÇKA), which was established in the TR62 region and included the cities of Mersin and Adana, became operational in 2008 and declared its first financial support in 2009. As seen, development agencies in Turkey form the first institutional structure marking the transition to a placed-based regional development paradigm.

Regional plans were prepared by the CDA in the TR62 region between 2010-2013 and 2014-2023. According to the current situation analysis in the Second Plan (ÇKA, 2014a, p. 7), the TR62 region accounted for 4.1% of the value added created in 2010 in Turkey and ranked 7th among the regions. CDA ranked 12th among the Level 2 regions in terms of per capita gross value. The Çukurova region ranked 9th according to the 2011 Survey of Socio-Economic Development of Provinces and Regions prepared by the Ministry of Development. Adana and Mersin ranked 16th and 24th, respectively, among the cities in the same study. In the Turkey inter-provincial competitiveness index conducted by the International Competition Research Institute (Turkish: Uluslararası Rekabet Araştırmaları Kurumu - URAK) during the 2009-2010 period, Adana and Mersin ranked 9th and 14th, respectively. Again, in the same study, Adana and Mersin ranked 18th and 22nd, respectively, in the human capital and quality of life sub-index. These data show that the quality of life and human capital in the provinces of the region are relatively worse compared to industry, production and competitiveness. On the other hand, due to the shift of global growth centers to the east in the Plan, the goal of the region being the leader in the region of the Eastern Mediterranean was set (ÇKA, 2016, p. 5). The CDA has taken on an active role in the planning, implementation and coordination of the Adana RIS and Mersin RIS Plus projects since 2015(ÇKA, 2014b, p. 17). New regional innovation system models can be utilized to evaluate the development potential and capacity of the region. Using its advantages, in terms of transportation networks and logistics, the region can improve investment opportunities and benefit from knowledge flows through global network chains and trade routes (World Bank, 2016, p. 28).

RIS Mersin Project (2005-2008)

The city of Mersin was the first province to implement the EU's RIS model in Turkey in 2005. The project, titled the Regional Innovation Strategy for Mersin Region of Turkey (RIS-MERSİN) received financial support from the Sixth Framework

Program (FP6) that was to be implemented between June 1, 2005 and January 31, 2008. The project was led by the Mersin Governorship and a consortium of ODTU TEKNOKENT. The members of the consortium included Mersin University, Mersin Chamber of Commerce and Industry, Mersin-Tarsus Organized Industrial Zone and EPIRUS Innovation Development Center of Greece. The aim of the project was to provide interaction between companies, public institutions, universities etc., increase the innovation capabilities of the enterprises, create new job opportunities and create a sustainable regional economy by using the valuable assets and resources of Mersin (Mersin Innovation Strategy 2006-2016, 2008, p. 3). Mersin became a member of the European Network of Innovative Regions (IRE) with the RIS project.

Agriculture and food, logistics, and tourism areas were identified as priority sectors, platforms were formed, and strategies and action plans were prepared based on the project. The projects, cooperation and capacity improvement activities performed as part of RIS Mersin have resulted in valuable experience and learning. However, some deficiencies in system design and institutional structure have caused some hindrances in the implementation of the project (Levent, 2016, p. 4; Gök, 2009, p. 94). Certain factors, such as failure to realize the planned R&D investments, lack of contribution by the university, failure to form platforms to support the joint work, and disregard for the spatial structure, have created significant constraints. The most common problems typically faced in innovation system applications were encountered in the RIS Mersin project as well (IRE, 2008, p. 13; OECD, 2010c). These problems are regarded as systemic failures.

Mersin RIS Plus Project and TR62 Regional Smart Specialization Strategies (2015-present)

The regional innovation system studies related to Mersin RIS Plus (SFC-Strategy for Competition[1]), were put into practice in Mersin and Adana on June 04, 2015 with the protocol signed under the coordination of ÇKA. (ÇKA, 2017e, p. 16). With this movements, first RIS Mersin Project (2005-2008) is tried to adopt with regional smart specialization strategies The study, titled, *Çukurova Smart Specialization Strategy* was launched with the aim of strengthening the region's innovation capacity and was carried out in cooperation with governorships, metropolitan municipalities, chambers of commerce and industry, the Adana Commodity Exchange, Çukurova University, Mersin University, Adana Science and Technology University, and the Adana Hacı Sabancı Organized Industry Region. As part of the Çukurova Regional Plan, priority sectors and clusters with high competitiveness will be identified for both cities, a strategy and action plan based on innovation in regional development will be developed, and sectoral action plans, which will be established after sectoral collaboration platforms are developed, will be implemented. Within the framework of the project, the plan is to create innovation-based strategies and actions in the sectoral and thematic areas, which will be determined using the smart specialization approach, and these strategies and actions will be implemented in cooperation with all relevant stakeholders in the region (ÇKA, 2018, pp. 13-18).

Although the smart specialization model was adopted in 2015, more comprehensive planning was able to be carried out first in the 2018 program of the CDA. Smart specialization model applications, such as digital transformation, key enabled technologies, global value chains, international networking activities, improvement of the investment environment, development of entrepreneurship eco-system, and capacity development, were planned. R&D and current innovation situation analyses were carried out for the Mersin RIS Plus and Adana RIS projects; moreover, innovation needs analysis studies were conducted for Mersin (ÇKA, 2017a; ÇKA, 2017b, 7; ÇKA, 2017c). These technical analyses will be used to determine priorities in the RIS3 model. The industrial sector cannot create enough employment in Mersin, yet Mersin is growing due to the increase in the overall growth rate in Turkey. Therefore, the RIS3 model should be well evaluated. Important clues were also found for systemic problems in the innovation needs analysis study conducted for Mersin. The following suggestions were developed based on the research results:

- **Need for İnnovation and Low İnnovation in Agriculture and Tourism:** Transportation and logistics sectors use the current infrastructure. The effects of path-dependence are strong and the lock-in can be strengthened by the interference eco-system. Initiative priorities and incentives should be determined through a holistic assessment.
- **Complementarity Relations of Some Food and Chemical Products are High due to the Geographical Proximity of Mersin to Adana:** Collaboration and clustering should be facilitated. Relatedness and specialization based on the resources of the provinces should be realized, and regional diversity should be enhanced. This diversification would positively affect the interventional exploration process by supporting economic complexity.
- **Exporters are More İnnovative:** Openness to knowledge flows increases through export, and learning processes emerge. Projects for export should be supported. Continuous interventional exploration should be improved.
- **As the Level of Product İnnovation İncreases, the Need for Product İnnovation Support increases:** Capacity can be increased through regional and sectoral network collaborations and Value chains. Top-down policy should be implemented more effectively.

SOLUTIONS AND RECOMMENDATIONS

When evaluated generally, the Mersin RIS Plus project compared to the RIS Mersin project has major application differences in terms of both model design and periodic conditions. The following should be taken into account when using the RIS3 as a development mechanism for the city of Mersin.

- Planning is carried out at the TR62 level
- In specialization, entrepreneurial discoveries at the product and process level take precedence over sectoral orientation
- It is affected by new industrialization and business models due to Industry 4.0
- Global-regional value chains and interconnectedness are effective in system design
- Integration into China-based One Belt One Road system is needed
- Quadruple helix model is applied
- Both bottom-up and top-down policies are implemented together
- Decentralization is important in the operation of the system
- Innovative initiatives have characteristics that transform regional structure
- It is a dynamic adaptive complex system
- Talented people are more required
- Cultural diversity is needed for creativity

RIS3, on the other hand, has a structure that requires innovation systems. In an open innovation model to be integrated into global value chains, it is very important for the system to be durable and have the ability to adapt to overcome the obstructions affecting underdeveloped regions (Akçomak & Bürken, 2019, p. 2; Asheim, 2019, p. 12; Papamichail et al., 2019, p. 67). The processes for the monitoring and evaluation of RIS3 are now being developed in European region. For this reason, a multi-layer and project-specific dynamic system design can be proposed for the innovation system management and development path for new Mersin RIS Plus Project model based on smart specialization concept.

Top Layers

- Global industry 4.0, digital transformation
- Global Sustainable Development Goals (SDGs)
- Global value chains, platforms
- AB FP9, Framework Programme for Research and Innovation-2021-2027: Digital Europe

National, Regional and Local Layers

1. Identification of smart specialization strategy expert. Monitoring and connecting (local level-Mersin, Adana)
2. Establishment of smart specialization team. Agility, team of experts, talent-based, monitoring, analyzing, evaluation, (regional level-TR62)
3. Formation of Çukurova Innovation Council: Determination of priorities, implementation
4. Quadruple helix model (regional level-TR62)
5. Establishment of regional development agencies system: Planning, network and collaboration (national level-Turkey)
6. Creation of smart specialization platform: Network and collaboration (national level-Turkey)

One of the important factors that will affect the Mersin RIS Plus period, unlike the RIS Mersin period, is that Mersin is a province that is open to mass migration due to the political turmoil in the Middle East. Referring to integrated, inclusive social innovation models to address this situation will be useful for RIS3 practices. According to the World Development Report (WDR) (2009, pp. 158-159), migration and an agglomeration economy support each other. In this context, the region either attracts the trained workforce or the migrants in the region are trained. As a result of the clustering, the increasing returns and the spread of knowledge on the scale reinforce the agglomeration. In addition, because the migrants will continue their connections with the places they come from, creativity and diversity are expected to increase as a result of tacit knowledge.

FUTURE RESEARCH DIRECTIONS

The Mersin RIS Plus project, which will continue under the coordination of the Çukurova Development Agency and Adana RIS, will be extremely sensitive to an open innovation system design, collaborations and dynamic network externalities. The regulatory function of the public will be limited to coordination and orientation. The tendency of decentralization in the operation of the system will become increasingly important. Moreover, interaction with digital flexible labor markets, platforms and value chains will highlight the process of interventional exploration. Therefore, it is also necessary to establish a smart specialization management system apart from the Agency mechanisms. By taking advantage of the innovations in digital transformation, rather than holding to the traditional approach that is based on knowledge, and using the sources available in the region, the Mersin RIS Plus project, as a model, aims to discover, create and implement new superiorities specific to the region, continuously influence the whole region, and create new growth paths. Taking into account this aim, the fact that the TR62 region becomes a center of attraction for talent and that its specialization policy functions as a catching-up mechanism requires the project to be handled within the framework of complexity science.

CONCLUSION

Smart specialization is a new industrialization strategy, one based on the system and evolution approach and knowledge production, and the EU adopted this strategy in the late 2000s because it lost its power of competitiveness in economic growth, employment and technology. Soon, smart specialization was used in the design of national and regional innovation systems and was implemented under the name of smart specialization strategy for research and innovation (RIS3). Along with the knowledge-based economy of the 21st century, the pressures of the Asian region as the center of the global economy has required new regulations and formations to be made in the American and European-based capitalist economic system and policy design. For example, when the process of globalization is considered in terms of knowledge flow, the specialization strategy of economic theory based on equilibrium in a closed system and decreasing returns has started to become inadequate in the modeling of complexity. This is the case because it has been scientifically affirmed that everything changes at the same time and that everything can be related to everything at the same time, complexity science generates multidisciplinary explanations on this basis. These innovations have influenced the economic, social and political policy proposals that central capitalist organizations like the OECD and the EU developed at the regional and international level.

The scientific and theoretical transformation of the knowledge-based digital economic structure suggests that the RIS3 model originating from the EU will co-evolve with complexity science. Turkey's partnership and membership processes with the EU have resulted in Turkey being affected by Europe's structural compliance and cohesion policies and being able to benefit from money funds. The RIS Mersin project was supported by EU funds between 2005-2008. It is the first regional innovation system within the context of a knowledge-based economy, and the experience it provided has led to significant learning effects. Based on the smart specialization model, the RIS Mersin Plus Project is being constructed on this accumulation of knowledge. As a system approach with its own mechanism, the RIS3 model was designed as a structure capable of evolving through trials and errors. The RIS3 model has many features and applications different from those of the RIS Mersin model. Therefore, the performance of the Mersin RIS Plus project launched in 2015 will help to facilitate a correct understanding of these innovations and their implementations.

ACKNOWLEDGMENT

I thank to my wife biologist Mustafa Berkan Yardımcı because my research has benefited from many discussions with him on theory of evolution and my son computer engineer İsmet Ata Yardımcı for graphic designing.

REFERENCES

Ackoff, R. L. (1979). The Future of Operational Research is Past. *The Journal of the Operational Research Society*, *30*(2), 93–104. doi:10.1057/jors.1979.22

Akçomak, İ. S., & Bürken, S. (2019). *The Middle-Technology Trap: The Case of the Automotive Industry in Turkey*. Maastricht University, Netherlands.

Antonelli, C. (2009). The Economics of Innovation: From the Classical Legacies to the Economics of Complexity. *Economics of Innovation and New Technology*, *18*(7), 611–646. doi:10.1080/10438590802564543

Antonelli, C. (Ed.). (2011). *Handbook on the Economic Complexity of Technological Change*. Edward Elgar. doi:10.4337/9780857930378

Antonelli, C. (2018). *The Evolutionary Complexity of Endogenous Innovation: The Engines of the Creative Response*. Edward Elgar. doi:10.4337/9781788113793

Archibugi, D., & Michie, J. (1997). Technological Globalisation or National Systems of Innovation? *Futures*, *29*(2), 121–137. doi:10.1016/S0016-3287(96)00072-9

Arthur, W. B. (2010). Complexity, The Santa Fe Approachi and Non-equilibrium Economics. *History of Economic Ideas*, *18*(2), 149–166.

Asheim, B. T. (2019). Smart Specialisation, Innovation Policy and Regional Innovation Systems: What About new Path Development in Less Innovative Regions? *Innovation (Abingdon)*, *32*(1), 8–25. doi:10.1080/13511610.2018.1491001

Asheim, B. T., Boschma, R., & Cooke, P. (2011). Constructing Regional Advantage: Platform Policies based on Related Variety and Differentiated Knowledge Bases. *Regional Studies*, *45*(7), 893–904. doi:10.1080/00343404.2010.543126

Asheim, B. T., & Coenen, L. (2006). Contextualizing Regional Innovation Systems in a Globalising Learning Economy: On Knowledge Bases and Institutional Frameworks. *The Journal of Technology Transfer*, *31*(1), 163–173. doi:10.100710961-005-5028-0

Asheim, B. T., Smith, H. L., & Oughton, C. (2011). Regional Innovation Systems: Theory, Empirics and Policy. *Regional Studies*, *45*(7), 875–891. doi:10.1080/00343404.2011.596701

Barca, F. (2009). *An Agenda for a Reformed Cohesion Policy: A Place-based Approach to Meeting European Union Challenges and Expectations*. Brussels: European Commission.

Bleda, M., & del Rio, P. (2013, June). (The Market Failure and the Systemic Failure Rationales in Technological Innovation Systems. *Research Policy*, *42*(5), 1039–1052. doi:10.1016/j.respol.2013.02.008

Boulding, K. (1956). General Systems Theory-The Skeleton of Science. *Management Science*, *2*(3), 197–208. doi:10.1287/mnsc.2.3.197

Boulding, K. (1997). *Yirminci Asrın Mânası (E. Güngör, Çev.)*. İstanbul: Ötüken.

Camplin, T., & Elliot, E. (2014). Innovation, Complex Systems and Computation: Technological Space and Speculations on the Future. *Studies in Emergent Order*, *7*, 184–206.

Charles, D.; Gross, F. & Bachtler, J. (2012). 'Smart Specialization' and Cohesion – A Strategy for All Regions? IQ.

Chorafakis, G., & Pontikakis, D. (2011). Theoretical Underpinnings and Future Directions of European Union Research Policy: A Paradigm Shift. *Prometheus*, *29*(2), 131–161. doi:10.1080/08109028.2011.600829

Cilliers, P. (2000). What Can We Learn From a Theory of Complexity? *Emergence*, *2*(1), 23–33. doi:10.1207/S15327000EM0201_03

ÇKA-Çukurova Kalkınma Ajansı. (2014a). Adana: Çukurova Bölge Planı.

ÇKA-Çukurova Kalkınma Ajansı. (2016). 10. Yılında Çukurova Kalkınma Ajansı. Adana.

ÇKA-Çukurova Kalkınma Ajansı. (2017a). RIS + Mersin Ar-Ge ve İnovasyon Mevcut Durum Analizi. Adana.

ÇKA-Çukurova Kalkınma Ajansı. (2017b). RIS + Mersin Yenilik İhtiyaç Analizi Raporu. Adana.

ÇKA-Çukurova Kalkınma Ajansı. (2017c). RIS + Adana Ar-Ge ve İnovasyon Mevcut Durum Analizi. Adana.

ÇKA-Çukurova Kalkınma Ajansı. (2017d). *Mersin Yatırım, Destek ve Tanıtım Stratejisi ve Eylem Planı, 2017-2023 Stratejik Planı-2017 Eylem Planı*. Adana: Mersin Yatırım Destek Ofisi.

ÇKA-Çukurova Kalkınma Ajansı. (2017e). Adana: Yılı Çalışma Programı.

ÇKA-Çukurova Kalkınma Ajansı. (2018). Adana: Yılı Çalışma Programı.

ÇKA-Çukurova Kalkınma Ajansı & TKA-Türkiye Kalkınma Ajansı. (2014b). *Mersin İli Potansiyel Yatırım Konuları Araştırması*. Ankara.

Coenen, L., Asheim, B., Bugge, M. M., & Herstad, S. J. (2017). Advancing Regional Innovation Systems: What does Evolutionary Economic Geography Bring to the Policy Table? *Environment and Planning C. Politics and Space*, *35*(4), 600–620.

Comim, F. (2000). The Santa Fe Approach to Complexity: A Marshallian Evolution. *Structural Change and Economic Dynamics*, *11*(1-2), 25–43. doi:10.1016/S0954-349X(99)00020-X

Cook, P. (1992). Regional Innovation Systems: Competitive Regulation in the New Europe. *Geoforum*, *23*(3), 365–382. doi:10.1016/0016-7185(92)90048-9

Cook, P. (1996). The New Wave of Regional İnnovation Networks: Analysis, Charactaristics and Strategy. *Small Business Economics*, *8*(2), 159–171. doi:10.1007/BF00394424

Cook, P., & Leydesdorff, L. (2006). Regional Development in the Knowledge-Based Economy: The Construction of Advantage. *The Journal of Technology Transfer*, *31*(1), 5–15. doi:10.100710961-005-5009-3

Cook, P., Uranga, M. G., & Etxebarria, G. (1998). Regional Systems of Innovation: An Evolutionary Perspective. *Environment & Planning A*, *30*(9), 1563–1584. doi:10.1068/a301563

De Bruijn, P., & Lagendijk, A. (2005). Regional Innovation Systems in The Lisbon Strategy. *European Planning Studies*, *13*(8), 1153–1172. doi:10.1080/09654310500336519

DeBresson, C. ve Hu, X. (1999). Identifying Clusters of Innovative Activity: A New Approach and A Toolbox. In Boosting Innovation The Cluster Approach (pp. 27-59). OECD Proocedings, OECD.

Dodgson, M., Hughes, A., Foster, J., & Metcalfe, J. S. (2010). *System Thinking, market failure, and the development of innovation policy: The Case of Australia*. Centre for Business Research. Retrieved from. http://www.uq.edu.au/economics/abstract/403.pdf

Dopfer, K. (1994). Kenneth Boulding: A Founder of Evolutionary Economics. *Journal of Economic Issues*, *28*(4), 1201–1204. doi:10.1080/00213624.1994.11505618

Drack, M. (2015). Ludwig von Bertalanffy's Organismic View on the Theory of Evolution. *The Journal of Experimental Zoology, 324B*, 77–90.

Dulupçu, M. A., & Okçu, M. (2000). Towards Quantum Economic Development: Transcending Boundaries. *Ankara Üniversitesi SBF Dergisi, 55*(3), 29–53.

EC-European Commission. (1993). *Growth, competitiveness, employment – The challenges and ways forward into the 21st Century*. Luxembourg: Office for Official Publications of the European Communities.

EC-European Commission. (2000). *Towards a European Research Area. COM(2000) 6 final*. Brussels: European Union.

EC-European Commission. (2009). *The Role of Community Research Policy in the Knowledge-Based Economy*. Brussels: European Union.

EC-European Commission. (2010). *Europe 2020 Flagship Initiative Innovation Union. SEC(2010) 1161 Final*. Brussels: European Union.

EC-European Commission. (2010a). *Europe 2020 A Strategy for Smart, Sustainable and Inclusive Growth. COM(2010) 2020*. Brussels: European Union.

EC-European Commission. (2010b). *Regional Policy Contributing to Smarth Growth in Europe 2020. COM(2010) 553 Final*. Brussels: European Union.

EC-European Commission. (2012, May). Guide to Research and Innovation Strategies for Smart Specializations (RIS3). Brussels: European Union.

EC-European Commission. (2017a). *Strenghtening Innovation in Europe's Region: Towards Resilient, Inclusive and Sustainable Growth at Territorial Level*. Brussels: European Union.

EC-European Commission. (2017b). *Open's Future: Open Innovation, Open Science, Open to the World*. Brussels: European Union.

Edler, J., & Fagerberg, J. (2017). Innovation Policy: What, Why, and How. *Oxford Review of Economic Policy, 33*(1), 2–23. doi:10.1093/oxrep/grx001

Edquist, C. (Ed.). (2005). *Systems of Innovation Technologies, Institutions and Organizations*. Routledge.

Edquist, C. (2011). Design of Innovation Policy Through Diagnostic Analysis: Identification of Systemic Problems (or Failures). *Industrial and Corporate Change, 20*(6), 1725–1753. doi:10.1093/icc/dtr060

Eraydın, A. (2016). Attributes and Characteristics of Regional Resilience: Defining and Measuring the Resilience of Turkish Regions. *Regional Studies*, *50*(4), 600–614. doi:10.1080/00343404.2015.1034672

Eren, E. (2018). İktisadi Modellemede Gelişmeler: Evrim Modellenebilir mi? *Efil Journal*, *1*(1), 58–87.

Ergin, A. (2016). Bilim ve Teknoloji Yüksek Kurulu Kararları ve Gelişmeleri. Toplantısı, Ankara. Retrieved from https://www.tubitak.gov.tr/sites/default/files/btyk29_web_2.pdf

European Council. (2000). Presidency Conclusions. Retrieved from http://www.europarl.europa.eu/summits/lis1_en.htm

Fagerberg, J., Martin, B. R., & Andersen, E. S. (2013). Innovation Studies: Towards a New Agenda. In J. Fagerberg, B.R. Martin, & E.S. Andersen (Ed.), Innovation Studies: Evolution & Future Challenges (pp. 1-17). UK:Oxford University Press.

Ferry, M., & McMaster, I. (2013). Cohesion Policy and the Evolution of Regional Policy in Central and Eastern Europe. *Europe-Asia Studies*, *65-8*(8), 1502–1528. doi:10.1080/09668136.2013.832969

Fontana, M. (2010). The Santa Fe Perspective on Economics: Emerging Patterns in the Science of Complexity. *History of Economic Ideas*, *18*(2), 167–196.

Foray, D. (2012). *Smart Specialisation and the New Industrial Policy Agenda.* Brussels: European Union.

Foray, D. (2014). From Smart Specialisation to Smart Specialisation Policy. *European Journal of Innovation Management*, *17*(4), 492–507. doi:10.1108/EJIM-09-2014-0096

Foray, D., David, P. A., & Hall, B. (2009). Smart Specialisation: the Concept. In Knowledge for Growth: Prospects for Science, Technology and Innovation (20-24). Report, EUR 24047, Brussels: European Union.

Foray, D., & Goenega, X. (2013). *The Goals of Smart Specialisation.* Brussels: European Union.

Foray, D., Morgan, K., & Radosevic, S. (2018). *The Role of Smart Specialization in the EU Research & Innovation Policy Landscape*. Retrieved from https://ec.europa.eu/regional_policy/en/information/publications/brochures/2018/the-role-of-smart-specialisation-in-the-eu-research-innovation-policy-landscape

Foray, D., & Rainoldi, A. (2013). *Smart Specialisation Programmes and Implementation.* Brussels: European Union.

Freeman, C. (1995). The 'National System of Innovation' in Historical Perspective. *Cambridge Journal of Economics, 19*, 5–24.

Frenz, M., & Oughton, C. (2005). *Innovation in the UK Regions and Devolved Administrations: A Review of the Literature*. Department of Trade and Industry, Governement of the UK. Retrieved from http://www.bis.gov.uk/files/file9651.doc

Gianella, C. Kyriakou; Cohen, C. & Przeor, M. (Ed.), (2016). Implementing Smart Specialisation: A Handbook. Brussels: European Union.

Godin, B. (2004). The Obsession of Competitiveness and its Impact on Statistics: The Construction of High-Technology Indicators. Project on The History and Sociology of S&T Statistics.

Godin, B. (2006). The Knowledge-Based Economy: Conceptual Framework or Buzzword? *The Journal of Technology Transfer, 31*(1), 17–30. doi:10.100710961-005-5010-x

Godin, B. (2007). National Innovation System: The System Approach in Historical Perspective. Project on The History and Sociology of S&T Statistics.

Gök, T. (2009). RIS Mersin Projesi Üzerine Bir Özet Değerlendirme. *Planlama, 3-4*, 93–95.

Gordon, R. J. (2004). Why Was Europe at the Station When America's Productivity Locomotive Departed? *NBER*.

Hammond, D. (2005). Philosophical and Ethical Foundations of System Thinking. *TripleC, 3*(2), 20–27. doi:10.31269/triplec.v3i2.20

Hart, N. (2013). *Alfred Marshall and Modern Economics: Equilibrium Theory and Evolutionary Economics*. Palgrave Macmillan. doi:10.1057/9781137029751

Hester, P. T., & Adams, K. M. (2014). *Systemic Thinking, Fundamentals for Understanding Problems and Messes*. Switzerland: Springer. doi:10.1007/978-3-319-07629-4

Hodgson, G. M. (2000). The Concept of Emergence in Social Science: Its History and Importance. *Emergence, 2*(4), 65–77. doi:10.1207/S15327000EM0204_08

Holt, R. P. F., Rosser, J. B. Jr, & Colander, D. (2011). The Complexity Era in Economics. *Review of Political Economy*, *23*(3), 357–369. doi:10.1080/09538259.2011.583820

Hutter, M. (1994). Organism as a Metaphor in German Economic Thought. In P. Mirowski (Ed.), *Natural Images in Economic Thought: Markets Read in Tooth and Claw* (pp. 289–321). USA: Cambridge University Press. doi:10.1017/CBO9780511572128.011

IRE-Innovation Regions in Europe. (2008). IRE Working Group Effective Regional Innovation Systems Final Report. Retrieved from https://wbc-rti.info/object/document/7823/attach/Fina_report_ERIS_final.pdf

Johnson, B., Edquist, C., & Lundvall, B. (2003, November). Economic Development and the National System of Innovation Approach. *Proceedings of the First Globelics Conference*, Rio De Janeiro. Academic Press. Retrieved from https://smartech.gatech.edu/bitstream/handle/1853/43154/BengtAkeLundvall_2.pdf

Katz, J. S. (2006). Indicators for Complex Innovation Systems. *Research Policy*, *35*(7), 893–909. doi:10.1016/j.respol.2006.03.007

Katz, J. S. (2016). What is a Complex Innovation System? *PLoS One*, *11*(6), 1–24. doi:10.1371/journal.pone.0156150 PMID:27258040

Kaufmann, A., & Wagner, P. (2005). EU Regional Policy and the Stimulation of Innovation: The Role of the European Regional Development Fund in the Objective 1 Region Burgenland. *European Planning Studies*, *13*(4), 581–599. doi:10.1080/09654310500107274

Kazgan, G. (2006). *İktisadi Düşünce Politik İktisadın Evrimi.* İstanbul: Baskı.

Kim, L., & Nelson, R. R. (Eds.). (2000). *Technology, Learning, and Innovation.* Cambridge, UK: Cambridge University Press.

Landabaso, M. (1997). The Promotion of Innovation in Regional Policy: Proposal for a Regional Innovation Strategy. *Entrepreneurship and Regional Development*, *9*(1), 1–24. doi:10.1080/08985629700000001

Levent, T. (2016). RIS-Mersin Project: The First Regional Innovation Strategy in Turkey and its Spatial Dimensions. *Folia Geographica Socia-Oeconomica*, *24*, 5–16.

Lewis, P. (2016). Systems, Structural Properties and Levels of Organisation: The Influence of Ludwig Von Bertalanffy on the Work of F.A. Hayek. In L. Fiorito, S. Scheall, & C. Eduardo Suprinyak (Ed.), *Including a Symposium on Austrian Economics in the Postwar Era (Research in the History of Economic Thought and Methodology* (pp. 125 – 159). Emerald Group Publishing Limited.

Lundvall, B.-A. (2007). National Innovation Systems—Analytical Concept and Development Tool. *Industry and Innovation, 14*(1), 95–119. doi:10.1080/13662710601130863

Lundvall, B.-A. (2016). *The Learning Economy and the Economics of Hope*. Anthem Press. doi:10.26530/OAPEN_626406

Lundvall, B.-A., Johnson, B., Andersen, E. S., & Dalum, B. (2002). National Systems of Production, Innovation and Competence Building. *Research Policy, 31*(2), 213–231. doi:10.1016/S0048-7333(01)00137-8

Madelin, R., & Ringrose, D. (2016). *Opportunity now: Europe's Mission to Innovate. Policy Review Report*. Brussels: European Union.

Mariussen, A., Rakhmatullin, R., & Stanionyte, L. (2016). *Smart Specialisation: Creating Growth through Trans-national Cooperation and Value Chains. Thematic Work on the Understanding of Transnational Cooperation and Value Chains in the Context of Smart Specialization*. Luxembourg: European Union.

Martin, R., & Sunley, P. (2007). Complexity Thinking and Evolutionary Economic Geography. *Journal of Economic Geography, 7*(5), 573–601. doi:10.1093/jeg/lbm019

Martin, R. B. (2013). Innovation Studies: An Emerging Agenda. In J. Fagerberg, B.R. Martin, & E.S. Andersen (Ed.), Innovation Studies: Evolution & Future Challenges (pp. 168-186). UK: Oxford University Press.

McCann, P., & Ortega-Argiles, R. (2013). Transforming European Regional Policy: A Result Driven Agenda and Smart Specialization. *Oxford Review of Economic Policy, 29*(2), 405–431.

Mckelvey, B. (2001). What is Complexity Science? It is Really Order-Creation Science. *Emergence, 3*(1), 137–157. doi:10.1207/S15327000EM0301_09

Mckelvey, B. (2004). Toward a Complexity Science of Entrepreneurship. *Journal of Business Venturing, 19*(3), 313–341. doi:10.1016/S0883-9026(03)00034-X

Mersin. (2008). Mersin İnovasyon Stratejisi 2006-2016.

Mirowski, P. (1991). *More Heat Than Light: Economics as Soscial Physics, Physics as Nature's Economics*. Cambridge University Press.

Mitleton-Kelly, E. (Ed.). (2003). *Complex Systems and Evolutionary Perspectives on Organizations: The Application of Complexity Theory to Organizations*. Elsevier.

Morgan, K. (2013). The Regional State in the Era of Smart Specialization. *Ekonomiaz, 83*(2), 102–125.

Mytelka, L. K., & Smith, K. (2002). Policy Learning and Innovation Theory: An Interactive and Co-evolving Process. *Research Policy, 31*(8-9), 1467–1479. doi:10.1016/S0048-7333(02)00076-8

Nelson, R. R., & Winter, S. G. (1982). *An Evolutionary Theory of Economic Change*. Belknap Press.

Noell, C. (2007). A Look into the Nature of Complex Systems and Beyond "Stonehenge" Economics: Coping with Complexity or Ignoring it in Applied Economics. *Agricultural Economics, 37*(2-3), 219–235. doi:10.1111/j.1574-0862.2007.00268.x

OECD. (1997). *National Innovation Systems*. Paris: OECD Publishing.

OECD. (1998). *The OECD Jobs Strategy Technology, Productivity and Job Creation Best Policy Practices*. Paris: OECD Publishing.

OECD. (1999). *Managing National Systems*. Paris: OECD Publishing.

OECD. (2005). Guidelines for Collecting and Interpreting Innovation Data — The Oslo Manual (3rd ed.). Paris: Eurostat Publishing.

OECD. (2009). *Investing for Growth: Building innovative regions. Policy Report, Meeting of the Territorial Development Policy Committee at Ministerial level (31 March 2009)*. Paris: OECD.

OECD. (2010a). *Regional Development Policies in OECD Countries*. Paris: OECD Publishing.

OECD. (2010c). Regional Innovation Strategies. Retrieved from. http://www.oecd.org/innovation/policyplatform/48137737.pdf

OECD. (2015). *System Innovation: Synthesis Report*. Paris: OECD Publishing.

Öğüt, K., & Sunal, S. (2017). Kompleks Adaptif Bir Sistem Olarak Ekonomi ve İktisat. In E. Eren & S. Şahin (Eds.), *Kompleksite ve İktisat* (pp. 44–57). İstanbul.

Oliva, G. (2015). The Road to Servomechanisms: The Influence of Cybernetics on Hayek from The Sensory Order to the Social Order. Duke University.

Papamichail, G., Rosiello, A., & Wield, D. (2019). Capacity-Building Barriers to S3 Implementation: An Empirical Framework for Catch-up Regions. *Innovation (Abingdon)*, *32*(1), 66–84. doi:10.1080/13511610.2018.1537844

Pellegrin, J. (2007). Regional Innovation Strategies in the EU or a Regionalized EU Innovation Strategy. *Innovation*, *20*(3), 203–221.

Prigogine, I. (1987). Exploring Complexity. *European Journal of Operational Research*, *30*(2), 97–103. doi:10.1016/0377-2217(87)90085-3

Prigogine, I., & Stengers, I. (1984). Order Out of Chaos: Man's New Dialogue With Nature. USA: A Bantham Book.

Reillon, V. (2017.September). EU Framework Programmes for Research and Innovation. Evolution and Key Data from FP1 to Horizon 2020 in View of FP9. European Union.

Robert, V., Yoguel, G., & Lerena, O. (2017). The Ontology of Complexity and the Neo-Schumpeterian Evolutionary Theory of Economic Change. *Journal of Evolutionary Economics*, *27*(4), 761–793. doi:10.100700191-017-0512-x

Rosser, J. B. Jr. (2011). *Complex Evolutionary Dynamics in Urban-Regional and Ecologic-Economic Systems: From Catastrophe to Chaos and Beyond*. London: Springer. doi:10.1007/978-1-4419-8828-7

Simon, H. A. (1962). The Architecture of Complexity. *Proceedings of the American Philosophical Society*, *106*(6), 467–487.

Simon, H. A. (2018). Can There be a Science of Complex Systems? In Y. Bar-Yam (Ed)., *Unifying Themes in Complex Systems* (pp. 3-14), CRC Press.

Temin, P. (2002). The Golden Age of European Growth Reconsidered. *European Review of Economic History*, *6*(1), 3–22. doi:10.1017/S1361491602000011

The World Bank. (2009). *Reshaping Economic Geography.*

Turkcan, B. (2014). Knowledge Externalities and Knowledge Spillovers in Social Networks: The Case of Izmir Metalwork Industrial District. *European Planning Studies*, *22*(7), 1425–1443. doi:10.1080/09654313.2013.789488

Uyarra, E., Sörvik, J., & Midtkandal, I. (2014). *Inter-regional Collaboration in Research and Innovation Strategies for Smart Specialisation (RIS3)*. European Union.

Valentinov, V. (2015). Kenneth Boulding's Theories of Evolutionary Economics and Organizational Change: A Reconstruction. *Journal of Economic Issues*, *49*(1), 71–88. doi:10.1080/00213624.2015.1013880

von Bertalanffy, L. (1950). The Theory of Open Systems in Physics and Biology. *Science*, *111*(2872), 23–29. doi:10.1126cience.111.2872.23 PMID:15398815

von Bertalanffy, L. (1969). *General Systems Theory: Foundation, Development, Applications*. New York, USA: George Braziller.

von Bertalanffy, L. (1972). The History and Status of General Systems Theory. *Academy of Management Journal*, *15*(4), 407–426.

Weaver, W. (1948). Science and Complexity. *American Scientist*, *36*(4), 536–544. PMID:18882675

White, R., Engelen, G., & Uljee, I. (2015). *Modeling Cities and Regions as Complex Systems: From Theory to Planning Applications*. London, England: MIT Press. doi:10.7551/mitpress/9780262029568.001.0001

World Bank. (2016). Bölgesel Yatırım Ortamı Değerlendirmesi Raporu, TR62 IBBS II Bölgesi Adana-Mersin, Ankara.

Wyckoff, A. (2017). Innovation and Complexity. In P. Love, Ve J. Stockdale-Otarola (Eds.), Debate The Issues: Complexity and Policy Making (pp. 80-83). Paris: OECD Publishing. doi:10.1787/9789264271531-en

KEY TERMS AND DEFINITIONS

Complexity Science: A new scientific and philosophical paradigm based on complex systems with a perspective of systemism prevailing in the 21st century.

Knowledge-Based Economy: An economy that depending on greatly knowledge input in which knowledge is created with systemic processes that become increasingly complex.

Innovation System: An institutional and organizational network for better innovating processes and creating new knowledge.

Systems Theory: Transdisciplinary field of science integrating and unifying principles in systems with isomorphism and wholeness.

ENDNOTE

1 RİS (Rekabet İçin Strateji) in Turkish.

Chapter 6
Irregular Migration and Economic Nationalism in EU

Tugba Aydin Halisoglu
Artvin Coruh University, Turkey

ABSTRACT

Nationalism is one of the controversial issues in political science studies. Nationalism includes rational approaches as well as emotional ones, both strong support and intense criticism. This chapter will apply the primordial approach of nationalism, considering its roots from before the French Revolution and as a result of human psychology. So, the sense of belonging, is the main argument of the primordial approach in nationalism studies, will be examined with its effect on the migration economy. The main focus of the chapter will be the European Union facing huge refugee flows from Syria, the economic impact of refugees by the effect of migration, and citizen reaction to immigrants and the economy.

DOI: 10.4018/978-1-7998-1037-7.ch006

INTRODUCTION

December 17, 2010: A politically important date when the crisis has exploded, which still oppress the Arab world, as well as Europe. The main actor of the day is Tarek al-Tayeb Mohamed Bouazizi, who was born March 29, 1984, in Sidi Bouzid. After his father's death when Bouazizi was 3-years-old, he became an important source for financial support of his family. Without graduation in high school, he tried to find a job that he could have taken care of his family. So, he worked as a street vendor, selling fruits on the streets to earn in a day, as usual, he did on December 17, 2010, too.

11:30 am: In the Tunisian town of Sidi Bouzid, it was an ordinary day till Bouazizi was slapped and harassed by policewoman together with two market inspectors to demand bribes. His crates and electronic weight scale were tried to expropriate. He had lost his capital, also was humiliated in the public. Bouazizi went to the local governor to complain, but he was denied. Later in the day, he set himself into the fire. Bouazizi died on January 4, 2011, but his fire did not inflame only his life, also millions of people just a week after.

So, the story above is not only the film strip of Bouazizi. This is also the story of the Jasmine Revolution, sprouting in Bouazizi's protest. As Jasmine is the national flower of Tunisia, it was sloganed as 'Let's give jasmine to the police!' by many media organizations, which has caused President Zine El Abidine Ben Ali to be forced out of the presidency. So, the new term 'Arab Spring' has been decided to use after those protest leap to Algeria with a domino effect.

One of the critical processes of the Arab Spring was observed in Syria, causing huge migration flow into neighboring and European countries. Since March 2011, over 5.6 million people have fled Syria. Still, European Union countries are one of the top favorite destinations for most of the Syrian immigrants. Among them, Germany, Italy, and France are the countries with a high number of asylum applications. Their balanced economy, high living standards, stable politics, and democracy are attractive factors for an immigrant to migrate. But, what about the other side of the coin? What difficulties do these countries have in the economy during the post-immigration process? So, in this study, the focus will be given to the economy to find out the impacts of immigration into the EU countries in the eye of nationalism. This research aims to answer how Syrian immigration affects the current economic situation of EU member states; and how a sense of belonging can affect the citizens choice in the economy.

The rest of the chapter is organized as follows: The first part of the chapter consists of discussions on nationalism in the light of several approaches, including their cultural, emotional and instrumental dimensions. The main focus will be given to economic nationalism, considering the primordial approach and its main component of the sense of belonging. The second part of this chapter will discuss the terminology of irregular migration and immigration statistics to indicate the current situation in the EU. The last part will focus on discussions on the economy and irregular migration. The main emphasis will be given to the economic impact of immigration including how EU member states manage the migration process.

NATIONALISM: A GENERAL CONCEPT

Nationalism has hardly annual concept and includes lack of concurrence the opinion. Surrounded by an ideological frame, it makes difficult to provide a common acceptance on the definition.

Nationalism has defined in several ways such as 'sleeping beauty' or 'the source of harm'. 'Good', 'bad', 'constructive' or 'destructive' developments in historical periods had influenced these emotional approaches. Constructive developments such as the power to unite nations, impulse force of state-building process or immersive influence on citizens at the time of war; as well as destructive developments such as laying low an empire or harboring to hatred may affect the conceptual definition of nationalism. So, the term can simply be introduced as a figure of speech or expressive formation (Gökalp, 2007:281).

While there is no simple definition on nationalism, discussion over its nature vary. For example, Berghe (1981) frames nationalism with its characteristic as 'original sin' referring to its stimulating nature of irrational ambitions. Also, Kedouire (1960) announces nationalism as an intellectual mistake of political history, that of including bad ideas community.

Adam Smith mirrors the emotional component of nationalism. Smith (1993) defines the term as a sentiment 'emphasizing the symbols, ceremonies, and custom of national identity. So, Smith emphasizes emotions and strengthening components of them. Within today, there are several symbols combining people together and providing unity within a state. The flag is one of them, with each color defining each nationalistic beliefs. For example, the French flag constitutes blue, white and red as the national emblem of the republic. These colors refer to King (white), and the city of Paris (blue and red), which forms the major symbols of French Revolution such as liberty, equality, and fraternity (The French Flag, 2019). The national anthem is another strong symbol to remind citizens about their battled past, the need to stay strong today and great hopes for the future of their own nation and state. A sample can be found in German national anthem "Deutschlandlied" (Song of Germany), which was originally adopted for its connection to the March 1848 Liberal Revolution. Also, the emphasis on unity, rights, and freedoms are embedded as the national motto of Germany:

Einigkeit und Recht und Freiheit
für das deutsche Vaterland!
Danach lasst uns alle streben
brüderlich mit Herz und Hand!
Einigkeit und Recht und Freiheit
sind des Glückes Unterpfand:
Blüh im Glanze dieses Glückes,
blühe, deutsches Vaterland! [1]

Gellner is another intellectual, defining nationalism without its natural characteristic. He introduces his view of nationalism in his book *Thought and Change,* published in 1964. In his words, nationalism is described such as 'the will of a group aiming for state-building and aiming at cultural development' (Gellner, 1983). Here, Gellner frames the culture as a social tie. Herder also provides close links between culture and nationalism, which stand for cultural nationalism. Herder says that a natural state is built on one national character and one nation. So, in his words, the state is the end and he defends the cultural unity of Germany for the sake of humanity (Schmidt, 1956, p. 407).

Apart from cultural manners, civic nationalism is another field in nationalism studies. John Stuart Mill is one of the intellectual, contributing to civic nationalism discussions with its 'values' dimension. Here, values are considered as 'civic values' by most academicians. But, Mill proposes virtue of strong ethnic foundations for the functioning of civic government in his words below:

Among a people without fellow-feeling, especially if they read and speak different languages, the united public opinion, necessary to the working of representative government, cannot exist...it is, in general, a necessary condition of free institutions that the boundaries of governments should coincide in the main with those of nationalities (Williams, 2004, p. 15).

John Breuilly contributes to nationalism discussions with a different dimension. Breuilly examines nationalism with comparative history methods in his book *Nationalism and the State.* In his definition, nationalism is considered as political movements aiming to struggle for power as vindicating nationalistic arguments (Breuilly, 1993). Also, Paul Brass provides an instrumental approach and shortly defines nationalism and ethnic identities as a tool to seizure and to hold the power (Brass, 1979).

As seen, there are several definitions and approaches on nationalism, which make this term analyze in a large scale such as liberal nationalism, micro-nationalism, civic nationalism, cultural nationalism, left-wing nationalism, economic nationalism and so on. As economic nationalism consists of the main approach of this paper, the next part will focus on its concept and relation with a sense of belonging.

Economic Nationalism

Economic nationalism is simply defined in the Cambridge Dictionary as *a situation in which a country tries to protect its own economy by reducing the number of imports and investments from other countries* (Cambridge Dictionary, n.d.). This definition seems to eliminate the wide components of economic nationalism and reduces it only into the 'trade' dimension. But the term includes more than the trade. It also covers protectionist politics, including trade. Protectionist politics here signifies a limited movement of capital, person and goods. According to Cooper (2007;4), economic nationalism is related to resistance to globalization, which dismantles economic barriers between nation-states. Hellenier defines the term in a different way. According to Hellenier (2002:308), the term is mostly used by liberal economists to describe their disliked politics. So Koffman (Koffman, quoted in Helleiner, 2002, p. 309) contributes these discussions such as everything incompatible with a liberal definition of economy and politics is reminded as doctrine.

In Pickel's work, a modern listing for economic nationalism covers four discussion points, arguing that economic nationalism can be seen in any form including also economic liberalism. For Pickel, economic nationalism is a specific dimension of nationalism studies and it is not an economic theory. So the term can not be doctrinized because of consisting a political action. Additionally, nationalism as an economic ideology can result in specific economic, cultural and political structures (Pickel, 2003, pp. 116-117).

Primordial Approach and The Sense of Belonging

There are two main approaches in nationalism studies: Primordial approach and modernist approach. Theorists, considering post- French Revolution period in history, examines nationalism on nation-state base. The modern approach can be counted on this frame. Modernists claim that nations are the result of modern conditions. Formation of nation-states, urbanization, capitalism, and industrialization are seen as the main components.

On the contrary, the primordial approach claims that the nation exists even before the nation-state. They argue that nations did not appear in any period of history; indeed, did subsist with elements consisting of community identities such as language and culture. This approach includes a sense of belonging and genetics. Another claim in the primordial approach is about its emotional dimension. So, primordialism is defined as "sentiment about a perceived essential continuity from group ancestry to progeny (perceived kith and kin), located symbolically in a specific territory or place (which may or may not be the current place of the people concerned)" (Weinrich et al, 2013, p. 119).

Primordialists presents three separate viewpoints such as naturalism, biological primordialism, and cultural primordialism. Naturalism recognizes ethnic identity as natural as speaking skill or gender. So, differentiation of human beings into several ethnic groups are accepted as the need for natural order. Biological primordialism seeks for ethnic ties inside the genetic instinct and characteristics. Lastly, cultural primordialism claims on given loyalty to social life (Özkırımlı, 2009, pp. 85-92).

While defining nations, the human factor should be considered as the main source of the sense of belonging. Because, human beings can unite and relate to each other with emotions, identities, and consciousness. Thus, human instincts and the need for social interaction base for nationalistic arguments in this field.

Sense of belonging also causes psychological results such as integrity, articulation, development of joint consciousness, giving meaning and relevancy. Belonging starts with the question of 'Who am I?'. Impersonations enclose groups adopted by birth or subsequently. Of course, the question of 'who am I?' has a shallow concept as its own alone. This question takes on a meaning when psychological, sociological, economic and cultural factors are assessed all together.

IRREGULAR MIGRATION IN EU

Irregular Migration: A Short Introduction

The migration is apart from solely basic human movements as from one place to another. These movements also have the ability to change individuals own life, as well as the social, political, economic and cultural structure of the hosting society.

Attractive factors such as high living standards, democracy or warm climate can affect individuals' decisions to migrate in a volunteer way. Here, individuals prefer to migrate without any forcing factor and the decision is on their own. But, in the case of forced factors such as war, unstable political structure, terror and so on, then the structure of decision dramatically change. So, the types and the needs of migration vary.

In this paper, the main focus will be given to irregular migration (the result of the Syrian civil war) within the EU. So, what is irregular migration? The term is defined in a global context by the International Organization for Migration as a "movement that takes place outside the regulatory norms of the sending, transit and receiving countries" (IOM, n.d). According to IOM, there is no universal definition of irregular migration. Each state explains this term regarding their position as hosting, sending or transit country. For example, hosting countries relate to irregular migration as entry, stay or work without necessary documents or authorization. Or, for sending countries, irregular migration is about "crossing international borders without a valid passport" (IOM, n.d).

Irregular migration can also be defined in a regional context. Migration and Home Affairs of European Commission claim irregular immigrant as "the irregular entry of third-country nationals in Schengen Area, without the fulfilling the conditions set out in Regulation (EU) 2016/399 (Schengen Borders Code)" (European Commission, n.d).

As seen above, irregular migration simply refers to the migratory situation of individuals in a given period, not to their irregularity. Here, irregularity includes lack of information to access to welfare, health and education services. Morehouse ve Blomfield (2011, p. 4) systemize components of irregularity such as: 1) illegal entry of the border; 2) entrance of borders with forged documents; 3) the entry with legal documents including wrong information; 4) excess of the valid resident permit; 5) not leaving the hosting country even negative decisions on stay; and 6) no forced governmental action for return.

Irregular Migration in the World and in EU

Considering refugee flow between 1980-2017, it is observable that two big migration waves affected the world order on the 1990s and just after 2005 (Please see figure-1). The first migration wave has raised on the 1990s, just at the end of the Cold War. Iraq's invention to Kuwait, conflicts in Balkans, genocide at Rwanda and war in Afghanistan are major cases in the international world order. These cases forced 20.023.531 people to migrate (The World Bank, n.d). Just after 1992, the number

Figure 1. World refugees: Total population and as proportion of world population, 1980-2017
Source: (UNHCR, n.d (a))

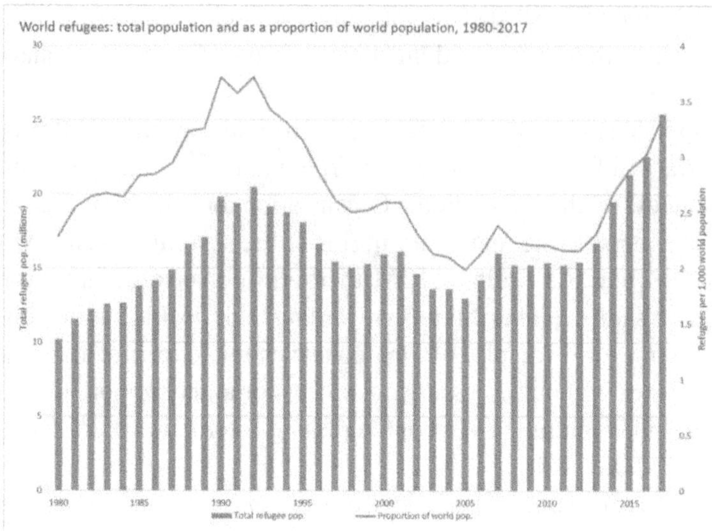

of refugees started to lessen until 2005. But due to conflicts in Iraq and Afghanistan and armed conflict in Colombia raised the numbers again. So, between 2005 to 2007, just in two years, the numbers of refugees has raised from 12.863.676 to 15.953.753. By the strong effect of Arab Spring and Syrian civil conflict, the number has raised into 25.376.316 in 2017 (The World Bank, n.d). Today in 2019, there are around 25.4 million of refugees and 3.1 million asylum seekers in the world (UNHCR, n.d (b)). Figure 1 illustrates the total change between 1980-2017.

European Union is one of the favorite destinations for refugees. By Syrian civil conflict, well- developed European countries attracted most of the immigrant because of having high-living standards, stable political structure, functioning democracy, rule of law, labor opportunity and stable economics. According to Eurostat data, first-time asylum applicants in the EU in fourth quarter of 2018 is 150690 in total. Syrian applicants are consisting of 12% amount of total application (17465 application). Refugees from Afghanistan consist of second in the list with the amount of 8% (12200 application). Figure 2 and 3 illustrate applications by citizenship in numbers.

The third figure illustrates first-time asylum applicants by citizenship in detail. Regarding the data, between Q4-2017 to Q4-2018, the number of Syrian applicants has declined. But still, Syrian applicants consist of the highest amount of applications (17465 applicants).

Figure 2. First time asylum applicants in the EU28 (Q4-2018)
Source: (Eurostat, n.d (a))

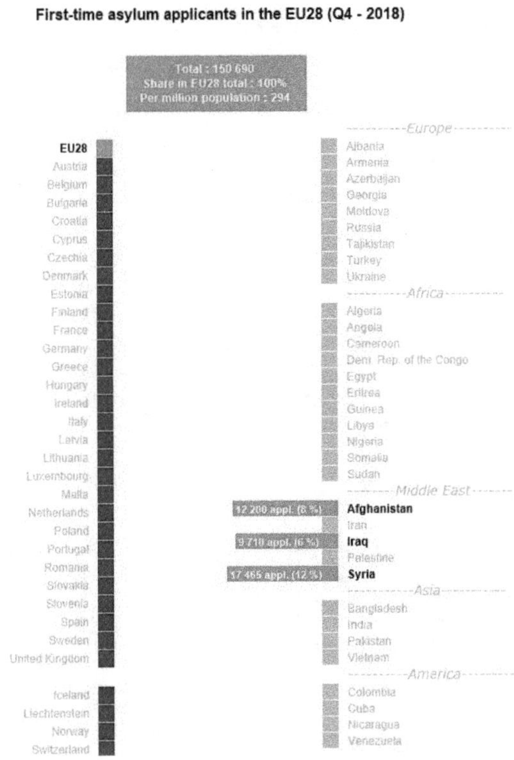

Figure 4 clearly demonstrates the most popular destinations of refugees for asylum applications. Germany (41795 application), France (28790 application), Greece, Spain, and Italy are seen the most attractive destinations for applicants by Q4-2018. Indeed Eastern European states such as Estonia, Slovakia, and Latvia have the minimum numbers in applications. Of course, migration policy and state control over the immigrants affected the results in these countries. Figure 4 illustrates asylum applicants' number for each EU countries in detail.

Figure 3. First-Time asylum applicants in the EU28 by citizenship
Source: (Eurostat, n.d. (b))

First-time asylum applicants in the EU-28 by citizenship, Q4 2017 – Q4 2018

	Q4 2017	Q1 2018	Q2 2018	Q3 2018	Q4 2018	Absolute change		Change in %		Last 12 months
						between Q3 2018 and Q4 2018	between Q4 2017 and Q4 2018	between Q3 2018 and Q4 2018	between Q4 2017 and Q4 2018	
Non-EU	154 400	141 760	141 445	146 945	150 690	3 740	-3 715	3	-2	580 845
Syria - (SY)	23 450	21 205	20 975	21 275	17 465	-3 810	-5 985	-18	-26	80 920
Afghanistan - (AF)	9 780	8 160	9 420	11 210	12 200	990	2 420	9	25	40 990
Iraq - (IQ)	12 945	10 870	8 965	10 055	9 710	-345	-3 235	-3	-25	39 595
Iran - (IR)	4 250	4 250	4 470	6 640	7 835	1 200	3 585	18	84	23 195
Pakistan - (PK)	6 955	5 835	5 605	6 235	7 030	800	80	13	1	24 705
Turkey - (TR)	4 630	3 745	4 535	7 435	6 255	-1 185	1 625	-16	35	21 965
Albania - (AL)	4 590	4 170	3 955	4 795	6 105	1 315	1 515	27	33	19 025
Venezuela - (VE)	3 625	4 110	7 555	4 435	5 825	1 390	2 195	31	61	21 920
Georgia - (GE)	3 615	5 030	3 745	3 725	5 485	1 760	1 865	47	52	17 980
Nigeria - (NG)	7 510	6 805	6 090	4 815	4 405	-410	-3 105	-9	-41	22 120
Guinea - (GN)	3 485	3 195	2 660	3 180	4 260	1 085	775	34	22	13 295
Colombia - (CO)	1 050	1 285	3 330	2 375	2 975	605	1 930	25	184	9 970
Bangladesh - (BD)	4 175	3 755	3 205	2 730	2 960	235	-1 215	9	-29	12 650
Eritrea - (ER)	4 340	4 235	4 095	3 670	2 945	-725	-1 395	-20	-32	14 945
Russia - (RU)	2 850	2 900	2 760	3 170	2 820	-350	-30	-11	-1	11 650
Somalia - (SO)	3 015	2 910	2 850	3 045	2 500	-545	-520	-18	-17	11 305
Algeria - (DZ)	2 665	2 550	2 095	2 100	2 440	335	-230	16	-9	9 185
Palestine - (PS)	1 030	1 290	1 425	2 185	2 275	90	1 245	4	121	7 175
Ukraine - (UA)	2 205	2 075	2 145	2 060	2 210	145	0	7	0	8 490
Ivory Coast - (CI)	2 775	2 300	2 120	1 900	2 125	225	-650	12	-23	8 445
Sudan - (SD)	2 240	1 690	1 880	2 785	1 835	-950	-405	-34	-18	8 185
Morocco - (MA)	1 970	1 970	1 810	1 920	1 810	-110	-155	-6	-8	7 510
Mali - (ML)	2 250	1 760	1 510	1 155	1 805	645	-450	56	-20	6 230
China - (CN)	1 435	1 145	1 250	1 580	1 770	190	335	12	23	5 745
CD (') - (CD)	1 625	1 755	1 650	1 650	1 715	65	85	4	5	6 775
India - (IN)	1 080	1 115	1 330	1 360	1 480	120	400	9	37	5 280
Cameroon - (CM)	1 445	1 270	1 170	1 305	1 355	50	-90	4	-6	5 100
El Salvador - (SV)	815	950	1 505	985	1 230	240	410	24	50	4 670
Egypt - (EG)	1 045	1 055	1 010	1 160	1 195	35	150	3	14	4 415
Senegal - (SN)	1 850	1 700	1 450	980	1 135	150	-715	15	-39	5 265
Other (non-EU)	29 700	26 695	24 865	25 035	25 545	510	-4 155	2	-14	102 135

Countries selected here are those with the highest number of asylum applicants registered during Q4 2018
(') CD – Congo, the Democratic Republic of the
Source: Eurostat (online data code: migr_asyappctzm)

eurostat

IRREGULAR MIGRATION AND THE IMPACT ON ECONOMY

Belonging and Economic Impacts of Refuges

The central approach to the sense of belonging is to receive feedback from the social environment and to adopt after an enthusiastic read. That is the main reason why some societies have a strong sense of belonging, while others are not. Thick

Figure 4. Asylum applicants Q4 2017-Q4 2018
Source: (Eurostat, n.d (c))

Asylum applicants, Q4 2017 – Q4 2018

	Q4 2017		Q1 2018		Q2 2018		Q3 2018		Q4 2018			First-time asylum applicants					
											Share of first-time asylum applicants (%)	absolute change		change in %		per million population (¹) Q4 2018	last 12 months
	First-time asylum applicants	Total asylum applicants	First-time asylum applicants	Total asylum applicants	First-time asylum applicants	Total asylum applicants	First-time asylum applicants	Total asylum applicants	First-time asylum applicants	Total asylum applicants		between Q3 2018 and Q4 2018	between Q4 2017 and Q4 2018	between Q3 2018 and Q4 2018	between Q4 2017 and Q4 2018		
EU-28	154 400	168 230	141 760	155 940	141 445	155 920	146 945	161 585	150 690	164 800	91	3 740	-3 715	3	-2	294	580 845
Belgium	3 660	4 830	4 000	5 290	3 610	4 855	5 565	6 635	4 950	5 780	86	-610	1 290	-11	35	434	18 130
Bulgaria	565	690	295	310	260	280	800	820	1 105	1 125	98	305	440	38	66	157	2 465
Czechia	280	365	300	385	295	385	360	430	400	490	82	40	120	11	42	38	1 350
Denmark	740	760	800	835	765	785	1 085	1 105	815	845	96	-270	75	-25	10	141	3 465
Germany	45 920	52 245	44 910	50 705	38 680	43 855	42 005	47 820	36 290	41 795	87	-5 710	-9 630	-14	-21	438	161 885
Estonia	25	25	10	10	15	15	50	50	20	20	100	-30	-10	-63	-31	14	90
Ireland	905	920	970	975	670	675	990	995	1 025	1 030	100	40	120	4	13	212	3 655
Greece	15 280	15 770	12 945	13 345	16 330	16 835	16 670	17 200	19 030	19 580	97	2 360	3 750	14	25	1 772	64 975
Spain	8 000	8 155	8 755	8 965	16 175	16 565	12 670	12 970	15 125	15 550	97	2 455	7 125	19	89	324	52 730
France	25 745	27 700	25 255	27 195	26 080	28 790	27 210	29 245	31 940	33 960	94	4 735	6 195	17	24	475	110 485
Croatia	255	280	215	245	140	165	185	215	135	170	79	-50	-120	-26	-47	33	675
Italy	22 990	23 615	17 690	18 755	13 640	15 005	9 075	10 060	8 750	9 875	89	-325	-14 235	-4	-62	145	49 165
Cyprus	1 285	1 320	1 325	1 395	1 430	1 455	2 145	2 175	2 705	2 745	99	560	1 420	26	110	3 131	7 610
Latvia	35	35	50	50	30	30	55	55	40	45	89	-10	5	-22	20	22	175
Lithuania	110	120	40	50	90	95	140	145	115	120	96	-30	0	-20	1	40	385
Luxembourg	585	605	445	465	425	455	660	690	700	730	96	40	110	6	19	1 159	2 225
Hungary	660	665	280	290	145	160	105	105	100	110	91	-10	-565	-8	-85	10	635
Malta	395	445	395	410	425	475	545	560	670	685	98	125	275	22	70	1 408	2 035
Netherlands	3 945	4 600	4 145	4 830	4 310	4 980	6 185	7 415	5 825	6 800	86	-360	1 880	-6	48	339	20 465
Austria	4 855	5 335	3 420	3 980	2 645	3 105	2 765	3 310	2 560	2 985	86	-210	-2 300	-8	-47	290	11 390
Poland	485	890	585	1 045	625	1 065	585	970	615	1 030	60	30	130	5	26	16	2 405
Portugal	270	315	245	270	215	220	375	395	405	405	100	30	135	8	51	39	1 240
Romania	900	945	355	415	450	490	570	635	575	605	95	5	-325	1	-36	29	1 945
Slovenia	435	465	510	525	895	905	905	925	490	520	94	-410	55	-46	13	238	2 800
Slovakia	45	50	45	50	45	55	30	30	35	40	88	5	-10	13	-21	6	155
Finland	925	1 135	765	1 000	710	900	770	1 235	700	1 370	51	-70	-220	-9	-24	127	2 945
Sweden	5 815	6 780	4 440	5 510	3 995	4 890	4 860	5 685	4 775	5 480	87	-85	-1 040	-2	-18	472	18 075
United Kingdom	9 175	9 285	8 575	8 675	8 345	8 435	9 585	9 710	10 785	10 910	99	1 200	1 610	12	18	183	37 290
Iceland	200	210	130	135	160	180	190	200	245	260	94	55	45	28	22	706	730
Liechtenstein	30	30	50	50	45	55	35	35	15	15	100	-20	-15	-60	-60	367	145
Norway	445	490	430	455	625	675	920	950	550	585	94	-365	105	-40	23	104	2 530
Switzerland	3 760	4 150	3 615	4 020	3 310	3 740	3 230	3 650	3 310	3 745	88	80	-450	3	-12	390	13 465

Note: total asylum applicants include first-time asylum applicants and repeat applicants.
(¹) Relative to population as of 1st of January 2018
Source: Eurostat (online data code: migr_asyappctzm)

eurostat

multiculturalism is also seen as an alternative approach, assuming that modern societies composed of different communities having a strong identity and belonging (Mulgan, 2009)

Sense of belonging is mostly put into question at unstable periods. The instability could appear such as huge migration flow, economic downfall or so on. For example, while refugee flow is at stake, immigrants, as well as citizens of the hosting country, may feel 'they do not belong'. Implicit messages from landlords, public authorities or labor forces cause this feeling. Positive components in the economy such as career development opportunity are one of the key feedback that individuals may receive as a positive message in the process of belonging (Mulgan, 2009).

Economic regression does not result as a sole problem in the economy itself. It also forecloses the social and economic integration of low skilled immigrants in the country. At regression times, discussions and expectations over immigrants grow. During these periods, immigrants are accepted as a burden on public finance. Even there is no clear evidence that immigrants are the reason for low wages and native employment displacement, still public opinion tends to believe in that way. So, these claims may provide to grow anti-immigrants discourses by the public in hosting country (Papademetriou et al., 2009, pp. 1-7).

Table 1. Summary of the impacts of the gaps/barriers and their estimated costs

Impact	Description	Estimated Annual Costs
Impacts on irregular migration	Costs related to control of irregular migration and cost of human trafficking	€19.7 - 33.2 billion
Impacts on external action and development cooperation	Costs associated with the attempt to limit departures from countries of origin and transit via external action tools	€1.7 billion
Impacts on employment and integration	Costs of limited labor market integration of refugees and tax loss due to the shadow economy	€2.1-2.7 billion
Impacts on living and health conditions of asylum-seekers	'Value of life losses', costs related to detention and poor reception facilities, healthcare costs	€11.8-17.7 billion
Impacts on the efficiency of procedures	Costs of inefficiencies in Dublin transfers, at the application stage and in case of returns	€2.5-4.9 billion
Total		€37.8-60.2 billion

Source: (EPRS, ibid:8)

Table 2. Typical assignment of responsibilities for refugee-related tasks and functions in decentralized countries

Central government	Sub-central government
Registration	Primary and secondary education
Asylum procedure	Social welfare, minimum income
Refugee camps, emergency housing	Housing after the refugee camp
Immediate first aid	Active labor market policy
Possibly basic language training	(Extended) language training
Civic integration training	
Returns	

Source: (OECD, 2017:2)

Recent research conducted by World Bank has also claimed that immigrants contribute more to the economy if hosting state provides convenient conditions for immigrants to find jobs and to improve their professional skills. So, hosting states should provide citizenship opportunity for permanent worker immigrants (Moving for Prosperity, 2018:25). Further, the OECD report assesses the economic impact of the refugee crisis in Europe (OECD, 2015, pp. 1-4). Jordan is considered one part of this research as hosting a huge amount of Syrian refugees (approx. 630000 in 2015). This report finds that the Syrian crisis did not have a negative impact on the formal labor market. But, informal employment and governmental expenses to meet humanitarian aid to Syrian refugees have raised (OECD, 2015, p. 3).

In relation with asylum seekers and refugees, asylum process remains important. At EU level, this processes is divided into four stages as a pre-arrival, arrival, the application, and post-application. At the pre-arrival stage, there is no common EU policy on resettlement and no legislative mechanisms at EU level, which makes asylum seekers rely on smugglers (EPRS, 2018: 6). To prevent illegal departures, the external dimension of the Common European Asylum System (CEAS) is used for two thematic areas such as resettlement and third-country support (External Dimension, (n.d)). Arrival and application stages are also problematic within the EU itself. For example, CEAS is criticized for disproportionate responsibility on the certain Member States and creating legal hurdles for the applicants. Consecutively, overburdening of member states causes inadequate reception conditions resulting in the weak application in some member states. In the end, insufficient arrival and application processes may harden immigrants not only for the application process but also for problems in labor market and economic integration during post-application stages such as lower-employment levels of asylum seekers and shadow economy (EPRS, ibid: 6-7). These economic impacts involve irregular migration, development cooperation, employment, integration, living and health conditions and efficiency of procedures. These impacts can be summarized together with estimated costs below:

Once immigrants complete administrative and legal process to stay in the hosting country, other factors such as social, cultural and economic aspects became important. At short term, immigrants provide positive impacts on the economy. Because they have to be fed, educated and be housed. In most hosting European Union member states, responsibilities for refugee-related tasks are undertaken by sub-centered governments. The table below classifies responsibilities in each central government and sub-central government in the case of Austria:

As seen on the table, very integration responsibilities such as extended education, language training, and housing are provided by local governments in Austria. The central government is responsible for documentation and basic training at the beginning level. Short term implementations on the governmental level are quite important because success at this level determines how long term impacts will be shaped. So, the more refugees find jobs, the more they are well educated and bring in the labor market, and the opportunity for career development provide a greater positive impact on economic growth.

What Do EU Citizens Say?: Refugees, Labor Market and Sense of Belonging

As well as other policy fields, the European Union has a dynamic character while migration policy is at stake. Thus previous integration experiences remain important to build more effective EU Migration Policy.

Syrian refugee crisis still remains important for policymakers at the EU level. Refugees are accepted as one of the vulnerable group (European Parliament, 2017) and should be considered to take more effective and sensitive steps for their better integration into society. Thus, integration into the labor market is one of the primary targets. But, since there has been no joint approach and attitudes by member states, the integration process is organized diversely. And each member states' attitudes towards integration can be affected by their own past immigration experiences. As a sample, Scandinavian countries have long-term immigration experiences, which make them build improved integration policies. Or, Eastern European countries have fewer integration experiences. So, past experience, together with social reactions on immigrants shape integration policies in the labor market (ICF, 2018, p. 5).

Some claims that sole access to the labor market is not enough for integration. Other critical elements such as housing needs, cultural orientation, the reaction of the host society should be also considered for further integration(ICF, ibid:6). Haveaux, the Director of the Red Cross EU Office also contributes these approach claiming that family reunification, access to health, legal consultancy and language training should also be considered ("How to make," 2016).

As the reaction of society is important to shape the integration policy, this research focuses on Eurobarometer survey results on public opinion. The last study by Eurobarometer has been applied in June 2019 with 27,464 EU citizens, who are over at the age of 15. This survey was conducted to find out citizens opinion about the post-electoral process of European Parliament The final report has not been published yet, but summary results show an important rise of public consciousness on current developments affecting EU such as economy, immigration, and the environment as below:

- 68% of respondents claim that their country has benefited from being in the EU.
- 56% of respondents believe that their voice is counted by the EU.
- The main motivations to vote in EP elections are economy and growth (44%) and immigration (34%) (Eurobarometer, 2019:1-19)

Another survey carried by TNS Political & Social network in the 28 Member States of the European Union (EU) between 21 and 30 October 2017 provides a clear understanding of public opinion about immigration and general perspective of citizens. The results are as below:

- 69% of respondents see immigration as a problem.
- Respondents from EU member countries such as Hungary (63%), Malta (63%), Greece (63%) Slovakia (54%), and Italy (51%) claim that immigration is a problem.
- Regarding the economy, 72% of respondents agree that immigrants make it easier to fill jobs in their country for which it is difficult to find workers. 51% of respondents think that immigrants have a positive impact on the economy. (49%) agree that immigrants bring new ideas and boost innovation in their country while 41% disagree.
- 39% of respondents agree that immigrants take jobs away from workers and 57% disagree (Special Eurobarometer 469, 2018, pp. 1-17)

What do these results tell us about the sense of belonging and economy? First, EU citizens are now more sensitive and supportive about their voice in the EU. Immigration is one of the top issues in citizens' agenda as well as other topics such as economy, security, and environment. Immigration is still seen a problem in many ways, even lesser than before. So, these reactions may be reflected by citizens towards to economy politics of governments as 'we' and 'others' and may harm integration process of immigrants and refugees into the society.

SOLUTIONS AND RECOMMENDATIONS

The main mistake in nationalism studies is the efforts to frame definitions in a subjective manner. Nationalism with a sense of belonging should be observed in full picture, assessing all other social, economic, cultural as well as international factors. Because nationalism is embedded in human psychology, thus human factor becomes important for societal development and acceleration of state. The human factor in the economy also remains important. When economic nationalism is considered, individuals reactions to economic activities and governmental decisions should be taken into account. Especially at unstable periods, anti-immigration discourses raise. These discourses demonstrate dissolving of a sense of belonging and the need to reconstruct the collective identity. So, new economic regulations on better conditions for immigrants should be organized, considering local people needs and expectations.

REFERENCES

Brass, P. (1979). *Elite Groups, Symbol Manipulation and Ethnic Identity among Muslims of South Asia. In D. Taylor and Y. Malcolm (Eds.), Political Identity in SouthAsia*. London: Curzon Press.

Breuilly, J. (1993). *Nationalism and the State. Manchester*. Manchester: UniversityPress.

Cambridge Dictionary. (n.d). Economic Nationalism. Retrieved from: https://dictionary.cambridge.org/tr/sözlük/ingilizce/economic-nationalism

Cooper, Z. (2007). *Economic Nationalism*. The Smith Institute.

Deutschlandied (Song of Germany). (n.d.). Britannica. Retrieved from https://www.britannica.com/topic/Deutschlandlied

EPRS. (2018). The Cost of Non-Europe in Asylum Policy, European Parliamentary Research Service. Retrieved from http://www.europarl.europa.eu/RegData/etudes/STUD/2018/627117/EPRS_STU(2018)627117_EN.pdf

Eurobarometer. (2019). The 2019 Elections: A pro-European –and young – electorate with clear expectations, First results of the European Parliament post-electoral survey. European Parliament. Retrieved from https://www.europarl.europa.eu/at-your-service/files/be-heard/eurobarometer/2019/election2019/EB915_SP_EUROBAROMETER_POSTEE19_FIRSTRESULTS_EN.pdf

European Commission. (n.d.). Irregular Migration. Migration and Home Affairs of European Commission. Retrieved from https://ec.europa.eu/home-affairs/content/irregular-migrant-0_en

European Parliament. (2017). Integration of Refugees in Europe. Retrieved from http://www.europarl.europa.eu/news/en/headlines/society/20170629STO78628/integration-of-refugees-in-europe

Eurostat. (n.d.a). First Time Asylum Applicant in the EU28 (Q4-2018). Retrieved from https://ec.europa.eu/eurostat/statistics-explained/index.php/Asylum_quarterly_report

Eurostat. (n.d.b). First-Time Asylum Applicants in the EU28 by citizenship. Retrieved from https://ec.europa.eu/eurostat/statistics-explained/index.php/Asylum_quarterly_report#Where_do_asylum_applicants_come_from.3F

Eurostat. (n.d.c). Asylum Applicants Q4 2017-Q4 2018. Retrieved from https://ec.europa.eu/eurostat/statistics-explained/index.php?title=File:Table_2_-_Asylum_applicants,_Q4_2017_%E2%80%93_Q4_2018.png

External Dimension. (n.d.). European Asylum Support Office. Retrieved from https://www.easo.europa.eu/operational-support/external-dimension

Gellner, E. (1983). *Nations and Nationalism*. Ithaca: CornellUniversityPress.

Gökalp, E. (2007). *Milliyetçilik: Kuramsal Bir Değerlendirme*. Anadolu Üniversitesi Sosyal Bilimler Dergisi.

Helleiner, E. (2002). Economic Nationalism as a Challenge to Economic Liberalism? Lessons from the 19th Century. *International Studies Quarterly*, *46*(3), 307–329. doi:10.1111/1468-2478.00235

How to Make the Integration of Refugees into the Labour Market Work. (2016). European Parliament News. Retrieved from http://www.europarl.europa.eu/news/en/headlines/world/20160218STO14834/how-to-make-the-integration-of-refugees-into-the-labour-market-work

ICF. (2018). *Peer Review on 'Integration of Refugees into the Labour Market*. Directorate-General for Employment, Social Affairs and Inclusion.

IOM. (n.d). Key Migration Terms, International Organization for Migration, Retrieved from https://www.iom.int/key-migration-terms#Irregular-migration

Kedourie, E. (1960). *Nationalism*. London: Hutchinson.

Mill, J. S. (1947). On Liberty, and Considerations on Representative Government. (Originally printed in 1861)

Morehouse, C., & Bloomfield, M. (2011). *Irregular Migration in Europe*. Migration Policy Institute.

Moving for Prosperity. (2018). *Policy Report*. The World Bank.

Mulgan, G. (2009). Feedback and Belonging: Explaining the Dynamics of Diversity. Migration Policy Institute. Retrieved from https://www.migrationpolicy.org/article/feedback-and-belonging-explaining-dynamics-diversity

OECD. (2015). How will the Refugee Surge Affect the European Economy? Migration Policy Debates. Retrieved from http://www.oecd.org/migration/How-will-the-refugee-surge-affect-the-European-economy.pdf

OECD. (2017). Who bears The Cost of Integrating Refugees? Migration Policy Debates. Retrieved from https://www.oecd.org/els/mig/migration-policy-debates-13.pdf

Özkırımlı. U. (2009). Milliyetçilik Kuramları: Eleştirel Bir Bakış. Ankara: Doğu Batı Yayınları.

Papademetriou, D., Sumption, M., & Somerville, W. (2009). *Migration and the Economic Downturn: What to Expect in the European Union*. Migration Policy Institute.

Pickel, A. (2003). Explaining, and Explaining with Economic Nationalism. *Journal of Nations and Nationalism*, *9*(1).

Schmidt, R. (1956). Cultural Nationalism in Herder. *Journal of the History of Ideas*, *17*(3), 407–417. doi:10.2307/2707552

Smith, A. (1993). *National Identity*. University of Nevada Press.

Special Eurobarometer 469. (2018). Integration of Immigrants in the European Union. Retrieved from Directorate-General for Migration and Home Affairs and co-ordinated by the Directorate-General for Communication& TNS opinion & social.

The French Flag. (2019). France Diplomatique. Retrieved from https://www.diplomatie.gouv.fr/en/coming-to-france/france-facts/symbols-of-the-republic/article/the-french-flag

The World Bank. (n.d.). Refugee Population by Country or Territory of Asylum. Retrieved from https://data.worldbank.org/indicator/sm.pop.refg?end=2017&start=1990

UNHCR. (n.d.a). Are the Refugee Numbers The Highest Ever? Retrieved from https://www.unhcr.org/blogs/statistics-refugee-numbers-highest-ever/

UNHCR. (n.d.b). Figures at a Glace. Retrieved from: https://www.unhcr.org/figures-at-a-glance.html

van den Berghe, P. (1981). *The Ethnic Phenomenon*. New York: Elsevier.

Weinreich, P., Bacova, V., & Rougier, N. (2003). Basic primordialism in ethnic and national identity. In P. Weinreich & W. Saunderson (Eds.), *Analysing Identity: Cross-cultural, Societal and ClinicalContexts*. Hove: Routledge.

Williams, H. (2014). Considerations on the Scottish Referendum and a Discourse on the British Conundrum: Mill, Price, and the Question of Nationalism. *Anali Hrvatskogpolitološkogdruštva, 11*(1), 7-25. Retrieved from https://hrcak.srce.hr/140172

KEY TERMS and DEFINITIONS

EU: The most favorite destination for irregular immigrants.

Irregular Migration: Undocumented, illegal or unauthorized movements.

Nationalism: There are several definitions considering its relation with sentiments, instrumental dimension, culture, destructive and constructive structure.

ENDNOTE

1 This is the last octave of the anthem. English translation of this part is: Unity and rights and freedom
for the German fatherland. Let us strive for it together, brotherly with heart and hand. Unity and rights and freedom are the basis of good fortune. Flower in the light of this good fortune, flower German fatherland. Retrieved from https://www.britannica.com/topic/Deutschlandlied

Chapter 7
Positive Economics From the Perspective of Kant's Thought

Ertuğrul İbrahim Kızılkaya
https://orcid.org/0000-0002-7657-9915
Istanbul University, Turkey

ABSTRACT

Departing from Kant's thought, we could argue that the portrait of homo economicus drawn by positive economics corresponds to a homo phainomenon as a heteronomous person of concrete economic reality. In addition, we could try to show that economics could not get rid of naturalism, materialism, and fatalism, justifying Kant's concerns. We could also emphasize that, while in the beginning the aim of being a positive science to be able to produce synthetic a posteriori propositions, positive economics tried to continue its way by the method of synthetic a priori. Finally, we must also point out the possibility for an autonomous or free homo noumenon to establish an original ethos by setting goals for itself.

DOI: 10.4018/978-1-7998-1037-7.ch007

INTRODUCTION

Immanuel Kant, the great thinker of the age of enlightenment, made a very important contribution to the rational delineation of human thought. He has developed a striking approach not only to the characteristics of knowledge, but also to the nature of man. Departing from his anthropological vision, Kant aimed to avoid the danger of falling into materialism, naturalism or fatalism. In this context, economics, like other sciences, has been exposed to these dangers. Will it be possible for economics, to escape the Kant's trilemma by generating synthetic a posteriori knowledge? Or aiming to obtain the physics of human behavior, will economics find itself in a situation drowned in mathematics? From this point on, it will be appropriate to find answers to these complicated questions.

KANT'S CONTRIBUTION

Kant has made important distinctions, which are often used today, revealing where the boundaries of knowledge began and where they ended. The distinction between analytic propositions and synthetic propositions, and the other distinction of *a priori* and *a posteriori* knowledge were used to reach a specific taxonomy in Kant's epistemology.

Analytic propositions, used to express reality, do not extend our knowledge and are insightful. In other words, the inclusion of the predicate in the concept are discussed. In contrast, synthetic propositions extend our knowledge of reality. The predicate is not included in the concept and may be true or false.

When it comes to the other distinction that Kant had used; it should be emphasized first that *a priori* knowledge is information that is not based on experience. From this point of view, we do not know the source, but we think that it contains information. The knowledge obtained from the experience is *a posteriori* knowledge. Kant does not doubt that our knowledge begins with experience.

As it is known, Kant considered these two differentiations together, and explored the ability of pure mind to produce knowledge and reach judgments. In this context, he has reached a classification that includes four different judgments:

Analytic a posteriori
Analytic a priori
Synthetic a posteriori
Synthetic a priori

The first category of *analytic a posteriori* is a fundamentally contradictory expression. Practices or propositions based on experience but not extending our knowledge are not possible.

Analytical ones (*analytic a priori*) that does not extend our knowledge of propositions are not based on experience. These are examples of metaphysical information. They cannot be experienced, cannot be proved, and how they are acquired is unknown. These types of information are self-referenced.

Those who do not rely on experience but expanding our knowledge are *synthetic a priori* propositions. These propositions, produced in some areas such as mathematics, astronomy and theoretical physics, are best known examples.[1] Even under conditions where experience is not possible, rational human thought should be considered as an important category because it provides the basis for producing information. In this respect, the tradition of thinking called *rationalism* should be pointed out. Human mind and thinking ability can produce knowledge, also understand reality from this perspective and construct cause and effect relations within the scope of facts.

Based on the experience, those who produce knowledge are *synthetic a posteriori* propositions. *Empiricism* should be evaluated in this context. While the human mind is a *tabula rasa* before the information acquisition activity, it is possible to grasp the reality with the information obtained after the experience. Probably the best example to be given is physics or natural sciences with a broader definition. From this point on, it will be appropriate to pass on Kant's perspective on human concept from his deep vision about our knowledge and the knowledge acquisition process or human capacity to produce judgments. As it is known, Kant has added a fourth to the three ancient questions of philosophy and has tended to address an anthropological problem. These questions are:

What can I know?
What ought I do?
What may I hope for?
Was ist der Mensch?

The answer to the first question is the classification of the propositions and / or judgments briefly discussed in the lines above, and is mainly the subject of the *Critique of Pure Reason*. The question of what man ought to do is discussed in the work of *Critique of Practical Reason* as the subject of moral philosophy with the question of ethics. In his book, Kant sets out a vision of the idea of human thought to know beyond necessity.

Before mentioning the fourth question, in other words the anthropological problem, it is necessary to give a different distinction about this vision. According to Kant, the human mind is his understanding and the principles produced by this power enable experience. Without experience, we cannot know any objects, and we cannot think of any object without reason.

Kant says that the ability to understand indeterminate objects of a possible experience should be called phenomenon when they are considered as determined objects. However, another characteristic of the human mind is its tendency to experience and / or to overcome nature. The use of reason in the process of experience causes only the production cycle of questions to be repeated infinitely. Human thought does not produce questions that have answers not only in the world of experience but in the plane of concepts to understand this world. Pure mind creates transcendental ideas to answer these questions. These concepts beyond being an object of experience or sensual vision are called noumenon by Kant.

Kant collects the mentioned subjects under three headings: firstly, the absolute unity of the thinking subject. In the context of this noumenon, which is also called a full subject or psychological idea, Spirit or Immortality etc. are discussed. The second one deals with the absolute unity of the sequence of the conditions of the appearances. The exact sequence of conditions or cosmological idea, is examined as the so-called cosmological ideology, such as Universe or Freedom. Thirdly, the absolute unity of the condition of all objects of thought emerges. The rule of what is the highest condition of the possibility of everything that can be considered, or within the scope of theological idea, is seen as the God noumenon.

Therefore, while the knowledge of man is limited by experience, what is called as *Ding an sich* is revealed by the pure mind of man. In other words, the objective reality of *Ding an sich* is something that is impossible to know, that any definite judgment can not be put forward, and it is not impossible to think of by human beings.

Kant argues that we cannot rationalize the area called metaphysics with a bold step and that we cannot go beyond the *analytic a priori* quality of the information that we will produce about it, and that we will come up with such mind-like implications. For this reason, according to Kant, metaphysics is the talk on the boundary between the sensible world (*mundus sensibilis*) and those who are the designs of the beyond. On the one hand, this limit is the limit of the field of experience, on the other hand it is the limit of the concepts (*mundus intelligibilis*). Thinking while standing on this boundary will expand our knowledge without being mistaken by mysticism and so on and thus will be of *synthetic a priori*.

The sentences of Kant in *Prolegomena* will not be overlooked in this context:

It is true: we cannot provide, beyond all possible experience, any determinate concept of what things in themselves may be. But we are nevertheless not free to hold back entirely in the face of inquiries about those things; for experience never fully satisfies reason; it directs us ever further back in answering questions and leaves us unsatisfied as regards their full elucidation, as everyone can sufficiently observe in the dialectic of pure reason, which for this very reason has its good subjective ground. Who can bear being brought, as regards the nature of our soul, both to the point of a clear consciousness of the subject and to the conviction that the appearances of that subject cannot be explained materialistically, without asking what then the soul really is, and, if no concept of experience suffices thereto, without perchance adopting a concept of reason (that of a simple immaterial being) just for this purpose, although we can by no means prove the objective reality of that concept? Who can satisfy themselves with mere cognition through experience in all the cosmological questions, of the duration and size of the world, of freedom or natural necessity, since, wherever we may begin, any answer given according to principles of experience always begets a new question which also requires an answer, and for that reason clearly proves the insufficiency of all physical modes of explanation for the satisfaction of reason? Finally, who cannot see, from the thoroughgoing contingency and dependency of everything that they might think or assume according to principles of experience, the impossibility of stopping with these, and who does not feel compelled, regardless of all prohibition against losing oneself in transcendent ideas, nevertheless to look for peace and satisfaction beyond all concepts that one can justify through experience, in the concept of a being the idea of which indeed cannot in itself be understood as regards possibility – though it cannot be refuted either, because it pertains to a mere being of the understanding – an idea without which, however, reason would always have to remain unsatisfied?[2]

Who is *looking for peace and satisfaction* should be considered in the fourth question of Kant (*Was ist der Mensch?*). It should be emphasized, in this context, that Kant is trying to address human in two different dimensions which can be considered as, philosophical anthropological attitude: *homo phainomenon* and *homo noumenon.*[3] This is a distinction referenced epistemologically rather than an ontological perspective.

As a matter of fact, Takiyettin Mengüşoğlu sheds light on this distinction of Kant with the following lines:

Kant says that on this. Human beings can only be examined from two perspectives; From one of these aspects of view, one can only see a natural being, a view, a homo phainomenon. From this point of view, human beings appear to us as an entity that is not free, heterologous, dependent on natural laws; for in such a case the human being, like every natural object, depends on the laws of nature. But if we change our point of view and look at man from a different point of view, then it appears to us as a human being, a homo noumenon, a free, autonomous entity. This is because human beings do not depend on the laws of nature, but on the laws of reason. These are only two different views. One of these points of view considers man as a natural being and once as a mental being. These explanations show that Kant's dual vision is not only a view that divides human beings in terms of existence, but also divides them into two distinct areas, but a gnoseological duality. [4]

It can be argued that Kant tried to take the human being as the actor of two different planes through this distinction. On the one hand, there is a human, who is subject to the natural world, called *mundus sensibilis*, to the nature, to matter, and therefore to natural laws such as all natural things in time-space. On the other side, we see another human who belongs to the world, which we can call *mundus intelligibilis*, who is autonomous, intelligent, free, who can put laws in itself and build his own world. That is the man who produces the world of noumenon.

Before we begin to discuss the human being who can establish his own world, we must emphasize that Kant hopes to benefit from this dualism in order to show man's autonomy and, of course, his freedom.[5] As a matter of fact, Kant demonstrates the benefits of moving away from various approaches that make human beings heteronomous or dependent:

Here I now find that the psychological idea, however little insight I may gain through it into the pure nature of the human soul elevated beyond all concepts of experience, at least reveals clearly enough the inadequacy of those concepts of experience, and thereby leadsme away from materialism, as a psychological concept unsuited to any explanation of nature and one that, moreover, constricts reason with respect to the practical. Similarly, the cosmological ideas, through the manifest inadequacy of all possible cognition of nature to satisfy reason in its rightful demands, serve to deter us from naturalism, which would have it that nature is sufficient unto itself. Finally, since all natural necessity in the sensible world is always conditioned, in that it always presupposes the dependence of one thing on another, and since unconditioned necessity must be sought only in the unity of a cause distinct from the sensible world, although the causality of that cause, in turn, if it were merely nature, could never make comprehensible the existence of the contingent as its consequence; reason, therefore, by means of the theological idea, frees itself from fatalism – from blind natural necessity both in the connection of nature itself, without a first principle, and in the causality of this principle itself – and leads the way to the concept of a cause through freedom, and so to that of a highest intelligence. The transcendental ideas therefore serve, if not to instruct us positively, at least to negates the impudent assertions of materialism, naturalism, and fatalism which constrict the field of reason, and in this way they serve to provide moral ideas with space outside the field of speculation; and this would, I should think, to some extent explain the aforementioned natural predisposition.[6]

His opposition and his courageous idea of rejections of *materialism, naturalism, and fatalism* led Kant to the concept of how freedom could be conceptualized and how man should behave.[7] The thinker of freedom associates man's anthropological dualistic structure with the categorical imperative. Man, who is not important as an animal creature, can increase his value as a thinking creature by building a life independent of the world of the senses through moral law.[8] The human being of Kant can think and make the universe understandable within the framework of the categories of pure mind consisting of time, space and causality. Considering this subject as a universal consciousness, both present in every individual; in other words, it is possible to open up new horizons in front of him by dealing with both empirical and transcendental dualism. In the world of morality that he establishes, one will hope to be able to take part in happiness by behaving in accordance with the categorical imperative. Man blessed with happiness and wisdom will be able to reach *Sittlichkeit* (objective moral life) or the ultimate good.

From this perspective, it is seen that Kant's approach, which determines the boundaries of access to knowledge, has a human dimension. When it is necessary to evaluate the typology of *homo economicus* of Positive Economics in this context, it would be appropriate to be able to avoid some tendencies that Kant emphasizes. As emphasized in the lines above, Kant thought that human thought could hold the opportunity to stay away from the trilemma of *materialism*, *naturalism* and *fatalism* with its *homo noumenon* character. However, when we look at the content of the portrait of *homo economicus* drawn by economics, it is seen that although it is a rationalist fiction, it is designed to be suitable as a *homo phainomenon*. There is a great benefit in repeating a previously highlighted point: the phenomenon for Kant is that the ability to understand the ambiguous objects of an experience is considered in the form of defined objects (concepts). To put it another way, the information that economics establishes based on concrete reality (the *homo economicus* typology or the self-functioning market mechanism) is a phenomenon. Therefore, the actor of this typology will be the heterologous human, *homo phainomenon* of the concrete economic reality.

Perhaps the most concrete indication of this is that the economic man has been defined as a maximization actor to overcome the law of scarcity. With the ultimate inadequacy of the resources that nature has to offer (naturalism), the lack of a human being without the need to construct life in a manner dependent on these scarce resources (materialism) and the emphasis on the impossibility of its ability to overcome these decisive conditions (fatalism); the science of economics problematize the human which was described by Kant as an existence of reason, only in the framework of instrumental reason or in the plane of phenomenon.

Kant, however, believed that human beings had the potential to be free from all of these necessities, while pointing to the *homo noumenon*. Indeed, the original potential of man is the ability to complete the deficiencies and thus his original creative nature. When Kant wanted to point it out, he was talking about the concepts of freedom and morality. Thus, instead of being limited to the instrumental rationality of a heterologous *homo phainomenon* (economics), it would be possible for an autonomous *homo noumenon* to set goals for himself and establish a unique *ethos*[9].

CONCLUSION

At this point, it should be questioned why economics is stuck in some part of the human, rather than using all of his cognitive abilities as producing knpwledge about man through reason. A possible answer to this can be produced by benefiting by Kant's thought. As previously emphasized, Kant used *analytical a priori*, *synthetic a priori* and *synthetic a posteriori* categories to classify the propositions. It is possible to rank the areas where the most examples of these are in metaphysics, mathematics and physics, respectively. It is known that with its methodological concerns since the beginning, economics aims to build a successful or a comprehensive theory similar to natural sciences in the field of social sciences. Thus, the ultimate goal of economics was to produce *synthetic posteriori* propositions. However, the inability to fully experience the endless possibilities of human behavior, and the inability to practice experiments on economic phenomena, have deprived the economics from accessing this *telos*.

In this case, for the economics that establishes its own autonomy and wishes to prove the same as other thoughtful quests, a theoretical activity in *synthetic a priori* content is the point of escape. Of course, in this process, if we use the term *Aufklarung*, *rationalization*, or Weber's *Entzauberung* [the phenomenon of the disenchantment of the World] term also has a considerable role.[10] Economics, which tries to make sense of the gigantic changes experienced in the flow of time, has been helpless in the face of the large number of changes and focused on the unchanged within the complex processes. In this respect, a conceptualisation and naming of the cases is separated. Then, they are directed to a quantitative calculation of the typology of the decomposed ones. If we try to express with Kant's concepts, economics which failed to obtain a *synthetic posteriori*, had to be content with *synthetic a priori*. Or as hoping to obtain the *physics* of human behavior, find itself in a situation drowned in mathematics.

In other words, the *homo economicus* of mainstream economics is trapped in the natural (naturalism), given (materialism) and universal (fatalism) trilemma. At this point, the positivist character of the process can also be focused. The scientific approach firstly defines the cases, then tries to measure them, tests them, and finally comes to the scene with the claim of determining cause-effect relationships has been the methodology adopted by the economy. In fact, there is no mistake to criticize the activity of producing knowledge considered so far; or we could already be trundled into a bottomless metaphysical pit.

However, the main problem is not to emphasize the knowledge produced by economics as a cross-sectional or partial information, but to begin to claim that it is the essence of human behavior. It is probably unthinkable that such an attitude cannot be dragged into a vortex of dogmatism in the face of the multitude of social, historical and institutional planes. As a matter of fact, the mainstream economics' over-abstracted, isolated, frozen, and then mathematized human behavior led many thinkers to criticize such as the passion of formalism. Positive economics breaking its connection with the endless multitude of human [social-political-economical-institutional-historical] reality, was produced postulates instead of the hypotheses. Instead of examining the specific (particular and even singular) experiences of the human reality, the molded identity produced within this scope is presented as a true substance. However, as seen in the thought of Kant, we can hope to rely on the ability of the human to think beyond the phenomenon, and try to direct the energy of the economics to noumenons. I think there are many philosophers who will guide us in this direction. Such as Hegel who wrotes in his Phänomenologie des Geistes the search for what is beyond experience:

Corresponding to this requirement is a laborious and almost petulant zeal to save mankind from its absorption in the sensuous, the vulgar, and the singular. It wishes to direct people's eyes to the stars, as if they had totally forgotten the divine and, as if they were like worms, each and all on the verge of finding satisfaction in mere dirt and water. There was a time when people had a heaven adorned with a comprehensive wealth of thoughts and images. The meaning of all existence lay in the thread of light by which it was bound to heaven and instead of lingering in this present, people's view followed that thread upwards towards the divine essence; their view directed itself, if one may put it this way, to an other-worldly present. It was only under duress that spirit's eyes had to be turned back to what is earthly and to be kept fixed there, and a long time was needed to introduce clarity into the dullness and confusion lying in the meaning of things in this world, a kind of clarity which only heavenly things used to have; a long time was needed both to draw attention to the present as such, an attention that was called experience, and to make it interesting and to make it matter. – Now it seems that there is the need for the opposite, that our sense of things is so deeply rooted in the earthly that an equal power is required to elevate it above all that. Spirit has shown itself to be so impoverished that it seems to yearn for its refreshment only in the meager feeling of divinity, very much like the wanderer in the desert who longs for a simple drink of water. That it now takes so little to satisfy spirit's needs is the full measure of the magnitude of its loss.[11]

REFERENCES

Badiou, A. (2013). Ethics: An Essay on the Understanding of Evil (P. Hallward, trans., 1st ed.). Verso.

Changeux, J. P. (2002). *The Physiology of Truth: Neuroscience and Human Knowledge*, Cambridge.

de La Mettrie, J. O. (1912). *Man a Machine, philosophical and historical notes by Gertrude C.* Chicago: Bussey.

Foucault, M. (2008). *Introduction to Kant's Anthropology* (R. Nigro, Ed., NigroR. BriggsK., Trans.). Los Angeles.

Hegel, G. W. F. (2018). *The Phenomenology of Spirit* (T. Pinkard, Trans. & Ed.). Cambridge.

Kant, I. (2002). *Critique of Practical Reason* (W. S. Pluhar, Trans.). Indianapolis.

Kant, I. (2004). *Prolegomena to Any Future Metaphysics* (G. Hatfield, Trans. & Ed.). Cambridge. doi:10.1017/CBO9780511808517

Kant, I. (2006). *Anthropology from a Pragmatic Point of View* (R. B. Louden, Trans. & Ed.). Cambridge.

Karatani, K. (2003). *Transcritique on Kant and Marx*. Cambridge. doi:10.7551/mitpress/6897.001.0001

Mengüşoğlu, T. (2015). *İnsan Felsefesi: I. İnsanın Varlık Yapısı ve Nitelikleri, II.* Ankara: İnsan ve Hayvan, Dünya ve Çevre.

Nutku, U. (2016). *Yeniçağ Felsefesinde A Priori Problemi*. Academic Press.

Schumpeter, J. A. (1954). *History of Economic Analysis*. Routledge.

Spinoza, B. (1985). *Collected Works of Spinoza* (Vol. 1). (E. Curley, Trans. & Ed.). Princeton.

ENDNOTES

1 The position of mathematics has been studied extensively by Kant: "Kant detected synthetic judgment in every domain of thinking except for logic, the domain of tautology. Mathematics was no exception. Or, more to the point,

Kant's radical contribution here was that he considered even mathematics — the very domain believed to be most stable and certain because of its being analytical— as an a priori synthetic judgment. During his lifetime, it was this stance that earned Kant the worst reputation of all of his ideas, and it has been constantly attacked ever since. But Kant maintained this stance because previous philosophy had insisted that only analytic judgment was apodictic, and accordingly took mathematics —which philosophy was convinced was the most analytic of judgments— as a norm." (Kojin Karatani, *Transcritique on Kant and Marx*, Cambridge, 2003, p. 55).

2 Immanuel Kant, *Prolegomena to Any Future Metaphysics*, translated and edited by Gary Hatfield, Cambridge, 2004, p. 103.

3 Michel Foucault puts an interesting contribution in this context: "We are touching on the essential point: in *Anthropology*, man is neither a *homo natura*, nor a purely free subject; he is caught by the syntheses already operated by his relationship to the world." Michel Foucault, *Introduction to Kant's Anthropology*, edited by Roberto Nigro, translated by Roberto Nigro and Kate Briggs, Los Angeles, 2008, pp. 54-55.

4 Takiyettin Mengüşoğlu, *İnsan Felsefesi: I. İnsanın Varlık Yapısı ve Nitelikleri, II. İnsan ve Hayvan, Dünya ve Çevre*, Ankara, 2015, p. 65. In this excerpt and other lines of Mengüşoğlu, it is necessary to draw attention to the use of gnoseology instead of epistemology. In the context of the conceptualization of man, it is important to refer to the knowledge of *gnosis*, which points to a wider scope rather than *episteme*, including *intuitio*.

5 In *Critique of Practical Reason*, Kant includes the following lines: "It is nothing other than personality, i.e., the freedom and independence from the mechanism of all of nature, yet regarded at the same time as a power of a being subject to pure practical laws that are peculiar to it, viz., are given by its own reason, so that the person as belonging to the world of sense is subject to his own personality insofar as he at the same time be longs to the intelligible world. Thus, it is not surprising if the human being, as belonging to both worlds, must regard his own being in reference to this second and highest vocation solely with veneration, and regard the laws of this vocation with the highest respect." (Immanuel Kant, *Critique of Practical Reason*, translated by Werner S. Pluhar, Indianapolis, 2002, pp. 111-112).

6 Kant, op. cit., 2004, pp. 113-114.

7 The *categorical imperatif*, expressed as the rule of conduct as valid as the principle of a universal law, refers to a behavior that does not relate human behavior to any external purpose, that is valid only for itself and that is directly

in its own right. At this point, it would be appropriate to emphasize that Kant puts forward freedom as the condition of moral law. There is also a mutual interaction: "(I) wish only to point out that whereas freedom is indeed the *ratio essendi* of the moral law, the moral law is the *ratio cognoscendi* of freedom. For if the moral law were not *previously* thought distinctly in our reason, we would never consider ourselves entitled to assume such a thing as freedom (even though freedom is no self-contradictory). But if there were no freedom, then the moral law could not be encountered in us at all." (Kant, op. cit., 2002, p. 5).

8 In this context, it is necessary to think on the following lines of Uluğ Nutku: "Numen appears in the phenomenon but does not originate from the phenomenon. The intellectual beings that have passed from the phenomenon of life have been involved in their naturalness because they have taken an influence from the numen. If there is any other person in the universe other than man, he will be bound and bound by the same moral law, even if he is not in that human form." (Uluğ Nutku, *Yeniçağ Felsefesinde A Priori Problemi*, Ankara, 2016, p. 94) We know *phenomenons* by this distinction. They can be known as they are included in the contexts of time and space, and passed through the filter of our understanding. The *noumenons* do not take place in time and space, so the intellect tends to fall into illusions about them.

9 I use the concept of *Ethos* to include two meanings, one character and the other moral. Benedict de Spinoza puts the connection between behavior, knowledge, freedom and reason in his *Ethics* (Part V: "On the Power of the Intellect, or on Human Freedom", Propositions X): "So long as we are not torn by affects contrary to our nature, we have the power of ordering and connecting "the affections of the Body according to the order of the intellect." Affects which are contrary to our nature, ...which are evil, are evil insofar as they prevent the Mind from understanding. Therefore, so long as we are not torn by affects contrary to our nature, the power of the Mind by which it strives to understand things is not hindered. So long, then, the Mind has the power of forming clear and distinct ideas, and of deducing some from others. And hence, so long do we have the power of ordering and connecting the affections of the Body according to the order of the intellect, q.e.d." (Benedict Spinoza, *Collected Works of Spinoza*, edited and translated by Edwin Curley, vol. I, Princeton, 1985, pp. 1276-1277). The quest for an original ethos continues today: "So Evil is possible only through an encounter with the Good. The ethic of truths which simply serves to lend consistency to that 'some-one' that we

are, and which must manage to sustain, with its own animal perseverance, the intemporal perseverance of a subject of truth - is also that which tries to ward off Evil, through its effective and tenacious indusion in the process of a truth. This ethics combines, then, under the imperative to 'Keep going! ', resources of discernment (do not fall for simulacra), of courage (do not give up), and of moderation (*réserve*) (do not get carried away to the extremes of Totality). The ethic of truths aims neither to submit the world to the abstract rule of a Law, nor to struggle against an external and radical Evil. On the contrary, it strives, through its own fidelity to truths, to ward off Evil - that Evil which it recognizes as the underside, or dark side, of these very truths." (Alain Badiou, *Ethics: An Essay on the Understanding of Evil*, translated and introduced by Peter Hallward, London, 2001, p. 97).

10 One of the earliest examples of efforts to address human life from a rationalist-materialist perspective (or in the perspective of French Materialism) is seen in the lines published by Julien Ofray de La Mettrie in 1748: "Man is so complicated a machine that it is impossible to get a clear idea of the machine beforehand, and hence impossible to define it. For thisreason, all the investigations have been vain, which the greatest philosophers have made *à priori*, that is to say, in so far as they use, as it were, the wings of the spirit. Thus it is only *à posteriori* or by trying to disentangle the soul from the organs of the body, so to speak, that one can reach the highest probability concerning man's own nature, even though one can not discover with certainty what his nature is." (Julien Ofray de La Mettrie, *Man a Machine*, philosophical and historical notes by Gertrude C. Bussey, Chicago, 1912, p. 89) However de La Mettrie's perspectives continued to expand and become more widespread. For example, Charles Babbage, in his work of 1832, *On the Economy of Machinery and Manufactures*, examined the rationalist-materialist approach of the adaptation of the human activity in the production to the machines with a rationalist-materialist approach, thus addressing the division of labor and productivity, and even a large aroused interest. (Joseph A. Schumpeter, *History of Economic Analysis*, London, 1954, p. 541) Nowadays, it can be claimed that a similar materialist approach attracts attention. For example, there are studies that establish links between fields such as neuroscience and human knowledge (Cf., Jean Pierre Changeux, *The Physiology of Truth: Neuroscience and Human Knowledge*, Cambridge, 2002).

11 Georg W. F. Hegel, *The Phenomenology of Spirit*, translated and edited by Terry Pinkard, Cambridge, 2018, pp. 7-8. The search for "what is beyond experience" is an ancient questionning which can be found clearly in the Platon's

thought. Platon, thinking on the ontological problem or aiming to attain to the contemplation of *aletheia*, pointed out the *ousia* and in this context he made specific distinctions such as *tauton – heteron*, *peras – apeiron* and *stasis – kynesis*. These could be seen in the complexity of *genesis* or the perpetual change of the *phainomenon*. Philosophy, searching the "never-changing" in this continuity, should determine the *eidos* besides the *arithmos*. Consequently focusing only on *arithmos* will leave our thought incomplete (or bounded) as in the case of the positive economics' *homo economicus*.

Chapter 8
An Analysis on Turkey's Urbanization Process in the Context of Urban Development Paradigms

Aygül Kılınç
https://orcid.org/0000-0003-2566-042X
Gaziantep University, Turkey

ABSTRACT

The ideological, economic, and technological phenomena experienced in the history of the world have affected the social order surprisingly. These phenomena have transformed the social order with their political, economic, and socio-cultural dimensions and have been effective in their reshaping. Since the first quarter of the 20th century, this has led to the emergence of three new paradigms of urban development. The first paradigm includes the period from the Second World War to the end of the 1970s, and this paradigm is defined as the state-based urban development period. The period from the 1980s to the mid-1990s was named the market-centered urban development period. Lastly, the period that continued since the mid-1990s has been named the governance period or the third way.

INTRODUCTION

Important political, economic and socio-cultural phenomena in human history have affected the social development process surprisingly. These phenomena which have left their traces in the process of social development have transformed and

DOI: 10.4018/978-1-7998-1037-7.ch008

reshaped the social structure as breaking points. These have led to the emergence of new paradigms / approaches. The effects of these paradigms on the urban space perception and urban development in the context of the political, economic and socio-cultural conditions of the period in which they were born contain significant differences that require attention. In each paradigm, the roles of urban actors and the field of action of these actors differ considerably. It is possible to mention three paradigms that have been consistently significant from the 1930s onwards. Historically, they emerged as the state-centered urban development period, market-centered urban development period, and governance-centered urban development period. These paradigms constitute the main axis of the study. These paradigms, which are relatively related to or cause of each other from the perspective of time have become apparent in the political and economic conjunctural conditions of the relevant period. They are also the perpetrators of the spatial, economic and socio-cultural processes in the cities of the period they are related to. For example; in the first period, the built environment in the urban area was perceived as a concrete living space where the value of use was relatively at the forefront. In the forthcoming period, these concrete living spaces have been attributed value over the market value (exchange value). In the urban development process, along with the significant efficiency of the state actor, it has been found that the actors became diversified by inclusion of the market and other urban actors in the process in time. In the temporal process, the logical context of this changing perception of cities becomes clear in the context of these changing paradigms. Political and urban practices of the state and other urban actors are also analyzed in the context of these changing paradigms. Political, economic, socio-cultural and spatial relation types are regenerated in the social-change process triggered by the paradigm change. This study periodically analyzes these three paradigms. These paradigms are discussed theoretically in the context of political and economic conjunctural conditions of the period in which they were effective. The perception of the city, and the direction and nature of the urban development in the relevant period has been shed in this context. In the study, firstly the conjunctural context of urban development has been clarified. Then, within the frame of the political and socio-economic conditions of the relevant period, the question of how each paradigm emerged has been examined. The distinctive features of these paradigms for urban development have been emphasized. Their diversified perceptions of urban space and urban development have been set forth. Finally, the urban development process of Turkey has been evaluated in the context of each paradigm.

ON URBAN DEVELOPMENT AND CONJUNCTURAL CONTEXT

Social transformation involves changes and transformations that take place at various degrees in all dimensions of social structure depending on time and space. Quality and quantity of social change that becomes evident in different degrees at the global, national and local scales varies from society to society. Although functional differentiation or change in urban areas takes place in a short period of time, the fact that this condition becomes apparent in physical tissue requires a much longer temporal process (Aktüre, 1987: 2). Variables such as changing and developing means of production in time, technical and scientific developments, style of capital accumulation, nature of state intervention and urban actors; and the social relations and values reproduced in this context define the conjunctural, in other words; the political, economic and socio-cultural status of a defined period.

The political, economic and socio-cultural phenomena experienced in the process of social development enure the social and physical processes in the urban area. This creates positive or negative results in the form of objective and subjective patterns in the urban tissue, and also becomes apparent in space. With all its components, this process creates the urban development evolution of a settlement. This structural transformation, which takes place in the social structure and urban space in parallel with social variables, is explained as urban development / change as a concept with a wide content including urbanization and urbanizing.

The important transformations with political, economic, scientific, technological and social dimensions, which deeply affected the social structure and caused significant changes on this structure, have been experienced in the world. These transformations developed the production forces of the countries in which they were born. It has laid the foundation for the emergence of new mode of production and relations from the old mode of production. The new mode of production and its relations have affected the texture of the social structure in a certain process platform and have caused structural changes in the political and institutional texture of the countries. It has been particularly effective in the production of new political and economic policies. In addition, these policies have been transferred or imposed to peripheral countries for the purpose of creating a hegemonic power in a pragmatic approach. These transformations; which create structural changes in the social structure of the countries in which they are born, and affect especially the countries of the periphery on international economic relations; were tried to be understood through four closely related scenarios. These scenarios are defined as the transition from an industrial society to an information society, the transition from a fordist mode of production to a post-fordist mode of production, the transition from a nation-state structure to a globalized world, and the transition from modernism to post-modernism (TÜBA, 2006: 12; Tekeli, 2001: 27-28).

All these phenomena have led to some remarkable and different transformations on the urban development and local government structures of the central and peripheral countries. In this process, three major paradigms have emerged. According to this, the period from the Second World War until the end of the 1970s constitutes the first period. This period became apparent as the period of state-based urban development. The second period, starting from the 1980s to the mid-1990s, was defined as the period of market-based urban development. The third period, which started in the mid-1990s and is still valid today, has been defined as a period of governance-based urban development (TÜBA, 2006: 31-32).

EVALUATION OF STATE-CENTERED URBAN DEVELOPMENT

The legitimacy of the state is based on the belief that human rights and freedoms will be protected. As a necessity of this belief and in order to reinforce the belief, the state has been defined as a device that has the task of fulfilling the services such as security, justice and the judiciary and the establishment of the institutional structure and the rules of social order (Özer, 2005: 126-127). Eroğul (2002: 159-161) mentioned three functions of the state. These functions are to improve production forces, to strengthen relations of production and to protect their interests. These functions attributed to the state are considered a requirement of the ontological existence of the state. On the other hand, according to Kepenek (.?.: 51-52), the concept of state has changed over time. It was stated that this conceptual change historically varied qualitatively from country to country. These differences are also considered depending on the country's mode of production, and political and social development. Thus, it is understood that the quality and quantity of the functions attributed to the state can move forward or backward in the context of political ideology valid at any defined time. In the words of Kepenek, the state has had to become developmentist in the process of capitalist accumulation. In Western capitalist countries, the state has started to provide new services such as education, health and social security as well as traditional functions. In addition, the state has taken on new tasks such as preventing unemployment and developing transportation and communication services. This shows that in Western capitalist countries there is a further expansion in the functions of the state.

As a result of the realization of the Industrial Revolution, the production process of the machine increased the product range. The economic production system based on agriculture has been replaced by a liberal economic production system based on the factory industry and this has led to the beginning of mass production (Özdemir, 2004: 145-146). The gradual development of the Industrial Revolution resulted in the articulation of almost all peripheral countries into industrial capitalism. This situation has led to an increase in social tensions and conflict in the industrialized countries and an increasingly sharp competition among the capitalist central countries has been raised (Şaylan, 2003: 71). This new situation has increased the vital importance of the interventionist, regulatory and redistributive functions of the state apparatus in the social order. Until the 1929 World Economic Crisis, liberalism became the dominant economic view in the world. The work of John Maynard Keynes, published during those dates, was intended to improve the economic conditions caused by the crisis in question. This work envisaged a new economic approach as a way out of the crisis. The work consisted of the principles of under-employment balance, ignoring Say's Law, and resorting to state expenditures with revenues to sustain demand (Galbraith, 2004: 204). In other words, Keynes and a group of other economists stated that public spending should be increased, a less restrictive credit policy should be adopted and public infrastructure investments should be encouraged. He also suggested abandoning the obsession to reduce wages. The economists, who are considered as authorities, have seen the solution in maintaining the current approach (Beaud, 2003: 211). However, in spite of the opposing views, a common protectionist approach was adopted under the leadership of Keynes's policies following the Great Economic Crisis. Due to world markets collapsing in World War II, in many countries after the war there was no free convertibility of national money. Capital transfers have been subject to strict control and internal financial markets have been strictly regulated. While many economic activities have been taken under protection against international competition, in many countries simultaneously the services sector and the agricultural sector have been protected (Özdemir, 2004: 157). Briefly, state intervention was necessary in order to ensure the economic sustainability of capitalism (Demirer et al., 1999: 96). In this sense, the policies proposed by Keynes led to the birth of the welfare state.

The welfare state approach aims to maximize social welfare. This approach foresees the comprehensive intervention of the state in the economy. In addition, the state understanding of this approach carries intrusive, regulatory, redistributive and entrepreneurial qualities (Özer, 2005: 130-133). The welfare state, symbolizing the state of the 20th century, was the ground for reconciliation between social forces (state, capital, organized labor). The important principle that created this compromise was the meeting of the interests of the state, capital and organized labor trio on a certain ground (Sezen, 1999: 43). Another characteristic that defines the welfare state is that the production structure is based on the fordist accumulation regime, which is characterized by mass production and consumption. The mass production required by this mode of production is designed to produce mass-standard goods in technological and organizational terms. It was mostly based on large-scale industrial enterprises operating on an assembly line basis, where semi-skilled or unskilled labor is controlled by Taylorist methods. Consumption patterns that are suitable for such a production process have been the high wage policy of the welfare state and social security expenditures. These patterns of consumption are supported by the creation of an ideological and cultural organization that highlights the consumption culture (Sezen, 1999: 44; Kara, 2004: 89). In other words; fordism, a production method, was supported by Keynesian economic policy and welfare state concept and developed as a capital accumulation regime (Şahin, 2004: 114). In this context; the welfare state, above all, undertook the role of interventionist, entrepreneur and regulatory state in social and economic life (Kara, 2004: 45).

EVALUATION OF MARKET-CENTERED URBAN DEVELOPMENT

The structural crisis of capitalism, which began in the late 1960s and became widespread in the mid-1970s, emerged as the crisis of the massive capital accumulation regime. As Demirer et al. (1999: 451) pointed out, the fordist capital accumulation regime first appeared in the US and Europe as the capital accumulation process began to break down in the late 1960s. It turned into a crisis in the 1970s. In the end, the capital accumulation regime was crowned by the debt crisis in the late 1970s and turned into a general economic crisis. In order to evaluate the oil-dollar funds accumulated in the banks as a result of the impact of the oil crisis in 1974, the capitalist central countries turned to the peripheral countries and created international debt markets. This market has started to grow rapidly and globalize. Yeldan (2002: 21) gathered the dynamics underlying the globalization process under four main headings. The first dynamic is the overproduction-based crisis created by the high tempo of accumulation throughout the golden age of capitalism. The second is the snow squeeze fed by the fordist relations of production, which has marked the capital-labor contradiction in the welfare state period. The third is the intensification of international capitalist competition. Fourthly, the rise in financial capital and speculative accumulation preferences as a result of the liberalization of the financial system moved ahead of the industrial investments. The increase in social expenditures, the growth of employment, the increase in tax rates and the active role of the state in the market particularly in the welfare state period have been seen as the main causes of the economic crisis experienced. In that crisis environment, neoliberalism has emerged as a new approach to the economy. Friedrich Von Hayek (1899-1992), the Austrian economist who received the Nobel Prize (in 1974), stated that state intervention in the economic sphere makes people dependent on the state. He pointed out that the economic crisis in many developed countries and the financial crisis faced by most nation-states constitute a reason to return to the free market. Hayek's teaching of neoliberalism was adopted by Margaret Thatcher in England and by Ronald Reagan in the United States (Kloby, 2005: 289). Very soon, the neoliberal doctrine has become the unique source of policies that determine the conditions for crediting, lending or deferring debt to international financial institutions such as the IMF and the WB (Sezen, 1999: 50). These policies were then implemented rapidly in the peripheral countries carrying out their economy with external debt.

Neoliberalism is an economic and political doctrine that rejects the state's intervention in the local economy or advocates its reduction. The main emphasis of the neoliberal doctrine is based on the 'small state'. It requires that the state be withdrawn from the economy as an entrepreneur and as an investor and that the state should only play a role as provider and regulator of the required services (Özgen, 2007: 167; Kazgan, 2005: 195-196). In this context, the distinctive features of this teaching can be listed as follows: minimizing state intervention to the market economy; creation of a market-driven market economy; competition with foreigners as an impulse to private enterprise and acceptance of the price element as the main element of control. In foreign policy, this teaching was aimed at opening the use of capital for the use of capital by political instruments including diplomacy, economic pressure, and even military interventions. In other words, it aimed to create a global market system with the help of these tools. In the context of the concept of globalization that will form the framework of this system, a new world and a new political authority structure are envisaged. In this predicted new world order, the state apparatus was not eliminated, but was attributed to it a new role. According to this, it was desired to implement a set of decisive qualities that included the least governmental support and incentives, the integration of financial markets, and the transfer of information and trade from national political administrations to the market. It was understood that this tendency was intended to give a minimized role to the state.

This crisis, in which the Keynes approach and import substitution development strategies fell into the 1970s; and the capital accumulation crisis system, which became prominent in the second half of the 1970s; necessitated the renewal of itself with a new accumulation regime and a new state approach. Hence, the prerequisites for the transition to the postfordist accumulation regime began to emerge. Postfordism is structured on the basis of differentiated forms of production and consumption, underemployment, subcontracting, non-unionization and individual contracts (Şahin, 2004: 115). In line with the assumption that all actors that make up the society will achieve a balance within the free market economy in accordance with the neoliberal doctrine, the withdrawal of the state from economic and social life has eroded the understanding of the welfare state. It has also radically changed the theory of national development. Under this amendment, the central planning in national development theory is replaced by the free market; privatization of public entrepreneurship; the import economy and protectionist policies that can create the national economy have been replaced by an understanding of development which is open to the global market (Şahin, 2004: 120). Therefore, starting from the

1980s, welfare state practices were abandoned. Instead, the free market economy created within the framework of policies to support capital was intended to be put. The market has been defined as an environment of contracting and competitive opportunities in which the rational decisions of the actors to maximize their interest are associated with their free will. The functioning of the market economy was based on certain preliminary assumptions. These preliminary assumptions are as follows; actors are self-interest; behaviors towards maximizing self-interest are rational; the contractual relationship is the product of free will; there will be those who benefit from opportunities as well as losers (Bayramoğlu, 2005: 189-190). Although the market is the main instrument of neoliberal applications, planning is not a tool and institutionalization in the neoliberal environment (Balamir, 2008: 168). This new role given to the state apparatus and the market mechanism that has been prioritized have formed the basis of the change in perception of urban development. This situation also triggered the formation of a new urban form.

Within the framework of neoliberal doctrine, policy changes related to state intervention in urban areas, began to appear. For example, the state has been withdrawn in terms of providing services such as education, health and transportation. It has also provided the private sector with the procurement of tenders and similar services for the areas where it has not been withdrawn. This orientation, in a sense, brought about the disintegration of the welfare state practices in the urban area. The local government has been withdrawn from the practices such as rent and unemployment benefit, especially for working people. In addition, the arrangements for urban space have become smoother and the planning agency has lost its power significantly (TÜBA, 2006: 35). In this process, the planning device has gradually begun to move away from the tendency of the public to take care of activities such as redistribution of resources, reorganization of property, reorganization of urban environments and urban development, planning of regional development (Özgen, 2007: 170).

Within the framework of neoliberal teaching, collective consumption has ceased to be a factor that makes cities unique, and cities have become the focus of economic development and real estate rent. Ertürk and Sam (2009: 104) emphasized four types of relations between the capital and the city. The city is where the surplus-value is created. It is the area where the mode of production is re-determined. The urban area is the capital accumulation itself with its infrastructure, production and service. Rent, residual product distribution and capital accumulation are directly affected by the processes taking place in the urban area. In the neoliberal doctrine where functionality of the powerful state apparatus and practices of the planning institution is not respected, the fact that the urban development phenomenon is left to the functioning of the free market has caused serious contradictions in the context of these relations between the capital and the city. In the post-1980 period, cities both in the capitalist countries and in the peripheral countries experienced a rapid transformation. The most important feature of this transformation is the reproduction of labor, in other words, the loss of the priority of collective consumption. Instead, policies to support capital are highlighted. In this process, the management of the cities has gone beyond the responsibility of the local government. The city management has begun to take responsibility for the coalitions in which the capital is actively involved (TÜBA, 2006: 36). In this period, where the channels of representation and the forms have also been rapidly transformed; the representation of local communities in urban areas has relatively remained (although there is a counter-discourse); and in such cases, where local community representation took place, the framework of participation is shaped around the concerns of obtaining more rent rather than creating more livable cities (Şengül, 2003: 197). Because, above all, urban space is a floating-rover issue and it is a distribution tool that is the determinant of unequal and complex power relations in the society (Öksüz et al., 2007: 255).

EVALUATION OF GOVERNANCE-CENTERED URBAN DEVELOPMENT

According to the perception of the state, which dominated the thinking environment in the 1980s, public administration was a non-glossy area with excessive spending and record. According to this; it was emphasized that the state-owned enterprises have been the subject of criticism with their over-employment and non-productive production characteristics; the institutions of representative democracy are a cumbersome political system that cannot respond to changes, and bureaucracy represents a rather rigid and self-conscious civic structure during the policy-making process (Bayramoğlu, 2005: 28). Keynesian and import substitution strategies have started to be solved within the framework of the negative perception of the state as a result of capital accumulation crisis. In this process, welfare state practices were put aside and the neoliberal accumulation regime was dominant. The central and local state started to undertake significant transformations on the global, national and local scale within the framework of the specific positions of the countries (Şengül, 2003: 183). In such an environment, the governance model has introduced a new political and institutional structure thesis with multiple actors on the basis of equality and democracy. The term governance was first mentioned in 1989 by the DB in a report prepared for Africa. This term was passed as a "subsidiarity" in the EU resource. This term is translated into Turkish as "yönetişim". International organizations such as WB, IMF and UNDP have played a decisive role in the rapid rise of the governance term during the 1990s (Bayramoğlu, 2005: 28).

The concept of governance was defined by the OECD Global Governance Commission in 1995 as the sum of the forms of joint management of individuals, institutions, public and private sectors. It is the process by which conflicting or different interests are mobilized by harmonization and cooperation. It covers formal institutions and regimes responsible for ensuring compliance, and also includes informal arrangements that arise when people or institutions are either compromised or convinced that this is in their own interest (Güler, 2003: 93-105). One of the prominent meanings of the concept of governance is managing without government. One of the basic principles of this new form of administration is the projection of an inter-equal relationship, rather than a hierarchical relationship in the bureaucracy. Another is the co-management principle instead of the ruling-managed distinction. In this context, although the issue of governance is presented as a union of state, civil society and market actors; civil society organizations have assumed the main role in this trio. In this approach, the institutional framework and the development of policies necessary for the establishment and assurance of market economy mechanisms have been defined as the priority. In the framework of this structure, this approach excluded workers as a class. However, individuals who belong to all social classes and positions within the social structure have a new role as individuals. In addition, it has linked the political, economic and social mechanisms with each other at local, national and global scale (Bayramoğlu, 2005: 29-46). In this context, the phenomenon of globalization was perceived as the articulation of the economic and social parts of the world economy with each other and with the world markets (Yeldan, 2002: 20).

Therefore, the governance approach has overlapped and complemented the same perceptions of globalization. During the period of the welfare state, the top-down policies of the central state were dominated by local governments. In the governance approach, local government is envisaged to produce and implement original policies within a relative independence from the central government. In other words, within the framework of the neoliberal governance approach, local government turned to policies to support capital, which led to a significant change in the understanding of urban management. Behind this change, the city management has now gained a dimension beyond the nation-state; state and market-based accumulation strategies have lost their validity; and it is seen that a multi-actor city management structure including capital and local communities is targeted (Şengül, 2003: 190-195). Therefore, the ontology of an institutionalized local government apparatus is based on the local structure. Accordingly, the different geographical characteristics and social conditions of a country made it necessary to produce policies on a local scale as well as on a national scale. The main reason for this is that the central state has not been able to provide services in all corners of the country on an equal and quality level. This thesis was the main driving factor for local government to create relatively independent local policies from the central government. The interventions of the state in the form of direct intervention, support and regulation within the framework of the policies it has established at the central and local level fulfill three basic functions at the urban level (Şengül, 2003: 188). Accordingly, the first function was related to the continuity of production and capital accumulation (transportation, infrastructure, communication, urban planning, urban renewal, education, health, etc.). The second function concerned the provision of labor reproduction through collective consumption (rented housing, health, education, cultural services, etc.). The third function was the provision of social order and control (police and police services, unemployment benefits, education, health, social assistance, etc.). Thus, when talking about the intervention of the central state or local government to the urban area at a certain moment, a specific combination of three different forms of intervention is mentioned in the form of direct interference (such as housing production or rental housing), support (such as rent assistance) and regulation. The main issue to be addressed here is the content, purpose and the consequences of these different forms of intervention.

Globalization and the inequalities it produces face many resistance on a local scale. Local communities, civil organizations and public interest organizations support this struggle. They even act together with the city dwellers to produce counter policy (Çavuşoğlu, 2010). In this context, the city has become a formation that is shaped by the interaction of more and more actors. Intervention to this formation has taken the form of interventions within the process of mutual learning by actors who are part of the process instead of external determinations. For the sustainable development of a society that has reached this level, it has been deemed obligatory that it has reached the understanding of participatory politics and governance (Tekeli, 2007: 39). However, there are various channels of representation within the state that are different and often contradictory.

EVALUATION OF TURKEY'S URBANIZATION PROCESS IN CONTEXT OF URBAN DEVELOPMENT PARADIGMS

Turkey's urbanization process, found in the context of the conjunctural situation since the foundation of the Republic, can be divided into four periods outlined. It is understood that the political environment in which the country is located, the economic policy applied and the capital accumulation process are based on this periodical attempt. Accordingly, the first period (1923-1945) points to a period in which the economic policy of statism was decisive in the nation-state process. This period extends from the declaration of the Republic to the end of the Second World War. It is a period in which the rate of urbanization is low in a single-party political system and in addition, legal and institutional arrangements that direct urban development and urban planning are being made in the implementation of a fundamentalist modernity project. The second period began after 1945 and dates back to 1960. This period is a transitional period. In the country, in the period of international political and economic conjunctural restructuring after the Second World War, migration from rural to urban areas started and liberal economic policy was reverted. The third period includes the period 1960-1980. In this period, the phenomenon of urbanization gained momentum. Due to the insufficient institutional system, the system was re-configured. In addition, a planned economy was searched and for the first time in the history of the country, urban planning education was institutionalized as a separate discipline. This period corresponds to the period in which national economic space and accumulation of economic capital came into prominence due to the policy of import substitution industrialization. The fourth period includes the post-1980 years. In this period extending to the present day, with the effect of neoliberal economic policy and globalization, the nation-state process started to weaken. Under the influence of neoliberal economic policy, globalization and localization, legal and institutional arrangements have changed in the country. Most importantly, the accumulation of economic capital has been predominantly determined in the transnational space (Şengül, 2008: 113).

The Republic of Turkey was founded in 1923. Based on this period, this process goes back to the end of the Second World War. In the early years of the foundation, a liberal economic policy was implemented for national development in the country. However, this policy did not yield the expected results. With the effect of the World Economic Crisis of 1929, it was decided to follow a soft statism policy as the economic policy in 1930-1932, which was the most depressive years of the country (Çavdar, 2003: 295). The statist economic policy was the product of the specific social and economic conditions of the relevant period (Kepenek, 2012: 57). In addition, this policy also has been decisive in the subsequent periods of Turkey's economy and on the structural features of the urban development process. Statist economic practices were effective between 1930 and 1940, and in these years state interventionism was enlarged by taking the form of a planned economy (DİE, 1973: 153).

In these years, there was no significant movement in the rural-urban structure of the population in the cities except Ankara, the capital. During this period, important initiatives were made in economic and socio-cultural fields, particularly in industrial investments such as mining, energy, iron and steel and railways within the scope of statism practices. However, this situation did not create a significant change in the rural-urban structure of the population (Kepenek, 2012: 79). The content of statist economic policy consisted of the industrial-based investments established by the state. The aim was to spread national development throughout the country. In this respect, Anatolian cities with a population of more than ten thousand were selected for investment. Public services and transport infrastructure in these small settlements were assumed to increase as a result of these investments. In this context, urbanization was expected to gain speed (Göksu, 2012: 244; Çalışkan, 2003: 16). However, the data for the period indicated that there was no significant change in rural-urban population movements and that the country's urbanization rate followed a slow course until the 1950s.

After the establishment of the Republic, the first census was held in 1927. According to this census the total population of the country was 13 million 648 thousand. Of this population, 3 million 306 thousand lived in cities and 10 million 342 thousand lived in rural areas. From the census results until 1950, it is understood that approximately 75% of the total population in the country lived in villages and the remaining 25% lived in cities. These data indicate that there was no significant change in the rural-urban ratio of the population, and that no significant urbanization process was experienced a in a twenty-three year period in Turkey (Erkan, 2002: 84; Çavdar, 2003: 269). In other words, the limited mobility observed in the urbanization phenomenon or population movements between the years when the Republic was established and the years of the Second World War can be attributed to the fact that Ankara was the capital city with state-established industrial enterprises (Çalışkan, 2003: 16). At the end of 1919, the population of Ankara, which was about 20 thousand, increased by ten times by reaching 74 thousand in 1927 and 226 thousand in 1945 (Yavuz, 1980: 13). In those years, Ankara has become almost the only city of the country with its rapid population growth.

The second period extends from 1945 to 1960. The foundations of the state-centered urban development in Turkey have begun to be laid in the statism period. However, the increase in the rate of urbanization began to be observed after the Second World War. Therefore, this period was marked by migration movements from rural to urban. The main political and economic characteristics of this period are the end of the Second World War, the closure of the single party period with the transition to the multi-party electoral system, and the transition from statist economic policy to liberal economic policy. In addition, after the Second World War, the current government then has endeavored to receive foreign aid (from the aid under the Marshall Plan) from the United States and international organizations established under its leadership; the government has followed a policy that attaches importance to foreign investment and seeks to provide the prerequisites for inclusion in the system introduced by the Bretton Woods Agreement; and the distinctive conditions of the country's preference for taking place in the US block in the bipolar world that emerged after the war are the major developments related to the external conjunctural situation of the relevant period (Tezel, 2002: 222-223; Tekeli & İlkin, 1974: 5).

In those years when liberal economic policy was prioritized, the 1947 Development Plan, which was prepared in line with the wishes of foreign aid circles, envisaged the transfer of economic enterprises other than mining, energy, iron-steel and railways to the private sector over time; namely privatization (Kepenek, 2012: 83). Turkey's 1947 Development Plan, which opted for the country's development sector has been agriculture. Other sectors are dealt with in a way that will help the agricultural development. In the Plan, agricultural development is conditioned on infrastructure, especially on the development of the road system. It was based on complete freedom for private enterprise. It was decided that the technology to be imported from abroad would be new (Tekeli & İlkin, 1974: 15-17). It is understood that, in that period when mechanization started in agriculture, said priority sectors were directly related to urban development. After the 1945s, when the demographic structure of the country is analyzed, it is seen that the unraveling has started in the countryside. During this period, there was an influx of immigrants from rural areas to major cities such as Ankara, Istanbul and Izmir. The rural population who came to the city and could not solve the housing problem became the trigger of the slum problem in the big cities of the country because of the informal houses they produced (İİB, 1973: 18). Particularly in the 1950s, the housing needs of the rapidly increasing number of new urban residents could not be met by the governments of the period. In those years, a planned land and housing policy could not be pursued for the resettlement of newcomers to the city. On the other hand, the migrants illegally built their houses on the urban boundaries, mostly on the public lands located far from the city center. This situation will lead to irregular growth of cities in the following years (Apan, 2008). In those years, governments have been silent against the phenomenon of slum because of populist policies. Over time, municipal services were taken to the slums due to concerns about voting. The Law on Slums in 1966 has been the source of the permanence of the slum areas (Adaman & Keyder, 2008). Therefore, if an urban policy is to be mentioned in these years, it can be said that this policy took place in the form of the spread of slum areas which would make the reproduction of labor cheaper (Göksu, 2012: 244).

The third period begins in 1960 and extends to 1980. This period was under the influence of political instability due to the military coups and the oil crisis which started in 1970 and deepened in 1973. During this period, there has been a return from liberal economic policy to planned statist economic policy. Since 1963, five-year development plans have been implemented within the framework of planned economic policy. In the planned economic model, which was implemented in those years, the import substitution industrialization policy was followed. This industrialization policy prioritizes the production of imported goods by the public sector or the state-funded private sector in order to avoid external dependence. Since the establishment of the country, the support to the domestic private enterprise to achieve the accumulation of domestic capital in the country has been among the primary objectives of the country. In accordance with this purpose, in order to ensure growth and accumulation of capital, the relevant legislation regulating the relations of production has been regulated in line with the interests of the capital groups. Five-year development plans, which are decisive on urban development, formed the main lines of the legal and institutional infrastructure of the Republic's urban management, urban development and urban planning concept until the 1980s (Tekeli, 2010: 62-63; Göçer, 1985: 55).

The fourth period, which was started in 1980, was entered with a military coup and economic policy change as in the previous period. Subsequent globalization and localization phenomenon, large-scale urban transformation projects emerged as the factors that differentiated this period from the previous ones. It is possible to start the effects of market-centered urban development in the country in those years. This is because the 1980 military coup and the 24 January Decisions (24 Ocak Kararları) put an end to the policy of import substitution industrialization in the country. New economic arrangements prepared within the framework of the neoliberal approach give the state a more passive role in the economic field. This new role of the state has been expressed as arbitrating relations between classes in society, avoiding interventions in favor of lower classes for the continuation of social reconciliation and allowing the privatization of some state services (Işık & Pınarcıoğlu, 2003: 125). Neoliberal economic policy has given priority to legal and organizational arrangements that will ensure the urbanization of capital (Göksu, 2012: 244). It has also changed the outlook on the built environment. In this economic approach in which a new capital accumulation strategy emerged, urban space became the focal point for capital accumulation. In this context, the usage value of the housing in urban area has begun to be replaced by the value of change (Şengül, 2012: 442). The old built environment in the city center and close to the city center began to collapse. Instead of the demolished old buildings, new buildings with high economic value were built. This demolition and rebuilding process, including also the handover of ownership of property, was expressed as urbanization of the capital. Urban transformation projects have been seen by some circles as projects aimed at achieving these goals.

The phenomenon of migration in Turkey's geography varies in terms of quality and diversity. Since then, there have been periodic migrations to the country. There have also been immigrants to foreign countries. The country has also been used as a transit country in migration movements. However, internal and external migrations in the country have always been in continuity even if they occur at different intensities. On the other hand, migration movements were particularly effective on the built environment. It has led to significant changes in the structural texture of big cities. During this period, rapid population increase due to migration increased the density of buildings in urban centers. On the other hand, the increasing housing demand of the lower and middle classes caused the slum areas to gain value. As a result, single-storey houses with small gardens in the big cities of the country were destroyed. They have been replaced by multi-storey slums. For example; asylum seekers, transit migrants, suitcase traders, women's household workers, European pensioners, high-skilled immigrants who came from the neighboring countries to major cities, especially to Istanbul after the 1985s, significantly affected the social structure. This distorted and irregular urban fabric was deteriorated as a result of mass forced migration in the 1990s due to terrorism (Adaman & Keyder, 2008; Danış, 2017). Due to the Syria crisis erupted in 2011, large number of Syrians took refuge in Turkey. More than two million immigrants who flocked to the country in this latest wave of migration have deeply affected the country's political, economic and social structure.

Governance-centered urban development entered the country in the 1990s within the framework of legal legislation. Turkey's European Union membership process continues. In this functioning process, Turkey is obliged to adapt its legislation to the European Union legislation. So far, some of the legal texts to which the country is a party have concerned the development of local autonomy and democracy. The European Charter of Local Self-Government is just one of these legal texts. As a result of this period, City Councils that encourages local participation in political and administrative decision-making process of local governments was put on the agenda of municipalities in Turkey. The European Charter of Local Self-Government prepared by the European Council was approved on December 9, 1992 by Turkey. It is possible to summarize the purpose of the European Charter of Local Self-Government in reaching the ideals of local democracy and autonomy (Keleş, 2009: 55; Himsworth, 2007: 276-277). The cooperation of the state, civil society / initiative and market actors was aimed to be realized through the so-called City Councils especially in local decision-making processes. The structure of the City Council is based on the governance model. The operation of this model is based on the principle of managing together. In other words, the principle of hierarchy that operates in the decision making processes will be replaced by the principle of co-governing upon the implementation of this model. Thus, a new form of governance with the principle of co-govern instead of governing-managed distinction will become operational in local governments.

To summarize, Turkey urbanization experience that took place in their own specific conditions coincide to a large extent on urban development paradigms. In fact, the urban policies of developed and developing countries and the course of urban development of these countries have progressed in quite different lines. However, the Keynesian economic approach is based on the state's understanding of the state's comprehensive intervention in the economy. In this context, Turkey has lived in the urban development process in the framework of statist and state-centered import substitution industrialization policy. Neoliberal economic policy is based on the assumption that all actors in society will achieve a balance within the free market economy. Therefore, it foresees the withdrawal of the state from economic and social life. In this context, the state has gradually withdrawn in providing urban services such as education, health, and transport. The provision of services related to the areas where the state is withdrawn is left to the private sector through bids and similar methods. In this sense; market-oriented urban development, even though in a different form and to a different extent, became operational in Turkey as a result of the January 24 Decisions. The governance model as a new management approach has put forward a new multi-actor political and institutional structuring thesis on the level of equality and democracy. This new form of governance is based on the principle of co-managing rather than governing-managed separation. In this framework, although the administration is presented as a combination of state, civil society / initiative and market actors, non-governmental organizations have played a major role in this trio. In addition; political, economic and social mechanisms are linked to each other at local, national and global scale. In this context, the phenomenon of globalization and localization is in harmony with the governance model, which is the new form of governance. Because it has paved the way for the economic and social parts of the world economy to be articulated with each other and increasingly with world markets. Turkey has been articulated in this running global political and economic process. Therefore, it can be said that governance-centered urban development has started to emerge in the country since the 1990s.

CONCLUSION

The state-centric urban development paradigm, the market-centric urban development paradigm, or the governance-centric urban development paradigm has not been able to produce lasting solutions to urban problems. None of these paradigms were able to develop mechanisms to manage urban development in a healthy way, and could not produce rational solutions to urban problems. The paradigms in the context of the political, economic and social conditions of each period have important differences in the perception of urban space and the perspective of urban development. In this context, the roles of urban actors have also changed. This situation has been pioneered in the formation of a new paradigm which is the anti-thesis of the current paradigm in every period. In the state-centered paradigm, where the state was the main actor, the value of use was prioritized, and cities became the places where government investments gained intensity. However, cities have begun to take shape within the framework of the market-centered paradigm in the context of the conjunctural change. Therefore, the cities, where the value of use is prioritized and appearing as a concrete living space, have started to be evaluated on the basis of market value (exchange value) in the context of market-centered approach, and the urban space has begun to be accepted as a commodity. This new understanding paved the way for a structural change in urban form and urban development, created a new urban culture with a consumption focus and made private enterprise a determinant of urban development as a strong urban actor. Cities, however, have been assessed over their market value and the urban space has been seen as a sold commodity. In a sense, the welfare of the inhabitants of the city has lost their priority. However, the inadequacies of both approaches in terms of healthy urban development led to a new approach outside the state and market-centered urban development policies. This approach has been a civil society-based approach. This new approach, which can be expressed as the third way, has suggested the development and implementation of a new urban policy based on governance. One of the most important results of this new situation is the direct transition channels between the local and the global scale. Since the establishment of the country, Turkey's urbanization experience is directly affected by external political and economic conjuncture. In other words, the domestic political and economic orientations of the country have been shaped to a great extent under the influence of external conjunctural conditions. Perhaps because of this, the country's urbanization process has been largely in parallel with the state-centered, market-centered and governance-centered urban development paradigms that have been effective since the Second World War.

REFERENCES

Aktüre, S. (1987). *19. Yüzyıl Sonunda Anadolu Kenti Mekânsal Yapı Çözümlemesi*. Ankara: ODTÜ Mimarlık Fakültesi Press.

Apan, A. (2008). *Türkiye'de İç Göç Olgusu: Nedenleri ve Sonuçları*. Retrieved from http://paribus.tr.googlepages.com/a_apan05.doc

Balamir, M. (2008). Küresel Gelişmeler, Neoliberal Politikalar, Risk Toplumu ve Planlama. 8 Kasın Dünya Şehircilik Günü 31. Proceedings of 'Planlama Meslek Alanı: Geçmişten Geleceğe', 167-194.

Bayramoğlu, S. (2005). *Yönetişim Zihniyeti: Türkiye'de Üst Kurullar ve Siyasal İktidarın Dönüşümü*. İstanbul: İletişim Publications.

Beaud, M. (2003). *Kapitalizmin Tarihi* (F. Başkaya, Trans.). Ankara: Dost Bookstore.

Çalışkan, O. (2003). Anadolu'da Bir Yarı-Çevre Modernite Deneyimi: Kemalizm'in Şehirciliği. In *Planlama (2003/3)* (pp. 14–23). Ankara: TMMOB Şehir Plancıları Oda Publication.

Çavdar, T. (2003). *Türkiye Ekonomisinin Tarihi (1900-1960)*. Ankara: İmge Bookstore.

Çavuşoğlu, E. (2010). *Hegemonik Bir Süreç Olarak Türkiye Kentleşmesi*. Retrieved from http://tez2.yok.gov.tr/

Danış, Ç. (2017). *Demografi: Nüfus Meselelerine Sosyolojik Bir Bakış*. Retrieved from http://www.acikders.org.tr/pluginfile.php/4144/mod_resource/content/2/TUBA1.pdf

Demirer, G. N., Demirer, T., & Duran, M. (1999). *Neoliberal Saldırı Kriz ve İnsanlık*. Ankara: Ütopya Publications.

DİE-Devlet İstatistik Enstitüsü. (1973). *Türkiye'de Toplumsal ve Ekonomik Gelişmenin 50 Yılı* (M. Düzgüneş, Ed.). Ankara: Başbakanlık Devlet İstatistik Enstitüsü Printing Press.

Erkan, R. (2002). *Kentleşme ve Sosyal Değişme*. Ankara: Bilimadamı Publications.

Eroğul, C. (2002). *Devlet Nedir?* Ankara: İmge Bookstore.

Ertürk, H., & Sam, N. (2009). *Kent Ekonomisi*. Bursa: Ekin Publications.

Galbraith, J. K. (2004). *İktisat Tarihi* (M. Günay, Trans.). Ankara: Dost Bookstore.

Göçer, O. (1985). Temel Sorunlar. In *Şehircilik* (pp. 47–112). İstanbul: İstanbul Teknik Üniversitesi Printing Press.

Göksu, S. (2012). Kentsel Politika ve Siyaset İlişkisi. In *Kentsel Planlama Ansiklopedik Sözlük*. İstanbul: Ninova Publications.

Güler, B. A. (2003). Yönetişim: Tüm İktidar Sermayeye. *Praksis Dergisi*, *9*, 93-116. Retrieved from http://www.praksis.org/files/00903.pdf

Himsworth, C. (2007). Yerel Yönetimlerin Özerkliğine İlişkin İlkelere Uyumun İzlenmesi. In Yerellik ve Politika: Küreselleşme Sürecinde Yerel Demokrasi. İstanbul: İmge Bookstore.

Işık, O., & Pınarcıoğlu, M. M. (2003). *Nöbetleşe Yoksulluk*. İstanbul: İletişim Publications.

İİB-İmar ve İskân Bakanlığı. (1973). *50 Yılda İmar ve Yerleşme (1923-1973)*. Ankara: İmar ve İskân Bakanlığı Publications.

Kara, U. (2004). *Sosyal Devletin Yükselişi ve Düşüşü*. Ankara: Maki Publications.

Kazgan, G. (2005). *Türkiye Ekonomisinde Krizler (1921-2001)*. İstanbul: İstanbul Bilgi Üniversitesi Publications.

Keleş, R. (2009). *Yerinden Yönetim ve Siyaset*. İstanbul: Cem Bookstore.

Kepenek, Y. (n.d.). Gelişmede Devletin 'Yeni' Yeri Sorunu. *Proceedings of 'Planlamanın Meşruiyeti ve Plancıların Konumları'*, 51-55.

Kepenek, Y. (2012). *Türkiye Ekonomisi*. İstanbul: Remzi Bookstore.

Kloby, J. (2005). *Küreselleşmenin Sefaleti* (O. Düz, Trans.). İstanbul: Güncel Publications.

Öksüz, A. M., Beyazlı, D. Ş., & Türk, Y. A. (2007). Planlamada Yer Seçimi Kararlarının Politik İçeriği ve Politikalara Yansıması. Proceedings of Planlama Siyaset Siyasalar, 255-271.

Özdemir, S. (2004). *Küreselleşme Sürecinde Refah Devleti*. İstanbul: İstanbul Ticaret Odası Publications.

Özer, M. A. (2005). *Yeni Kamu Yönetimi: Teoriden Uygulamaya*. Ankara: Platin Publications.

Özgen, L. (2007). Küreselleşmiş Dünyada Planlama, Devlet, Hükümet Üzerine: Türkiye Örneği. Proceedings of Planlama Siyaset Siyasalar, 161-174.

Sezen, S. (1999). Devletçilikten Özelleştirmeye Türkiye'de Planlama. Ankara: Todaie.

Şahin, Y. E. (2004). Sosyal Devlet Modelinden 'Good Governance' Modeline Geçiş Sürecinde Kalkınma ve Planlama Anlayışında Gerçekleşen Değişim. Proceedings of Şehircilikte Reform, 113-126.

Şaylan, G. (2003). *Değişim Küreselleşme ve Devletin Yeni İşlevi*. Ankara: İmge Bookstore.

Şengül, H. T. (2003). Yerel Devlet Sorunu ve Yerel Devletin Dönüşümünde Yeni Eğilimler. *Praksis Dergisi*, *9*,183-220. Retrieved from http://www.praksis.org/files/009-07.pdf

Şengül, H. T. (2008). Planlama Meslek Alanı ve Dönüşümü: Bir Çerçeve Önerisi. Proceedings of Planlama Meslek Alanı: Geçmişten Geleceğe, 105-127.

Şengül, H. T. (2012). *Türkiye'nin Kentleşme Deneyiminin Dönemlenmesi. In 1920'den Günümüze Türkiye'de Toplumsal Yapı ve Değişim* (pp. 407–553). Ankara: Phoenix Publications.

Tekeli, İ. (2001). Her Geçen Gün Geleceği Yeniden Yaratıyor ve Yeniden Kavrıyoruz. Proceedings of 'Geleceği Planlamak: Yeni Planlama Yöntemi, Dili, Yasal Geleceği', 27-32.

Tekeli, İ. (2007). Siyaset ve Planlama İlişkisi Yeniden Tanımlanırken. Proceedings of Planlama Siyaset Siyasalar, 37-51.

Tekeli, İ. (2010). *Sanayi Toplumu İçin Sanayi Yazıları*. İstanbul: Tarih Vakfı Yurt Publications.

Tekeli, İ., & İlkin, S. (1974). Savaş Sonrası Ortamında 1947 Türkiye İktisadi Kalkınma Planı. Ankara: Ortadoğu Teknik Üniversitesi İdari İlimler Fakültesi.

Tezel, Y. S. (2002). Cumhuriyet Döneminin İktisadi Tarihi (1923-1950). İstanbul: Tarih Vakfı Yurt Publications.

TÜBA-Türkiye Bilimler Akademisi. (2006). *Yerleşme Bilimleri/Çalışmaları İçin Öngörüler*. Ankara: Türkiye Bilimler Akademisi Publications.

Yavuz, F. (1980). Kentsel Topraklar: Ülkemizde ve Başka Ülkelerde. Ankara: Ankara Üniversitesi Siyasal Bilgiler Fakültesi.

Yeldan, E. (2002). Neoliberal Küreselleşme İdeolojisinin Kalkınma Söylemi Üzerine Değerlendirmeler. *Praksis Dergisi, 7*, 19-34. Retrieved from http://www.praksis.org/files/007-02.pdf

Chapter 9
A Challenge to Homo Economicus: Behavioral Economics

Hatice Isıl Alkan
Ondokuz Mayıs University, Turkey

ABSTRACT

Neoclassical economics is the mainstream economic paradigm of the present era and has certain assumptions such as rationality, perfect knowledge and unique equilibrium. In this regard, homo economicus, namely rational economic man is the main agent of mainstream economics. However, this main agent has aspects that are inconsistent with reality. In other words, decision units are likely to be irrational in the real word because individuals are emotional and social beings. Considering that this conception of rationality contradicts with the instability of economies and crises that have happened, it seems that the dominant economic view cannot exactly explain current events. This chapter questions the concept of homo economicus, the compatibility of homo economicus with homo sapiens and attempts to reveal the shortcomings of the dominant view. It substantially tries to explore why behavioral economics is necessary and how behavioral economics can make up for the shortcomings of the mainstream economic paradigm by the help of its branches; experimental economics and neuroeconomics.

DOI: 10.4018/978-1-7998-1037-7.ch009

INTRODUCTION

Economics is a science that, like other sciences, changes and evolves over time. Economic thought has undergone significant evolution since the emergence of mercantilist thought. Following every economic view, new schools have emerged that highlight the shortcomings of the previous one. It should here be noted that a neoclassical view has been the dominant view in economics for many years; thus, neoclassical economics has become the mainstream. However, neoclassical economics has shortcomings and aspects that are inconsistent with reality. In this regard, the term "homo economicus", which refers to the rational and unemotional individual who pursues his or her self-interest, stands out as one of the basic assumptions of neoclassical economics. It is an economic agent who acts inconsistently with reality and has low explanatory power in terms of economic decisions.

The dominant paradigm suggests that human beings always act rationally. It also ignores irrationality and bounded rationality and by extension the influence of psychological factors in behaviors and decisions. However, human beings are emotional and social; therefore, psychological traits are of importance in decisions. The rationality of individuals seems to be contradictory to the destabilization of economies as a result of the emergence of financial crises, thereby indicating that the current mainstream economics cannot fully explain individual decisions.

Against this background, the first section describes the concept of homo economicus as the main agent of the mainstream. The second section attempts to show how behavioral economics (BE) emerged as a result of the shortcomings of mainstream economics and illustrates the development of BE within the context of old and new BE. It also discusses the pioneers of BE and their significant contributions to economics. The third section focuses on the basic concepts and methodology of BE. It also looks at experimental economics and neuroeconomics, which are the branches of BE. Moreover, the third section asserts the methodological differences between BE and mainstream economics. The conclusion section explains the general implications of the study and discusses why BE is needed in our era.

THE MAIN ACTOR OF MAINSTREAM: HOMO ECONOMICUS

Mainstream economics generally refers to neoclassical economics, which has several assumptions such as rationality, perfect knowledge, unique equilibrium, and diminishing returns. In this respect, rationality is one of the main assumptions of neoclassical economics, which is correlated with maximizing the net revenue. Entities have the knowledge of all alternatives and limitations and thus makes the best possible choice to achieve the goals (Soukup, Maitah, & Svoboda, 2015, p. 2). Homo economicus[1] is the rational economic man who is the main agent of mainstream economics. In a more detailed sense, homo economicus is a person who tries to maximize his or her welfare under the budget constraint (Nyborg, 2000, p. 309), who has to make a choice with given and determinate preferences, who is self-interested and outcome-oriented, and who is concerned with social interactions as long as they affect his or her wealth (Gintis, 2000, p. 312). Homo economicus is an individual with complete knowledge of all economic issues such as goods and markets. This entity always makes a rational choice among available options, usually prefers many to less, and is always consistent (Candan & Hanedar, 2005).

Homo economicus is accepted to be one of the main assumptions of mainstream economics; however, the question to ask is to what extent the term "homo economicus" can function without problems. Doucouliagos discusses that the homo economicus of neoclassical thought has a set of characteristics such as (1) maximizing (optimizing) behavior, (2) the cognitive ability to exercise rational choice, and (3) individualistic behavior and independent tastes and preferences. However, the compatibility of homo economicus with homo sapiens has been questioned. There are two groups of criticisms. The first group is concerned with the bounded rationality that has three components: "(1) there are cognitive limitations to rational choice, (2) agents adapt but do not optimize; and (3) agents are not maximizers, they are satisficers". The second group is centered on "the role of institutions and group behavior, with two main criticisms: (1) agents may not act individualistically, and (2) agents' tastes and preferences are neither exogenous nor independent" (1994, pp. 877-878).

The concepts of homo economicus and rationality have been criticized by various schools since classical economics. Thus, criticisms about this issue are not new and cannot be attributed to only behavioral economists. For instance, the early criticism was voiced by the leader of classical school Adam Smith. In his first book "The Theory of Moral Sentiments", Smith argues (1976) that human beings would not be as selfish as envisaged, but would be influenced by what other people experienced[2]. Smith (1976) put significant emphasis on the concepts of sympathy, empathy, and antipathy (pp. 9-23). It is argued that Adam Smith laid the foundations of BE with his aforementioned book. Keynesians and New Keynesians have also questioned rationality in the short and long term. In his seminal work "General Theory", Keynes (2008) discusses that the decisions of individuals are not completely rational and are influenced by subjective factors (pp. 99-103). To put it succinctly, the concepts of homo economicus and rationality have been widely criticized and claimed to be insufficient to explain human behavior. Some economists argue that pure rationality cannot be talked about, as suggested by traditional economists, while they maintain the validity of bounded rationality. In this connection, BE is an economic school that investigates the applicability of related concepts. In recent years, the assumptions of neoclassical economics have been highly questioned in the economics literature. Daniel Kahneman and Vernon Smith (2002) and Richard Thaler (2017) were awarded the Nobel Prize in Economics for their work that led the questioning of the idea of homo economicus and rationality and by extension traditional economics. Kahneman has shown that human beings cannot make rational decisions in terms of uncertainty and risk and underlined that individuals are not always rational, as advocated by mainstream economists. Smith has established laboratory experiments as a tool in empirical analysis, especially in the study of alternative market mechanisms, thereby refuting the prevailing view that economists could not carry out controlled experiments as the way chemists or other scientists do ("Press release", 2019). Thaler analyzed the economic decision-making process using psychological insights and pointed to three psychological factors: the tendency to not behave completely rational (bounded rationality), social preferences, and self-control problems ("Richard H. Thaler Facts", n.d.).

DEVELOPMENT OF BEHAVIORAL ECONOMICS: OLD BEHAVIORAL ECONOMICS AND NEW BEHAVIORAL ECONOMICS

Although the traces of BE date back to earlier years as mentioned in the previous section, it should be noted that research on the emergence of BE has grown since the mid-twentieth century. Economists' avoidance of psychology has occurred with the neoclassical revolution although it seems to be paradoxical. In the 20th century, economists wished that economics would be natural science and did not find psychology, which emerged in that period, sufficiently scientific. They also thought that psychology could not provide a stable basis for economics. In fact, Fisher and Pareto speculated about the feelings and economic choices of people in the early 20th century. Keynes was also interested in psychological insights; however, psychology disappeared in the middle of the century. Throughout the second half of the century, George Katona and Herbert Simon wrote books and articles on psychological components and bounded rationality. Although they managed to attract attention, they could not change the direction of the economy. However, the anomalies that occurred in the economy could not be ignored and cognitive psychology rose to prominence in the 1960s (Camerer & Loewenstein, 2010, p. 4).

According to Peter Earl, the emergence of BE began at four different universities, namely Carnegie-Mellon University and the University of Michigan in the USA, and the University of Oxford and the University of Stirling in the UK (1988, p. 3). The first and most visible research group emerged at Carnegie University. This group carried out significant studies on bounded rationality, satisficing, and simulations. Richard Cyert, James March, and Herbert Simon were prominent researchers who were mainly sponsored by the Ford Foundation and the Office of Naval Research (ONR). Richard Nelson and Sidney Winter brought these studies to Yale University. The second group appeared at the University of Michigan. The pioneer of this group was George Katona, who tried to combine economics with psychology. While the researchers in the Carnegie group focused more on firm behavior, Katona's team focused more on consumer behavior and macroeconomic issues. The third group was working at Oxford University. This group was more concerned with uncertainty and coordination issues. The leading representatives of the third group were P. W. S. Andrews, D. M. Lamberton, H. Malmgren, J. Marschak, G. B.Richardson, and G. L. S. Shackle. The last fourth group emerged at the University of Stirling. Their main research areas were eclecticism and integration. The proponents of this group were Neil Kay, Brian Loasby, Richard Shaw, John Sutton, Andrew Tylecote, and Peter Earl (Sent, 2004, pp. 740-741).

Although there are several names that have made a significant contribution to the development of old BE, Katona and Simon can be considered to be the founding fathers of old BE. Simon is well-known for the notions of bounded rationality and satisficing. He was awarded the Nobel Prize for his contributions to economics; however, Katona has been overlooked. Katona was ignored by the historians of economic thought excluding Schumpeter. Katona was influenced by Gestalt psychology and worked on public policy issues. He endeavored to bring psychological dimension to economics (Hosseini, 2011, p. 978). Likert, Strümpel and Pratt are other scholars who hold this view earlier than Hosseini[3].

Another prominent founder Herbert Simon from Carnegie-Mellon University is one of the first critics of the rational choice model in economics. Simon argued for bounded rationality. From this perspective of rationality, he held the view that economic models of choice are deficient because they suppose substantive rationality. According to Simon, if the factors and interactions of the predicted behavior are simple, substantive rationality can be relevant. On the other hand, if the factors and interactions are complex, procedural rationality should be considered. Simon received the Nobel Prize in Economics in 1978 for his proposal that individual procedural rationality should be explicitly modeled (Simon, 1996, p. 25; Nagatsu, 2015, p. 444).

Thus, according to Simon, neoclassical economics cannot describe human choice behavior due to numerous cognitive limitations. His proposal "bounded rationality" is a better way of grasping the actual process of decision-making. However, the contributions of Katona and Simon to "new" BE was limited despite their efforts (Angner & Loewenstein, 2006, pp. 22-26).

BE is basically divided into two phases: old BE and new BE. Old BE generally includes the works of George Katona and Herbert Simon (between 1950 and 1970), while the new phase involves the studies of Daniel Kahneman, Amos Tversky, Richard Thaler, and others (since 1970) (Ayroza, Iwamoto, & Rodrigues, 2018, p. 53). New BE is an economic school that emerged in the 1970s. With respect to the emergence of new BE, the most important development in the 1970s was indeed the emergence of a new psychological model termed "behavioral decision making" (BDM) or "behavioral decision research" (BDR). BDR stemmed from the cognitive revolution. What distinguishes the BDR approach from other approaches is that it uses the theories of rational decision as the starting point (Angner & Loewenstein, 2006, pp. 26-28). According to Fischhoff (1988), economists traditionally optimize their decisions; however, the purpose of an empirically minded economist is not to test the hypothesis that people are optimizing but to determine what people are trying to optimize (p. 156). In this regard, the BDR approach differs from mainstream economics because an approach that does not exist in the rational choice model that characterizes mainstream economics exists in BDR. The rational choice theory has led to the emergence of the BDR approach and set up a difficult target for the BDR, which has led to the revelation of assumptions that could be investigated in the laboratory. BDR was used by Tversky and Kahneman and attracted the interest of economists in the second half of the 20th century (Angner & Loewenstein, 2006, pp. 27-30; Camerer & Loewenstein 2003, pp. 5-7).

The contributions of Kahneman and Tversky to BE can be examined under three headings. First, their manuscript titled "Judgment under Uncertainty: Heuristics and Biases" published in the journal Science in 1974, they examined how individuals decide under uncertainty and described three heuristics: representativeness, availability of instances or scenarios, and adjustment from an anchor. They claimed that a better understanding of these heuristics could improve decisions under uncertainty (Tversky & Kahneman, 1974). Second, in "Prospect Theory: An Analysis of Decision under Risk" published in the journal Econometrica in 1979, they criticized the expected utility theory and developed a new model for decision-making under risk, which is termed "prospect theory". They put emphasis on the reflection effect while explaining prospect theory. According to the authors, the certainty effect in a positive prospect leads to risk aversion. In other words, individuals prefer a sure gain to a probable higher gain. On the other hand, in a negative prospect, individuals exhibit "risk seeking preference". To put it differently, they prefer bigger potential losses to a smaller definite loss. In short, the same psychological principle "overweighting the risk" favors risk averse preference in the case of gains but risk seeking preference in case of losses. The authors termed the second effect as the reflection effect because "the preference between negative prospects is the mirror image of the preference between positive prospects" (Kahneman & Tversky, 1979, pp. 268-269). Table 1 shows a detailed description of the preferences in prospect theory. The preferences that appear in the problems indicated in the table confirm the reflection effect emphasized by the authors.

Another effect that the authors used to explain prospect theory is the isolation effect. According to the isolation effect, individuals prefer to focus on alternatives that attract their attention while ignoring other alternatives.

Problem: Suppose a two-stage game is played. In the first stage, the chance of finishing the game without winning anything is 0.75 and the probability of proceeding to the second stage is 0.25. In the second stage, two alternatives are available. The first one is gaining $4,000 with a probability of 0.80 and the second is the absolute gain of $3,000.

Among 141 individuals, 78% preferred the latter prospect. In fact, the initial offer here is a gain of $4,000 with a probability of 0.20 = (0.80 * 0.25) and the second offer is a gain of $3,000 with a probability of 0.25. When the same question was asked in this way earlier, the majority of individuals preferred (4000, .20); however, individuals ignored the first stage in this two-stage game and preferred the second choice. According to the authors, the isolation effect appears at this point (Kahneman & Tversky, 1979, pp. 271-272)

The utility function of Kahneman and Tversky is significantly different from the expected utility function. In prospect theory, decision-making is not related to the

Table 1. Preferences between positive and negative prospects (Kahneman & Tversky, 1979, p. 268)

	Positive Prospects		**Negative Prospects**	
Problem 3 (N = 95)	(4,000, .80) < 3,000		(-4,000, .80) > -3,000	
	[20]	[80]	[92]	[8]
Problem 7 (N = 66)	(3,000, .90) > (6,000, .45)		(-3,000, .90) > (-6,000, .45)	
	[86]	[14]	[8]	[92]

final value of wealth. The sensitivity of individuals to losses is much greater than the sensitivity to gains. In this context, expectations theory is a model that accounts for deviations from rationality (Kahneman & Tversky, 1979, pp. 277-279).

The framing effect is the third heading under which the contributions of Kahneman and Tversky to BE are examined. Expressing information in different ways causes individuals to feel different and these feelings affect their preferences or choices. Kahneman and Taversky (1981) refer to this fact as the framing effect and describe it with the aid of the following example:

Problem 1(N = 152): An unusual disease is expected to kill 600 people and two alternative programs are proposed to combat. If program A is conducted, 200 people will be saved. If program B is chosen, 600 people will be saved with 1/3 probability and no people will be saved with 2/3 probability.

Kahneman and Tversky asserted that the majority were risk averse and chose program A because it was more attractive than the risky choice B. Then, they reformulated problem 1 as follows:

Problem 2 (N = 155): An unusual disease is expected to kill 600 people and two alternative programs are proposed to combat. If program C is conducted, 400 people will die. If program D is chosen, no one will die with 1/3 probability and 600 people will die with 2/3 probability.

According to the authors, in the second problem, people were still risk averse and chose program D. Hence, choices involving gains are often risk averse and choices involving losses are often risk taking although the two problems are still identical (Kahneman & Tversky 1981, p. 53).

In the following years, Kahneman and Tversky advanced prospect theory and presented a new theory termed cumulative prospect theory. In the new theory, they examined preferences under uncertain and risky prospects. According to the authors, a distinctive fourfold pattern of risk attitudes emerged as a result of a new experiment: risk aversion for gains and risk seeking for losses of high probability; risk seeking for gains and risk aversion for losses of low probability (Tversky & Kahneman, 1992, p. 297).

Richard Thaler is another important contributor to BE. The first contributions of Thaler to BE can be found in his study "Toward a Positive Theory of Consumer Choice" wherein he criticized normative theory and discussed that the normative theory causes economists to make systemic and predictable mistakes in explaining or predicting consumer choices. He touched on the concept of "mental illusions" and prospect theory proposed by Kahneman and Tversky. He also underscored bounded rationality and pointed to the contributions of anomalies to the development of the descriptive theory of consumer choice. Opportunity costs and sunk costs are the other significant facts underlined in his study (Thaler, 1980, pp. 39-50). In "Mental Accounting and Consumer Choice", Thaler developed a new model of consumer decision using cognitive psychology and microeconomics. He put forward new concepts for different areas such as coding gains and losses, transaction utility, and budgetary rules. Thaler also made a considerable contribution to the marketing field, especially in the context of pricing (Thaler, 1985, pp. 199-213).

Thaler developed "Nudge Theory" with Sunstein. Thaler and Sunstein (2017) argued that when people are unable to think deeply, they can be misguided by approximate calculations and estimates. People are impulsive beings and can be affected in their most important decisions. Self-control is one of the problems of individuals. Conditions and the environment also affect individuals' behavior and choices. People use external systems to control themselves. For instance, people who know their weaknesses make shopping lists. People also have internal control systems such as planning and managing a family budget. This activity is called mental accounting. People may follow the likes of the majority due to social influences and the desire to adapt. For this reason, there may be a choice architecture that provides a better choice for consumers in uncomplicated situations (Thaler & Sunstein, 2017). Decision-makers make their decisions in a setting that have many features, not in a vacuum. People can make better decisions with the help of choice architecture. The six principles of choice architecture are iNcentives, Understand mappings, Defaults, Give feedback, Export error, and Structure complex choices, briefly NUDGES (Thaler, Sunstein, & Balz, 2010). According to Thaler and Sunstein, people do not always make perfect decisions as prescribed by the dominant economic paradigm and they need assistance in decision-making. In other words, in nudge theory, people's attitudes and behaviors can be changed without any difficulty with the aid of soft power (Altunöz & Altunöz, 2018, p. 125). The findings presented by Thaler and Sunstein are of great importance in terms of public policies because various policies that provide social benefits can be developed in this way. As a matter of fact, Sunstein was appointed by President Barack Obama as the head of the office responsible for the implementation of public policies in the USA and served from 2009 to 2012. This theory also attracted the attention of the former UK Prime Minister David Cameron and the policies that have been introduced since 2010 are enriched by the contributions of experimental and BE (Altunöz & Altunöz, 2018, pp. 127-131)

George Akerlof is another scholar who made a substantial contribution to BE. Akerlof was awarded the Nobel Prize in 2001 for his work on certainty and knowledge economy. In his book "Animal Spirits: How Human Psychology Drives the Economy and Why It Matters for Global Capitalism", he laid stress on the concept of "animal spirits" and defined it as moving and variable elements in the economy. Animal spirits sometimes paralyze and other times refreshes individuals (Akerlof & Schiller, 2010, p. 24). The study of Akerlof and Schiller emphasizes the weaknesses of mainstream economics in understanding economic activities and stipulates the substitution of mainstream economics with BE. The authors also assert that economics should benefit from psychology and sociology based on history and stories instead of traditional approaches to understand crises (Dinçer, 2011, p. 132).

FUNDAMENTAL CONCEPTS AND METHODOLOGY OF BEHAVIORAL ECONOMICS

Main concepts used in BE which are significantly different from those in mainstream economics are defined as follows (Altunöz & Altunöz, 2018, pp. 25-54):

1. Heuristics: People make their decisions using mental shortcuts. It also includes a share of inaccuracy as much as accuracy.
2. Loss Aversion: It is a concept related to prospect theory. As Kahneman and Tversky (1979) emphasize, it suggests that "losses loom larger than gains" (p. 279).
3. Self-Serving Bias: People tend to attribute positive events to their own character but negative events to external factors.
4. Hedonism and Hedonistic Consumption: Peopl often opt for forms of consumption that make them happy.
5. Bandwagon Effect: It means shaping decisions according to decisions of the majority (regardless own decision).
6. Snob Effect: A situation in which the demand for a certain good by individuals of higher income level is inversely related to the demand for the same good by those of lower income level.
7. Prejudices
8. Mental accounting[4]
9. Asymmetric Information: Lack of complete knowledge. "Asymmetric information, as the adjective indicates, refers to situations, in which some agent in a trade possesses information while other agents involved in the same trade do not." ("Asymmetric Information", n.d.)

10. Bounded rationality[5]
11. Anchor Effect: It is a type of cognitive bias which causes people to focus on the first information given to them in a decision-making process.
12. Framing effect[6]
13. The Illusion of Control: It is one's exaggerated belief that he or she can take necessary action when faced with an undesirable situation.
14. Hindsight Bias: "The tendency, upon learning an outcome of an event – such as an experiment, a sporting event, a military decision, or a political election – to overestimate one's ability to have foreseen the outcome." It is also known as the "I knew it all along phenomenon" (Inman, 2018).
15. Overoptimism: It is a type of cognitive bias that causes people to believe that they are more likely to experience good events rather than bad events.
16. Gambler Fallacy: A type of cognitive bias that a frequently occurring incident will occur less frequently in the future (or vice versa).
17. Money Illusion: Evaluation of income not with real but nominal value.
18. Mere Ownership Effect: Giving more value to individual possessions.
19. Escalation of Commitment: People's insistence on unsuccessful decisions.
20. Impact Bias: Positive or negative events that people face are thought to be long term, for instance, an endless economic crisis.
21. Transaction Utility: It is consumers' happiness that arises from the difference between the actual price and the reference price.

These concepts are the core concepts that are effective in the decision-making behavior of individuals according to BE. However, they are invisible in mainstream economics because in mainstream economics, individuals are fully informed, rational, thus unaffected by psychological factors when making decisions. In addition to core assumptions on which traditional and BE are based, their methodologies are quite different. Traditional economists often attempt to formulate a theory using numerical data and try to analyze correlations between incomes, prices, spendings, savings, and investments in markets. Behavioral economists are aware that the same stimuli can produce different responses at different times; therefore, they avoid broader generalizations. Behavioral economists do research based on experiments and observations rather than numerical data. While traditional theorists do not like surprises, behaviorists feel happy when they are surprised (Katona & Harris, 1978, pp. 14-18).

Although many studies in the 17th and 18th century suggested that the experimental method was one of the main sources of knowledge, the experimental method in the history of economics encountered great resistance until the mid-twentieth century.

The economic analyses were based on the abstract human model supported by homo economicus; therefore, the deductive method was preferred to the experimental method. The first acquaintance of economics with experimentation happened in the 1940s. The fact that Smith and Kahneman were awarded the Nobel Prize in 2002 for their contributions to BE is one of the clearest indications of the process of change in economics. Debates on whether the experimental method is suitable for economics have today been replaced by arguments on the methodology used in the experiments (Basılgan, 2013, pp. 62-80). In this respect, Edward Chamberlin is known as the first person who undertook experimental studies in economics. In his book "Economic Methodology", Maas (2014) explains that Chamberlin carried out experiments in classrooms of Harvard to test his theory of monopolistic competition and continued his experimental activities until the 1960s; Vernon Smith, as a student at Harvard in the 1950s, were in the classes where the experimental studies were conducted (p. 148).

Experimental economics has a lot in common with BE; the basis of both theories have traces of psychology. No inherent conflict can be seen between the two approaches. However, there are different aspects of these two approaches. Behavioral economists identify themselves as methodological eclectics. Their application of psychological insights to economics is their distinctive aspect. On the other hand, experimental economists underline the endorsement and use of experimentation as a research tool. According to behavioral economists, the developed rules of experimental economists are excessively restrictive. Behavioral economists find some types of data very useful such as demographics, self-reports, response times, and other cognitive measures. On the other hand, experimental economists rarely rely on these data (Loewenstein, 1999, pp. 25-34).

The following are the three main methods used by experimental economics (Akın & Urhan, 2009, pp. 7-8):

1. **Laboratory Experiments:** This is the first and the most widely used method which ensures maximum control. The researcher can continuously explore the experimental environment. Subjects act on a scenario while the motivating tool is money. Scores are converted to real money at the end of the experiment and payment is made accordingly. The experiment is then ended.
2. **Field Experiments:** Control is lost significantly in comparison with the laboratory experiments. Subjects are not isolated from their natural environment and are able to communicate with each other. The fact that they are insulated from

the real world to a minimum extent increases the power of these experiments. On the other hand, reproducibility of field experiments is lower compared to laboratory experiments. The difficulty in repeating the same setting causes these experiments not to be reproduced by other researchers. This method is criticized for its inability to show reactions to different cultural elements.

3. **Online Experiments:** With the development of internet technology, this method allows observations on hundreds of subjects. The use of such experiments is rapidly increasing.

In spite of these differences, BE attaches great importance to experimental economics and focuses on data obtained from experiments; however, it also moves beyond experimentation and embraces several different methods used by economists (Camerer & Loewenstein, 2010, pp. 6-8). In this regard, it is possible to say that BE has a wider perspective and experimental economics can be evaluated as a branch of BE.

Economic theory did not achieve great success in the 20th century, apart from a few exceptions in terms of empirical testability. The way to eliminate this failure is to go through a variety of scientific methods. Social sciences have recently attempted to use neurology. In this connection, increasing attempts have been made to establish a connection between the basic axioms of economic theory and the physical functioning of the brain. Brain imaging methods have been used to help understand the economic activities of individuals such as risk-taking behavior, production, consumption, and savings (Çiftçi, 2017, pp. 3-4). Behavioral economics' research on decision-making has led to the emergence of new methods and ideas on the subject and "Neuroeconomics" emerged in the late 1990s (Loewenstein, Rick, & Cohen, 2008, p. 649).

Neuroeconomics criticizes decision-making processes in traditional economic theory because decision-making processes cannot consist of a single process. Human behavior in real life is very complex and decision-making processes are multifaceted. According to neuroscientists, decision-making processes can be examined in two ways: controlled and automated decision making processes. Controlled processes are open and observable, while automated processes are not. One of the best examples of these processes is the use of a car with gear. The driving of an inexperienced driver is based on the controlled process. However, the driving of an experienced driver is based on the automated process. The experienced driver can easily perform activities such as chatting with others and using a phone. (Sanfrey, Loewenstein, Mcclure& Cohen, 2008, pp.108-116)

The development of neuroeconomics has progressed further with the development of neuroscience[7] techniques. Techniques for the non-invasive visualization of the human brain have made the relationship between the mental and neural functions of humans more clear; especially the functional magnetic resonance imaging (fMRI) technique has made it possible to display the brains of people in a non-invasive manner while they are engaged in a cognitive process (Demirel & Artan, 2016, p. 16). According to Zak (2004), neuroeconomics is an emerging field that aims to unearth the neural substrates related to economic decisions (p. 1737). He further describes it as a transdisciplinary field that focuses on decisions and thus is not limited to human studies. In this connection, the author makes reference to the first study in neuroeconomics focused on monkey's decisions, the 1999 *Nature* article by Michael Platt and Paul Glimcher.

Eventually, together with experimental economics and neuroeconomics, BE develops day by day and clearly demonstrates that the assumption of homo economicus does not reflect reality. It is likely that behavioral economics, which endeavors to create a more realistic theory, can produce a paradigm shift in economics in the near future.

CONCLUSION

Although neoclassical economics has been the dominant paradigm for many years, its basic assumptions have come under increasing criticism. In fact, the rational economic individual prototype "homo economicus" was criticized for a period from classical to Keynesian economics; however, these criticisms were ignored until the second half of the 20th century when Katona and Simon, who are considered to be founders of old BE, began to announce that the basic teachings of neoclassical economics were inaccurate. The authors tried to bring a psychological dimension to economics and paved the way for new behavioral economics by drawing attention to cognitive elements and bounded rationality in decision-making processes. Subsequently, Daniel Kahneman and Amos Tversky carried out significant research in the field of BE since the 1970s and added a distinct dimension to BE using the BDR approach in decision-making studies, thereby succeeding in attracting the attention of economists. Kahneman and Tversky emphasized decision-making under uncertainty, prospect theory, and risk-aversion, and were awarded the Nobel Prize in 2002, thereby proving the slowly changing framework of the economy. In more recent years, Richard Thaler has explored the consequences of factors such as bounded rationality, lack of social preferences, and lack of self-control, and demonstrated how these elements influence individual decisions and market processes. Thaler was awarded the 2017 Nobel Prize in Economics for his findings. Additionally, Thaler and Sunstein have shown through nudge theory that people cannot make perfect decisions as prescribed by mainstream economics and it is possible to influence human decisions with a soft force. These recent insights into decision-making processes have attracted the attention of various politicians in developed countries and affected public economic policies. In other words, developed countries have recently begun to benefit significantly from BE in the regulation and implementation of public policies.

Against this background, it is apparent that economics evolves and expands every day with new findings and theoretical concepts. In this process of evolution, the shortcomings of the dominant economic paradigm gradually become more evident. It is clear that decision-making units in markets do not usually exhibit rational behaviors as the dominant economic doctrine suggests, but rather they can make systematic errors. Thus, in some cases, they do not make rational choices that maximize their utility. Crises in recent years are the simplest examples of this situation because they have shown that uncertainty and psychological factors distract individuals from rationality and illustrated the importance of taking these factors into account in decision-making processes. If the dominant economic paradigm fails to explain the aforementioned anomalies, it is obvious that there is a need for a new paradigm to explain and make up for the shortcomings of the dominant paradigm. Here, the BE paradigm has emerged. With the aid of BE, the source of such abnormalities in the market can be located so that various regulatory elements can be activated to overcome such abnormalities. Recent research has revealed that BE exposes the shortcomings of neoclassical economics and more realistic decision-making methods are not in accord with the homo economicus prototype.

In conclusion, economics is a social science and economic outcomes emerge as a result of decision-making behavior. Thus, it is not possible for a science, detached from human, to fully reflect reality. New methodologies and testing of theories might pave the way for new efficient theories. The discussions and findings in this study clearly show that it is time to revise the dominant economic paradigm. In this respect, behavioral economics can be seen as a shining star of the new era and thus be evaluated as a significant shift to remedy the shortcomings of neoclassical economics.

REFERENCES

Akerlof, G. A., & Schiller, R. J. (2010). *Hayvansal güdüler: İnsan psikolojisi ekonomiyi nasıl yönlendirir ve küresel kapitalizm için niçin önemlidir?* (N. Domaniç & L. Konyar, Trans.). İstanbul: Scala Yayıncılık.

Akın, Z., & Urhan, B. (2009). *İktisat deneysel bir bilim olmaya mi başliyor?* TOBB University of Economics and Technology.

Altunöz, U., & Altunöz, H. (2018). *Davranışsal ekonomi (Nörofinans)*. Ankara: Seçkin Yayınevi.

Angner, E., & Loewenstein, G. (2007). Behavioral economics. In U. Mäki (Ed.), *Philosophy of economic* (pp. 641–690). Handbook of the philosophy of science Amsterdam: Elsevier.

Asymmetric information. (2003). World Bank. Retrieved from https://siteresources.worldbank.org/DEC/Resources/847971114437274304/Asymmetric_Info_Sep2003.pdf

Ayroza, I. F., Iwamoto, H., & Rodrigues, W. (2018). The old and the new Behavioral Economics: Highlights of a trajectory. *Textos De Economia*, *21*(2), 50–72. doi:10.5007/2175-8085.2018v21n2p50

Basılgan, M. (2013). İktisat ve deneysel yöntem: Deneyler, tartişmalar ve gelecek. İstanbul Üniversitesi Siyasal Bilgiler Fakültesi Dergisi, 48, 61-89.

Camerer, C. F., & Loewenstein, G. (2010). Behavioral economics: Past, present, future. Retrieved from http://www.its.caltech.edu/~camerer/ribe239.pdf

Camerer, C. F., Loewenstein, G., & Rabin, M. (Eds.). (2003). *Advances in behavioral economics*. New York: Russell Sage Foundation Press.

Candan, E., & Hanedar, A. Ö. (2005, October). İktisat neden bir kapalı kutudur? Hakim iktisadın değer yargısı-sinama ilişkisi. *Paper presented at Gazi Üniversitesi İİBF Ekonomik Yaklaşımlar Dergisi Kongreler Dizisi (IV)*, Ankara. Retrieved from http://debis.deu.edu.tr/userweb//onder.hanedar/dosyalar/gazi.pdf

Çiftçi, H. (2017). İktisadın farklı bir çehresi; nöroiktisat. *Ekonomi Bilimleri Dergisi*, *9*(1), 1–15.

Demirel, S. K., & Artan, S. (2016). Nöroiktisat ve iktisat biliminin geleceğine ilişkin tartışmalar. *Uluslararası Ekonomi ve Yenilik Dergisi*, *2*(1), 1–28. doi:10.20979/ueyd.07280

Dinçer, G. (2011). Hayvansal güdüler, insan psikolojisi ekonomiyi nasıl yönlendirir ve küresel kapitalizm için niçin önemlidir? [Review of the book Animal spirits: How human psychology drives the economy, and why it matters for global capitalism, by G. Akerlof & R. J. Shiller]. *Ekonomik Yaklaşım*, *22*(81), 129–132. doi:10.5455/ey.20020

Doucouliagos, C. (1994). A note on the evolution of homo economicus. *Journal of Economic Issues*, *28*(3), 877–883. doi:10.1080/00213624.1994.11505586

Earl, P. E. (1988). *Behavioural economics* (Vol. 1). Aldershot: Edward Elgar.

Fischhoff, B. (1988). Judgment and decision making. In R. J. Sternberg & E. E. Smith (Eds.), *The psychology of human thought* (pp. 153–187). New York: Cambridge University Press.

Gintis, H. (2000). Beyond Homo economicus: Evidence from experimental economics. *Ecological Economics*, *35*(3), 311–322. doi:10.1016/S0921-8009(00)00216-0

Hosseini, H. (2011). George Katona: A founding father of old behavioral economics. *Journal of Socio-Economics*, *40*(6), 977–984. doi:10.1016/j.socec.2011.04.002

Inman, M. (2018). *Hindsight bias*. Retrieved from https://www.britannica.com/topic/hindsight-bias

Kahneman, D., & Tversky, A. (1979). Prospect theory: An analysis of decision under risk. *Econometrica*, *47*(2), 263–291. doi:10.2307/1914185

Katona, G., & Harris, D. J. (1978). Behavioral economics. *The Challenge (Karachi)*, *21*(4), 14–18. doi:10.1080/05775132.1978.11470445

Keynes, J. M. (2008). *Genel teori, istihdam, faiz ve paranın genel teorisi* (U. S. Akalın, Trans.). İstanbul: Kalkedon Yayınları.

Likert, R. (1972). Courageous pioneers: Creating a new field of knowledge. In B. Strümpel, J. M. Morgan, & E. Zahn (Eds.), *Human behavior in economic affairs* (pp. 4–6). San Francisco: Jossey-Bass Inc.

Loewenstein, G. (1999). Experimental economics from the vantage-point of behavioural economics. *Economic Journal (London)*, *109*(453), 25–34. doi:10.1111/1468-0297.00400

Loewenstein, G., Rick, S., & Cohen, J. D. (2008). Neuroeconomics. *Annual Review of Psychology*, *59*(1), 647–672. doi:10.1146/annurev.psych.59.103006.093710 PMID:17883335

Maas, H. (2014). *Economic methodology: A historical introduction*. London: Routledge. doi:10.4324/9780203797679

Nagatsu, M. (2015). Behavioral economics, history of. In J. D. Wright (Ed.), *International encyclopedia of the social & behavioral sciences* (2nd ed., pp. 443–449). Oxford: Elsevier. doi:10.1016/B978-0-08-097086-8.03053-1

Nyborg, K. (2000). Homo economicus and homo politicus: Interpretation and aggregation of environmental values. *Journal of Economic Behavior & Organization*, *42*(3), 305–322. doi:10.1016/S0167-2681(00)00091-3

O'Boyle, E. J. (2007). Requiem for homo economicus. *Journal of Markets & Morality*, *10*(2), 321–337.

Pantaleoni, M. (1889). *Principii di economia pura*. Firenze: G. Barbèra.

Persky, J. (1995). The ethology of homo economicus. *The Journal of Economic Perspectives*, *9*(2), 221–231. doi:10.1257/jep.9.2.221

Pratt, R. W. (1972). Marketing applications of behavioral economics. In B. Strümpel, J. M. Morgan, & E. Zahn (Eds.), *Human behavior in economic affairs*. San Francisco: Jossey-Bass Inc.

Press release. (2002, October 9). Retrieved from https://www.nobelprize.org/prizes/economic-sciences/2002/press-release/

Richard, H. (n.d.). Thaler Facts. Retrieved from https://www.nobelprize.org/prizes/economic-sciences/2017/thaler/facts/

Sanfrey, A. G., Loewenstein, G., Mcclure, S. M., & Cohen, J. D. (2008). Neuroeconomics: Cross-currents in research on decision making. *Trends in Cognitive Sciences*, *10*(3), 108–116. doi:10.1016/j.tics.2006.01.009 PMID:16469524

Sent, E. M. (2004). Behavioral economics: How psychology made its (limited) way back into economics. *History of Political Economy*, *36*(4), 735–760. doi:10.1215/00182702-36-4-735

Simon, H. A. (1996). *The sciences of the artificial* (3rd ed.). Cambridge, MA: The M.I.T. Press.

Smith, A. (1976). *The theory of moral sentiments* (D. D. Raphael & A. L. Macfie, Eds.). Indianapolis: Liberty Classics.

Soukup, A., Maitah, M., & Svoboda, R. (2015). The concept of rationality in neoclassical and behavioural economic theory. *Modern Applied Science*, *9*(3), 1.

Strümpel, B., Morgan, J., & Zahn, E. (Eds.). (1972). *Human behavior in economic affairs*. San Francisco: Jossey-Bass Inc.

Thaler, R. (1980). Toward a positive theory of consumer choice. *Journal of Economic Behavior & Organization*, *1*(1), 39–60. doi:10.1016/0167-2681(80)90051-7

Thaler, R. (1985). Mental accounting and consumer choice. *Marketing Science*, *4*(3), 199–214. doi:10.1287/mksc.4.3.199

Thaler, R., Sunstein, C., & Balz, J. (2010). Choice architecture. doi:10.2139srn.1583509

Thaler, R. H., & Sunstein, C. R. (2017). *Dürtme: Sağlık, zenginlik ve mutlulukla ilgili kararları uygulamak* (E. Günsel, Trans.). İstanbul: Pegasus Yayınları.

Tversky, A., & Kahneman, D. (1974). Judgment under uncertainty: Heuristics and biases. *Science*, *185*(4157), 1124–1131. doi:10.1126cience.185.4157.1124 PMID:17835457

Tversky, A., & Kahneman, D. (1981). The framing of decisions and the psychology of choice. *Science*, *211*(4481), 453–458. doi:10.1126cience.7455683 PMID:7455683

Tversky, A., & Kahneman, D. (1992). Advances in prospect theory: Cumulative representation of uncertainty. *Journal of Risk and Uncertainty*, *5*(4), 297–323. doi:10.1007/BF00122574

Zak, P. J. (2004). Neuroeconomics. *Philosophical Transactions of the Royal Society*, *359*(1451), 1737–1748. doi:10.1098/rstb.2004.1544 PMID:15590614

ENDNOTES

1 There is no consensus on the exact occurrence of homo economicus. The first reference in this regard is "Principii di Economia Pura" authored by Maffeo Pantaleoni 1889. In "A History of Political Economy" authored by Ingram in 1888, the expression "economic man" was used for the first time in the literature. The first use of the term "oeconomicus" alone was in the German economic literature; Karl Raus used the term in in the 1847 and 1826 editions his work "Grundsätze Volkswirthschaftslehre" before Pantaleoni. Although John Stuart Mill has never used the term "economic man" in his essays, Mill's abstractions were thought to underline four human interest: accumulation, luxury, leisure, and procreation (O'Boyle, 2007, p. 322). Persky agrees with this assertion and notes that John Stuart Mill is known to be the creator of the concept "economic man", however, he never used this designation in his own writings and the rejections of historical school for Mill's theoretical abstractions gave rise to the appearance of the term (1995, p. 222).

2 The Theory of Moral Sentiments begins with the following sentences:
"How selfish soever man may be supposed, there are evidently some principles in his nature, which interest him in the fortune of others and render their happiness necessary to him, though he derives nothing from it except the pleasure of seeing it. Of this kind is pity or compassion, the emotion which we feel for the misery of others, when we either see it, or are made to conceive it in a very lively manner. That we often derive sorrow from the sorrow of others, is a matter of fact too obvious to require any instances to prove it, fort his sentiment, like all the other original passions of human nature, is by no means confined to the virtuous and humane, though they perhaps may feel it with the most exquisite sensibility." (Smith, 1976, p. 9)

3 Likert (1972) noted that Katona has a pioneer role in the emergence of BE. Strümpel (1972) asserted that Katona was the father of BE. Pratt (1972) argues that Katona and his colleagues in the University of Michigan made great effort for the growth of BE.

4 Explained in the previous section.

5 Explained in the previous section.

6 Explained in the previous section.

7 Neuroscience asserts that the brain cannot be evaluated as a homogeneous processor and in case of different types of problems, the brain contains different processes which are integrated in different ways (Loewenstein et al., 2008, p. 649).

Chapter 10
The Narh Prices of Various Comestibles in the First Half of the 19th Century

Ramazan Arslan
Bartın University, Turkey

ABSTRACT

Since the food prices are the essential needs of people, they have usually been a topical issue in every period. Therefore, this issue mobilized the administrators of aforementioned period, and necessitated to take measures on this issue. Perhaps one of the most significant measures were the narh (price fixing) system. In this study, narh prices of various comestibles have been approached according to dated 1241-1826 and numbered 09264 in the book of senior accountant (Başmuhasebe Kalemi Defteri). The purpose of study is to prove the given importance of the stability of food prices by Ottoman administration comparatively and to contribute to the studies that have been conducted or will be conducted. The documents in the Ottoman Archives of Turkish Presidency (COA in Turkish) have been used as a study method and other works have been used as well in terms of integrity of the topic. As a result of the study, it is found that Ottoman Empire prioritized the price stability in the comestibles, especially to the benefit of her people.

DOI: 10.4018/978-1-7998-1037-7.ch010

INTRODUCTION

Narh expresses the upper limit that is determined by the state in the prices of goods and services. The core of narh is the price stability. Price stability, on the other hand, provides the regulation of production, the abundance of goods in the markets and the first-hand delivery of goods from producers to consumers. Price stability is considered as one of the main objectives of economic policy.

Ottoman Empire followed a supply-oriented economic policy by paying regard to the welfare level of people. In the Ottoman political economy of classical period, supply-oriented economic policies based on justice became a priority for ruling class. Due to this, "ibadullahın terfi-i ahvali" expression was frequently emphasized. This expression means improving the conditions of the servants of Allah economically and socially. Therefore, providing this expression was considered as a criterion of "success" for all the administrators, notably sultan himself. In this regard, Ottoman thinkers evaluated the life as a whole by contrast with European mercantilists, they did not treat economic issues differently from social, political and moral issues and they approached to these issues in an integrity rather than individualism (Bulut, 2012, pp. 69-70). Administration had a tight control on both land and labor factor in the agricultural field with the purpose of providing the production system and satisfying the essential needs of people. Especially providing the essential comestibles to state and society was determined as priority and the prices were not set by the market (Bulut, 2012, pp. 77-78).

The aim of this study is to reveal the importance of price stability in basic foodstuffs of Ottoman Empire in the light of concrete archival documents. The study is considered important because it can offer solutions to similar economic problems of today. This study differs from its peers. Because the subject has been put forward on the concrete document without going into much detail. The regimentation of the book of senior accountant at the door of treasury (Bab-ı Ali Başmuhasebe Defteri) in the Ottoman Archives of Turkish Presidency (placed in D.BŞM.d9 and numbered 09264 book) has constituted the topic of this study. Narh book contains the various prices of foodstuffs and the prices of items belonging to the shopkeepers. These prices were compared with the other prices of Anatolia. As a result of the study, it was understood that price stability was given importance especially in basic food products in the Ottoman State, and there was no compromise in the conditions that disturbed price stability.

BACKGROUND

Ottoman Empire displayed a great responsibility to the supply of the essential needs of the people in the imperial lands. State especially pursued significant policies for several issues such as providing the essential needs such as bread, wheat, wood, coal, salt to markets, preventing escalations in the prices and the direct delivery of these products to consumers from producers. Various worthwhile works were conducted on this topic. In this study, however, only some of them will be mentioned.

Ömer Lütfü Barkan made significant contributions to the history of Ottoman finance with his studies on Ottoman budgets. Barkan's XVI. Head of the century in Turkey Price Movements article, has taken first place in the study of economic history. On the other hand, Halil Sahillioğlu is accepted as the authority on the history of money in the Ottoman Empire (Çakır, 2003: 34-39).

Şevket Pamuk made the most successful work on the money and prices in the Ottoman Empire. Pamuk (20017) examines the Ottoman monetary system in his study. The price revolution and its effects on the Ottoman economy. Focuses on the causes of financial crisis.

Korkut Boratav, A. Gündüz Ökçün and Şevket Pamuk worked together on the subject of wages in the Ottoman Empire and the developments in the world economy. In these studies, Ottoman money was considered as a time series. The study covers the period from the second quarter of the nineteenth century to the period before the First World War. In the long run due to the contraction in the world economy, rising tendencies in wages have been observed (Boratav, 1985:380).

In his study, Tabakoğlu (1987) approached the price control in Ottoman economy. The author indicated that the prices comprised according to the conditions of supply and demand in the market, a control policy is necessary in the market, otherwise, the competition would cause the monopolization and as a result of that, public authorities will have to intervene to the markets in various ways.

In his study, Solak (2008) detected that 80 species of fruit and vegetable produced in Anatolia in the period of Ottoman Empire and indicated that the cultivation of these products had importance in Anatolia.

In his study, Öztel (2012) examined the view of Ottoman administration to profiteering and the sentences given to profiteering. By highlighting profiteering will affect markets negatively, he wrote that Ottoman administration never capitulate in this issue and the criminals of profiteering punished heavily. He indicated that profiteering emerged in the market extensively and detected that it emerged in every production with buying and selling like manufacturing industry and agricultural products. He used archival documents to prove his study about profiteering. The view of administration on this topic was included as well and after indicating the responsibility of administration about providing the essential needs of people, he discoursed complaints to administration.

In his study, Öztel (2013) approached the profiteering problem in the Ottoman markets after Tanzimat period. The group who made profiteering was remarked by Öztel and he indicated that these people were usually the authorities who overlooked and different groups who could change periodically such as officials, taxmen and ship-owner merchants.

In his study, "Narh Regulation in Balıkesir", İlgürel (2003) identified the narh prices in the products such as bread, meat, onion, fresh grape, molasses, salt and Ramadan halva. Fidan (2017) analyzed the price dynamism in Kastamonu in Ottoman period and in his study, he revealed that the originated high price increases in Ottoman lands affected the sanjak of Kastamonu as well.

PRICE STABILITY AND CONCEPTS OF NARH

The word of stability means continuity and consistency. It expresses the situation that a serious fluctuation such as recession and overexpansion has appeared in economic activities (Seyidoğlu, 2002:301). Price stability can generally be expressed as the regulation of economy, the abundance of the amount of goods in the markets and first-hand delivery of goods to consumers from producers (Öztel, 2012:398-399). In this regard, price stability is accepted as one of the chief goals of economic policies. In general, price stability states that price increases should be kept in a moderate level. With price stability, more inflations will not occur in the economy as well (Seyidoğlu, 2002:203-204).

The instrument of "money" plays an important role in the economic relations of individuals. Because if money is not managed correctly in the economy, it can lead to inflation. This leads to price instability (Akdağ, 1999:166). Thus, one of the chief goals of market regulation in an economy is providing the price stability because price instability can alter the targets of goods distribution in the market at the same time as well. The high demands of rich class to specific goods can cause reduction the demands of poor class to those goods. As a result of that, the essential required goods by poor people could be allocated to the secondary needs of rich class. Hence, this condition occurred in provision area mostly in the Ottoman Empire. In this regard, the provision of Istanbul was considered as a serious problem[1]. Therefore, Ottoman Empire paid attention to the issue of provision of metropolises (Tabakoğlu, 1987:126). In this respect, meeting the basic needs of the people was found important in the framework of the provision principle in the Ottoman Empire (Genç, 2000, pp. 80-81). At the point of provision, the policy of state was to keep the population of city under control. Within this framework, some measures had been taken. For instance, preventing the peasants to settle in Istanbul, the people who has residence in Istanbul less than five years exiled from the city (Öztel, 2013, p. 569).

Narh expressed the upper limit that is determined by the state in the prices of goods and services in Ottoman Empire. Giving narh necessitated the price control as well. The duty of control was given to Ottoman constabulary (muhtesib). Constabulary was the assistant of kadis and was assigned to monitor the prices by patrolling bazaar and markets[2]. The business to give narhs continued until the mid-19th century and by the abolition of the ministry of public regularity (ihtisab nezareti) in 1854, the business of narh was connected to municipality (şehremaneti). Since 1856, there were no narh records in the registries (Kütükoğlu, 2006:390).

PRICE CONTROL IN OTTOMAN ECONOMY

As it is known, economic activities have largely been determined through price mechanism method in the monetary economies. In these economies, the prices have been made under the conditions of supply and demand. A tight control is inevitable for the market prices that have been made under these conditions because a control that will be made can transform the existing competition into monopolization. Therefore, public authorities were aware towards the intervention to market prices in the context of economic and social targets.

This awareness manifested itself as narh policy especially in the periods that prices were disadvantageous for the consumers. Although the necessity of narh policy changed based on the conditions of a period, mostly narh policy emerged in the conditions that supply was insufficient to demand, the transportation difficulties, financial factor and war periods. It was aimed that the essential supply of provisions for Ottoman people could not be sold above a certain price with narh policy (Tabakoğlu, 1987: 112).

The chief goal of narh execution was to prevent the unfair competition between tradesmen and merchants. Besides daily and seasonal price changes, after war, blockade, scarcity, natural disasters and coin adjustments, new pricings were made in the Ottoman Empire. Seasonal narhs mostly showed the prices on comestibles. The prices of bread, meat, milk and dairy products were different in winter and summer (Özdemir, 2017:7). The fixing of narh mostly concentrated on the essential supply of provisions of people. Thus, the issue that the essential necessaries would not be sold above the prices in current period had importance[3].

Narh system constituted the base of price policy in Ottoman Empire. Depending on reduction and expansion of markets, narh prices were rearranged. If the market reduction occurred, the narh prices would be increased and if the market expansion occurred, the prices would be decreased (Tabakoğlu, 1987, p. 122). Hence, breaking the monopolist tendencies was an issue that Ottomans dwelt on at the most. At the helm of these topics, there was profiteering (Tabakoğlu, 1987, p. 130).

Profiteering is described as collecting the essential needs of people such as food and beverage in cheap prices and when the time is right, selling them in high prices. In this sense, profiteering is known as engrossing in a sense (Devellioğlu, 2005, p. 419). Profiteering emerged mostly in essential production and consumption goods such as wood, coal, timber, meat, salt, wheat and cereals. Profiteering manifested itself in the market conditions that the prices have uptrend in extraordinary conditions such as scarcity, natural disasters and battles.

The position of administration for providing the stability against this practice which endanger the market order was among the most significant policies. The base of these policies was the narh system. Administration took macro prudential policies as a measure in order to prevent profiteering in these goods. The ones who were profiteers were punished with prison sentence such as exile,[4] confinement in a fortress[5] besides confiscation (Tabakoğlu, 1987, p. 130).

THE QUALITY OF NARH BOOK WHICH IS THE PRIMARY SOURCE OF THE STUDY

The regimentation of the book of senior accountant at the door of treasury (Bab-ı Ali Başmuhasebe Defteri) in the Ottoman Archives of Turkish Presidency (placed in D.BŞM.d9 and numbered 09264 book) has constituted the topic of this study. This book is paperback and unmarbled, has 16x49 dimensions and has three pages. The expression of "This declares the given narh in the June of 1241" is at the start of the book. Firstly, the essential comestibles or the sort of stuff are written in the book, and the unit of measure is given beneath. The monetary value is written under the unit of measure (Appendix-1). The data of book is given as lines rather than tables. The data is tabularized by the author, and the interpretations and evaluations has been made according to the table.

The book was regulated in 5 Dhu al-Qidah 1241/11 June 1826. The book contains 32 records belonging to various comestibles, 12 records belonging to butchers. The data in the book has been demonstrated the following titles in detail.

The Selected Comestibles and Narh Prices

The cereals were produced in Ottoman Anatolia at the most. The production of fruit and vegetable came after the cereals. The taxes became a matter of state when the crops of orchard and garden entered into the market. The subsistence production of peasant was not taken as a tax. In the study that Solak (Solak, 2008) made, it was confirmed that 80 species of fruit and vegetable were produced in Ottoman Anatolia. Pear, fig, watermelon, melon, apricot, grape, sour cherry and olive can be regarded in the group of fruits; while vine leaves, broad beans, pea, bean, spinach, squash, cabbage, lettuce, onion, mint, beet and eggplant can be counted in the group of vegetables (Solak, 2008: 221).

According to the dated 1241/1826 narh book that covers the topic of this study, the given narh in June can be seen in Table 1. While the narh price was given to the all products in the book, kıyye (an Ottoman unit of measure)[6] was based on as a quarter. While the 1 equivalent of products as kıyye could be different in terms of products, it was given as coin. Pursuant thereto, the total of 31 narh detection was made in the research period. These can be counted as purified oil, unpurified oil, simon-pure honey, licorice, red rice, the Diyarbekir grape, Persian red plum, Persian plum, cheese, molasses, chickpea, fruit leather, hazelnut, nut, churchkhela, roasted chickpea, fig, persimmon, olive, apple, cherry, apricot, milk, vine leave and bean in accordance with their line in the book (Table 1).

The narh was given to the total of 32 comestibles in the table. The highest three narh prices can be seen in simon-pure honey, purified and unpurified oils. The prices of these are respectively 90, 76 and 64 coins. The narh prices of goods which are the lowest as kıyye are respectively fresh milk, bean and vine leaves. Nut is considered as piece. 15 pieces of nut is prices as 1 coin in the document for instance.

The Narh Prices Belonging to Butchers

Celeb has been used in the dictionary for people in Turkish who transport butchers and especially sheep herds and sell them to butchers. Celep or voluntarily Celep, in Ottoman documents, means "animal merchant" (Türkhan, 2016: 255).

The drovers could sell their animals that they had led to Istanbul in two different ways. While they could sell the living sheep that they brought to the butchers at first, they could slaughter the sheep in the slaughterhouses that were assigned to them

Table 1. Ceiling prices of various foodstuffs as of June 1241/1826

Type / Unit of Measurement (kıyye)[7]	Narh Price (Money)
Refined oil	76
Unrefined oil	64
Genuine honey	90
Licorice honey	60
Superb rice	64
Diyarbekir grape	36
Superb Persian grape	38
Cheapjack Persian grape	36
Cheese	20
Superb Tortum	16
Grape molasses	20
Temasu plums	16
Chickpeas	12
Sweet dried fruit pulp	40
Cornelian cherry and sour dried fruit pulp	20
Hazelnuts	24
Nutmeat	40
Roasted nutmeat	48
Crushed walnut	32
Walnuts (5 pieces)	1
Churchkhela	32
Roasted chickpeas	20
Tortum figs	20
Superb date palm	60
Keşan figs	48
Rowan	12
Olives	20
Apples	8
Cherry, apricot and sour cherry	10
Fresh milk	6
Leaves	8
Beans	8

Source: COA. D.BSM.d, 09264, Jun 11, 1826 (5 Callum 1241):2

and they could sell them in the butcher shops that were assigned to them again as meat through the prices of current narh (Kal'a, 1992: 111). In June 1241, which is the subject of the study, it is given to the butcher shopkeepers. The price of these items is given under the related item. The data in the document were compiled by the author and tabulated (Table 2).

The total of 12 kind of goods was subjected to the narh. While mutton (lahm-ı ğanem), cow meat (lahm-ı bakar), engrafted wax, mottling, unmixed bread and loaves were considered as kıyye, tallow and biceps were considered as batman (an Ottoman unit of measure between 2 and 8 kilograms). It can be seen from the table that biceps had the highest narh. Onion and tallow followed it then. Loaves, bread and the unmixed bread of kebab makers comprised of the lowest products that narh was given.

FUTURE RESEARCH DIRECTIONS

Price stability is always important on the ground. Achieving this has been among the main duties of economic managers. For this purpose, price control were given importance. This is necessary for the prosperity and happiness of the people. In this respect, the narh system, which has been practiced in the Ottoman Empire for many

Table 2. The Narh Prices Belonging to Butchers

Type / Unit of Measurement (kıyye)	Narh Price
mutton /kıyye	14 money
cow meat /kıyye	12 money
candle oil /batman	4 penny, 10 money
infused candle /kıyye	54 money
lettuce /6 kıyye	7 money, 8 pennies
collards /batman	7 money, penny
onion /6 vineyard	1 money, 5 pennies
master's wage	70 money
workers wage	45 money
turnspit /2 şit=1 money	12 money
raw bread /kıyye	7 money
nut /okka	6 money

Source: COA. D.BSM.d, 09264, Jun 11, 1826 (5 Callum 1241): 2

years, is an important opportunity to solve possible economic problems. One aim of this study is to put forward the basic philosophy of Narh system and to understand economic logic. Narh issue will remain on the agenda when it comes to price control.

CONCLUSION

Narh expresses the upper limit that is determined by the state in the prices of goods and services. The primary objective of narh is to provide the price stability and price stability provides the regulation of production, the abundance of goods in the markets and the first-hand delivery of goods from producers to consumers. The price stability consisted of the base of economic policies. By the purpose of guarding the welfare level of people, Ottoman Empire followed a supply-oriented economic policy. These policies became the major priority for the administrators as well. In other words, improving the conditions of the servants of Allah both economically and socially was considered as a criterion of success for Ottoman administrators.

In order to reach that criterion of success, Ottoman administration acted responsibly for the supply of essential supply of provisions and the stable progress of their prices. In this regard, the administration kept the market under their control in order to provide the abundance of essential goods and not to raise their prices so much. While the administration was managing its duty of control, they had to be responsible. Narh policy especially manifested itself in the periods when the prices were disadvantageous for the consumers. The policy of giving narh could be changed based on transportation, scarcity of goods, cost element, war and seasonal conditions. If it was expressed very generally, when the reduction of market occurred, narh prices would be escalated and on the contrary, when the market expanded, narh prices would be reduced. In this regard, the chief goal of narh execution was to prevent the unfair competition which could be arisen between tradesmen and merchants.

In this study that the given narh prices to various goods in July 1241/1826 have been examined, the narh executed into the total of 44 products. The 32 of these were various comestibles while the 12 of these comprised of the given narh prices to butchers. Oil, honey, rice, grape, plum, cheese, chickpea, fruit leather, nut, churchkhela, roasted chickpea and fig can be regarded within the context of various goods. It is obtained that the highest three narhs were simon-pure honey (90 coins), purified oil (76 coins) and unpurified oil (64 coins). The goods that had the lowest narhs were fresh milk (6 coins), bean (8 coins) and vine leaves (8 coins).

When the given prices to the butchers in the same date have been analyzed, it can be seen that the narh was given to the products such as mutton, cow meat, tallow, mottling, biceps and onion. The highest narh of these is biceps. Onion and tallow followed it then. It is seen that the lowest given narhs were loaves, bread and the unmixed bread of kebab makers.

When the given information and obtained results have been evaluated together, it can be argued that the stable prices of goods and services, not keeping their prices highly and preventing people to have difficulties for the supply of their essential needs were the primary objectives of Ottoman administrators. As a result of this study, it is revealed that the administration was responsible against any kind of acts that could endanger the prosperity and welfare of people, dealt with any kind of acts that could lead unfair behaviors, took measures against the monopolization in the market and executed narhs in certain circumstances for the prevention of monopolization.

REFERENCES

Akdağ, M. (1999). Barış Yayınları. *Türkiye'nin İktisadî ve İçtimaî Tarihi, 2*, 1453–1559.

Akyel, S., & Savaş, S. (2015). Osmanlı Nüfus Defterlerinin Tarih Yazımındaki Yeri: 1840 Tarihli Çarsancak Kazası Gayrimüslim Nüfus Defteri Örneği. *Journal of History and Future, 1*(1), 78–98.

Boratav, K., Ökçün, A. G., & Pamuk, Ş. (1985). Ottoman Wages and the World-Economy, 1839-1913. *Review - Fernand Braudel Center, 8*(3), 379–406.

Bulut, M. (2012). Osmanlı Ekonomi Politiği'ne Yeniden Bir Bakış. Bilig, (62), 63-96.

Çakır, C. (2003). Türkiye'de İktisat Tarihi Çalışmalarının Tarihi Üzerine Bir Deneme. *Türkiye Araştırmaları Literatür Dergisi, 1*(1), 7–63.

COA. (1566, January). A. DVNSMHM.d..., 5/890, 6 Recep 973/27.

COA. (1568). The Ottoman Archives of Presidency of the Republic of Turkey (COA), A.{DVNSMHM.d.., 7/1270, 14 Shawwal 975/1 April .

COA. (1826, June). D.BSM.d, 09264, 5 Zilkade 1241/11.

COA. (1830, September). C.BLD., 31/1533, 29 Rabiülevvel 1246/17.

COA. (1851, August). A. MKT.NZD., 40/88, 17 Shawwal 1267/15.

COA. (1793, March). C.BLD. 39/1906, 23 Recep1207/6.

Devellioğlu, F. (2005). *Osmanlıca-Türkçe Ansiklopedik Lûgat "ihtikâr" maddesi (22 b.)*. Ankara: Aydın Kitabevi.

Emecen, F. (1992). Başmuhasebe Kalemi. *İslâm Ansiklopedisi Cilt, 5*, 133–135.

Fidan, M. (2017). Osmanlı Dönemi'nde Kastamonu'da Fiyat hareketliliği (M.1703-1776-1777-1796). Sosyal Bilimler Dergisi, 154-179.

Genç, M. (2000). *Osmanlı İmparatorluğu'nda Devlet ve Ekonomi*. İstanbul: Ötüken Neşriyat.

İlgürel, M. (2003). 1116-1119/1704-1707 Tarihleri Arasında Balıkesir'e Ait Narh Düzenlemeleri. İ. E. Halil İnalcık içinde. *Osmanlı Araştırmaları, XXIII*, 11–21.

Kal'a, A. (1992). 19. Yüzyılın İlk Yarısına kadar İstanbul Kasap Esnafının Organizasyonu. *Sosyal Siyaset Konferansları Dergisi*, *0*(37-38), 111–117.

Kütükoğlu, M. S. (2006). "Narh". Osmanlılar'da Narh. *İslâm ansiklopedisi Cilt*, *32*, 390–391.

Özdemir, R. (2017). Tarihte Tüketici Haklarına Yönelik Yapılan İlk Kanun: "Kanunname-i İhtisab- Bursa." Mecmua Uluslararası Sosyal Bilimler Dergisi, (4), 1-17.

Öztel, M. (2012). Osmanlı İdaresi'nin İhtikâra Bakışı ve İhtikâr Suçunun Cezası. *The International Journal of Social Sciences (Islamabad)*, *5*(6), 397–420.

Öztel, M. (2013). İstanbul Piyasasında Halkın Temel Tüketim Maddelerinden Ette Fiyat İstikrarı Sorunu (1850-1919). *Turkish Studies*, *8*(6), 567–589.

Pamuk, Ş. (2007). *Osmanlı-Türkiye İktisadî Tarihi 1500-1914*. İstanbul: İletişim Yayınları.

Şahin, E. (2017). *1754 Numaralı Çorum Şer'iyye Siciline Göre Çorum'da Sosyal ve Ekonomik Hayat (1826-1838)*. Yayınlanmamış Yüksek Lisans Tezi.

Seyidoğlu, H. (2002). *Ekonomik Terimler Ansiklopedik Sözlük (3rd ed.)*. İstanbul: Güzem Can Yayınları.

Solak, İ. (2008). Osmanlı İmparatorluğu Döneminde Anadolu'da Meyve ve Sebze Üretimi. Türkiyat Araştırmaları Dergisi, (24), 217-251.

Tabakoğlu, A. (1987). Osmanlı Ekonomisinde Fiyat Denetimi. İstanbul Üniversitesi İktisat Fakültesi Mecmuası, 43, 111-150.

Türkhan, M. (2016). "Celep". *İslâm Ansiklopedisi. Cilt Ek*, *1*, 255–257.

KEY TERMS AND DEFINITIONS

Celeb: Celeb has been used in the dictionary for people in Turkish who transport butchers and especially sheep herds and sell them to butchers. Means "animal merchant."

Constabulary: Constabulary was the assistant of kadi and was assigned to monitor the prices by patrolling bazaar and markets.

Narh: Expresses the upper limit that is determined by the state in the prices of goods and services.

Profiteering: Profiteering is described as collecting the essential needs of people such as food and beverage in cheap prices and when the time is right, selling them in high prices.

The Ottoman Archives: The archive, which contains the richest and most valuable archive material that was inherited from the Ottoman Empire, is located in the Ottoman Archive Complex in Istanbul. Today, it is known as "The Ottoman Archives of Presidency of the Republic of Turkey."

ENDNOTES

1 Since Istanbul has barley problem, it was requested that the barleys would be sold to the ranchero ships through narh by docking them into the piers and they would be sent to Istanbul after leaving the sufficient amount of barley for themselves from the people who has barleys in the places where sea is close (COA, A.{DVNSMHM.d..., 5/890, Recep 973/27 January 1566)

2 A quality control authority was given to constabulary in this regard. Another authority was given to constabulary for forbidding the people who sold the goods more than the determined prices according to their quality. In a document that was detected in this topic, a warning to non-muslims in Edirne who did not obey the rules about clothes was found. According to the warning, they had already been warned before and it was reported to the authorities as well. Constabulary was assigned to prevent shoemakers not to sell the shoes more than the determined prices and to warn the non-muslims to obey the clothing rule. "The instruction was given to constabulary for warning the non-muslims who had been warned before about their clothes; moreover, constabulary was charged to prevent the shoemakers for not selling the shoes more than the determined prices according to the quality in the edict which was given to constabulary (COA, A.{DVNSMHM.d.., 7/1270, 14 Shawwal 975/1 April 1568).

3 If an example will be given about this topic, it was requested that the meat should not be sold above the current narh prices from the people of Istanbul since the meat was an essential need. (COA, A.}MKT.NZD., 40/88, 17 Şevval 1267/August 15, 1851).

4 A cheese monger who caused losses to the people by selling cheese more than narh prices was exiled to Bozcaada (COA, C.BLD., 31/1533, 29 Rabiülevvel 1246/17 September 1830).

5 Bootmaker Ebubekir and Ahmed who sold boots more than narh prices were punished with confinement in a fortress (kalebendlik) at Sedd el Bahr (COA, C.BLD. 39/1906, 23 Recep1207 / 6 March 1793).

6 Kıyye (an Ottoman unit of measure) was a quarter that equaled to 400 drachma (dirhem) and it equaled to 1282 grams (Devellioğlu, 2005: 519).

7 For all items, the unit of measurement is 1 kıyye.

APPENDIX

Figure 1. Ceiling prices of various foodstuffs as of June 1241/1826
Source: COA. D.BSM.d, 09264, Jun 11, 1826 (5 Callum 1241):2

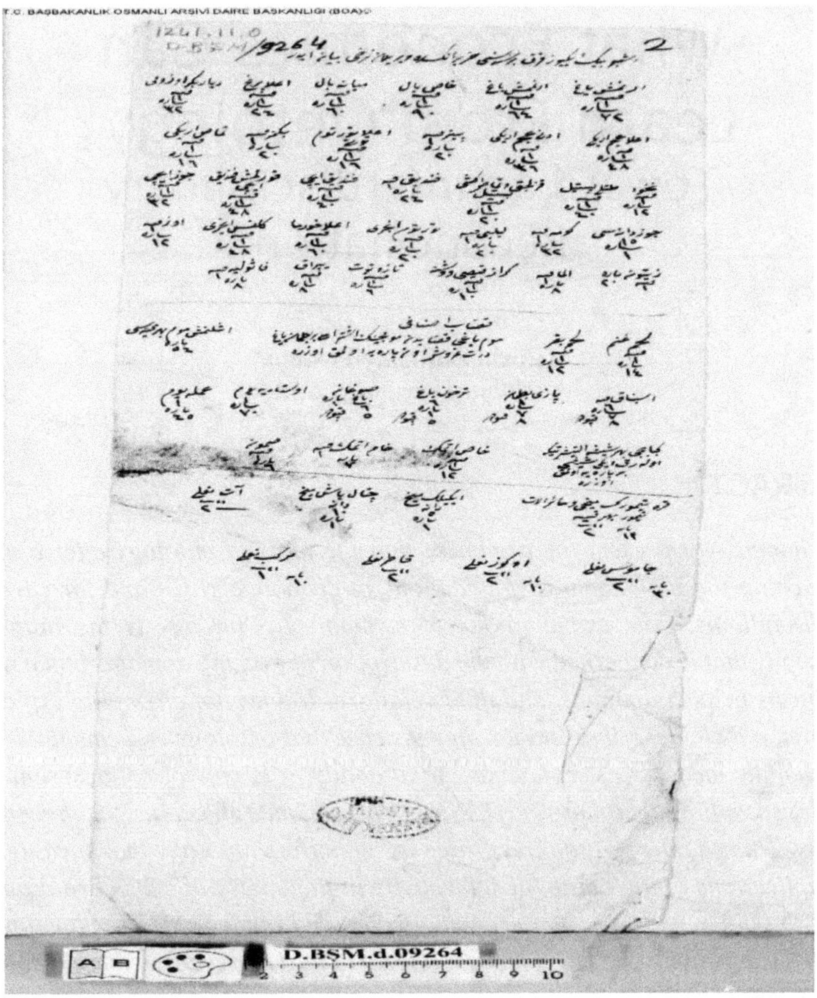

Chapter 11
What Economics Can Learn From Ontology:
Toward an Interdisciplinary Reconciliation

Gloria Zúñiga y Postigo
Ashford University, USA

ABSTRACT

This chapter will present the argument that the tools of ontology offer a means for teaching the philosophical foundations of economic value and for engaging interdisciplinarily the examinations of economics. Ontology is the branch of philosophy that is concerned with the description of existing domains in the world, the objects in such domains, and their relations. It does not attempt to explain or interpret, only to describe, and it is in this sense that ontology is reconcilable with the scientific methods of economics. Additionally, it is capable of describing the complex structures, relations, and emergence of economic objects in human economic activity. This chapter will address three insights from ontology that shed light on the implications of the notion of subjectivity in the theory of subjective economic value, the differences between economic value and other kinds of value, and the role that subjectivity and economic value have in the emergence of the social object we know as money.

DOI: 10.4018/978-1-7998-1037-7.ch011

INTRODUCTION

Although there have been important seed ideas advanced by the ancient Greek philosophers,[1] the literature on the ontology of economics starts more formally in economics and with Carl Menger at the turn of the 20th Century (1976). Menger's breakthrough was influential in the work of F. A. Hayek and others, but it lost its momentum around the end of the first half of the 20th Century. Ontological investigations have enjoyed a recent rise in popularity and the contemporary contributions are quite significant.[2] The practical contribution from this resurgence of interest in the ontology of economics is that it has facilitated the understanding of complex economic processes for non-specialists, and fueled the rise of interdisciplinary specializations such as philosophy of economics, and interdisciplinary programs such as philosophy, politics and economics, known most commonly now as PPE. A mechanism that set the stage for the renewed interest in these interdisciplinary activities was the growing awareness of moral problems in business, which was part of the wave in philosophy in the 1970s of developing specific applications of ethics to each specialized area of human activity—e.g., medicine, psychiatry, engineering, animal husbandry, to name a few—and of the methods in which human beings grew, harvested, mined, or hunted, the natural resources in the world, including the treatment of the human labor hired for such activities. Business ethics is one of the most successful applications of ethics insofar as it has become a required course in many business and economics programs at most universities. Specializing in business ethics requires not only the knowledge of ethical theory but also of business methods and economic concepts. Courses in business ethics are thus a challenge for both economists and philosophers.

Ontology can assist to ameliorate this challenge. The tools of ontology can easily present the differences among different ethical theories, starting from the notion of the moral good employed as the criterion of justification in each ethical theory, to the description of the fundamental and background characteristics for each of the theories. The same can be achieved for economic concepts. Even if the more technical aspects of economic analysis will still remain inaccessible to non-specialists taking business ethics courses, the tools of ontology can make possible for students (who will form part of society as consumers and voters) to understand that they have a role in guiding the forces of supply and demand, that price increases are not set by companies (the Shkreli incident with the price of Daraprim, notwithstanding), that taxing only the rich brings negative unintended consequences, and the role of incentives in our decisions to spend or save. This continuing dissemination of economic knowledge to those who will not become economists does indeed fill a gap that had previously remained neglected.

The motivation for this paper is to further promote this interdisciplinary interaction by advancing the argument that ontology can make a significant contribution to economics that will allow its body of knowledge to be more accessible to non-specialists in academia and broader society. Why should economists be interested in this? An important reason is that economists can empower ordinary members of society. Economics has greater power than any other discipline in influencing fiscal and monetary policy in nations. The problem is that ordinary citizens vote for elected officials based on platforms that assume a particular economic position, and they must do this without having even a rudimentary understanding of basic economic concepts. The optimal situation would be that voters could access material from which they can grasp basic economic principles which will help them identify mere rhetoric and emotional appeal from fact. Even if ordinary citizens cannot grasp the more technical aspects of economic analysis, understanding basic principles will be enough for making better decisions that will affect whole societies.

The first step, then, is to clarify what is economics. According to the American Economics Association, "economics can be defined in a few different ways. It is the study of scarcity, the study of how people use resources and respond to incentives, or the study of decision making."[3] Economics indeed provides us with the tools for understanding the choices that we have under conditions of scarcity as we pursue what we want or need, at any given point in time. It is important to note that this is also how we can understand our recognition of economic value. According to Carl Menger, economic value is the importance that individual goods or quantities of goods attain because we perceive these as causal factors to the satisfaction of our needs in concrete choices.[4] We could say, then, that economics is the study of economic value and this makes the mechanics of how economic value arises central to economic investigations—e.g., the recognition of a need or want, the availability of what we need or want, the consideration of alternatives, the function of incentives in these considerations, the discovery of new needs or wants, and the mechanics of choosing something at the cost of sacrificing something in its stead. However, neither the American Economics Association website, or standard textbooks in economics employed at American universities, introduce economic value explicitly, nor define it.[5] This is surprising since economics is the only discipline that has achieved an elegant presentation of its particular brand of value. And it is most certainly an uncelebrated feat in light of the fact that value is a difficult concept to define and it has escaped definition in various areas of philosophy thus far (ethics, aesthetics, political philosophy, and so on).

We could speculate on the reasons for the absence of an explicit definition of economic value in the teaching tools for economists, and the economics literature more generally. Perhaps it is because the subjectivity of economic value is already assumed in economic theory that it is deemed too obvious, or too unnecessary, to address explicitly. Or, possibly, the unsung importance of economic value is a respectful nod to the influential views by prominent economists who held that economics is a science devoid of values (Friedman, 1953; Samuelson, 1963). Regardless of what is the case, it seems clear that a characteristic of contemporary economics is to play down its own value-based foundation (Ferraro, et al., 2005; Dierksmeier, 2011; Zúñiga y Postigo, 2017; Racko, 2019).

Although the separation of economics from its philosophical foundation has raised problems that have been addressed in the literature (Seligman, 1969; Sen, 1973; Mirowski, 1989; Buchanan, 1997), the goal of this paper is to focus more narrowly on economic value—its subjectivity and the implication that it has on other economic phenomena such as money. Since the terrain for this paper is at the disciplinary borderlines of economics and philosophy, we are immediately confronted with the matter of specialized language. In order to avoid this obstacle, the only technical term in philosophy that we shall employ here is "ontology." In the "Background" section following immediately, we shall endeavor to clarify its meaning and applications. In the subsequent section titled "Three Insights from Ontology," we shall proceed with the arguments for what we propose ontology can offer to economics.

Background

Let us, then, proceed by introducing ontology and describing how it functions as a method of analysis. Ontology is the branch of philosophy that is concerned with the description of a domain, the objects in such a domain, and the relations that exist among these objects. Economics is one such domain that enjoys a complex ontology, not merely because of its dynamic processes of production, allocation, and distribution but, principally because its objects are social objects.

We are going to present a distinction among a few types of objects in what follows because the social world is complex. One of the tasks of social ontology—which is a branch of ontology—is to distinguish the different kinds of objects that are part of our human social world. Social objects are objects that are constituted by beliefs attached to physical things. This may sound odd at first but as human beings we are all familiar with these even if we haven't thought of these as such. Let us set aside economics for a moment and consider "justice."

We are familiar with the term "justice" if at the very least for pointing out to others (one's parents, spouse, friends, teachers, or colleagues) whenever we find a situation that is unjust. If we were presenting an ontology of law, we would include "justice" as an object in this domain. What kind of object is "justice"? We are not seeking definitions here but our natural intuitions about this object. So, let's just think of "justice" right now and consider what is the referent for this thought. Is it a physical thing in the world? Intuitively, justice is not a physical thing like mountains and trees, so it is clear that justice does not exist independently of human beings and our beliefs about what is justice. In this sense, we *could* say that justice is an ideal object, that is, an object that exists only in idea, just like unicorns do.

However, there is a difference between unicorns and justice. The difference is that we will never find a real unicorn in ordinary human experience. We can think of unicorns and this gives them an ideal existence, but not a real existence. In contrast, we encounter "justice" in ordinary human experience. We do this whenever we recognize that our beliefs about justice—however vague these beliefs may be—are realized in concrete, physical things in the world. And it is from our encounters of these instances of justice that we may draw our understanding of it, even when we encounter the absence of justice. The more we interact with others, the more our understanding of justice becomes more defined in our minds. An instance of justice could be a handshake confirming an agreement accepted by both parties because each believes that he or she is both contributing and receiving a fair share in the exchange. Another instance of justice could be a document such as The Declaration of Independence of the United States. In both instances, justice is not reducible to the physical aspects of the instances—i.e., the act of shaking another person's hand, or the parchment of paper on which The Declaration of Independence was written—but, rather, it is an un-severable combination of beliefs and physical things. This is the nature of a social object and, accordingly, justice is a social object. But keep in mind that social objects are formed spontaneously from our interactions with others. In other words, justice is not what we have written in law books. Rather, law books are merely an attempt to formalize what we have understood to be justice in our interactions with others. Law books are thus not social objects but another kind of objects: artefacts.

Let us, then, turn to artefacts. There may be physical things to which we may not consciously attach any particular beliefs, such as walls or chairs. Nonetheless, the fact remains that these physical things have a particular function. Walls protect our living spaces, and we employ chairs for sitting. Even when we do not think about it consciously, we create artefacts even if temporally. Suppose that we are hiking and find the need to rest. We will probably look for a ledge on the path or a large rock in order for it to serve the same purpose as a chair. When we attach to the ledge or the rock the function that we otherwise attribute to chairs, we have created an artefact. Neither the ledge, nor the rock, will cease to have their physical attributes but for that moment in which either serves as a place to sit, then they have become artefacts. Hence, artefacts are things that we create, and our act of creation may be as undisruptive as finding the right side of a rock to sit on, to building bridges and cities. Artefacts are objects that we design for a particular use or function. Houses, cars, computers, sofas, beds, are all examples of artefacts.

Let us sum up what we know thus far. We know that there are social objects which are constituted by physical things to which we attach particular beliefs, and that these objects arise spontaneously in human action. And we know that there are artefacts, which are objects that we create deliberately to serve a particular purpose. Having made this summation, we are ready to move to a more complex object, one constituted by social objects that inhere not merely in any particular physical basis but in artefacts. This is the case of money, which is a social object that inheres in what we know as currencies, which are artefacts since they are create means for exchanging money. Money is thus instantiated in currencies, which are constituted in our ordinary experience by the bills and coins that are part of a formal monetary system in a nation. Money is not an artefact because it is not a deliberate human creation. Rather, money has emerged spontaneously in human interaction as part of the belief that something can be employed as a medium of exchange. In the same way that justice is instantiated in a handshake or a document, the belief that some physical thing serves as a medium of exchange makes that thing money. Historically, money has taken many forms, from shells, gold pieces, and other physical things in the world. In contrast, currencies have been deliberately designed to serve the function of a medium of exchange. Hence, money can be instantiated in an artefact such as a dollar bill because we believe that that piece of paper can be used in an exchange. The moment we cease to believe this, as it has happened historically with extinct currencies, the dollar bill would be simply a historical piece of paper too. Hence, while money is a social object, the dollar bill is an artefact, but the former inheres in the latter whenever individuals hold the belief that the dollar bill is money.

Money is thus one object in an ontology of economics that we will address in the section that follows. Let us now consider two others: exchange and economic value.[6] Suppose that we hear news reports about a rise in the exchange rate of the dollar. The term "exchange" in this context refers to the belief that we will trade something we deem of less economic value for something of more economic value to us, and this belief is attached to the actual transaction of trading one thing for another. In other words, when a person is willing to pay for some thing, the person believes that the foregone opportunity cost of the best alternative use of that money is less than the value of the thing being acquired. Accordingly, one of the reasons for a rise in the exchange rate of a currency is when there is an increase in the demand for that currency. In other words, other currencies are being exchanged for dollars and, thereby, this reflects a rise in the economic value of the dollar. Economic growth, financial stability, and trust in a nation's leadership, are some of the factors that lead individuals to form beliefs about the economic value of a particular currency. But this can change at any time. Economic value is thus subjective because it depends on the beliefs that people have about some good and the causal relation to the satisfaction of a need or want at a particular point in time.

In the foregoing, we have introduced the descriptive nature of ontology, described three kinds objects, and presented examples of instances of these objects and some of the possible relations among them. This is intended to be only a brief sketch of the nature of some of the objects in the ontology of economics in order to show the descriptive power of ontology to make complex relations simpler to understand. Armed with these tools, we can now proceed with the further development and application of these tools.

Although at first sight it might appear trivial and perhaps unproductive for economists to attempt to slice known objects in economic theory for a closer analysis of their structure and relations, ontology offers an important advantage for economists. It serves as a tool for meta-analysis. As such, ontology can help settle the truth or falsity of certain claims motivated by subjective preferences and by virtue of which are seen as non-falsifiable. In other words, ontology can show that even a subjective valuation can be false, despite the fact that preferences are subjective. In what follows, we shall explain how this is the case, and present three insights from ontology that may open the door to interesting collaboration between economists and ontologists.

THREE INSIGHTS FROM ONTOLOGY

Subjectivity and Economic Value

The received understanding of economic value is that it is subjective. However, as pointed out in the foregoing, value phenomena have been treated in the same way as the experience of pain: the agent knows that he or she values something, but economic value is not observable, measurable, or disputable by any third party.

This has fueled the assumption that because economic value is not intrinsic in things, then economic value must be merely reducible to the mind. This would mean that agents are never wrong in their value judgments. However, this assertion is problematic because it doesn't correspond to real instances in which we discover that our economic valuation was indeed wrong.

Suppose that a working mother orders garments online for her children based on the expectations formed by the description and images provided on the merchant's website. Further suppose that when she receives the garments, she discovers that the actual garments do not meet her expectations. At that moment, the garment ceases to have value for her. We have all experienced similar instances in which things acquire value to us but then they lose their value shortly thereafter. This is the case of food. We value it when we are hungry, but it loses its value to us once we are full. But there is a distinction between, on the one hand, a thing ceasing to have value because our needs have been met and, on the other, to a thing ceasing to have value because it has not met our expectations in the first place. The latter is the case of unmet expectations presented in the preceding illustration.

If we examine the structure of the Mengerian definition of economic value, then to say that economic value is subjective does not only refer to the value judgment by an economic agent. It also refers to the facts of the object to which the judgment is directed. This distinction has also been presented in philosophy by John Searle (1995) as two senses of subjective: the epistemic sense and the ontological sense of subjective. The epistemic sense of subjective refers to judgments whose truth or falsity depend on the subject's attitudes, feelings, preferences, points of view. For example, if a food expert states that French food is the finest cuisine in the world, the truth or falsity of this judgment could not be settled by facts for it is a matter of taste and preference. There is also the ontological sense of subjective which refers to judgments about facts. If the same food expert claims that French cuisine predates Chinese cuisine, the truth or falsity of this claim can be settled by facts. If we bring Menger and Searle together, then we would have the following description:

A judgment of economic value has an epistemic sense of subjective that, by definition, is dependent on the subject's preferences. But a judgment of economic value also has an ontological sense insofar as the judgment refers to facts in the world. Hence, there are facts that can settle the truth or falsity of an economic value judgment.

This more robust value analysis will account for instances such as the working mother in our illustration above whose expectations were not met by the actual things she ordered. Her response is not merely a subjective matter, for the thing that is valued must meet the expectation created by the description and photographic depiction of the garments. If, for example, the description is that the garments are made of silk but they are made, instead, of satin, then this discrepancy can settle the truth of her claim that the garments are not as presented.

Let us consider another example: Jacob is feeling hungry so he considers the alternatives at his disposal at the restaurant where he is having lunch. He can choose from pizza, a hamburger, or a hot dog. Although Jacob likes all of these, he has a particular desire for the hamburger because he has been thinking of having a hamburger all morning and, at this time, Jacob believes that the hamburger is the best option to satisfy his appetite at that moment. This is, of course, a subjective judgment of value. But Jacob's judgment is also about facts in the world, such as the hamburger from a particular restaurant, with a particular preparation performed at that restaurant, at a particular price, and with a particular description. Jacob thus makes his judgment in favor of this particular hamburger based on these facts presented to him about this hamburger and on this basis he will form certain expectations about the hamburger. The two senses of subjective in this act of economic valuation can be illustrated as follows:

1. The evaluation of an object perceived by an individual as having a causal connection with the satisfaction of an urgent need.
2. The subject-dependent status of objects in their role as economic goods.

Notice that after eating the hamburger, the idea of the hamburger's value will cease in Jacob's estimation. Accordingly, if Jacob is presented with a second hamburger, this will not have the same value as the first one did, and it is more likely that the second hamburger will not hold any value at all because Jacob might feel already satiated. Jacob might even associate a disvalue to the second hamburger, if the thought of eating another hamburger is disagreeable.

Fig. 1 illustrates an epistemic sense of 'subjective' because it provides an account of choice given the constraint of limited resources despite unlimited wants. Hence, Fig. 1 depicts Jacob's subjective preference at the time of his choice. Fig. 2 presents the ontological sense of subjective since it is based on the facts that pertain to that particular choice and the economic character that inhered in Jacob's choice in light of his expectations based on such facts.

We know that not every hamburger is delicious even if it appears delicious. Appearances cannot reveal to us the facts that are not visible in unaided visual perception such as, say for example, the presence of e-coli in the hamburger. We

Figure 1. The process of choice

Figure 2. The process of valuing

will not know from appearances alone whether our expectations will be actually met. It is not until we make the choice and are able to test the valued object against our expectations that the value of the chosen object comes into its full realization. Above all, the awareness that subjectivism in valuations is not equivalent to perfect choices every time can allow economists to account for the correspondence between our perceptions and facts in order to arrive at either confirmations of right choices or explanations of wrong ones.

Menger (1976) draws this elegant ontology of valuing acts from his discovery of marginal utility. Economic value is, thus, subjective not merely because people prefer whatever they prefer. Rather, economic value is subjective because things that acquire economic value to us are dependent on the relation between a want and the thing actually satisfying that want. By virtue of being chosen, value inheres in the chosen thing (albeit temporarily) thus changing the character of a good to an object of economic value.[7]

The significance of Menger's contribution lies in the fine-grained description of what we are calling here "social objects." While most accounts of value tend to reduce value either to the mind or to some intrinsic property of things, Menger's description helps us in realizing that some social phenomena is composed of varying combinations of beliefs and entities, judgments and facts, preferences and matter. He then provided a description of exact laws of value phenomena.[8] In order to achieve such an account of value, our descriptions must be grounded on the experience of the valuing individual.

Not all Value is Economic Value

A second important insight from ontology is the distinction that economic value has from other kinds of value. Indeed, not all value phenomena are the same, and not all value is reducible to economic value. Consider the following comparison. In human experience, sand is a source of pleasure for many people because of the way it feels under bare feet at the beach. Unlike the case of economic value, this experience has a different value quality for it is characterized by *disinterestedness*. This means that the experience of value is not tied with the possession, consumption, or satisfaction of the valued thing in order for the value to be fully realized. Philosopher Immanuel Kant clarified that in aesthetic judgments, the satisfaction obtained from what is perceived as beautiful has an entirely disinterested character.[9] Think, for example, of the attitude we have when perceiving a sunset, or beautiful music. Kant explained that the satisfaction derived from beauty finds no grounds in the judging subject's situation or private conditions. An agent might be in the midst of securing lunch and yet, a beautiful sight will capture the agent's full attention even if this distracts the present economic judgment directed at making a choice for lunch. Kant's explanation of disinterested judgment allows us to grasp the distinction between judgments which consider a personal gain—as is the case with economic judgments—and those which are not bound up with concepts, feelings, or deliberations unique to the judging subject given particular circumstances.

Returning to our sand example, then, we value beach sand for its own sake in the same way that we may value the sight of fields of lavender. The grasping of aesthetic value in things does not embody the means for another end. Rather, the grasping *is* the end in itself. The delight of feeling sand on bare feet at the beach, the spectacular colors of a sunset, and the richness of purple in vast fields of lavender, are all instances of aesthetic experiences and each brings forth the recognition of the intrinsic intelligibility of the aesthetic value of the object. And aesthetic experiences capture our attention and emotions in a way that does not move us to attempt to possess the object of our aesthetic experience, but merely to grasp the aesthetic experience that the object affords us. Beach sand is then, in this sense, an aesthetic object because it is the object of an aesthetic experience.

It is important to recognize, however, that sand does not have an intrinsic property that makes it a source of pleasure to bare feet. Consider the contrast of the experience of beach sand to the experience of desert sand. Each experience has qualitative difference. Desert sand might be perceived as a negative experience because it hinders quick movement, and it often lays barren in a great expanse. Hence, rather than feeling soothed by the sand in a desert, a person might feel distress at the thought of not finding a way out of the desert, at least not quickly enough to survive. Although both experiences are aesthetic in nature, the experience of beach sand is characterized by pleasure while the experience of desert sand presented here can be characterized by pleasure in certain circumstances (if the desert is small and well marked for tourism) but it can also be characterized by distress and fear in other circumstances (in the midst of the Sahara, for example).

Let us now contrast the aesthetic experiences of sand that we have examined to the judgment of sand as a commodity instead of an economic good or a bad. Owing to its silica content, sand has been deployed for the production of computer components. Perceived in this way, sand takes the character of a commodity, which makes it a valuable raw material for agents in the computer manufacturing industry. The economic value that inheres in sand, qua commodity, is different than the aesthetic value that inheres in sand in aesthetic experiences of beach sand. These differences shed light on the qualitative differences in the experiences of economic value and aesthetic value. But there are many other sorts of values that exist which are also qualitatively different from economic value.

Take moral value, for example. The experience of moral value also has the character of disinterestedness but the quality of the experience is not aesthetic even though acting virtuously can lead to the experience of pleasure. However, the fundamental character of moral value is not revealed in our feeling good but, rather, in targeting the moral good. The examination then becomes a matter of identifying the kind of moral good that is the best guide for our morally-relevant actions. Each ethical theory that we find in philosophy has a unique moral good that underlies its practical rules or reasoning.

Utilitarians, for example, accept the consequences of any act as morally good if it brings about benefits to the majority of those affected by the act. A utilitarian argument, for example, could be useful to justify the death penalty precisely because even though the death penalty involves the killing of a person, the consequences of this act are deemed to be beneficial to most in society. The beneficial consequences could be that the members of society feel safer by eliminating a criminal and that this punishment does not impose an incremental cost to society for the length of the natural life of the criminal had the criminal been allowed to remain in prison for life. But there is vast disagreement about what is the moral good, so not all will accept the utilitarian justification for the death penalty.

The chief point that I would like to draw from the comparisons we have presented of three different kinds of values—economic, aesthetic, and moral values—is that economic value is but one kind of value and it has a unique nature, quality and boundaries that distinguish it. Perhaps the only unifying quality between economic value and all other kinds of values is that knowledge or beliefs play a central role, particularly in demarcating boundaries (Hayek, 1945). But the knowledge or beliefs that pertain to each kind of value are quite different.

Whenever more than one kind of value inheres in a single object, then the examination becomes even more formidable. Suppose we are examining the value phenomena of a cryptocurrency. What can be done if this object is under scrutiny for the economic analysis of a public policy, and it conflicts with another kind of value, such as moral value? In these cases, the economic analysis will target the phenomena in its relevant economic sphere. But moral valuations have not escaped economic recommendations regarding an issue of public policy. Since the New Deal, for example, antitrust discussions have involved considerations such as "ensuring all producers a fair opportunity to compete, preventing the exploitation of consumers and farmers, and limiting the political power of large firms."[10] The language of fairness, exploitation, and power is clearly directed at making a moral point. Even after the Chicago School's revolution in the 1980s against involving political or social goals in economic analysis, the politics of liberty redirected the focus to production efficiency by favoring competition as the moral effort to pursue. Staying within one's disciplinary boundaries is indeed not easy, especially on matters of value, not even for economists who see economics as a science devoid of any value. Since economics engages matters of public policy which often have different values interwoven in the narrative, distinguishing economic recommendations from moral recommendations that are difficult to extricate from the analysis can be a tall order.

Ontology can help economists navigate the value geography more easily, especially when certain conditions serve as boundary markers. Consider the following set of conditions drawn from Menger's investigations[11]:

1. Economic value is the significance attached to a good resulting from a conceptualization of the good in terms of a desired end. Such a conceptualization can be characterized as an interested evaluation since the agent perceives a causal connection between the possession of the good and the fulfillment of an end.
2. Economic value is the result of the recognition of a perceived utility stemming from concrete quantities of a good in relation to an end.
3. Economic value instantiates the feature of scarcity in a good on the basis of the agent's perceived lack of concrete quantities of such a good in relation to the fulfillment of his total utility.
4. Economic value has a dependence relation between the assigned importance to any one need or want and the relative importance of other needs or wants.
5. Economic value has a dependence relation between the relative importance of any need or want and the agent's overall degree of fullest satisfaction expected.
6. Economic value has a dependence relation between the importance of higher-order goods and the importance of first-order goods.
7. Economic value has a dependence relation between the future value of things and the present value of things.
8. The nature of the significance attached to a good varies according to the relation between wants and things. Hence, the putative significance of a good in a judging subjects mind is transitory since such significance arises and disappears as wants arise and disappear.
9. The economic value of the services of particular goods such as land, capital, and labor are subject to the same laws of value, outlined above, as for any other economic good.

The above conditions can be useful in value-diverse interdisciplinary examinations in academic or public policy circles.

Money is Not Exclusively Institutional

Let us now turn our examination to money. In economics, money is a domain that contains a few categories such as M1, M2, and M3. Although what belongs in each category, or the range of categories might vary slightly across practices, the objects that constitute each are roughly the same.[12] The M1 category is the one we are most familiar with in our ordinary experience: physical currency in the form of bills and coins. M1 also includes those forms of money that are easily converted into physical currency, such as travelers checks, demand deposits, deposits against which checks can be written, and NOW accounts. M1 is thus known as narrow money. Now, if to M1 we add savings accounts, short-term time deposits under $100,000, balances in retail money market mutual funds, 24-hour money market funds, we obtain M2. In the US, M3 is the aggregate of M2 plus long-term large denomination time deposits, balances in institutional money funds, money market funds with more than 24-hour maturity, repurchase liabilities issued by repository institutions, and Eurodollars held by residents of the United States at foreign branches of American banks. In the past, M3 has been the measure of money supply but this, too, has changed to the M2 measure. In the United Kingdom, there is an additional category: M4, and it is similar to the M3 measure of broad money in other countries, and it is constituted by M2 plus other deposits with an original maturity of up to five years, other claims on financial institutions such as repos and bank acceptances, debt instruments issued by financial institutions including commercial paper and bonds with a maturity of up to five years. This typology of money aids the role of central banks of measuring the money supply and taking adequate monetary policy measures.

The above typology of money may seem sufficiently clear for the meta-monetary decisions that central banks take, but how is it reconcilable with the common-sense understanding of money as the ultimate medium for exchange that ordinary users have? In the United States, for example, credit cards are often employed to pay for consumption goods on a regular basis. As such, credit cards may feel, mistakenly, like money to ordinary users. The description of money in economics offers a good clarification why this is a mistaken belief. First, credit cards do not fall under M1 or M2 and, thus, they are not part of the money supply. Second, and more importantly, although credit cards can be used to acquire goods and services, credit cards are nothing more than an obligation to pay, sometimes with accrued interest. Accordingly, an obligation (aka debt) cannot be measured in the money supply calculations despite their being part of the banks' lending and relending operations. This is a clear and useful explanation. However, can the M-typology of money offer an explanatory apparatus that extends beyond the institutional sphere of centrally-controlled money?

In ordinary transactions, people's understanding of money is broader than the typology of institutionalized money since alternatives to institutionalized money are employed concurrently with institutionalized money. Cigarettes, for example, have emerged as a medium of exchange in situations in which currency cannot be employed, such as prisons or drug rehabilitation centers. But alternatives to institutionalized money are also employed in non-restricted realms of life. Consider, for instance, gold, baseball cards, stamps, or art, to name a few. Until recently, informal money has not been a concern for economists since informal money has not had an effect on monetary policy. But the emergence of cryptocurrencies has been recognized as a concern for central banks.[13]

Anything that can serve as money in a given exchange—whether it is a physical thing as a diamond bracelet or a non-physical thing such as my rights to purchase a property—can be collectively accepted as money if this corresponds to (or gives rise to) collective beliefs. And this value phenomena continues to occur even if the thing that is accepted as money ceases to be accepted as money, and the beliefs are then transferred to some other thing that is accepted as money in its stead. This fungibility confirms that social objects are things constituted by beliefs upon a physical basis, and the physical basis can change. Understanding this kind of existence and relations among objects in social reality is essential for their adequate description.

In this light, we can obtain a finer grained picture of the phenomenon of money. Although money is a medium of exchange, it is not the result of design, even if it serves a purpose. Accordingly, money is not an artifact. Although money can take the form of an institutionalized object such as units of a particular currency, money is not reducible to its institutionalized form. Rather, money emerges spontaneously in all sorts of other forms even nowadays in which most nations issue institutionalized currency.

CONCLUSION

Why should these fine-grained ontological examinations matter to economics? The most practical answer is that ontology offers a scientific check in the examination of epistemological questions regarding central economic objects such as value, and ubiquitous economic objects such as money. The contributions of economics with regard to the phenomena of choice and valuation under conditions of scarcity are vast, admirable, and scientifically sound. Unfortunately, these are often obscured not only by mathematics in economics that makes it inaccessible to most in academia and society at large, but also by cultural memes that misrepresent economics in a narrow and unflattering light. For example, Adam Smith's magnificent elucidation of the notion of self-interest has been reduced to the caricature of greedy entrepreneurs in political rhetoric, and popular films. To make matters worse, some economists might have inadvertently fueled this misunderstanding. Most notably, George Stigler, characterized the Wealth of Nations as "a stupendous palace erected upon the granite of self-interest," although Smith never states that self-interest is the only motivation for human action.[14] Other interpretations of Smith that depict the Wealth of Nations as a departure from his moral examinations in his Theory of Moral Sentiments, have further fueled the conflation of self-interest with selfishness or greed.

Recent attention has been directed at the phenomenon of collective intentionality, which refers to those acts in which a group of people are directed to the same object and hold the same beliefs about it and act accordingly as if they were all of the same mind about it. Economic concepts have been prominently employed in these investigations, and economists should be a part of the discussion too (Hédoin, 2003; Bardsley, 2007; Papadopoulous, 2015). Regardless of the direction of the many strands that economic research may take, the examination of choice in conditions of scarcity, and the economic value that this reveals is fundamental in economics and distinguish it from any other discipline. Economics is indeed inextricably bound up with philosophy, and this marriage can be very fruitful.

REFERENCES

Baker, J. (2013). Economics and Politics: Perspectives on the Goals and Future of Antitrust. *Fordham Law Review, 81*(5), 2175–2196.

Bardsley, N. (2007). On Collective Intentions: Collective Action in Economics and Philosophy. *Synthese, 157*(2), 141–159. doi:10.100711229-006-9034-z

Buchanan, J. M. (1997). *Has Economics Lost Its Way? Reflections on the Economists' Enterprise at Century's End.* Fairfax, VA: Institute for Humane Studies.

Coase, R. H. (1976). Adam Smith's View of Man. *The Journal of Law & Economics, 19*(3), 529–546.

Crespo, R. F. (2006). The ontology of 'the economic': An Aristotelian Perspective. *Cambridge Journal of Economics, 30*(5), 767–781. doi:10.1093/cje/bei106

Dierksmeier, C. (2011). The freedom-responsibility nexus in management philosophy and business ethics. *Journal of Business Ethics, 101*(4), 263–283. doi:10.100710551-010-0721-9

Elster, J. (1989). *Nuts and Bolts for the Social Sciences.* Cambridge University Press. doi:10.1017/CBO9780511812255

Ferraro, F., Pfeffer, J., & Sutton, R. I. (2005). Economics language and assumptions: How theories can become self-fulfilling. *Academy of Management Review, 30*(1), 8–24. doi:10.5465/amr.2005.15281412

Hausman, D. M. (1999). Ontology and Methodology in Economics. *Economics and Philosophy, 15*(2), 283–288. doi:10.1017/S0266267100004028

Hayek, F. A. (1945). The Use of Knowledge in Society. *The American Economic Review, 25*(4), 519–530.

Hédoin, C. (2003). Collective Intentionality in Economics: Making Searle's Theory of Institutional Facts Relevant for Game Theory. *Erasmus Journal for Philosophy and Economics, 6*(1), 1–27. doi:10.23941/ejpe.v6i1.117

Kant, I. (1914). *Critique of Judgment* (J. H. Bernard, Trans.). London: McMillan. (Original work published 1892)

Lawson, T. (1994). A Realist Theory for Economics. In R. E. Backhouse (Ed.), *New Directions in Economic Methodology* (pp. 257–285). doi:10.4324/9780203204085.ch13

Mäki, U. (Ed.). (2001). *The Economic World View: Studies in the Ontology of Economics*. Cambridge University Press. doi:10.1017/CBO9780511752049

Menger, C. (1976). *Principles of Economics*. New York: New York University Press. (Original work published 1871)

Papadopoulous, G. (2015). Collective Intentionality and the State Theory of Money. *Erasmus Journal for Philosophy and Economics*, *8*(2), 1–20. doi:10.23941/ejpe.v8i2.198

Racko, G. (2019). The Values of Economics. *Journal of Business Ethics*, *154*(1), 35–48. doi:10.100710551-017-3442-5

Searle, J. (1995). *The Construction of Social Reality*. New York: The Free Press.

Seligman, B. B. (1969). The Impact of Positivism in Economic Thought. *History of Political Economy*, *1*(2), 256–278. doi:10.1215/00182702-1-2-256

Sen, A. (1989). Behavior and the Concept of Preference. *Economica*, *40*(159), 241–259. doi:10.2307/2552796

Smith, B. (1990). Aristotle, Menger, Mises: An Essay in the Metaphysics of Economics. *History of Political Economy*, *22*, 263–288.

Smith, V. (2013). Adam Smith: From Propriety and Sentiments to Property and Wealth. *The Forum for Social Economics*, *42*(4), 283–297. doi:10.1080/07360932.2013.798241

Zúñiga y Postigo, G. (1999). An Ontology of Economic Objects. *American Journal of Economics and Sociology*, *58*(2), 299–312. doi:10.1111/j.1536-7150.1998.tb03474.x

Zúñiga y Postigo, G. (2000). *A General Theory of Value: Axiology in the Central European Philosophical Tradition* [Doctoral dissertation]. University at Buffalo, Buffalo, New York

Zúñiga y Postigo, G. (2017). On the Transformation of Economic Value. *Axiomathes*, *27*(5), 561–576.

KEY TERMS AND DEFINITIONS

Economic Objects: These are the objects that fall under classifications that define the fundamental denizens of economics, such as good, price, money, commodity, value, exchange.

Economic Value: The causal connection that is perceived by an agent between a thing and the satisfaction of his or her present and urgent need.

Epistemic: Refers to the real of knowledge and justified belief known in philosophy as epistemology. Epistemology is concerned with the necessary and sufficient conditions of knowledge, its sources, its limits, theories of truth, what constitutes a justified belief, and whether the justification should be internal or external to the mind. and the truth conditions for propositions that represent.

Money: (a) In macroeconomics, money has been understood in terms of a classification of institutionalized currency that starts from the most liquid forms (M1) to broad money (M2, M3, or M4, depending on the practice) for the purposes of measuring the money supply for monetary policy considerations. (b) In economics and common-sense knowledge by ordinary users, money is the most efficient medium for exchange. In its institutionalized form, money is understood as being equivalent to the currency in a nation. More generally, money has taken many forms from shells, cigarettes, stamps, baseball cards, etc., and, more recently, cryptocurrencies.

Ontology: Ontology is the branch of philosophy that is concerned with the description of a domain, the objects in such a domain, and their relations that exist among these objects.

Philosophy: An activity of clarifying ideas—e.g., distinguishing an object, term, or idea from its closest conceptual neighbors, discovering its relevant domain(s) and boundaries, and advancing descriptions or definitions for it. In the course of roughly three millennia, this activity has resulted in the formation of well-defined bodies of knowledge that have given rise to disciplines in academia. Less formally, the activity of clarifying ideas assists individuals in self-reflection, character improvement, greater awareness of their moral agency, identifying goals, pursuing them, and seeking happiness.

Social Objects: Objects that come into being by spontaneous orders from human interactions that are not the result of human design or deliberation. They are constituted by beliefs that typically have a physical basis. Concepts, rules, and physical things, for example, can all be social objects.

Subjective: (a) The epistemic sense of subjective refers to an agent's judgments whose truth or falsity depends on his or her attitudes, feelings, beliefs, points of view. For example, "I like chocolate" is a subjective judgment. As such, subjective judgments are reducible to the mind. (b) The ontological sense of subjective refers to judgments about facts in the world that can settle the truth or falsity of such judgments. For example, "I like Belgian chocolate" is a judgment that refers to the fact that there is such a thing as Belgian chocolate, and these facts can settle the truth of the kind of chocolate that I like. However, I if say "I like Antarctican chocolate," then this judgment has no correspondence with a fact in the world since there isn't such a thing as chocolate grown or made in Antarctica.

ENDNOTES

1 Examinations of these contributions can be found in Smith, B. (1990), "Aristotle, Menger, Mises: An Essay in the Metaphysics in Economics;" Crespo, R. F. (2006), "The ontology of 'the economic': an Aristotelian Perspective."

2 See, for example, Lawson, T. (1994), "A Realist Theory for Economics;" Hausman, D.M. (1999), "Ontology and Methodology in Economics;" Zúñiga y Postigo, G. (1999), "An Ontology of Economic Objects;" Mäki, U. (2001), "Economic Ontology: What? Why? How?" in *The Economic World View: Studies in the Ontology of Economics.*

3 Under the tab titled "What is Economics?" in the American Economics Association website (https://www.aeaweb.org/resources/students/what-is-economics).

4 Carl Menger (1976), *Principles of Economics*, 115-116.

5 See, for example, *Microeconomics*, 9th ed., Pyndick R S and Rubinfeld D L (2018), Pearson; *Intermediate Economics: A Modern Approach*, 8th ed., Varian H (2010), Norton W.W.; *A Course in Microeconomic Theory*, Kreps M E (1990), Princeton University Press; and *Principles of Economics*, Frank, R (2008), McGraw-Hill.

6 The term "value" is qualified here because, arguable, there are other kinds of value—such as moral value or aesthetic value—that have a different nature than economic value. This argument has been advanced in G. Zúñiga y Postigo (2000), "A General Theory of Value: Axiology in the Central European Philosophical Tradition."

7 The same could apply to a bad. For example, garbage could be safely classified as a bad unless garbage is the prime material for an innovative garbage disposal mechanism that converts it into a productive composite.

8 See "An Ontology of Economic Objects," Gloria Zúñiga y Postigo (1999).

9 Immanuel Kant, *Critique of Judgment* (1968), pp. 38-46.

10 See Jonathan Baker, "Economics and Politics: Perspectives on the Goals and Future of Antitrust," p. 2182.

11 In Gloria Zúñiga y Postigo (1999), "An Ontology of Economic Objects"), p. 306.

12 We shall be using here the definitions according to the Federal Reserve Bank of New York. See "The Money Supply," Federal Reserve Bank of New York, retrieved from https://www.newyorkfed.org/aboutthefed/fedpoint/fed49.html

13 Speaking at the Financial Stability and Fintech Conference in 2017, Randal Quarles (U.S. Reserve Bank Vice-Chairman) asserted that decentralized currencies could have spillover effects on the broader financial system (https://www.bloomberg.com/news/articles/2017-11-30/guess-who-s-not-joining-bitcoin-revolution-fed-s-bank-watchdog). In 2018, Agustin Carstens (head of Bank for International Settlements) warned that cryptocurrencies could threatened financial stability (https://www.wsj.com/articles/cryptocurrencies-could-threaten-financial-stability-says-head-of-bis-1517911251).

14 George Stigler (1971), "Smith's Travels on the Ship of State," *History of Political Economy*, 3 (2): 265. Of course, more sober commentaries have been advanced since then. R. H. Coase (1976, 529) explained that "Self-interest is certainly, in Adam Smith's view, a powerful motive in human behavior, but it is by no means the only motive." Jon Elster (1989, 54) observed that "the assumption that all behavior is selfish is the most parsimonious that we can make...[and] we cannot conclude that selfishness is the more widespread motivation... [because] the world is messy, and the most parsimonious explanation is wrong." Vernon Smith (2013, 285) also recognized the magnification of self-interest among the commentators when he writes, "There is a vulgar representation of Adam Smith as championing the unconstrained pursuit of self-love to the exclusion of other values by humans..."

Chapter 12
Challenges of Developing Countries in Imitating Technological Progress

Ikbal Maulana
https://orcid.org/0000-0002-3727-3809
Indonesian Institute of Sciences (LIPI), Indonesia

ABSTRACT

Technological progress has become an important characteristics of economic progress. The most economically developed nations are also the most technologically advanced ones, that is, the ones that not only make a proper and innovative utilization of technology, but also develop it on their own. Newly developed countries, such as South Korea and China, have economically surpassed many Western countries, because they can catch up and surpass the technological capability of the latter. However, the technological progress of one country cannot be just imitated by another. Technological development is much more than just allocating a large budget for research and development. It involves and transform a heterogeneous network of actors, and hence requires a complex set of institutions and governance that enable the network to upgrade their collective capabilities.

DOI: 10.4018/978-1-7998-1037-7.ch012

INTRODUCTION

Technology and society are inseparable, they both coevolve and constitute each other. Human civilization grows with the development of technology, which they use to solve problems or overcome their limitations. Technology extends our body and cognition (McLuhan, 1994), enabling us to do many things that would be otherwise impossible. Without technology, only relying on our muscles and mind, we would be not too different from other species. Therefore, "It is easy to imagine human beings as pre-literate, but it is difficult to imagine them as pre-technological" (Nye, 2006, p. 5).

Since the industrial revolution, or more precisely since the capitalist system had become dominant in the Western world, technology development and diffusion have intensified. Under this system technological capabilities have become the determining factor of survival and success for both companies and countries. As the difference of technological capabilities among countries widen significantly, their inequality also increases greatly (North, 2005). The most economically developed nations are also the most technologically advanced ones, that is, the ones that not only make a proper and innovative utilization of technology, but also develop it on their own. Newly developed countries, such as South Korea and China, have economically surpassed many Western countries, because they can catch up and surpass the technological capabilities of the latter.

Many developing countries want to catch up with the advanced ones. Experts from the developed countries have always been keen to advise developing countries to achieve what the former have achieved for a long time. They regard their success as an irrefutable proof of their developmental prescriptions. Not only developing countries have been encouraged, but also being pressured by the developed world and the international development policy establishment to adopt free market economy, through implementing a set of "good policies" and establishing "good institutions" to foster their economic development (Chang, 2002). In technological capability development, the prescriptions includes inviting foreign direct investment (FDI) to establish manufacturing industries; establishing science and technology (S&T) institutions as those in developed countries; and establishing engineering higher education institutions.

Despite the long-term involvement of Western experts in advising developing countries as well as persistent pressures on the latter to liberalize their economy, most of them remain economically and technologically lagging behind. It is either they cannot implement the Western recommendations, or the Western experts provide wrong prescriptions. The successes of East Asian countries, such as South Korea, Taiwan and, most recently, China, have inspired developing countries to consider another path of development. This path combines the power and stability of state control and the agility of business enterprises. In the early development of technological capability, when market for the technological products do not exist, or competitive technological businesses still have to emerge, what the East Asian countries have done seems to make more sense to developing countries than what have been prescribed by Western countries. Eventually, they soon find out that there is no easy path to progress, even though the path might be believed to be the right one.

This chapter seek to unravel the complexity of imitating the technological progress achieved by other countries by examining the ontological and epistemological aspects of technology. The former addresses the what of technology and the latter addresses how we can understand, develop and utilize the what. Philosophical examination of technology will inform us whether our current policy and other efforts of developing technology do not contradict the nature of the technology and technological knowledge. Misunderstanding the nature of technology and technological knowledge will lead us to strive for the unachievable goals.

WHAT IS TECHNOLOGY?

Being in the world and alive, we are always confronted by the world and our own limitations, and being burdened with needs and driven by desires. Technology helps us to control and exploit the world, overcome our limitations, and satisfy our needs and desires. Drucker (1959), the founding father of the study of management, suggests that the purpose of doing or making technology is to overcome human limitation. Using technology, humans can overcome their poor body insulation, enabling them to expand their habitat to all climate zones. Without gills, fins or wings, human can be at home in the water and in the air. Other species can only adapt to their new environment through long period of genetic mutation, humans can do that within shorter time through technological development and utilization.

As a mortal, we can never fully remove our imperfections. There will always be limitations to overcome, hence, there will always be new technology to develop. Besides that, our needs are not fixed, but continue to change and can be changed. Existing technology can only temporarily satisfy us. After that, we need to be enchanted by new technology, otherwise we will get bored. So, there is a spiral of mutual influences between our needs and technology.

With technology we cannot conquer our own greed. Nevertheless, it makes us increasingly stronger vis-a-vis nature, which leads us to live in the Anthropocene epoch, in which human uses of technology have significant impacts on climate and ecosystem. Many people, especially technologists, believe that the problems caused by technology can be solved by further development of technology. There is always opportunity to further develop technology, albeit through solving problems caused by existing technology.

Technology is technology only if it can be used for practical purposes. Technology does not mean anything in itself, but is only defined in relation to human users who take advantage from it directly or indirectly. A man-made object whose function is not known to some people is not technology to them, even though it is for others. Broken objects for some people, hence no technology for them, may still be useful instruments for others. Therefore, for a technological artifact to be useful, it must be complemented with knowledge of its utilization. Failing to understand this connections leads to the wasting of many technological artifacts being diffused to those who cannot use them properly or at all. Recent technological development has given us increasingly user-friendly instruments into which more operating knowledge that previously had to be mastered by users is embedded. But, human knowledge about its utilization or purposes still determines it as technology.

In addition to artifact and knowledge, activity is another important aspect of technology (Mitcham, 1994). Modern technological artifacts are manufactured as decontextualized and simplified objects, and in the activities of technological utilization these artifacts are being "combined with each other and re-embedded in the natural environment" (Feenberg, 1999, p. 205). Technological artifacts, which Heidegger calls instrument, are used in combination with each other in order to solve practical problems. "Taken strictly, there 'is' no such thing as an equipment. To the Being of any equipment there always belongs a totality of equipment, in which it can be this equipment that it is. Equipment is essentially 'something in-order-to ["etwas um-zu…"]. A totality of equipment is constituted by various ways of the 'in-order-to', such as serviceability, conduciveness, usability, manipulability" (Heidegger, 1962, p. 97). An object as simple as a cup is not used in isolation from other objects. We use a cup to drink coffee. We put it on a table, and sit on a chair while drinking the coffee. And for brewing the coffee, we use a coffee maker, which also needs electricity that is produced by an even more complex technological network.

Regular and repeated activities of using technology will transform the doers (Feenberg, 1999). They will develop familiarity with that technology, and even become experts in that technological utilization. If the activities have economic significance, these will become vocation or profession. Through activities, a technological artifact will be combined with other technological artifacts to make it function properly. Since different artifacts are used or operated by different people in their activities, so each artifact is embedded in a socio-technical ensemble (Bijker, 1995). Putting the artifact into a different socio-technical ensemble may cause it not to function or not to function properly and sustainably, because it does not fit into the targeted ensemble.

For most of human history, prior to the pervasiveness of capitalism, technology was invented to serve existing human needs. Today capitalism has not only created technology, but also the needs for that technology. Many technological objects have been created even before the demands for them exist. When a technological means was developed, technologists might have no clear idea of the ends it will serve. "The relation of means to ends is not unilinear but circular. Familiar ends of long standing may find better satisfaction by new technologies whose genesis they had inspired. But equally-and increasingly typical-new technologies may suggest, create, even impose new ends, never before conceived, simply by offering their feasibility" (Jonas, 1979, p. 35). Businesses do believe that the demands for their technological innovations can be invented, promoted and instilled in consumers' mind.

Technology is not straightforward application of science. It can take advantage of science as well as other knowledge which is not scientifically proven yet. The design of technology is shaped by the problem that it tries to solve, available technological components and tools, and, most of all, the creativity of the human inventors. The creativity also plays a role because the functions of technology are multiple realizable, "the multiple realizability of function means that material cultures often contain several types of things all designed to serve basically the same function" (Preston, 2009, p. 215). For instance, spoons, which are made out of rigid material and take shape as a handle attached to a bowl, have been realized in many different ways. In different places, you can find spoon made from metal, wood, pottery, porcelain, plastic, and so on. And their forms can vary, the bowl may be oval, round or pointed, and the handle can be long or short, flat or bowl, decorated or plain. It is also possible then in one culture people use spoon for one thing, while in another culture people use chopstick.

Existing technology, whose functions currently satisfy consumer needs, sooner or later will be replaced by another technology that functions better. The current globalized capitalist world intensifies competition, which consequently speeds up the replacement of either technological objects or knowledge that underlies all the same functioning objects. This replacement gives consumers new, better or cheaper goods, but may also push companies out of business and workers out of employment. This is the process of creative destruction, "that incessantly revolutionizes the economic structure from within, incessantly destroying the old one, incessantly creating a new one" (Schumpeter, 2003, p. 83).

Severe creative destruction occurs when the so-called disruptive technology starts to displace dominant technology (Christensen, 2000). The established industry is being disrupted and gives the way for a completely new industry. For example, industry that produced camera based on celluloid film has been replaced by the one that produces digital camera. The new industry has different players, and the players from the old replaced industry have to struggle entering into the new one, because even though the technology seems to serve the same function, the underlying knowledge is radically different.

Technological development can be unpredictable, because technology is developed to serve human purposes, which can develop and change. Hence, to come into existence, technological objects have to be made, "they are existentially dependent not merely on some intentional human activities or others, but rather on intentions to create that very kind of object" (Thomasson, 2009, p. 195). Technology development at industry level is often unpredictable, because technologists have limited knowledge about possible technical solutions. They seek to improve their knowledge by doing research and development (R&D), through which they may discover something unexpected and unanticipated. They also have limited knowledge about market preferences, while at the same time these preferences keep shifting. Users also are sources of innovative ideas, either indirectly by complaining about the existing products, or directly by suggesting new features for existing products or demanding totally new products, and some users even modify the products by themselves (von Hippel, 2005). Many technological artifacts are multiple utilizable (Preston, 2009). Sometimes it is intentionally designed to serve multiple purposes. Sometimes users can find new functions unexpected by technologists who design it. For example, a kitchen knife that is designed only to cut vegetable, might be used as screwdriver or to open fish can by creative users.

Even a simple technological artifact cannot be created only by a single intentional individual like a novel or a poem could. In making an artifact we need to apply knowledge and use tools that have been developed by other people. Technology development is both a collective and inter-generational enterprise. Humanity have accumulated knowledge that allows them to continually improve technology or create new invention better than the existing ones. And the new technology is always being developed not only in reference to the existing technology it would replace, but also with the help of other existing technologies. Normally a technological artifact consists of different components, each of which has been produced by other people or companies. "Machines and devices are obviously composite, heterogeneous, and physically localized. Although they point to an end, a use for which they have been conceived, they also form part of a long chain of people, products, tools, machines, money, and so forth" (Akrich, 1992, p. 205).

Autonomous Technology Development

Civilization develops with the help of technology but, technology also has unwanted and unexpected side effects that threatens our existence as a species. We are now living in a worrying era of Anthropocene. However, the view that is mostly shared by engineers is that technology is neutral and its utilization and development are under human control. "Technology was thought to be neutral since it did not alter these natural ends but merely shortened the path to them" (Feenberg, 1999, p. 2). According to instrumentalist view, technology is neither good nor bad, morality and value cannot be attributed to technology, which is man-made. It could be used for either exploitative or humanitarian ends (Roszak, 1969). The views other than instrumentalism are regarded as underestimating human agency and weakening or even removing human responsibility.

Technological development is a collective enterprise, which is beyond any individual's control. And the result of this development is "a world of interdependence and universal externalities, and in consequence a whole new set of uncertainties" (North, 2005, p. 20). Technology seems to advance by its own "laws of motion" (Jonas, 1979), or is driven by the autonomous force from "the alien realm of reason" (Feenberg, 1999, p. vii). Indeed, humans do the development of technology, but they will be led by the autonomous force of technological development that they cannot control (Heidegger, 1977). They will be happily comply to the force, because the benefits are there and challenging it will not only be costly but also doomed to lose.

What has happened in capitalist system is in accordance with Heidegger's thought. The autonomous force that drives technology development is the capitalist endless pursuit for profit and growth. Within the capitalist framework everything – technology, production system, organization, or business model – is designed to maximize profit and growth. Sources of inefficiency and uncertainty will be eliminated or minimized. Human workers, who are often considered as the sources of efficiency and uncertainty have been partly replaced by machines and increasingly being controlled. Even though the technologists are responsible in designing production systems, they cannot avoid but obey the capitalist interests. Otherwise, they will be replaced as well. Even businesses also have to play the capitalist game if they do not want to be eliminated from the competition.

Within capitalist framework people lose control of directing technological development. It has its own path, and "that path is discovered through the pursuit of efficiency" (Feenberg, 1999, p. 77). Modern technology, according to Heidegger, is more than just human doing, but "sets upon man to order the real as standing-reserve in accordance with the way in which it shows itself. That challenging gathers man into ordering. This gathering concentrates man upon ordering the real as standing-reserve" (Heidegger, 1977, p. 19). Technology seems to develop autonomously out of our control. Even, when it disrupts existing industry or social order, we seem not to have any choice but accept it. People either believe that technology development cannot be stopped or technological progress is always good and considered as improvement. Many people are still confident that the many problems caused by technology can also be solved by technology (Maulana, 2019). While some people are concerned with the much talked about industrial revolution 4.0 that can push workers out of the jobs, yet many other people believe that the new technology will create new jobs. Capitalist society just do not want to slow down technological progress whatever the risk they are facing.

Technological progress is often a double-edged sword. As a technological artifact has its own source of energy and can be programmed, technologists can embed prescriptive knowledge into it, which makes it easy to operate. For instance, prescriptive knowledge of making bread has been embedded into bread maker, a home appliance for making bread (Johannesson & Perjons, 2014), allowing anyone who has no skill of making bread can make it just by putting the right ingredient into the appliance. While this development eases anyone to operate any technological artifact. In production system it makes corporations less dependent on their workers, so they can easily eliminate skilled workers, replacing them with less skilled ones, or using fewer number of workers to operate the production system. Those who are still at work are in vulnerable positions, sooner or later they might be replaced as well. Increasingly, their roles are being weakened because "The more science is incorporated into the labor process, the less the worker understands of the process; the more sophisticated an intellectual product the machine becomes, the less control and comprehension of the machine the worker has. In other words, the more the worker needs to know in order to remain a human being at work, the less does he or she know" (Braverman, 1974, p. 425). The negative impact of technology was anticipated by Marx.

Marx argued that capitalism would collapse not only because it was unjust and immoral, and not only because poverty and inequality would goad the workers to revolt, but also because it would create economic crises of increasing intensity. These crises were not caused by greed or oppression, and they would occur no matter how well meaning capitalists themselves might be. For Marx, the logic of capitalism led to continual investment in better machines and factories, which tied up resources in "fixed capital," leaving less money available for wages ("variable capital"). As investments shifted from labor power to machinery, the amount available for wages and the number of workers employed had to decrease; otherwise the capitalist could not make a profit. (Nye, 2006, p. 23).

The above development threatens the fate of workers in developed countries, but, opens the opportunities for the spread of industrialization in developing countries. Multinational corporations with new easy-to-operate production technology can move their production to developing countries having less skilled but less demanding workers. This kind of industrialization is only temporarily helping developing countries. When the wages are getting higher or the conditions are more demanding, the corporations may response by disassembling their production systems and moving them to other less demanding countries.

Autonomous technology development, however, is not a relevant issue to developing countries. Even they still have to struggle to encourage and stimulate technological capability development. Multi-National Corporations (MNCs) do establish manufacturing facilities, but local workers are more like components of production systems rather than determining agents. Global capitalists treat them only as market and low skill production sites. Momentum of technology development still needs to be created, before it can move autonomously. Alternative explanation is given by the social shaping model that argues that socio-cultural conditions determine the development specific technologies in a country, "technology is not following its own momentum or a sort of rational, goal-directed, problem-solving path but is instead shaped by social factors" (Bijker, 1995, p. 241).

Technological Knowledge

Technology is not a straightforward application of science, even though the development of modern technology is increasingly dependent on science. "Science aims at understanding, and its central element is a scientific law that purports to describe the way the world is. The problems of technology, by contrast, are practical.

Technology aims at control, and its central element is a rule (sometimes called a law) that purports to prescribe the way the world can be manipulated" (Mitcham, 1994, p. 198). People who develop technological knowledge must emphasize the usefulness, rather than the accuracy, of their theories and models. The main purpose of technology is to serve to satisfy human needs. Therefore, those who design technology must also understand the nature of human needs.

Based on the works of other writers, Mitcham (1994) identifies different elements of our technological capabilities, from the least to the most conceptual. Firstly, it is know-how or sensory motor skill, which was acquired intuitively or through learning by doing or trial and error. It cannot be categorized as knowledge in the strict sense, but more unarticulated skill, or tacit knowledge (Polanyi, 1966, 2005). Secondly, it is technical maxim, rule of thumb, or recipe, which constitutes a description of successful application of skills. Thirdly, it is descriptive law, or technological rule, in the form "if A then B", which is derived or generalized from experiences, but without systematic integration into the existing body of technological knowledge. It is not scientific yet, because there is no theoretical framework that can explain it. Lastly, technological theories, which are according to Mario Bunge, consist of substantive and operative knowledge. Substantive technological knowledge is essentially the application of scientific theories in real situation to solve real problem, "whereas operative theories are born in applied research and may have little if anything to do with substantive theories - this being why mathematicians and logicians with no previous scientific training can make important contributions to them" (Bunge, 1967, p. 122).

There are different kinds of technological activities that require different combinations and proportions of the above technological capabilities. Operating a machine does not require technological theories. Operators need to understand the know-how and master their skills through learning by doing. On the other side, designing complex production system requires complex technological theories, and the design must be explicitly produced to communicate to other stakeholders and to justify the needed funding to realize the design.

To successfully innovate, technologists not only have to know how to create a technological artifact, but also understand who will use it, and how and where it will be used. To function properly and sustainably, the artifact has to be used by a person who knows how to operate it, and it must be supported by local socio-technical system. It can easily access local sources of energy, and find spare parts and technicians when it is broken. In addition to substantive knowledge, technology development also involves creative processes and compliance with various social, technical and legal forces that simultaneously shape the development of any technological artifact. For example, the selection of materials for a car will take into account the loads and stresses it has to bear. The expected speed of the car is the product of a compromise between consumer preferences, regulation, law enforcement, and technical performance of various components of the car (Akrich, 1992). Other than the technical considerations are reflections of social values, what is called by Feenberg as the technical codes, which defines "the object in strictly technical terms in accordance with the social meaning it has acquired. These codes are usually invisible because, like culture itself, they appear self-evident" (Feenberg, 1999, p. 88).

When a new technological artifact does not fit an existing socio-technical system, either it will be refuted by that system, or, if it is forcefully inserted, it will disturb the stability of the existing system. Both disturbance and stabilization do occur in technological development. Strong disturbance occurs when disruptive technology is starting to be adopted widely, challenging the dominant one. Disturbance will be eventually followed by stabilization.

To minimize the cost of introducing new technology, technologists have to take into account the various objects that make up the world into which their technological object will be utilized, and also users and other people who will influence the adoption and utilization of that technology. Generally, technology has been designed to fit into particular socio-technical context (Akrich, 1992; Latour, 1992). Even the so-called disruptive technologies (Christensen, 2000) do fit its niche market in their early introduction.

The design of technology establishes a script (Akrich, 1992; Latour, 1992) that defines the framework of actions taken by users and the space where the actions take place. However, the users do not necessarily follow the script set by the technologists. There is a "negotiation" or "mutual enforcement" between the technologists' projected users and the real users. If the technology providers are strong enough, they may be able to dictate the users. A corporation, such as Apple, can dictate its scripts to its users. Apple has millions of loyal customers, many of them are willing to queue for hours in front of Apple stores to buy new products. While the customers of other brands may raise the compatibility issue, Apple's customers are proud that Apple product is incompatible with anything else. In production/manufacturing environment, it is not the technology producers that dictate workers, but the corporations, which have bought the technological systems.

Technological development most often has to consider that it will pay off, that the technology will improve productivity or business competitiveness. Technological innovation is expensive and risky that not everyone dares to do it. Therefore, it is more than just a problem of expertise. Therefore, technology development also requires entrepreneurs, people who have the courage (and access to capital and knowledge) to take uncertain venture of technological innovation "by exploiting an invention or, more generally, an untried technological possibility for producing a new commodity or producing an old one in a new way, by opening up a new source of supply of materials or a new outlet for products, by reorganizing an industry and so on" (Schumpeter, 2003, p. 132). The needs for this breed of entrepreneurs cannot be replaced by academics or researchers involved in technology development.

In developed countries, large corporations have routinized innovative activities by making them the business of R&D units or teams of trained specialists (Schumpeter, 2003). The technologists can focus on their invention, and not worry about the risk and cost of their efforts. On the contrary, most industries in developing countries lack R&D activities. Engineering higher educations or public R&D organizations are often not well connected with the relevant technological problems in industries. The difficulty of determining what to develop and how to do it leads developing countries to focus on investment in human capital, and at the same time inviting foreign investors to bring 'ready-made' technology, and select segment area of technology development and attempt to master that technology (Lall, 1996). Only relying on foreign companies or imported technology will not give a country a competitive advantage, because it is likely that many other developing countries do the same. This is often the case with industrialization in developing countries, the machineries are continually upgraded, but their position in global value chain does not improve.

Assembling complex socio-technical system requires collective learning by interacting that takes time, because people have to align their activities, knowledge and interests with each other. Every element of the system needs to adapt to fit with its surrounding in both economic and social interactions. In technological development, no one makes decision or thinks independently from others (Mannheim, 1954). In collective enterprises, such as industry and technology development, "thinking is a social activity; human culture and cognition are aspects of a single process. People learn from one another, not only facts but methods for processing those facts" (Kennedy, 1998, p. 57). In technological development, thinking, doing and interacting are often inseparable. More often, large parts of what they have learned are tacit and tacitly embedded in relationship among actors. People often overlook the interdependence among themselves in advancing national technological capability. The various interdependence among various activities, technical, social, economic and political, is too complex for a single actor to take all considerations into account. "It is solved not by somebody beforehand drawing up a comprehensive plan and everybody then acting according to this plan, as a technological problem would be solved, but by the individuals so mutually adjusting their actions that an order is formed" (Hayek, 2014, p. 406).

Users are the important elements of socio-technical system. Not only because they are the ones who eventually pay for the end products. They can also be sources of idea and knowledge. In some area, where technology is used for productive activity or solving complex problems, users do not just actively give suggestions, they can even modify the technology they use. "Empirical studies show that many users—from 10 percent to nearly 40 percent—engage in developing or modifying products. About half of these studies do not determine representative innovation frequencies; they were designed for other purposes. Nonetheless, when taken together, the findings make it very clear that users are doing a lot of product modification and product development in many fields" (von Hippel, 2005, p. 4).

Users in developing countries can be as demanding as those in advanced countries. If the demand cannot be met by local technology developers, then they will increasingly rely on imported technology. Investing in technological capability development is costly and risky, even more for developing countries, which are still burdened with other more basic needs. Therefore, not many developing countries dare to take the risk of allocating significant budget for that. The vision and courage to do that will depend on what Jasanoff (2015) and Kim (2015) call as socio-technical imaginary, that is, "collectively held, institutionally stabilized, and publicly performed visions of desirable futures, animated by shared understandings of forms of social life and social order attainable through, and supportive of, advances in science and technology" (Jasanoff, 2015, p. 4). This technological development is a learning process at national level, and this is "an incremental process filtered by the culture of a society which determines the perceived pay-offs.... the learning process appears to be a function of the way in which a given belief system filters the information derived from experiences; and of the different experiences confronting individuals and societies at different times" (North, 2005, p. 69).

Because the development of technological capability is expensive and uncertain, it needs strong and long-term supports from important members of society. Successful countries, such as East Asian countries have been familiar with technological discourse for quite a long time. The need for science and technology has developed from within. South Korean intellectuals have already discussed the entanglement of science and technology with nationalism and developmentalism even since the late nineteenth century (Kim, 2015). The importance of technology has been shared by their elites for quite a long time. And even of equal importance, they also realize the important of institutional development to support technological capability development. The development of technological capability is the result of interaction between technological characteristics and institutional settings, including corporate organization, industrial structure, and the role of the public sector (Hwang & Choung, 2014).

Technological progress has different impacts on different people. There are people who benefit from it, but there are also those who have experienced the cruelty of disruptive technology. Technological progress can increase the wealth of a nation as a whole, but it can also increase the inequality among population. Even for those who seem to benefit from the technological progress, they cannot avoid but to be incorporated as elements of a production system. Their creativity and knowledge are not their virtues as humans, but commodities that bind them to their alienation from themselves, from society and from nature. Technological progress is not only difficult to achieve, but also contains uncertainty and contradictions. According to Suarez-Villa (2009), "This degradation of human values is not grounded in technology, in and of itself. It is grounded in the character of a new kind of corporatism and its authoritarian control over technology" (p. 2). This view is still an instrumentalist view of technology. But, technology cannot be separated from the interests of those who develop and pay for its development.

PROMOTING TECHNOLOGICAL DEVELOPMENT

There are high costs for technological development, yet it can also give economic opportunities that encourage developed countries and their companies to heavily invest in it. In developed countries the larger part of R&D funding is provided by private sector, while in developing countries it is provided by government. In the developed countries, market competition stimulates innovations, including technological progress (North, 2005; Porter, 1990; Schumpeter, 1934), but in the developing ones market failed to give the same effect. Local companies and their employees are inept at using technology and acquiring technological knowledge, which makes them unable "to upgrade the technologies they have mastered, or diversify into new technologies as conditions change. Thus, they may stay at the low value-added end of the industrial spectrum, falling behind world technological frontiers as others forge ahead" (Lall, 1996, p. 27).

For experts from developed countries and the international development policy establishments, free market cannot fail and, therefore, developing countries should correct and improve their market. Inspired by neoclassical economics, they believe that "markets are basically efficient and governments basically inefficient, resource allocation is optimised by agents responding to free markets, and the best development policy is to remove all interventions in the functioning of free markets" (Lall, 1996, p. 1). Developing countries just have to adopt the "good policies" and "good institutions", which are to be found especially in the Anglo-American countries (Chang, 2002). They should implement free trade and investment, privatization and deregulation, and they should establish transparent and market-oriented corporate governance and financial institutions. However, Chang shows that "when they were developing countries themselves, today's developed countries used very few of the policies and institutions that they recommend to, or even force upon, today's developing countries" (Chang, 2002, p. 64). Based on his study on the success of East Asian countries, Lall (1996) suggests that developing countries cannot let their technological future to market, the pervasive market failures in developing countries calls for remedial and highly selective and targeted interventions.

To make appropriate interventions, policy makers should understand technological development at micro and meso level. Technology is developed through a highly localized processes (Porter, 1990) in which entrepreneurs play decisive roles (Schumpeter, 1934). Either at individual or organizational level, this development is driven by economic motivations, profit and growth, and it is achieved through the pursuit of efficiency. To engineers, "A good technological design is one that uses materials and energy efficiently" (Mitcham & Schatzberg, 2009, p. 30).

Under the framework of capitalism, economic and technical efficiencies have become the main criteria of technological development. Values and practices that embody human meaning have been shifted aside. "Efficiency sweeps away all other norms and determines an autonomous process of technological development" (Feenberg, 1999, p. viii). Technology has been continuously developed to eliminate any source of inefficiency. Unfortunately, from the perspective of capitalists, human labor is often regarded as the source of inefficiency, hence it is "to be reduced to a minimum if it cannot be eliminated altogether, say, by automation" (Schumacher, 2014, p. 421). The development of technology has been attempted to minimize the role of workers, "... the new work that technology stimulates is associated with the mechanization of labor. Machines are more frequently employed in manufacturing in order to produce commodities with greater rapidity and efficiency—meaning that work is less and less involved with the personal manufacture of artifacts and more and more with the maintenance and operation of machines that make parts for artifacts" (Verbeek, 2005, p. 18).

The pursuit for efficiency also leads to the development of increasingly user-friendly machineries, which allow MNCs to move their production system to any part of the world that has lower-wage workers and weak environmental protection laws. This gives the opportunities to developing countries to have manufacturing industries with least efforts, because everything has been provided by the MNCs. Developing countries can make more risky efforts of establishing their own industries by importing machineries available in the marketplaces. They can rely on technology vendors that are willing to provide anything they need. But, without the knowledge of which technology to choose, they can waste their financial resources and not get the best available technology. At whatever level of technological development, knowledge does help. If a country does not develop their technology, even though they have manufacturing industries, they will be forever kept in the lowest part of global value chain.

Developing countries cannot expect that their technological capabilities shall be upgraded by MNCs without making their own effort. At the initial stage of technological development, government's active role is necessary (Lall, 1996). Otherwise, challenging mature technology and industries from overseas will be a losing game. Generic interventions, such as establishing public R&D institutions and engineering higher educations that support many sectors is necessary, but targeting specific technology-based industries to protect and develop has been the key success in countries, such as South Korea and Taiwan. However, the infant industry protection must be gradually withdrawn, market for local technology must be strengthened, otherwise technological development will keep burdening government budget. The intervention that is needed is technology policy that stimulates market. The protection must eventually be lifted and the industry has to face the competition. "It is necessary to mobilize market forces, directly or indirectly, in those technological activities where the market mechanism has a competitive advantage over non-market mechanisms, but when it cannot yet achieve correct allocations on its own: policy interventions play a crucial interim role as markets are developed." (Lall & Teubal, 1998, p. 1374).

Under government's protection, the uncertainty of competition will be reduced or even removed. However, the uncertainty of technological R&D cannot be eliminated, trials and errors are inevitable. It is not only about finding technical solutions to a technical problem, but, most importantly, finding technical solutions that can compete against existing solutions and prospective solutions that may be given by competitors.

At national level, when market does not work, the development of national technological capability is more challenging, because it involves more actors with different knowledge and possible conflicting interests. No single actor has a complete knowledge of the socio-technical system in question. The knowledge "never exists in concentrated or integrated form but solely as the dispersed bits of incomplete and frequently contradictory knowledge which all the separate individuals possess" (Hayek, 1945, p. 519). National technological development cannot be fully planned out in advanced by a central planner. The problem is that people often do not realize that their knowledge incomplete. Conflicting views due to different perspectives do occur. For instance, in Indonesia there was a quarrel between economists and technologists to define the nation's developmental strategy and in allocating budget for technology development. The former gave more emphasis on the role of market forces, while the latter on the government's protection of infant industries (Amir, 2013).

Even though policy makers are able to convincingly show their good intent and the policy is directed to improve economic efficiency and progress, "it is not obvious that the government players will possess sufficient economic sophistication to achieve that objective" (North, 2005, p. 123). Hence, technology policy should encourage learning among industry players, technologists, and, not less importantly, government (Lall & Teubal, 1998). Either through market or non-market mechanism, what needs to be implemented the right incentive structure that will direct technological progress and stimulate local entrepreneurship and innovation, and the policy makers need to be aware that "economic change will require continual alteration in the institutional structure in order to maintain efficiency" (North, 2005, p. 123).

Developing countries tend to focus on developing tangible resources in overcoming technological backwardness, such as buying machineries or laboratory instruments and increasing the formal level of education of their populations. It is often overlooked that their inability to exploit the prospects of modern technology reflects an institutional framework that constrain what they can do collectively (North, 2005), and underlying beliefs that determine what future should and can be pursued (Jasanoff, 2015).

Institutional innovation must accompany or precede technological innovation. The success of East Asian Countries in catching up technological progress shows the importance of institutional innovation in addition to technological and developmental strategy innovations (Hobday, 2003). Institutions, as humanly devised constraints, are being established to reduce uncertainty and to structure incentives in human exchanges (North, 1990). "The major role of institutions in a society is to reduce uncertainty by establishing a stable (but not necessarily efficient) structure to human interaction" (p. 6). The economic agents will maximize their profits either by making choices within the existing set of constraints or attempting to alter the constraints.

In technological development, besides interacting with each other under particular rules, people also follow other sets of rules in creating technological artifacts. These latter rules, which define good design and acceptable features of technology, incorporate technical principles, user preferences, as well as regulation and law enforcement (Akrich, 1992). One set of rules are not separated from the other sets of rules, but are linked together to form a semi-coherent system called a regime. These rules coevolve and stabilize with each other, that makes it difficult to change a single rule without changing the others (Geels, 2004). As people working in the same area interact with one another, they will develop the same set of rules or regime. Different social or professional groups are likely to develop different regimes. With relation to technology development, various stakeholders may develop their own regimes that do not support each other. The technological regime of engineers working in industry is generally different from the regimes of those working in public R&D organizations or academics, which means that those regimes are having different incentive structures.

The performance of economic system is determined by the interdependent institutions, "changing just one institution in an attempt to get the desired performance is always an incomplete and sometimes a counter-productive activity" (North, 2005, p. 157). The institutions in use are not only the formal ones, people also comply with the informal rules "that modify, qualify, or even negate the formal rules" (p. 123). The formal institutions that hamper progress can be changed through formal procedures, but the informal institutions are difficult to change, because these are the product of a long and tacit social consensus. But, it does not imply that informal rules cannot be changed. Formal rules can be enacted and enforced to replace the informal rules.

The institutional innovation is complicated and unique for each country because they have unique combinations of interdependent formal and informal rules. Government cannot just change some rules and expect their problems to be solved. Institutional innovation always needs to be considered because the economy of capitalist society never reaches stability or continually experiences a process of creative destruction (Schumpeter, 2003), "that incessantly revolutionizes the economic structure from within, incessantly destroying the old one, incessantly creating a new one" (Schumpeter, 2003, p. 83).

The institutions that might have stimulated progress at one time may later prevent it. Business and technological environment keep changing, and old institutions are no longer suitable to deal with present challenges and circumstances. Hence, it is important for an economic system to have an adaptive efficiency, which "entails a set of institutions that readily adapt to the shocks, disturbances, and ubiquitous uncertainty that characterize every society over time" (North, 2005, p.78). A society or economic system that has adaptive efficiency is more open to see their own weakness and low performance, and ready to adjust their institutions or even question their belief system to resolve their problems. Without this openness, government can fail to intervene or make harmful interventions that are counter-productive, and "the costs of government failure always exceed those of market failure" (Lall & Teubal, 1998, p. 1370).

The world has changed and is no longer the same with the conditions when the successful East Asian countries started their technological development. The participations in the World Trade Organization (WTO) and free trade areas, such as the Asia-Pacific Economic Cooperation (APEC) and the ASEAN Free Trade Area (AFTA), impose particular institutions that will limit developing countries' capabilities to protect their infant industries. With the free trades and intensifying global competition, it is increasingly difficult for new industrializing newcomers to find empty spot in global market for their exported products.

Determining the correct interventions is not easy, since we are now in different economic environment from the era when China and South Korea started their technological development. Another important difference between them and many developing countries is that when starting their technological development, China and South Korea had already had strong state apparatus and visionary governments that not any country can easily imitate due to different historical and political context. "The risk of government failure has to be faced whenever policy solutions are recommended for market deficiencies. The widespread intervention of well-meaning governments has been the cause of enormous waste and inefficiency in the developing world" (Lall, 1996, p. 52). If governments and nations have adaptive efficiency, they can readily learn, especially learning from their failures. They will improve with time and efforts.

The present technological progress of developed countries can be seen as the result of historical process of institutional development (North, 2005). But, developing countries seem to imitate the outward features of current achievement of developed countries. Organizations with the same name, but with much weaker functionalities, have been established. Formal institutions copied from the advanced countries have also been established without sufficient evaluation about their implementations and appropriateness to local context. Even, if people upheld the deterministic view of technological development, what many developing countries do to imitate the facade of the innovation system of developed countries by themselves or by following the advice of experts from the latter, often ignore the process or path of development. Because what is imitated is only the last achievement of long process of development.

SOLUTIONS AND RECOMMENDATIONS

National technology development occurs in a network of various actors, businesses and industries, R&D organizations, higher education institutions, financial or funding organizations, policy makers, etc. The configuration of the network has been shaped by their long-term interactions and transactions. Their capabilities and knowledge coevolve and grow interdependent with each other, while each actor seeks to maximize the satisfaction of their needs, either of profits, growth, reputation, career, or else. While anyone can improve one's knowledge independently from others, one has limited choices to act with relation to technology utilization and development, because what one does is dependent on what others do or supply. However, the interconnection among actors cause them to be interlocked with each other, which prevents technological upgrading through market forces.

When market cannot be expected to stimulate technological upgrading, government should come to intervene. Since the intervention is directed toward heterogeneous actors, mix of different but integrated policies are needed rather than a single policy. Each policy addresses different aspect or part of technological development, but as a whole all policies are expected to help actors to coevolve further and to transform the configuration of the network to the higher level.

Technological development can be unmanageably complex, but, given their limited resources, developing countries need to target the least complex area of technological development, which however will have significant leverage. They can choose to target horizontally (specific area of intervention that applies for all sectors) or vertically (selecting specific actors).

FUTURE RESEARCH DIRECTIONS

Technological development is much more than just acquiring and applying knowledge and technology. Government cannot just allocate allocate a large amount of money for R&D activities then expect the nation will technologically advance. It is about coordinating and stimulating various parts of complex network to upgrade their knowledge and technologies while at the same time they can reconfigure themselves to fit with new capabilities and demands. When market does not work, government should provide incentive and demand to stimulate and push technological development. It is more than just providing funding, but more importantly establishing proper institutions and governance. Therefore, the future research can be directed toward the relationship between the nature of technological development, institutions and governance. Developing countries need to know when targeting particular technological development which institutions and governance will stimulate the development and which one will constrain it.

CONCLUSION

Humans develop technology to solve their problems or to overcome their limitation. Technology extends their body and mind. It manifests as a complex network of interdependent artifacts, knowledge and activities. It is a way of humans controlling the nature and production systems, which include human workers. Technological artifacts, especially those belong to production systems, are heterogeneous, each component may be produced by different people involving in different activities using different knowledge and equipment and machineries. Even a simple technological artifact often belongs to the complex socio-technical system. It might be possible to send the artifact to any part of the world. But, if it does not fit with the socio-technical system of use, it cannot be used at all, or cannot be used properly or sustainably. And, more importantly, it cannot be made locally, because there are more technological artifacts, knowledge and activities are needed.

Misunderstanding the nature of technology may result in wrong decision in technological capability development. People who perceive technology as merely artifact will regard that their technological capability can be improved by buying new and more sophisticated machineries. They will not invest in R&D, which do not guarantee any benefit. By keeping up with the latest machineries available in market, businesses can maintain their competitive positions, at least equal to those having the same machineries.

Developing countries cannot expect that market or foreign direct investment can steadily improve their technological capability without making significant efforts by themselves. Learning from the success of East Asian countries, developing countries can develop their technological capability by selective government's interventions, even though at the same time they have to stimulate their market as well. The protection of infant industry must be steadily withdrawn so that it does not continuously burden government's budget.

In addition to innovations in technology and developmental strategy, institutional innovations is essential but often overlooked by developing countries. The institutions have been developed to reduce uncertainty and structure incentives, but these do not necessarily stimulate progress and can even weaken the progress. Institutions need to be carefully designed and their impacts must be continuously evaluated. When they no longer support the performance of the economic system, they have to be altered.

ACKNOWLEDGMENT

This research received no specific grant from any funding agency in the public, commercial, or not-for-profit sectors.

REFERENCES

Akrich, M. (1992). The De-Scription of Technical Objects. In W.E. Bijker & J. Law (Eds.), Shaping Technology/Building Society: Studies in Sociotechnical Change (pp. 205–224). Cambridge, MA: MIT Press.

Amir, S. (2013). *The Technological State in Indonesia: The co-constitution of high technology and authoritarian politics*. New York, NY: Routledge.

Bijker, W. E. (1992). The Social Construction of Fluorescent Lighting, Or How an Artifact Was Invented in Its Diffusion Stage. In W.E. Bijker & J. Law (Eds.), Shaping Technology/Building Society: Studies in Sociotechnical Change (pp. 75–102). Cambridge, MA: The MIT Press.

Bijker, W. E. (1995). Sociohistorical Technology Studies. In S. Jasanoff, G. E. Markle, J. C. Petersen, & T. Pinch (Eds.), Handbook of Science and Technology Studies (Rev. ed., pp. 229–256). Thousand Oaks, CA: Sage.

Braverman, H. (1974). *Labor and Monopoly Capital: The Degradation of Work in the Twentieth Century*. New York, NY: Monthly Review Press. doi:10.14452/MR-026-03-1974-07_1

Bunge, M. (1967). *Scientific Research II: The Search for Truth*. Berlin: Springer-Verlag. doi:10.1007/978-3-642-48138-3

Chang, H.-J. (2002). Kicking Away the Ladder: An Unofficial History of Capitalism, Especially in Britain and the United States. *Challenge*, *45*(5), 63–97. doi:10.1080/05775132.2002.11034173

Christensen, C. M. (2000). *The Innovator's Dilemma*. New York, NY: HarperBusiness.

Drucker, P. F. (1959). Work and Tools. *Technology and Culture*, *1*(1), 28–37. doi:10.2307/3100785

Feenberg, A. (1999). *Questioning Technology*. New York, London: Routledge.

Geels, F. W. (2004). From sectoral systems of innovation to socio-technical systems: Insights about dynamics and change from sociology and institutional theory. *Research Policy*, *33*(6-7), 897–920. doi:10.1016/j.respol.2004.01.015

Guignon, C. B. (1983). *Heidegger and the Problem of Knowledge*. Indianapolis, IN: Hackett Publishing Company.

Hayek, F. A. (1945). The Use of Knowledge in Society. *The American Economic Review*, *XXXV*(4).

Hayek, F. A. (2014). Lecture III: Economics and Technology. In B. Caldwell (Ed.), *The Market and Other Orders* (pp. 402–414). Chicago: The University of Chicago Press. doi:10.7208/chicago/9780226089690.001.0001

Heidegger, M. (1962). *Being and Time*. Oxford, UK: Blackwell.

Heidegger, M. (1977). *The Question Concerning Technology and Other Essays* (Lovitt W, Trans.). New York, NY: Garland Publishing.

Hobday, M. (2003). Innovation in Asian Industrialization: A Gerschenkronian Perspective. *Oxford Development Studies*, *31*(3), 293–314. doi:10.1080/1360081032000111715

Hwang, H.-R., & Choung, J.-Y. (2014). The Co-evolution of Technology and Institutions in the Catch-up Process: The Case of the Semiconductor Industry in Korea and Taiwan. *The Journal of Development Studies*, *50*(9), 1240–1260. doi:10.1080/00220388.2014.895817

Jasanoff, S. (2015). Future Imperfect: Science, Technology, and the Imaginations of Modernity. In S. Jasanoff & S.-H. Kim (Eds.), *Dreamscapes of Modernity : Sociotechnical Imaginaries and the Fabrication of Power*. Chicago: The University of Chicago Press. doi:10.7208/chicago/9780226276663.003.0001

Johannesson, P., & Perjons, E. (2014). *An Introduction to Design Science*. Dordrecht, Holland: Springer. doi:10.1007/978-3-319-10632-8

Jonas, H. (1979). Toward a Philosophy of Technology. *The Hastings Center Report*, *9*(1), 34–43. doi:10.2307/3561700 PMID:429061

Kennedy, J. (1998). Thinking Is Social: Experiments with the Adaptive Culture Model. *The Journal of Conflict Resolution*, *42*(1), 56–76. doi:10.1177/0022002798042001003

Kim, S.-H. (2015). Social Movements and Contested Sociotechnical Imaginaries in South Korea. In S. Jasanoff & S.-H. Kim (Eds.), *Dreamscapes of Modernity: Sociotechnical Imaginaries and the Fabrication of Power* (pp. 152–173). Chicago: The University of Chicago Press.

Lall, S. (1996). *Learning from the Asian Tigers: Studies in Technology and Industrial Policy*. Hampshire, UK: Macmillan. doi:10.1057/9780230389892

Lall, S., & Teubal, M. (1998). "Market-Stimulating" Developing Technology Policies in Countries: A Framework with Examples from East Asia. *World Development*, *26*(8), 1369–1385. doi:10.1016/S0305-750X(98)00071-0

Latour, B. (1992). Where Are the Missing Masses? The Sociology of a Few Mundane Artifacts. In W. Bijker & J. Law (Eds.), *Shaping Technology/Building Society: Studies in Sociotechnical Change*. Cambridge, MA: MIT Press.

Mannheim, K. (1954). *Ideology and Utopia*. London: Routledge & Kegan Paul.

Maulana, I. (2019). Big Brothers Are Seducing You: Consumerism, Surveillance, and the Agency of Consumers. In O. Ozgen (Ed.), *Handbook of Research on Consumption, Media, and Popular Culture in the Global Age*. Hershey, PA: IGI Global. doi:10.4018/978-1-5225-8491-9.ch004

McLuhan, M. (1994). *Understanding Media: The Extensions of Man*. Cambridge, MA: The MIT Press.

Mitcham, C. (1994). *Thinking through Technology: The Path between Engineering and Philosophy*. Chicago: The University of Chicago Press.

Mitcham, C., & Schatzberg, E. (2009). Defining Technology and the Engineering Sciences. In A. Meijers (Ed.), *Philosophy of Technology and Engineering Sciences* (Vol. 9, pp. 27–64). Amsterdam. doi:10.1016/B978-0-444-51667-1.50006-9

North, D. (1990). *Institutions, Institutional Change and Economic Performance*. Cambridge, MA: Cambridge University Press. doi:10.1017/CBO9780511808678

North, D. C. (2005). *Understanding the Process of Economic Change*. Princeton, NJ: Princeton University Press. doi:10.1515/9781400829484

Nye, D. E. (2006). *Technology Matters: Questions to Live With*. Cambridge, MA: The MIT Press.

Polanyi, M. (1966). *The Tacit Dimension*. Chicago: The University of Chicago Press.

Polanyi, M. (2005). *Personal Knowledge: Towards a Post-Critical Philosophy*. London: Routledge.

Porter, M. E. (1990). *The Competitive Advantage of Nations*. Hampshire: Macmillan. doi:10.1007/978-1-349-11336-1

Preston, B. (2009). Philosophical Theories of Artifact Function. In A. Meijers (Ed.), *Philosophy of Technology and Engineering Sciences* (Vol. 9, pp. 213–234). Amsterdam: Elsevier. doi:10.1016/B978-0-444-51667-1.50013-6

Rosenberg, N. (2000). *Schumpeter and the Endogeneity of Technology*. London: Routledge. doi:10.4324/9780203465356

Roszak, T. (1969). *The Making of Counter Culture: Reflections on the Technocratic Society and Its Youthful Opposition*. New York, NY: Anchor Books.

Schumacher, E. F. (2014). Buddhist Economics. In R. C. Scharff & V. Dusek (Eds.), *Philosophy of Technology – The Technological Condition: An Anthology* (2nd ed., pp. 421–425). Chichester, UK: John Wiley & Sons, Inc.

Schumpeter, J. A. (1934). *The Theory of Economic Development*. Cambridge, MA: Harvard University Press.

Schumpeter, J. A. (1983). *The Theory of Economic Development*. New Brunswick, NJ: Transaction Publishers.

Schumpeter, J. A. (2003). *Capitalism, Socialism and Democracy*. London: Routledge.

Suarez-Villa, L. (2009). *Technocapitalism: A Critical Perspective on Technological Innovation and Corporatism*. Philadelphia, PA: Temple University Press.

Thomasson, A. L. (2009). Artifacts in Metaphysics. In A. Meijers (Ed.), *Philosophy of Technology and Engineering Sciences* (pp. 191–212). Amsterdam: Elsevier. doi:10.1016/B978-0-444-51667-1.50012-4

Verbeek, P.-P. (2005). *What Things Do: Philosophical Reflections on Technology, Agency, and Design*. University Park, PA: The Pennsylvania State University Press.

von Hippel, E. (2005). *Democratizing Innovation*. Cambridge, MA: The MIT Press. doi:10.7551/mitpress/2333.001.0001

Compilation of References

Acemoglu, D., & Robinson, J. A.(2012). Why Nations Fail? The Origins of Power, Prosperity and Poverty. New York: Crown Business. doi:10.1355/ae29-2j

Acemoğlu, D., Simon, J., & Robinson, J. (2001). The Colonial Origins of Comparative Development: An Empirical Investigation. *American Economic Literature*, *91*(5), 1369–1401.

Ackoff, R. L. (1979). The Future of Operational Research is Past. *The Journal of the Operational Research Society*, *30*(2), 93–104. doi:10.1057/jors.1979.22

Adorno, T. W., & Horkheimer, M. (2010). *Aydınlanmanın diyalektiği*. Kabalcı Yayınevi.

Akansel, I. (2004). *The Situation Of Woman Labourforce in the Art Sector, An Investigation on Ankara State Opera and Ballet (ASOB)*. Unpublished MSc dissertation, University of Gazi, Ankara, Turkey.

Akansel, I. (2017). Reading the Relationship between Public Relations and Economics by the Mediation of Thorstein Veblen. *Proceedings of the 3rd International Annual Meeting of SosyoEkonomi Society* (pp. 145-150). Academic Press.

Akçomak, İ. S., & Bürken, S. (2019). *The Middle-Technology Trap: The Case of the Automotive Industry in Turkey*. Maastricht University, Netherlands.

Akdağ, M. (1999). Barış Yayınları. *Türkiye'nin İktisadî ve İçtimaî Tarihi*, *2*, 1453–1559.

Akerlof, G. A. (1970). The market for "lemons": Quality uncertainty and the market mechanism. *The Quarterly Journal of Economics*, *84*(3), 488–500. doi:10.2307/1879431

Akerlof, G. A., & Schiller, R. J. (2010). *Hayvansal güdüler: İnsan psikolojisi ekonomiyi nasıl yönlendirir ve küresel kapitalizm için niçin önemlidir?* (N. Domaniç & L. Konyar, Trans.). İstanbul: Scala Yayıncılık.

Akın, Z., & Urhan, B. (2009). *İktisat deneysel bir bilim olmaya mi başliyor?* TOBB University of Economics and Technology.

Akrich, M. (1992). The De-Scription of Technical Objects. In W.E. Bijker & J. Law (Eds.), Shaping Technology/Building Society: Studies in Sociotechnical Change (pp. 205–224). Cambridge, MA: MIT Press.

Aktüre, S. (1987). *19. Yüzyıl Sonunda Anadolu Kenti Mekânsal Yapı Çözümlemesi*. Ankara: ODTÜ Mimarlık Fakültesi Press.

Akyel, S., & Savaş, S. (2015). Osmanlı Nüfus Defterlerinin Tarih Yazımındaki Yeri: 1840 Tarihli Çarsancak Kazası Gayrimüslim Nüfus Defteri Örneği. *Journal of History and Future*, *1*(1), 78–98.

Alston, L. J., & Bernardo, M. (2005). Property Rights and the State. In C. Menard & M. Shirley (Eds.), *Handbook of New Institutional Economics* (pp. 573–590). Netherlands: Springer.

Althusser, L. (1965). *For Marx*. The Penguin Press.

Altunöz, U., & Altunöz, H. (2018). *Davranışsal ekonomi (Nörofinans)*. Ankara: Seçkin Yayınevi.

Amir, S. (2013). *The Technological State in Indonesia: The co-constitution of high technology and authoritarian politics*. New York, NY: Routledge.

Angner, E., & Loewenstein, G. (2007). Behavioral economics. In U. Mäki (Ed.), *Philosophy of economic* (pp. 641–690). Handbook of the philosophy of science Amsterdam: Elsevier.

Antonelli, C. (2009). The Economics of Innovation: From the Classical Legacies to the Economics of Complexity. *Economics of Innovation and New Technology*, *18*(7), 611–646. doi:10.1080/10438590802564543

Antonelli, C. (2018). *The Evolutionary Complexity of Endogenous Innovation: The Engines of the Creative Response*. Edward Elgar. doi:10.4337/9781788113793

Antonelli, C. (Ed.). (2011). *Handbook on the Economic Complexity of Technological Change*. Edward Elgar. doi:10.4337/9780857930378

Aoki, M. (2001). *Toward A Comparative Institutional Analysis*. Massachusetts: MIT Press. doi:10.7551/mitpress/6867.001.0001

Archibugi, D., & Michie, J. (1997). Technological Globalisation or National Systems of Innovation? *Futures*, *29*(2), 121–137. doi:10.1016/S0016-3287(96)00072-9

Arrunada, B., & Veneta, A. (2005). Market Institutions and Judicial Rulemaking. In C. Menard & M. Shirley (Eds.), Handbook of New Institutional Economics (pp. 229-251). Netherlands: Springer. doi:10.1007/0-387-25092-1_11

Arthur, W. B. (2010). Complexity, The Santa Fe Approachi and Non-equilibrium Economics. *History of Economic Ideas*, *18*(2), 149–166.

Asheim, B. T. (2019). Smart Specialisation, Innovation Policy and Regional Innovation Systems: What About new Path Development in Less Innovative Regions? *Innovation (Abingdon)*, *32*(1), 8–25. doi:10.1080/13511610.2018.1491001

Asheim, B. T., Boschma, R., & Cooke, P. (2011). Constructing Regional Advantage: Platform Policies based on Related Variety and Differentiated Knowledge Bases. *Regional Studies*, *45*(7), 893–904. doi:10.1080/00343404.2010.543126

Asheim, B. T., & Coenen, L. (2006). Contextualizing Regional Innovation Systems in a Globalising Learning Economy: On Knowledge Bases and Institutional Frameworks. *The Journal of Technology Transfer*, *31*(1), 163–173. doi:10.100710961-005-5028-0

Asheim, B. T., Smith, H. L., & Oughton, C. (2011). Regional Innovation Systems: Theory, Empirics and Policy. *Regional Studies*, *45*(7), 875–891. doi:10.1080/00343404.2011.596701

Aslanbeigui, N., & Medema, S. G. (1998). Beyond the dark clouds: Pigou and Coase on social cost. *History of Political Economy*, *30*(4), 601–625. doi:10.1215/00182702-30-4-601

Asymmetric information. (2003). World Bank. Retrieved from https://siteresources.worldbank.org/DEC/Resources/847971114437274304/Asymmetric_Info_Sep2003.pdf

Auronen, L. (2003, May). Asymmetric information: Theory and applications. *Proceedings of the Seminar in Strategy and International Business*. Academic Press.

Ayer, A. J. (1952). *Language, truth, and logic* (2nd ed.). Dover Publications. (Original work published 1936)

Ayroza, I. F., Iwamoto, H., & Rodrigues, W. (2018). The old and the new Behavioral Economics: Highlights of a trajectory. *Textos De Economia*, *21*(2), 50–72. doi:10.5007/2175-8085.2018v21n2p50

Azar, R. (2015). Neoliberalism, Austerity and Authoritarianism. Retrieved from newpol.org/issue_post/neoliberalism-austerity-and-authoritarianism/

Bacchi, C., & Rönnblom, M. (2014). Feminist Discursive Institutionalism-A Poststructural Alternative. *NORA*, *22*(3), 170–186. doi:10.1080/08038740.2013.864701

Badiou, A. (2013). Ethics: An Essay on the Understanding of Evil (P. Hallward, trans., 1st ed.). Verso.

Baker, J. (2013). Economics and Politics: Perspectives on the Goals and Future of Antitrust. *Fordham Law Review*, *81*(5), 2175–2196.

Balamir, M. (2008). Küresel Gelişmeler, Neoliberal Politikalar, Risk Toplumu ve Planlama. Proceedings of 'Planlama Meslek Alanı: Geçmişten Geleceğe, Kasım 7-9 (pp. 167-194). Ankara: TODAİE.

Barca, F. (2009). *An Agenda for a Reformed Cohesion Policy: A Place-based Approach to Meeting European Union Challenges and Expectations*. Brussels: European Commission.

Bardsley, N. (2007). On Collective Intentions: Collective Action in Economics and Philosophy. *Synthese*, *157*(2), 141–159. doi:10.100711229-006-9034-z

Barzel, Y. (1997). *Economic Analysis of Property Rights*. Cambridge: Cambridge University Press. doi:10.1017/CBO9780511609398

Basılgan, M. (2013). İktisat ve deneysel yöntem: Deneyler, tartişmalar ve gelecek. İstanbul Üniversitesi Siyasal Bilgiler Fakültesi Dergisi, 48, 61-89.

Bator, F. M. (1958). The anatomy of market failure. *The Quarterly Journal of Economics*, *72*(3), 351–379. doi:10.2307/1882231

Bayramoğlu, S. (2005). *Yönetişim Zihniyeti: Türkiye'de Üst Kurullar ve Siyasal İktidarın Dönüşümü*. İstanbul: İletişim Publications.

Beaud, M. (2003). *Kapitalizmin Tarihi* (F. Başkaya, Trans.). Ankara: Dost Bookstore.

Benáček, V. (1992). Market failure versus government failure - The optıons of the emerging market economies. Retrieved from ww1.ceses.cuni.cz/benacek/FAILURE.pdf

Bénicourt, E., & Guerrien, B. (2017). Neoklasik İkisat Teorisi [The Theory of Neoclassical Economics]. Istanbul: The Publishing House of Kabalci.

Berik, G., Rodgers, Y., & Seguino, S. (2009). Feminist Economics of Inequality, Development, and Growth. *Feminist Economics*, *15*(3), 1–33. doi:10.1080/13545700903093524

Bhaskar, R. (1978). *A realist theory f science*. Great Britain: Harvester Wheatsheaf.

Bijker, W. E. (1992). The Social Construction of Fluorescent Lighting, Or How an Artifact Was Invented in Its Diffusion Stage. In W.E. Bijker & J. Law (Eds.), Shaping Technology/Building Society: Studies in Sociotechnical Change (pp. 75–102). Cambridge, MA: The MIT Press.

Bijker, W. E. (1995). Sociohistorical Technology Studies. In S. Jasanoff, G. E. Markle, J. C. Petersen, & T. Pinch (Eds.), Handbook of Science and Technology Studies (Rev. ed., pp. 229–256). Thousand Oaks, CA: Sage.

Bleda, M., & del Rio, P. (2013, June). (The Market Failure and the Systemic Failure Rationales in Technological Innovation Systems. *Research Policy*, *42*(5), 1039–1052. doi:10.1016/j.respol.2013.02.008

Bohman, J. (2005). *Critical theory*. Stanford. Retrieved from http://plato.stanford.edu/entries/critical-theory

Boratav, K., Ökçün, A. G., & Pamuk, Ş. (1985). Ottoman Wages and the World- Economy, 1839-1913. *Review - Fernand Braudel Center*, *8*(3), 379–406.

Boulding, K. (1956). General Systems Theory-The Skeleton of Science. *Management Science*, *2*(3), 197–208. doi:10.1287/mnsc.2.3.197

Boulding, K. (1997). *Yirminci Asrın Mânası (E. Güngör, Çev.)*. İstanbul: Ötüken.

Bowen, H. R. (1943). The interpretation of voting in the allocation of economic resources. *The Quarterly Journal of Economics*, *58*(1), 27–48. doi:10.2307/1885754

Brass, P. (1979). *Elite Groups, Symbol Manipulation and Ethnic Identity among Muslims of South Asia. In D. Taylor and Y. Malcolm (Eds.), Political Identity in SouthAsia*. London: Curzon Press.

Braverman, H. (1974). *Labor and Monopoly Capital: The Degradation of Work in the Twentieth Century*. New York, NY: Monthly Review Press. doi:10.14452/MR-026-03-1974-07_1

Breuilly, J. (1993). *Nationalism and the State. Manchester*. Manchester: UniversityPress.

Brown, W. S. (1999)... *Thorstein Veblen in the Twenty-First Century.*, *33*(4), 1035–1037.

Bruff, I. (2013, October 23). The Rise of Authoritarian Neoliberalism. A Journal of Economics. *Cultura e Scuola*, *26*, 113–129.

Buchanan, J. M., & Stubblebine, W. C. (1962). Externality. In Classic papers in natural resource economics (pp. 138-154). London: Palgrave Macmillan.

Buchanan, J. M. (1997). *Has Economics Lost Its Way? Reflections on the Economists' Enterprise at Century's End*. Fairfax, VA: Institute for Humane Studies.

Buchanan, J. M. (1999). *The collected works of James M. Buchanan (Volume-5): The Demand and Supply of Public Goods*. Indianapolis: Liberty Fund. (Original work published 1968)

Buckey, M. (2013). Locating Neoliberalism in Dubai: Migrant Workers and Class Struggle in the Autocratic City. *Antipode*, *45*(2), 256–274. doi:10.1111/j.1467-8330.2012.01002.x

Buğra, A. (1989). *İktisatçılar ve insanlar*. İstanbul: İletişim Yayınları.

Bulut, M. (2012). Osmanlı Ekonomi Politiği'ne Yeniden Bir Bakış. Bilig, (62), 63-96.

Bunge, M. (1967). *Scientific Research II: The Search for Truth*. Berlin: Springer-Verlag. doi:10.1007/978-3-642-48138-3

Çakır, C. (2003). Türkiye'de İktisat Tarihi Çalışmalarının Tarihi Üzerine Bir Deneme. *Türkiye Araştırmaları Literatür Dergisi*, *1*(1), 7–63.

Caldari, K., & Masini, F. (2011). Pigouvian versus Marshallian tax: Market failure, public intervention and the problem of externalities. *European Journal of the History of Economic Thought*, *18*(5), 715–732. doi:10.1080/09672567.2011.629300

Calderon-Agenjo, A., & Munoz-Galvez, L. (2019). Feminist Economics, Theoretical and Political Dimensions. *American Journal of Economics and Sociology*, *78*(1), 137–166. doi:10.1111/ajes.12264

Calhoun, C. (2002). *Authoritarianism, Dictionary of the Social Sciences*. Oxford: Oxford University Press.

Cambridge Dictionary. (n.d). Economic Nationalism. Retrieved from: https://dictionary.cambridge.org/tr/sözlük/ingilizce/economic-nationalism

Camerer, C. F., & Loewenstein, G. (2010). Behavioral economics: Past, present, future. Retrieved from http://www.its.caltech.edu/~camerer/ribe239.pdf

Camerer, C. F., Loewenstein, G., & Rabin, M. (Eds.). (2003). *Advances in behavioral economics*. New York: Russell Sage Foundation Press.

Camplin, T., & Elliot, E. (2014). Innovation, Complex Systems and Computation: Technological Space and Speculations on the Future. *Studies in Emergent Order*, *7*, 184–206.

Candan, E., & Hanedar, A. Ö. (2005, October). İktisat neden bir kapalı kutudur? Hakim iktisadın değer yargısı-sinama ilişkisi. *Paper presented at Gazi Üniversitesi İİBF Ekonomik Yaklaşımlar Dergisi Kongreler Dizisi (IV)*, Ankara. Retrieved from http://debis.deu.edu.tr/userweb//onder.hanedar/dosyalar/gazi.pdf

Carnap, R. (1966). The philosophical foundations of physics (M. Gardner, Ed.). Basic Books.

Carnap, R. (1937). *Logical syntax of language*. New York: Harcourt, Brace and Company.

Case, W. (1993). Semi-Democracy in Malaysia: Withstanding The Pressures for Regime Change. *Pacific Affairs*, 66(2), 183-205.

Çavuşoğlu, E. (2010). *Hegemonik Bir Süreç Olarak Türkiye Kentleşmesi*. Retrieved from http://tez2.yok.gov.tr/

Changeux, J. P. (2002). *The Physiology of Truth: Neuroscience and Human Knowledge*, Cambridge.

Chang, H.-J. (2002). Kicking Away the Ladder: An Unofficial History of Capitalism, Especially in Britain and the United States. *Challenge*, *45*(5), 63–97. doi:10.1080/05775132.2002.11034173

Charles, D.; Gross, F. & Bachtler, J. (2012). 'Smart Specialization' and Cohesion – A Strategy for All Regions? IQ.

Chorafakis, G., & Pontikakis, D. (2011). Theoretical Underpinnings and Future Directions of European Union Research Policy: A Paradigm Shift. *Prometheus*, *29*(2), 131–161. doi:10.1080/08109028.2011.600829

Christensen, C. M. (2000). *The Innovator's Dilemma*. New York, NY: HarperBusiness.

Çiftçi, H. (2017). İktisadın farklı bir çehresi; nöroiktisat. *Ekonomi Bilimleri Dergisi*, *9*(1), 1–15.

Cilliers, P. (2000). What Can We Learn From a Theory of Complexity? *Emergence*, *2*(1), 23–33. doi:10.1207/S15327000EM0201_03

ÇKA-Çukurova Kalkınma Ajansı & TKA-Türkiye Kalkınma Ajansı. (2014b). *Mersin İli Potansiyel Yatırım Konuları Araştırması*. Ankara.

ÇKA-Çukurova Kalkınma Ajansı. (2014a). Adana: Çukurova Bölge Planı.

ÇKA-Çukurova Kalkınma Ajansı. (2016). 10. Yılında Çukurova Kalkınma Ajansı. Adana.

ÇKA-Çukurova Kalkınma Ajansı. (2017a). RIS + Mersin Ar-Ge ve İnovasyon Mevcut Durum Analizi. Adana.

ÇKA-Çukurova Kalkınma Ajansı. (2017b). RIS + Mersin Yenilik İhtiyaç Analizi Raporu. Adana.

ÇKA-Çukurova Kalkınma Ajansı. (2017c). RIS + Adana Ar-Ge ve İnovasyon Mevcut Durum Analizi. Adana.

ÇKA-Çukurova Kalkınma Ajansı. (2017d). *Mersin Yatırım, Destek ve Tanıtım Stratejisi ve Eylem Planı, 2017-2023 Stratejik Planı-2017 Eylem Planı*. Adana: Mersin Yatırım Destek Ofisi.

Clague, C., Keefer, P., Knack, S., & Olson, M. (1996, June). Property and Contract Rights in Autocracies and Democracies. *Journal of Economic Growth*, *1*(2), 243–276. doi:10.1007/BF00138864

COA. (1566, January). A. DVNSMHM.d..., 5/890, 6 Recep 973/27.

COA. (1568). The Ottoman Archives of Presidency of the Republic of Turkey (COA), A.{DVNSMHM.d.., 7/1270, 14 Shawwal 975/1 April .

COA. (1793, March). C.BLD. 39/1906, 23 Recep1207/6.

COA. (1826, June). D.BSM.d, 09264, 5 Zilkade 1241/11.

COA. (1830, September). C.BLD., 31/1533, 29 Rabiülevvel 1246/17.

COA. (1851, August). A. MKT.NZD., 40/88, 17 Shawwal 1267/15.

Coase, R. H. (1976). Adam Smith's View of Man. *The Journal of Law & Economics*, *19*(3), 529–546.

Coase, R. (1999, September 17). The Task of the Society. *International Society for New Institutional Economics Newsletter*, *2*(2), 3–6.

Coase, R. H. (1960). The problem of social cost. *The Journal of Law & Economics*, *3*(October), 1–44. doi:10.1086/466560

Coenen, L., Asheim, B., Bugge, M. M., & Herstad, S. J. (2017). Advancing Regional Innovation Systems: What does Evolutionary Economic Geography Bring to the Policy Table? *Environment and Planning C. Politics and Space*, *35*(4), 600–620.

Cohen, J. (2018). What's "Radical" about [Feminist] Radical Political Economy? *The Review of Radical Political Economics*, *50*(4), 716–726. doi:10.1177/0486613418789704

Comim, F. (2000). The Santa Fe Approach to Complexity: A Marshallian Evolution. *Structural Change and Economic Dynamics*, *11*(1-2), 25–43. doi:10.1016/S0954-349X(99)00020-X

Cook, P. (1992). Regional Innovation Systems: Competitive Regulation in the New Europe. *Geoforum*, *23*(3), 365–382. doi:10.1016/0016-7185(92)90048-9

Cook, P. (1996). The New Wave of Regional İnnovation Networks: Analysis, Charactaristics and Strategy. *Small Business Economics*, *8*(2), 159–171. doi:10.1007/BF00394424

Cook, P., & Leydesdorff, L. (2006). Regional Development in the Knowledge-Based Economy: The Construction of Advantage. *The Journal ofTechnology Transfer*, *31*(1), 5–15. doi:10.100710961-005-5009-3

Cook, P., Uranga, M. G., & Etxebarria, G. (1998). Regional Systems of Innovation: An Evolutionary Perspective. *Environment & Planning A*, *30*(9), 1563–1584. doi:10.1068/a301563

Cooper, Z. (2007). *Economic Nationalism*. The Smith Institute.

Cornia, G. A. (1999). *Liberalization, globalization and ıncome distribution, UNU World Institute for Development Economics Research*. UNU/WIDER.

Crespo, R. F. (2006). The ontology of 'the economic': An Aristotelian Perspective. *Cambridge Journal of Economics*, *30*(5), 767–781. doi:10.1093/cje/bei106

De Bruijn, P., & Lagendijk, A. (2005). Regional Innovation Systems in The Lisbon Strategy. *European Planning Studies*, *13*(8), 1153–1172. doi:10.1080/09654310500336519

de La Mettrie, J. O. (1912). *Man a Machine, philosophical and historical notes by Gertrude C.* Chicago: Bussey.

DeBresson, C. ve Hu, X. (1999). Identifying Clusters of Innovative Activity: A New Approach and A Toolbox. In Boosting Innovation The Cluster Approach (pp. 27-59). OECD Proocedings, OECD.

Demirel, S. K., & Artan, S. (2016). Nöroiktisat ve iktisat biliminin geleceğine ilişkin tartışmalar. *Uluslararası Ekonomi ve Yenilik Dergisi*, *2*(1), 1–28. doi:10.20979/ueyd.07280

Demirer, G. N., Demirer, T., & Duran, M. (1999). *Neoliberal Saldırı Kriz ve İnsanlık*. Ankara: Ütopya Publications.

Demir, Ö., & Acar, M. (1997). *Sosyal Bilimler Sözlüğü.* Ankara: Vadi Publications.

Deutschlandied (Song of Germany). (n.d.). Britannica. Retrieved from https://www.britannica.com/topic/Deutschlandlied

Develliоğlu, F. (2005). *Osmanlıca-Türkçe Ansiklopedik Lûgat "ihtikâr" maddesi (22 b.).* Ankara: Aydın Kitabevi.

Dierksmeier, C. (2011). The freedom-responsibility nexus in management philosophy and business ethics. *Journal of Business Ethics, 101*(4), 263–283. doi:10.100710551-010-0721-9

Dinçer, G. (2011). Hayvansal güdüler, insan psikolojisi ekonomiyi nasıl yönlendirir ve küresel kapitalizm için niçin önemlidir? [Review of the book Animal spirits: How human psychology drives the economy, and why it matters for global capitalism, by G. Akerlof & R. J. Shiller]. *Ekonomik Yaklaşım, 22*(81), 129–132. doi:10.5455/ey.20020

Dodgson, M., Hughes, A., Foster, J., & Metcalfe, J. S. (2010). *System Thinking, market failure, and the development of innovation policy: The Case of Australia.* Centre for Business Research. Retrieved from. http://www.uq.edu.au/economics/abstract/403.pdf

Doğan, A. E. (2001). Türkiye Kentlerinde Yirmi Yılın Bilançosu. *Praksis Dergisi, 2*, 97-123. Retrieved from http://www.praksis.org/files/002Doğan.pdf

Dolfsma, W., & Hoppe, H. (1996). The Challenges of Feminist Economics. *Freiburger FrauenStudien, 2*, 59–72.

Dolfsma, W., & Hoppe, H. (2003). On Feminist Economics. *Feminist Review, 73*, 1–17.

Donath, S. (2000). The Other Economy, A Suggestion for a Distinctively Feminist Economics. *Feminist Economics, 6*(1), 115–123. doi:10.1080/135457000337723

Dopfer, K. (1994). Kenneth Boulding: A Founder of Evolutionary Economics. *Journal of Economic Issues, 28*(4), 1201–1204. doi:10.1080/00213624.1994.11505618

Doucouliagos, C. (1994). A note on the evolution of homo economicus. *Journal of Economic Issues, 28*(3), 877–883. doi:10.1080/00213624.1994.11505586

Drack, M. (2015). Ludwig von Bertalanffy's Organismic View on the Theory of Evolution. *The Journal of Experimental Zoology, 324B*, 77–90.

Drucker, P. F. (1959). Work and Tools. *Technology and Culture, 1*(1), 28–37. doi:10.2307/3100785

Dulupçu, M. A., & Okçu, M. (2000). Towards Quantum Economic Development: Transcending Boundaries. *Ankara Üniversitesi SBF Dergisi, 55*(3), 29–53.

Earl, P. E. (1988). *Behavioural economics* (Vol. 1). Aldershot: Edward Elgar.

EC-European Commission. (1993). *Growth, competitiveness, employment – The challenges and ways forward into the 21st Century*. Luxembourg: Office for Official Publications of the European Communities.

EC-European Commission. (2000). *Towards a European Research Area. COM(2000) 6 final.* Brussels: European Union.

EC-European Commission. (2009). *The Role of Community Research Policy in the Knowledge-Based Economy*. Brussels: European Union.

EC-European Commission. (2010). *Europe 2020 Flagship Initiative Innovation Union. SEC(2010) 1161 Final*. Brussels: European Union.

EC-European Commission. (2010a). *Europe 2020 A Strategy for Smart, Sustainable and Inclusive Growth. COM(2010) 2020*. Brussels: European Union.

EC-European Commission. (2010b). *Regional Policy Contributing to Smarth Growth in Europe 2020. COM(2010) 553 Final*. Brussels: European Union.

EC-European Commission. (2012, May). Guide to Research and Innovation Strategies for Smart Specializations (RIS3). Brussels: European Union.

EC-European Commission. (2017a). *Strenghtening Innovation in Europe's Region: Towards Resilient, Inclusive and Sustainable Growth at Territorial Level.* Brussels: European Union.

EC-European Commission. (2017b). *Open's Future: Open Innovation, Open Science, Open to the World.* Brussels: European Union.

Edler, J., & Fagerberg, J. (2017). Innovation Policy: What, Why, and How. *Oxford Review of Economic Policy*, *33*(1), 2–23. doi:10.1093/oxrep/grx001

Edquist, C. (2011). Design of Innovation Policy Through Diagnostic Analysis: Identification of Systemic Problems (or Failures). *Industrial and Corporate Change*, *20*(6), 1725–1753. doi:10.1093/icc/dtr060

Edquist, C. (Ed.). (2005). *Systems of Innovation Technologies, Institutions and Organizations.* Routledge.

Eggertsson, T. (2013). Quick Guide to New Institutional Economics. *Journal of Comparative Economics*, *41*(1), 1–5. doi:10.1016/j.jce.2013.01.002

Elster, J. (1989). *Nuts and Bolts for the Social Sciences*. Cambridge University Press. doi:10.1017/CBO9780511812255

Emecen, F. (1992). Başmuhasebe Kalemi. *İslâm Ansiklopedisi Cilt*, *5*, 133–135.

EPRS. (2018). The Cost of Non-Europe in Asylum Policy, European Parliamentary Research Service. Retrieved from http://www.europarl.europa.eu/RegData/etudes/STUD/2018/627117/EPRS_STU(2018)627117_EN.pdf

Eraydın, A. (2016). Attributes and Characteristics of Regional Resilience: Defining and Measuring the Resilience of Turkish Regions. *Regional Studies*, *50*(4), 600–614. doi:10.1080/00343404.2015.1034672

Eren, E. (2018). İktisadi Modellemede Gelişmeler: Evrim Modellenebilir mi? *Efil Journal*, *1*(1), 58–87.

Ergin, A. (2016). Bilim ve Teknoloji Yüksek Kurulu Kararları ve Gelişmeleri. Toplantısı, Ankara. Retrieved from https://www.tubitak.gov.tr/sites/default/files/btyk29_web_2.pdf

Eroğul, C. (2002). *Devlet Nedir?* Ankara: İmge Bookstore.

Ertürk, H., & Sam, N. (2009). *Kent Ekonomisi*. Bursa: Ekin Publications.

Etzioni, A. (1999). *Essays in socio-economics*. New York: Springer. doi:10.1007/978-3-662-03900-7

Eurobarometer. (2019). The 2019 Elections: A pro-European –and young – electorate with clear expectations, First results of the European Parliament post-electoral survey. European Parliament. Retrieved from https://www.europarl.europa.eu/at-your-service/files/be-heard/eurobarometer/2019/election2019/EB915_SP_EUROBAROMETER_POSTEE19_FIRSTRESULTS_EN.pdf

European Commission. (n.d.). Irregular Migration. Migration and Home Affairs of European Commission. Retrieved from https://ec.europa.eu/home-affairs/content/irregular-migrant-0_en

European Council. (2000). Presidency Conclusions. Retrieved from http://www.europarl.europa.eu/summits/lis1_en.htm

European Parliament. (2017). Integration of Refugees in Europe. Retrieved from http://www.europarl.europa.eu/news/en/headlines/society/20170629STO78628/integration-of-refugees-in-europe

Eurostat. (n.d.a). First Time Asylum Applicant in the EU28 (Q4-2018). Retrieved from https://ec.europa.eu/eurostat/statistics-explained/index.php/Asylum_quarterly_report

Eurostat. (n.d.b). First-Time Asylum Applicants in the EU28 by citizenship. Retrieved from https://ec.europa.eu/eurostat/statistics-explained/index.php/Asylum_quarterly_report#Where_do_asylum_applicants_come_from.3F

Eurostat. (n.d.c). Asylum Applicants Q4 2017-Q4 2018. Retrieved from https://ec.europa.eu/eurostat/statistics-explained/index.php?title=File:Table_2_-_Asylum_applicants,_Q4_2017_%E2%80%93_Q4_2018.png

External Dimension. (n.d.). European Asylum Support Office. Retrieved from https://www.easo.europa.eu/operational-support/external-dimension

Fagerberg, J., Martin, B. R., & Andersen, E. S. (2013). Innovation Studies: Towards a New Agenda. In J. Fagerberg, B.R. Martin, & E.S. Andersen (Ed.), Innovation Studies: Evolution & Future Challenges (pp. 1-17). UK:Oxford University Press.

Feenberg, A. (1999). *Questioning Technology*. New York, London: Routledge.

Feigl, H., & Blumberg, A. E. (1931). Logical positivism. *The Journal of Philosophy*, *28*(3), 281–296.

Ferraro, F., Pfeffer, J., & Sutton, R. I. (2005). Economics language and assumptions: How theories can become self-fulfilling. *Academy of Management Review*, *30*(1), 8–24. doi:10.5465/amr.2005.15281412

Ferry, M., & McMaster, I. (2013). Cohesion Policy and the Evolution of Regional Policy in Central and Eastern Europe. *Europe-Asia Studies*, *65-8*(8), 1502–1528. doi:10.1080/09668136.2013.832969

Fidan, M. (2017). Osmanlı Dönemi'nde Kastamonu'da Fiyat hareketliliği (M.1703-1776-1777-1796). Sosyal Bilimler Dergisi, 154-179.

Findlay, T. (2012). Feminist Institutionalism and Feminist Political Economy, A Dialogue on Gender, the State and Representation. *Proceeding of the Annual Meeting of the Canadian Political Science Association*. Academic Press.

Fischhoff, B. (1988). Judgment and decision making. In R. J. Sternberg & E. E. Smith (Eds.), *The psychology of human thought* (pp. 153–187). New York: Cambridge University Press.

Fontana, M. (2010). The Santa Fe Perspective on Economics: Emerging Patterns in the Science of Complexity. *History of Economic Ideas*, *18*(2), 167–196.

Foray, D., David, P. A., & Hall, B. (2009). Smart Specialisation: the Concept. In Knowledge for Growth: Prospects for Science, Technology and Innovation (20-24). Report, EUR 24047, Brussels: European Union.

Foray, D., Morgan, K., & Radosevic, S. (2018). *The Role of Smart Specialization in the EU Research & Innovation Policy Landscape*. Retrieved from https://ec.europa.eu/regional_policy/en/information/publications/brochures/2018/the-role-of-smart-specialisation-in-the-eu-research-innovation-policy-landscape

Foray, D. (2012). *Smart Specialisation and the New Industrial Policy Agenda*. Brussels: European Union.

Foray, D. (2014). From Smart Specialisation to Smart Specialisation Policy. *European Journal of Innovation Management*, *17*(4), 492–507. doi:10.1108/EJIM-09-2014-0096

Foray, D., & Goenega, X. (2013). *The Goals of Smart Specialisation.* Brussels: European Union.

Foray, D., & Rainoldi, A. (2013). *Smart Specialisation Programmes and Implementation.* Brussels: European Union.

Foucault, M. (2008). *Introduction to Kant's Anthropology* (R. Nigro, Ed., NigroR.BriggsK., Trans.). Los Angeles.

Freeman, C. (1995). The 'National System of Innovation' in Historical Perspective. *Cambridge Journal of Economics*, *19*, 5–24.

Frenz, M., & Oughton, C. (2005). *Innovation in the UK Regions and Devolved Administrations: A Review of the Literature.* Department of Trade and Industry, Governement of the UK. Retrieved from http://www.bis.gov.uk/files/file9651.doc

Friedman, M. (1953). The methodology of positive economics. In *Essays in positive economics.* University of Chicago Press.

Fukuyama, F. (1992). *The End of History and the Last Man.* New York: Macmillan Press Ltd.

Galbraith, J. K. (2004). *İktisat Tarihi* (M. Günay, Trans.). Ankara: Dost Bookstore.

Geels, F. W. (2004). From sectoral systems of innovation to socio-technical systems: Insights about dynamics and change from sociology and institutional theory. *Research Policy*, *33*(6-7), 897–920. doi:10.1016/j.respol.2004.01.015

Gellner, E. (1983). *Nations and Nationalism.* Ithaca: CornellUniversityPress.

Genç, M. (2000). *Osmanlı İmparatorluğu'nda Devlet ve Ekonomi.* İstanbul: Ötüken Neşriyat.

Gianella, C. Kyriakou; Cohen, C. & Przeor, M. (Ed.), (2016). Implementing Smart Specialisation: A Handbook. Brussels: European Union.

Gidens, A. (1979). *Central problems in social theory.* California: University of California Press. doi:10.1007/978-1-349-16161-4

Gilman, N. (1999). Thorstein Veblen's Neglected Feminism. *Journal of Economic Issues*, *33*(3), 689–711. doi:10.1080/00213624.1999.11506193

Gintis, H. (2000). Beyond Homo economicus: Evidence from experimental economics. *Ecological Economics*, *35*(3), 311–322. doi:10.1016/S0921-8009(00)00216-0

Glass, J. (1996). Review, Beyond Economic Man, Feminist Theory and Economics, Marianne A.Ferber and Julie A. Nelson; The Economic Status of Women under Capitalism, Institutional Economics and Feminist Theory, Janice Peterson and Doug Brown; Unequal Burden, Economic Crises, Persistent Poverty and Women's Work, Lourdes Beneria and Shelley Feldman. *Signs*, *21*(2), 499–502. doi:10.1086/495084

Godin, B. (2004). The Obsession of Competitiveness and its Impact on Statistics: The Construction of High-Technology Indicators. Project on The History and Sociology of S&T Statistics.

Godin, B. (2007). National Innovation System: The System Approach in Historical Perspective. Project on The History and Sociology of S&T Statistics.

Godin, B. (2006). The Knowledge-Based Economy: Conceptual Framework or Buzzword? *The Journal of Technology Transfer*, *31*(1), 17–30. doi:10.100710961-005-5010-x

Gökalp, E. (2007). *Milliyetçilik: Kuramsal Bir Değerlendirme*. Anadolu Üniversitesi Sosyal Bilimler Dergisi.

Gök, T. (2009). RIS Mersin Projesi Üzerine Bir Özet Değerlendirme. *Planlama*, *3-4*, 93–95.

Goldfinch, S. (2015). Property Rights and The Mystery of Capital: A Review of the Soto's Simplistic Solution to Development. *Progress in Development Studies*, *15*(I), 87–96. doi:10.1177/1464993414546971

Gordon, R. J. (2004). Why Was Europe at the Station When America's Productivity Locomotive Departed? *NBER*.

Gramsci, A. (1971). *Selections From the Prison Notebooks*. London: Lawrence and Wishart.

Greene, J. E. (2012). *Public finance: An international perspective*. Singapore: World Scientific Publishing.

Greif, A. (2006). *Institutions and the Path to the Modern Economy: Lessons from Medieval Trade*. Cambridge: Cambridge University Press. doi:10.1017/CBO9780511791307

Greif, A., & David, L. (2004, November). A Theory of Endogenous Institutional Change. *The American Political Science Review*, *98*(4), 633–652. doi:10.1017/S0003055404041395

Grief, A. (2005). Commitment, Coercion and Markets: the Nature and Dynamics of Institutions Supporting Exchange. In C. Menard & M. Shirley (Eds.), Handbook of New Institutional Economics (pp. 727-786). Netherlands: Springer. doi:10.1007/0-387-25092-1_29

Gruber, J. (2016). *Public finance and public policy* (5th ed.). New York: Worth Publishers.

Guignon, C. B. (1983). *Heidegger and the Problem of Knowledge*. Indianapolis, IN: Hackett Publishing Company.

Güler Aydın, D. (2010). Kapitalist sistemde bireyin sorgulanması: Yabancılaşma ve demir kafes. *Amme Idaresi Dergisi*, *43*(2), 17–32.

Güler, B. A. (2003). Yönetişim: Tüm İktidar Sermayeye. Praksis Dergisi, 9, 93-116. Retrieved from http://www.praksis.org/files/00903.pdf

Habermas, J. (1993). *İdeoloji olarak teknik ve bilim* (M. Tüzel, Trans.). İstanbul: Yapıkredi Yayınları.

Habermas, J. (2001). *İletişimsel eylem kuramı* (M. Tüzel, Trans.). İstanbul.

Hadfield, G. K. (2005). The Many Legal Institutions that Support Contractual Commitments. In C. Menard & M. Shirley (Eds.), Handbook of New Institutional Economics (pp. 175-205). Netherlands: Springer. doi:10.1007/0-387-25092-1_9

Haggard, S., Mac Intyre, A., & Tiede, L. (2008). The Rule of Law and Economic Development. *Annual Review of Political Science, 11*(1), 205–234. doi:10.1146/annurev.polisci.10.081205.100244

Haggard, S., & Tiede, L. (2011). The Rule of Law and Economic Growth: Where Are We? *World Development, 39*(5), 673–685. doi:10.1016/j.worlddev.2010.10.007

Hall, D., Hirsch, P., & Li, T. M. (2011). *Powers of Exclusion: Land Dilemmas in Southeast Asia*. Singapore: NUS Press.

Hall, S. (1985). Authoritarian Populism: A Reply to Jessop et al. *New Left Review, 151*(May-June), 115–124.

Hamilton, H., & Palmer, N. (2017). Co-Investment and Clientelism as Informal Institutions: Beyond 'Good Enough' Property Rights Protection. *Studies in Comparative International Development, 52*(4), 416–435. doi:10.100712116-017-9250-1

Hammond, D. (2005). Philosophical and Ethical Foundations of System Thinking. *TripleC, 3*(2), 20–27. doi:10.31269/triplec.v3i2.20

Hanson, N. R. (1965). *Patterns of discovery*. Cambridge: Cambridge University Press.

Hardin, G. (1968). The tragedy of the commons. *Science, 162*(3859), 1243–1248. doi:10.1126cience.162.3859.1243 PMID:5699198

Hart, N. (2013). *Alfred Marshall and Modern Economics: Equilibrium Theory and Evolutionary Economics*. Palgrave Macmillan. doi:10.1057/9781137029751

Harvey, D. (2005). *A Brief History of Neoliberalism*. Oxford: Oxford University Press.

Hausman, D. M. (1999). Ontology and Methodology in Economics. *Economics and Philosophy, 15*(2), 283–288. doi:10.1017/S0266267100004028

Hausman, D. M. (2008). Introduction. In D. M. Hausman (Ed.), *The Philosophy of Economics An Anthology*. Cambridge: Cambridge University Press.

Hayek, F. A. (1942). Scientism and the study of society. Part I. *Economica, 9*(35), 267–291. doi:10.2307/2549540

Hayek, F. A. (1945). The Use of Knowledge in Society. *The American Economic Review, 25*(4), 519–530.

Hayek, F. A. (2004). *The road to serfdom, Caldwell, B.* Westminster: The Institute of Economic Affairs.

Hayek, F. A. (2014). Lecture III: Economics and Technology. In B. Caldwell (Ed.), *The Market and Other Orders* (pp. 402–414). Chicago: The University of Chicago Press. doi:10.7208/chicago/9780226089690.001.0001

Hédoin, C. (2003). Collective Intentionality in Economics: Making Searle's Theory of Institutional Facts Relevant for Game Theory. *Erasmus Journal for Philosophy and Economics*, *6*(1), 1–27. doi:10.23941/ejpe.v6i1.117

Hegel, F. (1977). *The phenomenology of spirit.* Oxford: Clarendon Press.

Hegel, G. W. F. (2018). *The Phenomenology of Spirit* (T. Pinkard, Trans. & Ed.). Cambridge.

Heidegger, M. (1962). *Being and Time.* Oxford, UK: Blackwell.

Heidegger, M. (1977). *The Question Concerning Technology and Other Essays* (Lovitt W, Trans.). New York, NY: Garland Publishing.

Helleiner, E. (2002). Economic Nationalism as a Challenge to Economic Liberalism? Lessons from the 19th Century. *International Studies Quarterly*, *46*(3), 307–329. doi:10.1111/1468-2478.00235

Hempel, C. (1966). *Philosophy of natural science.* Oxford, England: Prentice-Hall.

Hester, P. T., & Adams, K. M. (2014). *Systemic Thinking, Fundamentals for Understanding Problems and Messes.* Switzerland: Springer. doi:10.1007/978-3-319-07629-4

Hill, E. L. (1968). A critique of positive economics. *American Journal of Economics and Sociology*, *27*(3), 259–266. doi:10.1111/j.1536-7150.1968.tb01047.x

Hillman, A. L. (2009). *Public finance and public policy: responsibilities and limitations of government* (2nd ed.). Cambridge: Cambridge University Press. doi:10.1017/CBO9780511813788

Hobday, M. (2003). Innovation in Asian Industrialization: A Gerschenkronian Perspective. *Oxford Development Studies*, *31*(3), 293–314. doi:10.1080/1360081032000111715

Hodgson, G. M. (2000). The Concept of Emergence in Social Science: Its History and Importance. *Emergence*, *2*(4), 65–77. doi:10.1207/S15327000EM0204_08

Hollis, M., & Nell, E. J. (1975). *Rational economic man: A Philosophical critique of neo-classical economics.* Cambridge University Press. doi:10.1017/CBO9780511554551

Holt, R. P. F., Rosser, J. B. Jr, & Colander, D. (2011). The Complexity Era in Economics. *Review of Political Economy*, *23*(3), 357–369. doi:10.1080/09538259.2011.583820

Hopkins, B. E., & Duggan, L. (2001). A Feminist Comparative Economic Systems. *Feminist Economics*, *17*(3), 35–69. doi:10.1080/13545701.2011.582847

Horkhemier, M. (1982). *Critical theory*. New York: The Continiuum Publishing Company.

Horkhemier, M. (1986). *Akıl Tutulması*. İstanbul: Metis Yayınları.

Hosseini, H. (2011). George Katona: A founding father of old behavioral economics. *Journal of Socio-Economics*, *40*(6), 977–984. doi:10.1016/j.socec.2011.04.002

How to Make the Integration of Refugees into the Labour Market Work. (2016). European Parliament News. Retrieved from http://www.europarl.europa.eu/news/en/headlines/world/20160218STO14834/how-to-make-the-integration-of-refugees-into-the-labour-market-work

Huffman, W. E. (2009). Does information change behaviour? *Proceedings of the OECD World Forum, Statistics, Knowledge and Policy*, Buson, Korea, October 27-30. Academic Press.

Hugh, E. (1919). *Modern science and materialism*. London: Longmans Green and Co.

Hutchinson, F., & Burkitt, B. (1997, March). An economic silence: Women and social credit. *Women's Studies International Forum*, *20*(2), 321–327.

Hutchison, T. W. (1984). Institutionalist economics old and new. *Journal of Institutional and Theoretical Economics*, *140*(1), 20–29.

Hutter, M. (1994). Organism as a Metaphor in German Economic Thought. In P. Mirowski (Ed.), *Natural Images in Economic Thought: Markets Read in Tooth and Claw* (pp. 289–321). USA: Cambridge University Press. doi:10.1017/CBO9780511572128.011

Hwang, H.-R., & Choung, J.-Y. (2014). The Co-evolution of Technology and Institutions in the Catch-up Process: The Case of the Semiconductor Industry in Korea and Taiwan. *The Journal of Development Studies*, *50*(9), 1240–1260. doi:10.1080/00220388.2014.895817

Hyman, D. N. (2010). *Public finance: A contemporary application of theory to policy* (10th ed.). Ohio: South-Westen Cengage Learning.

ICF. (2018). *Peer Review on 'Integration of Refugees into the Labour Market*. Directorate-General for Employment, Social Affairs and Inclusion.

İlgürel, M. (2003). 1116-1119/1704-1707 Tarihleri Arasında Balıkesir'e Ait Narh Düzenlemeleri. İ. E. Halil İnalcık içinde. *Osmanlı Araştırmaları*, *XXIII*, 11–21.

Inman, M. (2018). *Hindsight bias*. Retrieved from https://www.britannica.com/topic/hindsight-bias

IOM. (n.d). Key Migration Terms, International Organization for Migration, Retrieved from https://www.iom.int/key-migration-terms#Irregular-migration

IRE-Innovation Regions in Europe. (2008). IRE Working Group Effective Regional Innovation Systems Final Report. Retrieved from https://wbc-rti.info/object/document/7823/attach/Fina_report_ERIS_final.pdf

İşler, R. (2010). Feminist İktisadın Geleneksel İktisada Metedolojik Açıdan Getirdiği Eleştiriler [The Methodological Criticism of Feminist Economics to the mainstream economics]. *Ekonomi Bilimleri Dergisi [The Journal of Economics Science]*, *2*(1), 115–122.

Jasanoff, S. (2015). Future Imperfect: Science, Technology, and the Imaginations of Modernity. In S. Jasanoff & S.-H. Kim (Eds.), *Dreamscapes of Modernity : Sociotechnical Imaginaries and the Fabrication of Power*. Chicago: The University of Chicago Press. doi:10.7208/chicago/9780226276663.003.0001

Jessop, B. (2002). Liberalism, Neoliberalism, and Urban Governance: A State Theoretical Perspective. In *Antipode* (pp. 452–472). Oxford: Blackwell Publishers. doi:10.1002/9781444397499.ch5

Johannesson, P., & Perjons, E. (2014). *An Introduction to Design Science*. Dordrecht, Holland: Springer. doi:10.1007/978-3-319-10632-8

Johnson, B., Edquist, C., & Lundvall, B. (2003, November). Economic Development and the National System of Innovation Approach. *Proceedings of the First Globelics Conference*, Rio De Janeiro. Academic Press. Retrieved from https://smartech.gatech.edu/bitstream/handle/1853/43154/BengtAkeLundvall_2.pdf

Jonas, H. (1979). Toward a Philosophy of Technology. *The Hastings Center Report*, *9*(1), 34–43. doi:10.2307/3561700 PMID:429061

Juego, B. (2015). Elite Capture and Elite Conflicts in Southeast Asian Neoliberalization Processes. In South South Tricontinental Collaborative Programme (Ed.), Inequality, Democracy and Development under Neoliberalism and Beyond (pp. 68-93). Buenos Aires: CLACSO – Latin American Council of Social Sciences.

Juego, B. (2018). The Institutions of Authoritarian Neoliberalism in Malaysia: A Critical Review of the Development Agendas under the Regimes of Mahathir, Abdullah, and Najib. *Austrian Journal of South-East Asian Studies*, *11*(1), 53–79.

Kahneman, D., & Tversky, A. (1979). Prospect theory: An analysis of decision under risk. *Econometrica*, *47*(2), 263–291. doi:10.2307/1914185

Kal'a, A. (1992). 19. Yüzyılın İlk Yarısına kadar İstanbul Kasap Esnafının Organizasyonu. *Sosyal Siyaset Konferansları Dergisi*, *0*(37-38), 111–117.

Kant, I. (1914). *Critique of Judgment* (J. H. Bernard, Trans.). London: McMillan. (Original work published 1892)

Kant, I. (2002). *Critique of Practical Reason* (W. S. Pluhar, Trans.). Indianapolis.

Kant, I. (2004). *Prolegomena to Any Future Metaphysics* (G. Hatfield, Trans. & Ed.). Cambridge. doi:10.1017/CBO9780511808517

Kant, I. (2006). *Anthropology from a Pragmatic Point of View* (R. B. Louden, Trans. & Ed.). Cambridge.

Karatani, K. (2003). *Transcritique on Kant and Marx*. Cambridge. doi:10.7551/mitpress/6897.001.0001

Kara, U. (2004). *Sosyal Devletin Yükselişi ve Düşüşü*. Ankara: Maki Publications.

Katona, G., & Harris, D. J. (1978). Behavioral economics. *The Challenge (Karachi)*, *21*(4), 14–18. doi:10.1080/05775132.1978.11470445

Katz, J. S. (2006). Indicators for Complex Innovation Systems. *Research Policy*, *35*(7), 893–909. doi:10.1016/j.respol.2006.03.007

Katz, J. S. (2016). What is a Complex Innovation System? *PLoS One*, *11*(6), 1–24. doi:10.1371/journal.pone.0156150 PMID:27258040

Kaufmann, A., & Wagner, P. (2005). EU Regional Policy and the Stimulation of Innovation: The Role of the European Regional Development Fund in the Objective 1 Region Burgenland. *European Planning Studies*, *13*(4), 581–599. doi:10.1080/09654310500107274

Kaul, I., Grunberg, I., & Stern, M. A. (1999). *Global public goods: Concepts, policies and strategies, Kaul, I., Grunberg, I., & Stern, M. A: Global Public Goods: International Cooperation in the 21st Century*. New York: Oxford University Press.

Kayıran, M. (2013). Kamu malları: Piyasa başarısızlığı mı teorilerin başarısızlığı mı? [Public Goods: Market Failure or the Failure of the Theories?]. *Ankara Universty SBF Juornal*, *68*(4), 147–184.

Kazgan, G. (2005). *Türkiye Ekonomisinde Krizler (1921-2001)*. İstanbul: İstanbul Bilgi Üniversitesi Publications.

Kazgan, G. (2006). *İktisadi Düşünce Politik İktisadın Evrimi*. İstanbul: Baskı.

Keane, D., & Mc Geehan, N. (2008). Enforcing Migrant Workers' Rights in the United Arab Emirates. *International Journal on Minority and Group Rights*, *15*(1), 81–115.

Kedourie, E. (1960). *Nationalism*. London: Hutchinson.

Keefer, P., & Knack, S. (1997). Why Don't Poor Countries Catch Up? A Cross-National Test of An Institutional Environment. *Economic Inquiry*, *35*(3), 590–602. doi:10.1111/j.1465-7295.1997.tb02035.x

Kennedy, J. (1998). Thinking Is Social: Experiments with the Adaptive Culture Model. *The Journal of Conflict Resolution*, *42*(1), 56–76. doi:10.1177/0022002798042001003

Kepenek, Y. (n.d.). Gelişmede Devletin 'Yeni' Yeri Sorunu. Proceedings of 'Planlamanın Meşruiyeti ve Plancıların Konumları (pp. 51-55). Ankara. *TMMOB Şehir Plancıları Odası*.

Keskinok, H. Ç. (2007). Planlama ve Siyaset İlişkisi Üzerine: Kimin İçin Siyaset, Kimin İçin Planlama? Proceedings of Planlama Siyaset Siyasalar, Dokuz Eylül Üniversitesi Kaynaklar Yerleşkesi, İzmir (pp. 97-100). Academic Press.

Keynes, J. M. (2008). *Genel teori, istihdam, faiz ve paranın genel teorisi* (U. S. Akalın, Trans.). İstanbul: Kalkedon Yayınları.

Kiddie, G.L. (2010). Perceived Security of Tenure and Housing Consolidation in Informal Settlements: Case Studies from Urban Fiji. *Pacific Economic Bulletin*, *25*, 193–214.

Kim, L., & Nelson, R. R. (Eds.). (2000). *Technology, Learning, and Innovation*. Cambridge, UK: Cambridge University Press.

Kim, S.-H. (2015). Social Movements and Contested Sociotechnical Imaginaries in South Korea. In S. Jasanoff & S.-H. Kim (Eds.), *Dreamscapes of Modernity: Sociotechnical Imaginaries and the Fabrication of Power* (pp. 152–173). Chicago: The University of Chicago Press.

Kızılçelik, S. (2008). *Frankfurt okulu*. Ankara: Anı Yayıncılık.

Klein, P. G. (1998). New Institutional Economics. Department of Economics, University of Georgia.

Kloby, J. (2005). *Küreselleşmenin Sefaleti* (O. Düz, Trans.). İstanbul: Güncel Yayıncılık.

Knutsen, C. H. (2011). Democracy, Dictatorship and Protection of Property Rights. *The Journal of Development Studies*, *47*(1), 164–182. doi:10.1080/00220388.2010.506919

Knutsen, C. H., & Hanne, F. (2013). Property Rights in Dictatorships: Kings Protect Property Better Than Generals or Party Bosses. *Contemporary Politics*, *19*(1), 94–114. doi:10.1080/13569775.2013.773205

Krieger, L. (1962). The uses of Marx for history. *Political Science Quarterly*, *75*(3), 355–378. doi:10.2307/2146388

Kuhn, T. (1962). *The structure of scientific revolutions*. University of California Press.

Kütükoğlu, M. S. (2006). "Narh". Osmanlılar'da Narh. *İslâm ansiklopedisi Cilt*, *32*, 390–391.

Lall, S. (1996). *Learning from the Asian Tigers: Studies in Technology and Industrial Policy*. Hampshire, UK: Macmillan. doi:10.1057/9780230389892

Lall, S., & Teubal, M. (1998). "Market-Stimulating" Developing Technology Policies in Countries: A Framework with Examples from East Asia. *World Development*, *26*(8), 1369–1385. doi:10.1016/S0305-750X(98)00071-0

Landabaso, M. (1997). The Promotion of Innovation in Regional Policy: Proposal for a Regional Innovation Strategy. *Entrepreneurship and Regional Development*, *9*(1), 1–24. doi:10.1080/08985629700000001

Latour, B. (1992). Where Are the Missing Masses? The Sociology of a Few Mundane Artifacts. In W. Bijker & J. Law (Eds.), *Shaping Technology/Building Society: Studies in Sociotechnical Change*. Cambridge, MA: MIT Press.

Lawson, T. (1994). A Realist Theory for Economics. In R. E. Backhouse (Ed.), *New Directions in Economic Methodology* (pp. 257–285). doi:10.4324/9780203204085.ch13

Le Grand, J. (1991). The theory of government failure. *British Journal of Political Science*, *21*(4), 423–442. doi:10.1017/S0007123400006244

Leblang, D. (1996). Property Rights, Democracy and Economic Growth. *Political Research Quarterly*, *49*(1), 5–26. doi:10.1177/106591299604900102

Levent, T. (2016). RIS-Mersin Project: The First Regional Innovation Strategy in Turkey and its Spatial Dimensions. *Folia Geographica Socia-Oeconomica*, *24*, 5–16.

Lewis, P. (2016). Systems, Structural Properties and Levels of Organisation: The Influence of Ludwig Von Bertalanffy on the Work of F.A. Hayek. In L. Fiorito, S. Scheall, & C. Eduardo Suprinyak (Ed.), *Including a Symposium on Austrian Economics in the Postwar Era (Research in the History of Economic Thought and Methodology* (pp. 125 – 159). Emerald Group Publishing Limited.

Lexico. (n.d.). Gender. Retrieved from www.lexico.com/en/definition/gender

Li, S. (1999). The Benefits and Costs of Relation-Based Governance: An Explanation of the East Asian Miracle and Crisis. *Paper presented at the American Economic Association Annual Meeting*, New York. Academic Press.

Likert, R. (1972). Courageous pioneers: Creating a new field of knowledge. In B. Strümpel, J. M. Morgan, & E. Zahn (Eds.), *Human behavior in economic affairs* (pp. 4–6). San Francisco: Jossey-Bass Inc.

Lindahl, E. (1958). *Just taxation – A positive solution, Musgrave, R. A. & Peacock, A. T.: Classics in the Theory of Public Finance*. London: The Macmillan Press. (Original work published 1919)

Linz, S., & Lipset, S. M. (Eds.). (1999). *Democracy in Developing Countries*. Boulder: Lynne Rienner.

Li, S. (2004). Why is Property Right Protection Lacking in China? An Institutional Explanation. *California Management Review*, *46*(3), 100–115. doi:10.2307/41166223

Loewenstein, G. (1999). Experimental economics from the vantage-point of behavioural economics. *Economic Journal (London)*, *109*(453), 25–34. doi:10.1111/1468-0297.00400

Loewenstein, G., Rick, S., & Cohen, J. D. (2008). Neuroeconomics. *Annual Review of Psychology*, *59*(1), 647–672. doi:10.1146/annurev.psych.59.103006.093710 PMID:17883335

Lundvall, B.-A. (2007). National Innovation Systems—Analytical Concept and Development Tool. *Industry and Innovation*, *14*(1), 95–119. doi:10.1080/13662710601130863

Lundvall, B.-A. (2016). *The Learning Economy and the Economics of Hope*. Anthem Press. doi:10.26530/OAPEN_626406

Lundvall, B.-A., Johnson, B., Andersen, E. S., & Dalum, B. (2002). National Systems of Production, Innovation and Competence Building. *Research Policy*, *31*(2), 213–231. doi:10.1016/S0048-7333(01)00137-8

Maas, H. (2014). *Economic methodology: A historical introduction*. London: Routledge. doi:10.4324/9780203797679

Madelin, R., & Ringrose, D. (2016). *Opportunity now: Europe's Mission to Innovate. Policy Review Report*. Brussels: European Union.

Mäki, U. (Ed.). (2001). *The Economic World View: Studies in the Ontology of Economics*. Cambridge University Press. doi:10.1017/CBO9780511752049

Mankiw, N. G. (2001). *Principles of economics* (2nd ed.). USA: Harcourt.

Mannheim, K. (1954). *Ideology and Utopia*. London: Routledge & Kegan Paul.

Marcuse, H. (1964). *One-dimensional man: Studies in the ideology of advanced industrial society*. Boston: Beacon.

Mariussen, A., Rakhmatullin, R., & Stanionyte, L. (2016). *Smart Specialisation: Creating Growth through Trans-national Cooperation and Value Chains. ThematicWork on the Understanding of Transnational Cooperation and Value Chains in the Context of Smart Specialization*. Luxembourg: European Union.

Martin, R. B. (2013). Innovation Studies: An Emerging Agenda. In J. Fagerberg, B.R. Martin, & E.S. Andersen (Ed.), Innovation Studies. Evolution & Future Challenges (pp. 168-186). UK: Oxford University Press.

Martin, R., & Sunley, P. (2007). Complexity Thinking and Evolutionary Economic Geography. *Journal of Economic Geography*, *7*(5), 573–601. doi:10.1093/jeg/lbm019

Marx, K. (1970). *A contribution to the critique of political economy*. New York: International Publishers.

Marx, K. (1979). *Grundrisse*. Birilim Yayıncılık.

Marx, K. (2007). *Economic and philosophic manuscripts of 1844*. Dover Publications.

Marx, K., & Engels, F. (1970). *The German ideology*. London: Lawrence & Wishart.

Maulana, I. (2019). Big Brothers Are Seducing You: Consumerism, Surveillance, and the Agency of Consumers. In O. Ozgen (Ed.), *Handbook of Research on Consumption, Media, and Popular Culture in the Global Age*. Hershey, PA: IGI Global. doi:10.4018/978-1-5225-8491-9.ch004

Mazurkiewicz-Zachorowska, A. (2015). The Concept of Care in Institutional and Feminist Economics and Its Impact on Public Policy. *Journal of Economic Issues*, *49*(2), 405–413. doi:10.1080/00213624.2015.1042747

McCann, P., & Ortega-Argiles, R. (2013). Transforming European Regional Policy: A Result Driven Agenda and Smart Specialization. *Oxford Review of Economic Policy*, *29*(2), 405–431.

Mckelvey, B. (2001). What is Complexity Science? It is Really Order-Creation Science. *Emergence*, *3*(1), 137–157. doi:10.1207/S15327000EM0301_09

Mckelvey, B. (2004). Toward a Complexity Science of Entrepreneurship. *Journal of Business Venturing*, *19*(3), 313–341. doi:10.1016/S0883-9026(03)00034-X

McLuhan, M. (1994). *Understanding Media: The Extensions of Man*. Cambridge, MA: The MIT Press.

McMahon, W. W. (1987). *Externalities in education, Psacharopoulos, G.: Economics of Education, Research and Studies* (pp. 133–137). Oxford: Pergamon.

Menard, C., & Mary, M. S. (2005). *Handbook of new institutional economics*. Netherlands: Springer. doi:10.1007/b106770

Menard, C., & Shirley, M. M. (2005). Introduction. In C. Menard & M. M. Shirley (Eds.), *Handbook of New Institutional Economics*. Netherlands: Springer.

Menger, C. (1976). *Principles of Economics*. New York: New York University Press. (Original work published 1871)

Mengüşoğlu, T. (2015). *İnsan Felsefesi: I. İnsanın Varlık Yapısı ve Nitelikleri, II.* Ankara: İnsan ve Hayvan, Dünya ve Çevre.

Mersin. (2008). Mersin İnovasyon Stratejisi 2006-2016.

Mill, J. S. (1947). On Liberty, and Considerations on Representative Government. (Originally printed in 1861)

Milne, R. S., & Mauzy, D. K. (1999). *Malaysian Politics under Mahathir*. London: Routledge; doi:10.1007/0-387-25092-1_1.

Milne, S. (2013). *The Revenge of History: The Battle For the 21st Century*. London: Verso.

Mirowski, P. (1991). *More Heat Than Light: Economics as Soscial Physics, Physics as Nature's Economics*. Cambridge University Press.

Mirrlees, J. A. (1999). The theory of moral hazard and unobservable behaviour: Part I. *The Review of Economic Studies*, *66*(1), 3–21. doi:10.1111/1467-937X.00075

Mitcham, C. (1994). *Thinking through Technology: The Path between Engineering and Philosophy*. Chicago: The University of Chicago Press.

Mitcham, C., & Schatzberg, E. (2009). Defining Technology and the Engineering Sciences. In A. Meijers (Ed.), *Philosophy of Technology and Engineering Sciences* (Vol. 9, pp. 27–64). Amsterdam. doi:10.1016/B978-0-444-51667-1.50006-9

Mitleton-Kelly, E. (Ed.). (2003). *Complex Systems and Evolutionary Perspectives on Organizations: The Application of Complexity Theory to Organizations*. Elsevier.

Morehouse, C., & Bloomfield, M. (2011). *Irregular Migration in Europe*. Migration Policy Institute.

Morgan, K. (2013). The Regional State in the Era of Smart Specialization. *Ekonomiaz*, *83*(2), 102–125.

Moving for Prosperity. (2018). *Policy Report*. The World Bank.

Mulgan, G. (2009). Feedback and Belonging: Explaining the Dynamics of Diversity. Migration Policy Institute. Retrieved from https://www.migrationpolicy.org/article/feedback-and-belonging-explaining-dynamics-diversity

Murzi, M. (2007) *Logical positivism*. Retrieved from http://www.murzim.net/Articles/Positivism.pdf

Musgrave, R. A. (1959). *The theory of public finance: A study in pubic economy*. Bombay: Tata-McGraw Hill.

Mytelka, L. K., & Smith, K. (2002). Policy Learning and Innovation Theory: An Interactive and Co-evolving Process. *Research Policy*, *31*(8-9), 1467–1479. doi:10.1016/S0048-7333(02)00076-8

Nagatsu, M. (2015). Behavioral economics, history of. In J. D. Wright (Ed.), *International encyclopedia of the social & behavioral sciences* (2nd ed., pp. 443–449). Oxford: Elsevier. doi:10.1016/B978-0-08-097086-8.03053-1

Nelson, J. (1996). Feminism, Objectivity and Economics. New York: Routledge.

Nelson, J. (1996). What is Feminist Economics All About? *Challenge*, *39*(2), 4–8.

Nelson, R. R., & Winter, S. G. (1982). *An Evolutionary Theory of Economic Change*. Belknap Press.

Noell, C. (2007). A Look into the Nature of Complex Systems and Beyond "Stonehenge" Economics: Coping with Complexity or Ignoring it in Applied Economics. *Agricultural Economics*, *37*(2-3), 219–235. doi:10.1111/j.1574-0862.2007.00268.x

North, D. C. (1981). Structure and Change in Economic History. New York: Norton.

North, D. (1990). *Institutions, Institutional Change and Economic Performance*. Cambridge: Cambridge University Press. doi:10.1017/CBO9780511808678

North, D. (1993). Institutions and Credible Commitment. *Journal of Institutional and Theoretical Economics*, *149*(1), 11–23.

North, D. (1994). Economic Performance Through Time. *The American Economic Review*, *84*(3), 359–368.

North, D. (1995). The New Institutional Economics and Third World Development. In J. Harris & J. Hunter (Eds.), *The New Institutional Economics and Third World Development* (pp. 17–26). London: Routledge. doi:10.4324/9780203444290.pt1

North, D. (2005). *Understanding the Process of Institutional Change*. New Jersey: Princeton University Press. doi:10.1515/9781400829484

North, D. C., & Barry, R. W. (1989). Constitutions and Commitment: The Evolution of Institutions Governing Public Choice in Seventeenth-Century England. *The Journal of Economic History*, *49*(4), 803–832. doi:10.1017/S0022050700009451

Nutku, U. (2016). *Yeniçağ Felsefesinde A Priori Problemi*. Academic Press.

Nyborg, K. (2000). Homo economicus and homo politicus: Interpretation and aggregation of environmental values. *Journal of Economic Behavior & Organization*, *42*(3), 305–322. doi:10.1016/S0167-2681(00)00091-3

Nye, D. E. (2006). *Technology Matters: Questions to Live With*. Cambridge, MA: The MIT Press.

O'Boyle, E. J. (2007). Requiem for homo economicus. *Journal of Markets & Morality*, *10*(2), 321–337.

OECD. (1997). *National Innovation Systems*. Paris: OECD Publishing.

OECD. (1998). *The OECD Jobs Strategy Technology, Productivity and Job Creation Best Policy Practices*. Paris: OECD Publishing.

OECD. (1999). *Managing National Systems*. Paris: OECD Publishing.

OECD. (2005). Guidelines for Collecting and Interpreting Innovation Data — The Oslo Manual (3rd ed.). Paris: Eurostat Publishing.

OECD. (2009). *Investing for Growth: Building innovative regions. Policy Report, Meeting of the Territorial Development Policy Committee at Ministerial level (31 March 2009)*. Paris: OECD.

OECD. (2010a). *Regional Development Policies in OECD Countries*. Paris: OECD Publishing.

OECD. (2010c). Regional Innovation Strategies. Retrieved from. http://www.oecd.org/innovation/policyplatform/48137737.pdf

OECD. (2015). How will the Refugee Surge Affect the European Economy? Migration Policy Debates. Retrieved from http://www.oecd.org/migration/How-will-the-refugee-surge-affect-the-European-economy.pdf

OECD. (2015). *System Innovation: Synthesis Report*. Paris: OECD Publishing.

OECD. (2017). Who bears The Cost of Integrating Refugees? Migration Policy Debates. Retrieved from https://www.oecd.org/els/mig/migration-policy-debates-13.pdf

Öğüt, K., & Sunal, S. (2017). Kompleks Adaptif Bir Sistem Olarak Ekonomi ve İktisat. In E. Eren & S. Şahin (Eds.), *Kompleksite ve İktisat* (pp. 44–57). İstanbul.

Öksüz, A. M., Beyazlı, D.Ş., & Türk, Y.A. (2007). Planlamada Yer Seçimi Kararlarının Politik İçeriği ve Politikalara Yansıması. Proceedings of Planlama Siyaset Siyasalar, Dokuz Eylül Üniversitesi Kaynaklar Yerleşkesi, İzmir (pp. 255-271). Academic Press.

Oliva, G. (2015). The Road to Servomechanisms: The Influence of Cybernetics on Hayek from The Sensory Order to the Social Order. Duke University.

Olson, M. (1993). Democracy, Dictatorship and Development. *The American Political Science Review*, *87*(3), 567–576. doi:10.2307/2938736

Opper, S. (2008). New Institutional Economics and Its Application on Transition and Developing Countries. In E. Brousseau & J.-M. Glachant (Eds.), New Institutional Economics: A Guidebook (pp. 389-407). Cambridge: Cambridge University Press.

Ostrom, E. (2000). Collective action and the evolution of social norms. *The Journal of Economic Perspectives*, *14*(3), 137–158. doi:10.1257/jep.14.3.137

Ostrom, E., & Basurto, X. (2011). Crafting analytical tools to study institutional change. *Journal of Institutional Economics*, *7*(3), 317–343. doi:10.1017/S1744137410000305

Özdemir, R. (2017). Tarihte Tüketici Haklarına Yönelik Yapılan İlk Kanun: "Kanunname-i İhtisab- Bursa." Mecmua Uluslararası Sosyal Bilimler Dergisi, (4), 1-17.

Özdemir, S. (2004). *Küreselleşme Sürecinde Refah Devleti*. İstanbul: İstanbul Ticaret Odası Publications.

Özer, M. A. (2005). *Yeni Kamu Yönetimi: Teoriden Uygulamaya*. Ankara: Platin Yayınları.

Özgen, L. (2007). Küreselleşmiş Dünyada Planlama, Devlet, Hükümet Üzerine: Türkiye Örneği. Proceedings of Planlama Siyaset Siyasalar, Dokuz Eylül Üniversitesi Kaynaklar Yerleşkesi, İzmir (pp. 161-174). Academic Press.

Özkırımlı. U. (2009). Milliyetçilik Kuramları: Eleştirel Bir Bakış. Ankara: Doğu Batı Yayınları.

Öztel, M. (2012). Osmanlı İdaresi'nin İhtikâra Bakışı ve İhtikâr Suçunun Cezası. *The International Journal of Social Sciences (Islamabad)*, *5*(6), 397–420.

Öztel, M. (2013). İstanbul Piyasasında Halkın Temel Tüketim Maddelerinden Ette Fiyat İstikrarı Sorunu (1850-1919). *Turkish Studies*, *8*(6), 567–589.

Pamuk, Ş. (2007). *Osmanlı-Türkiye İktisadî Tarihi 1500-1914*. İstanbul: İletişim Yayınları.

Pantaleoni, M. (1889). *Principii di economia pura*. Firenze: G. Barbèra.

Papademetriou, D., Sumption, M., & Somerville, W. (2009). *Migration and the Economic Downturn: What to Expect in the European Union*. Migration Policy Institute.

Papadopoulous, G. (2015). Collective Intentionality and the State Theory of Money. *Erasmus Journal for Philosophy and Economics*, *8*(2), 1–20. doi:10.23941/ejpe.v8i2.198

Papamichail, G., Rosiello, A., & Wield, D. (2019). Capacity-Building Barriers to S3 Implementation: An Empirical Framework for Catch-up Regions. *Innovation (Abingdon)*, *32*(1), 66–84. doi:10.1080/13511610.2018.1537844

Parsons, T. (1967). *The structure of social action*. New York: Free Press.

Pavlovskaya, M. (2013). Between neoliberalism and difference: Multiple Practices of Property in Post-Soviet Russia. *Europe-Asia Studies*, *65*(7), 1295–1323. doi:10.1080/09668136.2013.822708

Peck, J., & Tickell, A. (2002). Neoliberalizing Space. *Antipode*, *34*(3), 380–404. doi:10.1111/1467-8330.00247

Pellegrin, J. (2007). Regional Innovation Strategies in the EU or a Regionalized EU Innovation Strategy. *Innovation*, *20*(3), 203–221.

Peng, M. (2003). Institutional Transactions and Strategic Choices. *Academy of Management Review*, *28*(2), 275–296. doi:10.5465/amr.2003.9416341

Peng, M., & Luo, Y. (2000). Managerial ties and firm performance in a transition economy: The nature of a micro-macro link. *Academy of Management Journal*, *43*(3), 486–501.

Perloff, J. M. (2007). *Microeconomics* (4th ed.). USA: Pearson Addison Wesley.

Persky, J. (1995). The ethology of homo economicus. *The Journal of Economic Perspectives*, *9*(2), 221–231. doi:10.1257/jep.9.2.221

Peterson, J. (1995). For Whom? Institutional Economics and Distributional Issuses in the Economics Classroom. *Journal of Economic Issues*, *29*(2), 567–574. doi:10.1080/00213624.1995.11505693

Peterson, J. (2012). The Great Crisis and the Significance of Gender in the U.S. Economy. *Journal of Economic Issues*, *46*(2), 277–290. doi:10.2753/JEI0021-3624460203

Pickel, A. (2003). Explaining, and Explaining with Economic Nationalism. *Journal of Nations and Nationalism*, *9*(1).

Pigou, A. C. (1912). *Wealth and welfare*. London: Macmillan.

Pigou, A. C. (1920). *Welfare economics, Londra.* Macmillan.

Polanyi, M. (1966). *The Tacit Dimension.* Chicago: The University of Chicago Press.

Polanyi, M. (2005). *Personal Knowledge: Towards a Post-Critical Philosophy.* London: Routledge.

Popper, K. R. (1979). Objective knowledge: An evolutionary approach (rev. ed.). Oxford: Clarendon Press.

Porter, M. E. (1990). *The Competitive Advantage of Nations.* Hampshire: Macmillan. doi:10.1007/978-1-349-11336-1

Poulantzas, N. (1978). *State, Power, Socialism.* London: Verso.

Power, M. (2004). Social Provisioning as a Starting Point for Feminist Economics. *Feminist Economics, 10*(3), 3–19. doi:10.1080/1354570042000267608

Pratt, R. W. (1972). Marketing applications of behavioral economics. In B. Strümpel, J. M. Morgan, & E. Zahn (Eds.), *Human behavior in economic affairs.* San Francisco: Jossey-Bass Inc.

Press release. (2002, October 9). Retrieved from https://www.nobelprize.org/prizes/economic-sciences/2002/press-release/

Preston, B. (2009). Philosophical Theories of Artifact Function. In A. Meijers (Ed.), *Philosophy of Technology and Engineering Sciences* (Vol. 9, pp. 213–234). Amsterdam: Elsevier. doi:10.1016/B978-0-444-51667-1.50013-6

Prigogine, I., & Stengers, I. (1984). Order Out of Chaos: Man's New Dialogue With Nature. USA: A Bantham Book.

Prigogine, I. (1987). Exploring Complexity. *European Journal of Operational Research, 30*(2), 97–103. doi:10.1016/0377-2217(87)90085-3

Przeworski, A., Alvarez, M., Chaibub, J. A., & Limongi, F. (2000). *Democracy & Development: Political Institutions and Well-Being in the World, 1950-1990.* Cambridge: Cambridge University Press. doi:10.1017/CBO9780511804946

Quora. (n.d.). Role of Philosophy. Retrieved from https://www.quora.com/What-is-the-role-of-philosophy-in-economics

Racko, G. (2019). The Values of Economics. *Journal of Business Ethics, 154*(1), 35–48. doi:10.100710551-017-3442-5

Razeen, S. (2002). *Classical liberalism and international economic order.* New York: Routledge.

Reihenbech, H. (1951). *The rise of scientific philosophy.* University of California Press.

Reillon, V. (2017.September). EU Framework Programmes for Research and Innovation. Evolution and Key Data from FP1 to Horizon 2020 in View of FP9. European Union.

Richard, H. (n.d.). Thaler Facts. Retrieved from https://www.nobelprize.org/prizes/economic-sciences/2017/thaler/facts/

Robert, V., Yoguel, G., & Lerena, O. (2017). The Ontology of Complexity and the Neo-Schumpeterian Evolutionary Theory of Economic Change. *Journal of Evolutionary Economics*, *27*(4), 761–793. doi:10.100700191-017-0512-x

Rosenberg, N. (2000). *Schumpeter and the Endogeneity of Technology*. London: Routledge. doi:10.4324/9780203465356

Rosser, J. B. Jr. (2011). *Complex Evolutionary Dynamics in Urban-Regional and Ecologic-Economic Systems: From Catastrophe to Chaos and Beyond*. London: Springer. doi:10.1007/978-1-4419-8828-7

Roszak, T. (1969). *The Making of Counter Culture: Reflections on the Technocratic Society and Its Youthful Opposition*. New York, NY: Anchor Books.

Ryan, B. E. (1982). Thorstein Veblen, A New Perspective. *Mid-American Review of Sociology*, *7*(2), 29–47.

Sachs, J. (1992). Privatization in Russia: Some Lessons from Eastern Europe. *The American Economic Review*, *82*(2), 43–48.

Şahin, Y. E. (2004). Sosyal Devlet Modelinden 'Good Governance' Modeline Geçiş Sürecinde Kalkınma ve Planlama Anlayışında Gerçekleşen Değişim. Proceedings of Şehircilikte Reform 2003 Mersin Üniversitesi-TMMOB Şehir Plancıları Odası, Mersin (pp. 113-126). Academic Press.

Şahin, E. (2017). *1754 Numaralı Çorum Şer'iyye Siciline Göre Çorum'da Sosyal ve Ekonomik Hayat (1826-1838)*. Yayınlanmamış Yüksek Lisans Tezi.

Samuelson, P. A. (1954). The pure theory of public expenditure. *The Review of Economics and Statistics*, *36*(4), 387–389. doi:10.2307/1925895

Samuelson, P. A. (1955). Diagrammatic exposition of a theory of public expenditure. *The Review of Economics and Statistics*, *37*(4), 350–356. doi:10.2307/1925849

Sanfrey, A. G., Loewenstein, G., Mcclure, S. M., & Cohen, J. D. (2008). Neuroeconomics: Cross-currents in research on decision making. *Trends in Cognitive Sciences*, *10*(3), 108–116. doi:10.1016/j.tics.2006.01.009 PMID:16469524

Şaylan, G. (2003). *Değişim Küreselleşme ve Devletin Yeni İşlevi*. Ankara: İmge Kitabevi.

Schlick, M. (1996). *The emergence of logical empiricism*. Garland Publishing Inc.

Schmidt, R. (1956). Cultural Nationalism in Herder. *Journal of the History of Ideas*, *17*(3), 407–417. doi:10.2307/2707552

Schumacher, E. F. (2014). Buddhist Economics. In R. C. Scharff & V. Dusek (Eds.), *Philosophy of Technology – The Technological Condition: An Anthology* (2nd ed., pp. 421–425). Chichester, UK: John Wiley & Sons, Inc.

Schumpeter, J. A. (1934). *The Theory of Economic Development*. Cambridge, MA: Harvard University Press.

Schumpeter, J. A. (1954). *History of Economic Analysis*. Routledge.

Schumpeter, J. A. (2003). *Capitalism, Socialism and Democracy*. London: Routledge.

Searle, J. (1995). *The Construction of Social Reality*. New York: The Free Press.

Seidman, L. S. (2009). *Public finance*. NewYork: McGraw Hill/Irwin.

Seiz, J. (1995). Bargaining Models, Feminism and Institutionalism. *Journal of Economic Issues*, *29*(2), 609–618. doi:10.1080/00213624.1995.11505698

Seligman, B. B. (1969). The Impact of Positivism in Economic Thought. *History of Political Economy*, *1*(2), 256–278. doi:10.1215/00182702-1-2-256

Sen, A. (1989). Behavior and the Concept of Preference. *Economica*, *40*(159), 241–259. doi:10.2307/2552796

Şengül, H. T. (2003b). Yerel Devlet Sorunu ve Yerel Devletin Dönüşümünde Yeni Eğilimler. *Praksis Dergisi*, *9*, 183-220. Retrieved from http://www.praksis.org/files/009-07.pdf

Şengül, H. T. (2009a). *Kentsel Çelişki ve Siyaset*. İstanbul: İmge Bookstore.

Sent, E. M. (2004). Behavioral economics: How psychology made its (limited) way back into economics. *History of Political Economy*, *36*(4), 735–760. doi:10.1215/00182702-36-4-735

Serdaroglu, U. (2008). Feminist İktisat Bilimi Sorguluyor [Feminist Economics queries Science] *Ekonomik Yaklşaşım [Ekonomik Yaklaşım Association]*, *19*(66), 1–28. doi:10.5455/ey.10658

Seyidoğlu, H. (2002). *Ekonomik Terimler Ansiklopedik Sözlük (3rd ed.)*. İstanbul: Güzem Can Yayınları.

Sezen, S. (1999). Devletçilikten Özelleştirmeye Türkiye'de Planlama, Ankara: Todaie.

Sharkey, W. W. (1983). *The theory of natural monopoly, Cambridge Books*. Cambridge University Press.

Shirley, M. M. (2005). Institutions and Development. In C. Menard & M.M. Shirley (Eds.), Handbook of New Institutional Economics (pp. 611-638). Netherlands: Springer. doi:10.1007/0-387-25092-1_25

Simon, H. A. (2018). Can There be a Science of Complex Systems? In Y. Bar-Yam (Ed)., *Unifying Themes in Complex Systems* (pp. 3-14), CRC Press.

Simon, H. A. (1962). The Architecture of Complexity. *Proceedings of the American Philosophical Society*, *106*(6), 467–487.

Simon, H. A. (1996). *The sciences of the artificial* (3rd ed.). Cambridge, MA: The M.I.T. Press.

Smith, A. (1976). *The theory of moral sentiments* (D. D. Raphael & A. L. Macfie, Eds.). Indianapolis: Liberty Classics.

Smith, A. (1993). *National Identity*. University of Nevada Press.

Smith, B. (1990). Aristotle, Menger, Mises: An Essay in the Metaphysics of Economics. *History of Political Economy*, *22*, 263–288.

Smith, V. (2013). Adam Smith: From Propriety and Sentiments to Property and Wealth. *The Forum for Social Economics*, *42*(4), 283–297. doi:10.1080/07360932.2013.798241

Solak, İ. (2008). Osmanlı İmparatorluğu Döneminde Anadolu'da Meyve ve Sebze Üretimi. Türkiyat Araştırmaları Dergisi, (24), 217-251.

Soukup, A., Maitah, M., & Svoboda, R. (2015). The concept of rationality in neoclassical and behavioural economic theory. *Modern Applied Science*, *9*(3), 1.

Special Eurobarometer 469. (2018). Integration of Immigrants in the European Union. Retrieved from Directorate-General for Migration and Home Affairs and co-ordinated by the Directorate-General for Communication& TNS opinion & social.

Spinoza, B. (1985). *Collected Works of Spinoza* (Vol. 1). (E. Curley, Trans. & Ed.). Princeton.

Staveren, I. V. (2010). Post-Keynesianism meets feminist economics. *Cambridge Journal of Economics*, *34*(6), 1123–1144.

Stiglitz, J. E. (2000). Economics of the public sector (3rd ed.). New York: W.W. Norton & Company.

Strober, M. H. (1994). Can Feminist Thought Improve Economics Rethinking Economics Through a Feminist Lens. *AEA Papers and Proceedings*, *84*(2), 143–147.

Strümpel, B., Morgan, J., & Zahn, E. (Eds.). (1972). *Human behavior in economic affairs*. San Francisco: Jossey-Bass Inc.

Suarez-Villa, L. (2009). *Technocapitalism: A Critical Perspective on Technological Innovation and Corporatism*. Philadelphia, PA: Temple University Press.

Sugden, R. (1991). Rational Choice: A Survey of Contributions from Economics and Philosophy. *Economic Journal (London)*, *101*(407), 751–785. doi:10.2307/2233854

Swami Krishnananda. (n.d.). Philosophy. Retrieved from https://www.swami-krishnananda.org/phil/phil_01.html

Tabakoğlu, A. (1987). Osmanlı Ekonomisinde Fiyat Denetimi. İstanbul Üniversitesi İktisat Fakültesi Mecmuası, 43, 111-150.

Tankut, G. (2002). Kentler. In *Bilim ve Teknik Dergisinin Ücretsiz Eki.* Academic Press. Retrieved from http://www.biltek.tubitak.gov.tr/bdergi/yeniufuk/icerik/kentler.pdf

Tansel, C. B. (2017). *States of Discipline: Authoritarian Neoliberalism and the Contested Reproduction of Capitalist Order.* London: Rowman & Littlefield International.

Tejani, S. (2019). What's feminist about feminist economics? *Journal of Economic Methodology, 26*(2), 99–117. doi:10.1080/1350178X.2018.1556799

Tekeli, İ. (2001b). Her Geçen Gün Geleceği Yeniden Yaratıyor ve Yeniden Kavrıyoruz. Proceedings of 'Geleceği Planlamak: Yeni Planlama Yöntemi, Dili, Yasal Geleceği', TMMOB Şehir Plancıları Odası, Ankara (pp. 27-32). Academic Press.

Tekeli, İ. (2007). Siyaset ve Planlama İlişkisi Yeniden Tanımlanırken. Proceedings of Planlama Siyaset Siyasalar, Dokuz Eylül Üniversitesi Kaynaklar Yerleşkesi, İzmir (pp. 37-51). Academic Press.

Temin, P. (2002). The Golden Age of European Growth Reconsidered. *European Review of Economic History, 6*(1), 3–22. doi:10.1017/S1361491602000011

Thaler, R., Sunstein, C., & Balz, J. (2010). Choice architecture. doi:10.2139srn.1583509

Thaler, R. (1980). Toward a positive theory of consumer choice. *Journal of Economic Behavior & Organization, 1*(1), 39–60. doi:10.1016/0167-2681(80)90051-7

Thaler, R. (1985). Mental accounting and consumer choice. *Marketing Science, 4*(3), 199–214. doi:10.1287/mksc.4.3.199

Thaler, R. H., & Sunstein, C. R. (2017). *Dürtme: Sağlık, zenginlik ve mutlulukla ilgili kararları uygulamak* (E. Günsel, Trans.). İstanbul: Pegasus Yayınları.

The French Flag. (2019). France Diplomatique. Retrieved from https://www.diplomatie.gouv.fr/en/coming-to-france/france-facts/symbols-of-the-republic/article/the-french-flag

The World Bank. (2009). *Reshaping Economic Geography.*

The World Bank. (n.d.). Refugee Population by Country or Territory of Asylum. Retrieved from https://data.worldbank.org/indicator/sm.pop.refg?end=2017&start=1990

Thomasson, A. L. (2009). Artifacts in Metaphysics. In A. Meijers (Ed.), *Philosophy of Technology and Engineering Sciences* (pp. 191–212). Amsterdam: Elsevier. doi:10.1016/B978-0-444-51667-1.50012-4

TÜBA-Türkiye Bilimler Akademisi. (2006). *Yerleşme Bilimleri/Çalışmaları İçin Öngörüler, Çalışma Grubu: İlhan Tekeli vd.* Ankara: Türkiye Bilimler Akademisi Publications.

Turkcan, B. (2014). Knowledge Externalities and Knowledge Spillovers in Social Networks: The Case of Izmir Metalwork Industrial District. *European Planning Studies*, *22*(7), 1425–1443. doi:10.1080/09654313.2013.789488

Türkhan, M. (2016). "Celep". *İslâm Ansiklopedisi. Cilt Ek*, *1*, 255–257.

Tversky, A., & Kahneman, D. (1974). Judgment under uncertainty: Heuristics and biases. *Science*, *185*(4157), 1124–1131. doi:10.1126cience.185.4157.1124 PMID:17835457

Tversky, A., & Kahneman, D. (1981). The framing of decisions and the psychology of choice. *Science*, *211*(4481), 453–458. doi:10.1126cience.7455683 PMID:7455683

Tversky, A., & Kahneman, D. (1992). Advances in prospect theory: Cumulative representation of uncertainty. *Journal of Risk and Uncertainty*, *5*(4), 297–323. doi:10.1007/BF00122574

Ulbrich, H. H. (2011). *Public finance in theory and practice* (*2nd ed.*). London: Routledge.

UNHCR. (n.d.a). Are the Refugee Numbers The Highest Ever? Retrieved from https://www.unhcr.org/blogs/statistics-refugee-numbers-highest-ever/

UNHCR. (n.d.b). Figures at a Glace. Retrieved from: https://www.unhcr.org/figures-at-a-glance.html

Uyarra, E., Sörvik, J., & Midtkandal, I. (2014). *Inter-regional Collaboration in Research and Innovation Strategies for Smart Specialisation (RIS3).* European Union.

Valentinov, V. (2015). Kenneth Boulding's Theories of Evolutionary Economics and Organizational Change: A Reconstruction. *Journal of Economic Issues*, *49*(1), 71–88. doi:10.1080/00213624.2015.1013880

van den Berghe, P. (1981). *The Ethnic Phenomenon*. New York: Elsevier.

van Straven, I. (2005). Feminist Economics, Settiong out the Parametres. In C. Bauhardt & G. Caglar (Eds.), Feministiche Kritik der politischen Ökonomie (pp. 18-48). Wiesbaden: VS Verlag für Sozialwissenschaften.

Varian, H. R. (2010). *Intermediate microeconomics: A modern approach* (*8th ed.*). New York: W. W. Norton & Company.

Veblen, T. B. (2015). Aylak Sınıfın Teorisi Kurumların İktisadi İncelemesi [The Theory of Leisure Class An Economic Study of Institutions]. Ankara: Heretik Yayınları.

Verbeek, P.-P. (2005). *What Things Do: Philosophical Reflections on Technology, Agency, and Design*. University Park, PA: The Pennsylvania State University Press.

Vernon, R. (1983). Organizational and Institutional Responses to Political Risk. In R. Herring (Ed.), *Managing International Risk* (pp. 191–216). Cambridge: Cambridge University Press. doi:10.1017/CBO9780511664601.011

von Bertalanffy, L. (1950). The Theory of Open Systems in Physics and Biology. *Science*, *111*(2872), 23–29. doi:10.1126cience.111.2872.23 PMID:15398815

von Bertalanffy, L. (1969). *General Systems Theory: Foundation, Development, Applications*. New York, USA: George Braziller.

von Bertalanffy, L. (1972). The History and Status of General Systems Theory. *Academy of Management Journal*, *15*(4), 407–426.

von Hippel, E. (2005). *Democratizing Innovation*. Cambridge, MA: The MIT Press. doi:10.7551/mitpress/2333.001.0001

Waddoups, J., & Tilman, R. (1992). Thorstein Veblen and Feminism of Institutional Economics. *International Review of Sociology*, *3*(3), 182–204. doi:10.1080/03906701.1992.9971127

Weaver, W. (1948). Science and Complexity. *American Scientist*, *36*(4), 536–544. PMID:18882675

Weingast, B. R. (1993). Constitutions as Governance Structures: The Political Foundations of Secure Markets. *Journal of Institutional and Theoretical Economics*, *149*(1), 286–311.

Weinreich, P., Bacova, V., & Rougier, N. (2003). Basic primordialism in ethnic and national identity. In P. Weinreich & W. Saunderson (Eds.), *Analysing Identity: Cross-cultural, Societal and ClinicalContexts*. Hove: Routledge.

White, R., Engelen, G., & Uljee, I. (2015). *Modeling Cities and Regions as Complex Systems: From Theory to Planning Applications*. London, England: MIT Press. doi:10.7551/mitpress/9780262029568.001.0001

Wicksell, K. (1958). *A new principle of just taxation. In R.A. Musgrave & A.T. Peacock (Eds.), Classics in the theory of public finance* (pp. 72–118). London: The Macmillan Press. (Original work published 1896)

Williams, H. (2014). Considerations on the Scottish Referendum and a Discourse on the British Conundrum: Mill, Price, and the Question of Nationalism. *Anali Hrvatskogpolitološkogdruštva*, *11*(1), 7-25. Retrieved from https://hrcak.srce.hr/140172

Williamson, O. E. (2000). The New Institutional Economics: Taking Stock, Looking Ahead. *Journal of Economic Literature*, *38*(3), 595–613. doi:10.1257/jel.38.3.595

Winston, C. (2006). *Government failure versus market failure: microeconomics policy research and government performance*. Washington, D.C.: AEI-Brookings.

Woolley, F. (2005). The Citation Impact of Feminist Economics. *Feminist Economics*, *11*(3), 85–106. doi:10.1080/13545700500301312

World Bank. (2016). Bölgesel Yatırım Ortamı Değerlendirmesi Raporu, TR62 IBBS II Bölgesi Adana-Mersin, Ankara.

Wyckoff, A. (2017). Innovation and Complexity. In P. Love, Ve J. Stockdale-Otarola (Eds.), Debate The Issues: Complexity and Policy Making (pp. 80-83). Paris: OECD Publishing. doi:10.1787/9789264271531-en

Yeldan, E. (2002). Neoliberal Küreselleşme İdeolojisinin Kalkınma Söylemi Üzerine Değerlendirmeler. *Praksis Dergisi*, *7*, 19-34. Retrieved from http://www.praksis.org/files/007-02.pdf

Yi, J., Peng, M., Yang, X., & Mutlu, C. (2015). Privatization, Governance and Survival: MNE Investments in Private Participation Projects in Emerging Economies. *Journal of World Business*, *50*(2), 294–301. doi:10.1016/j.jwb.2014.10.006

Yırtıcı, H. (2009). *Çağdaş Kapitalizmin Mekânsal Örgütlenmesi*. İstanbul: İstanbul Bilgi Üniversitesi Publications.

Zakaria, H. A. (1989). Malaysia: Quasi-democracy in a Divided Society. In Democracy in Developing Countries (pp. 347-381). Boulder: Rienner.

Zak, P. J. (2004). Neuroeconomics. *Philosophical Transactions of the Royal Society*, *359*(1451), 1737–1748. doi:10.1098/rstb.2004.1544 PMID:15590614

Zúñiga y Postigo, G. (2000). *A General Theory of Value: Axiology in the Central European Philosophical Tradition* [Doctoral dissertation]. University at Buffalo, Buffalo, New York

Zúñiga y Postigo, G. (1999). An Ontology of Economic Objects. *American Journal of Economics and Sociology*, *58*(2), 299–312. doi:10.1111/j.1536-7150.1998.tb03474.x

Zúñiga y Postigo, G. (2017). On the Transformation of Economic Value. *Axiomathes*, *27*(5), 561–576.

Related References

To continue our tradition of advancing information science and technology research, we have compiled a list of recommended IGI Global readings. These references will provide additional information and guidance to further enrich your knowledge and assist you with your own research and future publications.

Abtahi, M. S., Behboudi, L., & Hasanabad, H. M. (2017). Factors Affecting Internet Advertising Adoption in Ad Agencies. *International Journal of Innovation in the Digital Economy*, *8*(4), 18–29. doi:10.4018/IJIDE.2017100102

Agrawal, S. (2017). The Impact of Emerging Technologies and Social Media on Different Business(es): Marketing and Management. In O. Rishi & A. Sharma (Eds.), *Maximizing Business Performance and Efficiency Through Intelligent Systems* (pp. 37–49). Hershey, PA: IGI Global. doi:10.4018/978-1-5225-2234-8.ch002

Alnoukari, M., Razouk, R., & Hanano, A. (2016). BSC-SI: A Framework for Integrating Strategic Intelligence in Corporate Strategic Management. *International Journal of Social and Organizational Dynamics in IT*, *5*(2), 1–14. doi:10.4018/IJSODIT.2016070101

Alnoukari, M., Razouk, R., & Hanano, A. (2016). BSC-SI, A Framework for Integrating Strategic Intelligence in Corporate Strategic Management. *International Journal of Strategic Information Technology and Applications*, *7*(1), 32–44. doi:10.4018/IJSITA.2016010103

Altındağ, E. (2016). Current Approaches in Change Management. In A. Goksoy (Ed.), *Organizational Change Management Strategies in Modern Business* (pp. 24–51). Hershey, PA: IGI Global. doi:10.4018/978-1-4666-9533-7.ch002

Alvarez-Dionisi, L. E., Turner, R., & Mittra, M. (2016). Global Project Management Trends. *International Journal of Information Technology Project Management, 7*(3), 54–73. doi:10.4018/IJITPM.2016070104

Anantharaman, R. N., Rajeswari, K. S., Angusamy, A., & Kuppusamy, J. (2017). Role of Self-Efficacy and Collective Efficacy as Moderators of Occupational Stress Among Software Development Professionals. *International Journal of Human Capital and Information Technology Professionals, 8*(2), 45–58. doi:10.4018/IJHCITP.2017040103

Aninze, F., El-Gohary, H., & Hussain, J. (2018). The Role of Microfinance to Empower Women: The Case of Developing Countries. *International Journal of Customer Relationship Marketing and Management, 9*(1), 54–78. doi:10.4018/IJCRMM.2018010104

Arsenijević, O. M., Orčić, D., & Kastratović, E. (2017). Development of an Optimization Tool for Intangibles in SMEs: A Case Study from Serbia with a Pilot Research in the Prestige by Milka Company. In M. Vemić (Ed.), *Optimal Management Strategies in Small and Medium Enterprises* (pp. 320–347). Hershey, PA: IGI Global. doi:10.4018/978-1-5225-1949-2.ch015

Aryanto, V. D., Wismantoro, Y., & Widyatmoko, K. (2018). Implementing Eco-Innovation by Utilizing the Internet to Enhance Firm's Marketing Performance: Study of Green Batik Small and Medium Enterprises in Indonesia. *International Journal of E-Business Research, 14*(1), 21–36. doi:10.4018/IJEBR.2018010102

Atiku, S. O., & Fields, Z. (2017). Multicultural Orientations for 21st Century Global Leadership. In N. Baporikar (Ed.), *Management Education for Global Leadership* (pp. 28–51). Hershey, PA: IGI Global. doi:10.4018/978-1-5225-1013-0.ch002

Atiku, S. O., & Fields, Z. (2018). Organisational Learning Dimensions and Talent Retention Strategies for the Service Industries. In N. Baporikar (Ed.), *Global Practices in Knowledge Management for Societal and Organizational Development* (pp. 358–381). Hershey, PA: IGI Global. doi:10.4018/978-1-5225-3009-1.ch017

Ávila, L., & Teixeira, L. (2018). The Main Concepts Behind the Dematerialization of Business Processes. In M. Khosrow-Pour, D.B.A. (Ed.), Encyclopedia of Information Science and Technology, Fourth Edition (pp. 888-898). Hershey, PA: IGI Global. doi:10.4018/978-1-5225-2255-3.ch076

Bartens, Y., Chunpir, H. I., Schulte, F., & Voß, S. (2017). Business/IT Alignment in Two-Sided Markets: A COBIT 5 Analysis for Media Streaming Business Models. In S. De Haes & W. Van Grembergen (Eds.), *Strategic IT Governance and Alignment in Business Settings* (pp. 82–111). Hershey, PA: IGI Global. doi:10.4018/978-1-5225-0861-8.ch004

Bashayreh, A. M. (2018). Organizational Culture and Organizational Performance. In W. Lee & F. Sabetzadeh (Eds.), *Contemporary Knowledge and Systems Science* (pp. 50–69). Hershey, PA: IGI Global. doi:10.4018/978-1-5225-5655-8.ch003

Bedford, D. A. (2018). Sustainable Knowledge Management Strategies: Aligning Business Capabilities and Knowledge Management Goals. In N. Baporikar (Ed.), *Global Practices in Knowledge Management for Societal and Organizational Development* (pp. 46–73). Hershey, PA: IGI Global. doi:10.4018/978-1-5225-3009-1.ch003

Benmoussa, F., Nakara, W. A., & Jaouen, A. (2016). The Use of Social Media by SMEs in the Tourism Industry. In I. Lee (Ed.), *Encyclopedia of E-Commerce Development, Implementation, and Management* (pp. 2159–2170). Hershey, PA: IGI Global. doi:10.4018/978-1-4666-9787-4.ch155

Berger, R. (2016). Indigenous Management and Bottom of Pyramid Countries: The Role of National Institutions. In U. Aung & P. Ordoñez de Pablos (Eds.), *Managerial Strategies and Practice in the Asian Business Sector* (pp. 107–123). Hershey, PA: IGI Global. doi:10.4018/978-1-4666-9758-4.ch007

Bharwani, S., & Musunuri, D. (2018). Reflection as a Process From Theory to Practice. In M. Khosrow-Pour, D.B.A. (Ed.), Encyclopedia of Information Science and Technology, Fourth Edition (pp. 1529-1539). Hershey, PA: IGI Global. doi:10.4018/978-1-5225-2255-3.ch132

Bhatt, G. D., Wang, Z., & Rodger, J. A. (2017). Information Systems Capabilities and Their Effects on Competitive Advantages: A Study of Chinese Companies. *Information Resources Management Journal, 30*(3), 41–57. doi:10.4018/IRMJ.2017070103

Bhushan, M., & Yadav, A. (2017). Concept of Cloud Computing in ESB. In R. Bhadoria, N. Chaudhari, G. Tomar, & S. Singh (Eds.), *Exploring Enterprise Service Bus in the Service-Oriented Architecture Paradigm* (pp. 116–127). Hershey, PA: IGI Global. doi:10.4018/978-1-5225-2157-0.ch008

Bhushan, S. (2017). System Dynamics Base-Model of Humanitarian Supply Chain (HSCM) in Disaster Prone Eco-Communities of India: A Discussion on Simulation and Scenario Results. *International Journal of System Dynamics Applications, 6*(3), 20–37. doi:10.4018/IJSDA.2017070102

Biswas, A., & De, A. K. (2017). On Development of a Fuzzy Stochastic Programming Model with Its Application to Business Management. In S. Trivedi, S. Dey, A. Kumar, & T. Panda (Eds.), *Handbook of Research on Advanced Data Mining Techniques and Applications for Business Intelligence* (pp. 353–378). Hershey, PA: IGI Global. doi:10.4018/978-1-5225-2031-3.ch021

Bücker, J., & Ernste, K. (2018). Use of Brand Heroes in Strategic Reputation Management: The Case of Bacardi, Adidas, and Daimler. In A. Erdemir (Ed.), *Reputation Management Techniques in Public Relations* (pp. 126–150). Hershey, PA: IGI Global. doi:10.4018/978-1-5225-3619-2.ch007

Bureš, V. (2018). Industry 4.0 From the Systems Engineering Perspective: Alternative Holistic Framework Development. In R. Brunet-Thornton & F. Martinez (Eds.), *Analyzing the Impacts of Industry 4.0 in Modern Business Environments* (pp. 199–223). Hershey, PA: IGI Global. doi:10.4018/978-1-5225-3468-6.ch011

Buzady, Z. (2017). Resolving the Magic Cube of Effective Case Teaching: Benchmarking Case Teaching Practices in Emerging Markets – Insights from the Central European University Business School, Hungary. In D. Latusek (Ed.), *Case Studies as a Teaching Tool in Management Education* (pp. 79–103). Hershey, PA: IGI Global. doi:10.4018/978-1-5225-0770-3.ch005

Campatelli, G., Richter, A., & Stocker, A. (2016). Participative Knowledge Management to Empower Manufacturing Workers. *International Journal of Knowledge Management, 12*(4), 37–50. doi:10.4018/IJKM.2016100103

Căpusneanu, S., & Topor, D. I. (2018). Business Ethics and Cost Management in SMEs: Theories of Business Ethics and Cost Management Ethos. In I. Oncioiu (Ed.), *Ethics and Decision-Making for Sustainable Business Practices* (pp. 109–127). Hershey, PA: IGI Global. doi:10.4018/978-1-5225-3773-1.ch007

Carneiro, A. (2016). Maturity in Health Organization Information Systems: Metrics and Privacy Perspectives. *International Journal of Privacy and Health Information Management, 4*(2), 1–18. doi:10.4018/IJPHIM.2016070101

Chan, R. L., Mo, P. L., & Moon, K. K. (2018). Strategic and Tactical Measures in Managing Enterprise Risks: A Study of the Textile and Apparel Industry. In K. Strang, M. Korstanje, & N. Vajjhala (Eds.), *Research, Practices, and Innovations in Global Risk and Contingency Management* (pp. 1–19). Hershey, PA: IGI Global. doi:10.4018/978-1-5225-4754-9.ch001

Chandan, H. C. (2016). Motivations and Challenges of Female Entrepreneurship in Developed and Developing Economies. In N. Baporikar (Ed.), *Handbook of Research on Entrepreneurship in the Contemporary Knowledge-Based Global Economy* (pp. 260–286). Hershey, PA: IGI Global. doi:10.4018/978-1-4666-8798-1.ch012

Charlier, S. D., Burke-Smalley, L. A., & Fisher, S. L. (2018). Undergraduate Programs in the U.S: A Contextual and Content-Based Analysis. In J. Mendy (Ed.), *Teaching Human Resources and Organizational Behavior at the College Level* (pp. 26–57). Hershey, PA: IGI Global. doi:10.4018/978-1-5225-2820-3.ch002

Chaudhuri, S. (2016). Application of Web-Based Geographical Information System (GIS) in E-Business. In U. Panwar, R. Kumar, & N. Ray (Eds.), *Handbook of Research on Promotional Strategies and Consumer Influence in the Service Sector* (pp. 389–405). Hershey, PA: IGI Global. doi:10.4018/978-1-5225-0143-5.ch023

Choudhuri, P. S. (2016). An Empirical Study on the Quality of Services Offered by the Private Life Insurers in Burdwan. In U. Panwar, R. Kumar, & N. Ray (Eds.), *Handbook of Research on Promotional Strategies and Consumer Influence in the Service Sector* (pp. 31–55). Hershey, PA: IGI Global. doi:10.4018/978-1-5225-0143-5.ch002

Dahlberg, T., Kivijärvi, H., & Saarinen, T. (2017). IT Investment Consistency and Other Factors Influencing the Success of IT Performance. In S. De Haes & W. Van Grembergen (Eds.), *Strategic IT Governance and Alignment in Business Settings* (pp. 176–208). Hershey, PA: IGI Global. doi:10.4018/978-1-5225-0861-8.ch007

Damnjanović, A. M. (2017). Knowledge Management Optimization through IT and E-Business Utilization: A Qualitative Study on Serbian SMEs. In M. Vemić (Ed.), *Optimal Management Strategies in Small and Medium Enterprises* (pp. 249–267). Hershey, PA: IGI Global. doi:10.4018/978-1-5225-1949-2.ch012

Daneshpour, H. (2017). Integrating Sustainable Development into Project Portfolio Management through Application of Open Innovation. In M. Vemić (Ed.), *Optimal Management Strategies in Small and Medium Enterprises* (pp. 370–387). Hershey, PA: IGI Global. doi:10.4018/978-1-5225-1949-2.ch017

Daniel, A. D., & Reis de Castro, V. (2018). Entrepreneurship Education: How to Measure the Impact on Nascent Entrepreneurs. In A. Carrizo Moreira, J. Guilherme Leitão Dantas, & F. Manuel Valente (Eds.), *Nascent Entrepreneurship and Successful New Venture Creation* (pp. 85–110). Hershey, PA: IGI Global. doi:10.4018/978-1-5225-2936-1.ch004

David, F., van der Sijde, P., & van den Besselaar, P. (2016). Enterpreneurial Incentives, Obstacles, and Management in University-Business Co-Operation: The Case of Indonesia. In J. Saiz-Álvarez (Ed.), *Handbook of Research on Social Entrepreneurship and Solidarity Economics* (pp. 499–518). Hershey, PA: IGI Global. doi:10.4018/978-1-5225-0097-1.ch024

David, R., Swami, B. N., & Tangirala, S. (2018). Ethics Impact on Knowledge Management in Organizational Development: A Case Study. In N. Baporikar (Ed.), *Global Practices in Knowledge Management for Societal and Organizational Development* (pp. 19–45). Hershey, PA: IGI Global. doi:10.4018/978-1-5225-3009-1.ch002

Delias, P., & Lakiotaki, K. (2018). Discovering Process Horizontal Boundaries to Facilitate Process Comprehension. *International Journal of Operations Research and Information Systems*, *9*(2), 1–31. doi:10.4018/IJORIS.2018040101

Denholm, J., & Lee-Davies, L. (2018). Success Factors for Games in Business and Project Management. In *Enhancing Education and Training Initiatives Through Serious Games* (pp. 34–68). Hershey, PA: IGI Global. doi:10.4018/978-1-5225-3689-5.ch002

Deshpande, M. (2017). Best Practices in Management Institutions for Global Leadership: Policy Aspects. In N. Baporikar (Ed.), *Management Education for Global Leadership* (pp. 1–27). Hershey, PA: IGI Global. doi:10.4018/978-1-5225-1013-0.ch001

Deshpande, M. (2018). Policy Perspectives for SMEs Knowledge Management. In N. Baporikar (Ed.), *Knowledge Integration Strategies for Entrepreneurship and Sustainability* (pp. 23–46). Hershey, PA: IGI Global. doi:10.4018/978-1-5225-5115-7.ch002

Dezdar, S. (2017). ERP Implementation Projects in Asian Countries: A Comparative Study on Iran and China. *International Journal of Information Technology Project Management*, *8*(3), 52–68. doi:10.4018/IJITPM.2017070104

Domingos, D., Martinho, R., & Varajão, J. (2016). Controlled Flexibility in Healthcare Processes: A BPMN-Extension Approach. In M. Cruz-Cunha, I. Miranda, R. Martinho, & R. Rijo (Eds.), *Encyclopedia of E-Health and Telemedicine* (pp. 521–535). Hershey, PA: IGI Global. doi:10.4018/978-1-4666-9978-6.ch040

Domingos, D., Respício, A., & Martinho, R. (2017). Reliability of IoT-Aware BPMN Healthcare Processes. In C. Reis & M. Maximiano (Eds.), *Internet of Things and Advanced Application in Healthcare* (pp. 214–248). Hershey, PA: IGI Global. doi:10.4018/978-1-5225-1820-4.ch008

Dosumu, O., Hussain, J., & El-Gohary, H. (2017). An Exploratory Study of the Impact of Government Policies on the Development of Small and Medium Enterprises in Developing Countries: The Case of Nigeria. *International Journal of Customer Relationship Marketing and Management*, *8*(4), 51–62. doi:10.4018/IJCRMM.2017100104

Durst, S., Bruns, G., & Edvardsson, I. R. (2017). Retaining Knowledge in Smaller Building and Construction Firms. *International Journal of Knowledge and Systems Science*, *8*(3), 1–12. doi:10.4018/IJKSS.2017070101

Edvardsson, I. R., & Durst, S. (2017). Outsourcing, Knowledge, and Learning: A Critical Review. *International Journal of Knowledge-Based Organizations*, *7*(2), 13–26. doi:10.4018/IJKBO.2017040102

Edwards, J. S. (2018). Integrating Knowledge Management and Business Processes. In M. Khosrow-Pour, D.B.A. (Ed.), Encyclopedia of Information Science and Technology, Fourth Edition (pp. 5046-5055). Hershey, PA: IGI Global. doi:10.4018/978-1-5225-2255-3.ch437

Ejiogu, A. O. (2018). Economics of Farm Management. In *Agricultural Finance and Opportunities for Investment and Expansion* (pp. 56–72). Hershey, PA: IGI Global. doi:10.4018/978-1-5225-3059-6.ch003

Ekanem, I., & Abiade, G. E. (2018). Factors Influencing the Use of E-Commerce by Small Enterprises in Nigeria. *International Journal of ICT Research in Africa and the Middle East*, *7*(1), 37–53. doi:10.4018/IJICTRAME.2018010103

Ekanem, I., & Alrossais, L. A. (2017). Succession Challenges Facing Family Businesses in Saudi Arabia. In P. Zgheib (Ed.), *Entrepreneurship and Business Innovation in the Middle East* (pp. 122–146). Hershey, PA: IGI Global. doi:10.4018/978-1-5225-2066-5.ch007

El Faquih, L., & Fredj, M. (2017). Ontology-Based Framework for Quality in Configurable Process Models. *Journal of Electronic Commerce in Organizations*, *15*(2), 48–60. doi:10.4018/JECO.2017040104

El-Gohary, H., & El-Gohary, Z. (2016). An Attempt to Explore Electronic Marketing Adoption and Implementation Aspects in Developing Countries: The Case of Egypt. *International Journal of Customer Relationship Marketing and Management*, *7*(4), 1–26. doi:10.4018/IJCRMM.2016100101

Entico, G. J. (2016). Knowledge Management and the Medical Health Librarians: A Perception Study. In J. Yap, M. Perez, M. Ayson, & G. Entico (Eds.), *Special Library Administration, Standardization and Technological Integration* (pp. 52–77). Hershey, PA: IGI Global. doi:10.4018/978-1-4666-9542-9.ch003

Faisal, M. N., & Talib, F. (2017). Building Ambidextrous Supply Chains in SMEs: How to Tackle the Barriers? *International Journal of Information Systems and Supply Chain Management, 10*(4), 80–100. doi:10.4018/IJISSCM.2017100105

Fernandes, T. M., Gomes, J., & Romão, M. (2017). Investments in E-Government: A Benefit Management Case Study. *International Journal of Electronic Government Research, 13*(3), 1–17. doi:10.4018/IJEGR.2017070101

Fouda, F. A. (2016). A Suggested Curriculum in Career Education to Develop Business Secondary Schools Students' Career Knowledge Management Domains and Professional Thinking. *International Journal of Technology Diffusion, 7*(2), 42–62. doi:10.4018/IJTD.2016040103

Gallardo-Vázquez, D., & Pajuelo-Moreno, M. L. (2016). How Spanish Universities are Promoting Entrepreneurship through Your Own Lines of Teaching and Research? In L. Carvalho (Ed.), *Handbook of Research on Entrepreneurial Success and its Impact on Regional Development* (pp. 431–454). Hershey, PA: IGI Global. doi:10.4018/978-1-4666-9567-2.ch019

Gao, S. S., Oreal, S., & Zhang, J. (2018). Contemporary Financial Risk Management Perceptions and Practices of Small-Sized Chinese Businesses. In I. Management Association (Ed.), Global Business Expansion: Concepts, Methodologies, Tools, and Applications (pp. 917-931). Hershey, PA: IGI Global. doi:10.4018/978-1-5225-5481-3.ch041

Garg, R., & Berning, S. C. (2017). Indigenous Chinese Management Philosophies: Key Concepts and Relevance for Modern Chinese Firms. In B. Christiansen & G. Koc (Eds.), *Transcontinental Strategies for Industrial Development and Economic Growth* (pp. 43–57). Hershey, PA: IGI Global. doi:10.4018/978-1-5225-2160-0.ch003

Gencer, Y. G. (2017). Supply Chain Management in Retailing Business. In U. Akkucuk (Ed.), *Ethics and Sustainability in Global Supply Chain Management* (pp. 197–210). Hershey, PA: IGI Global. doi:10.4018/978-1-5225-2036-8.ch011

Giacosa, E. (2016). Innovation in Luxury Fashion Businesses as a Means for the Regional Development. In L. Carvalho (Ed.), *Handbook of Research on Entrepreneurial Success and its Impact on Regional Development* (pp. 206–222). Hershey, PA: IGI Global. doi:10.4018/978-1-4666-9567-2.ch010

Giacosa, E. (2018). The Increasing of the Regional Development Thanks to the Luxury Business Innovation. In L. Carvalho (Ed.), *Handbook of Research on Entrepreneurial Ecosystems and Social Dynamics in a Globalized World* (pp. 260–273). Hershey, PA: IGI Global. doi:10.4018/978-1-5225-3525-6.ch011

Gianni, M., & Gotzamani, K. (2016). Integrated Management Systems and Information Management Systems: Common Threads. In P. Papajorgji, F. Pinet, A. Guimarães, & J. Papathanasiou (Eds.), *Automated Enterprise Systems for Maximizing Business Performance* (pp. 195–214). Hershey, PA: IGI Global. doi:10.4018/978-1-4666-8841-4.ch011

Gianni, M., Gotzamani, K., & Linden, I. (2016). How a BI-wise Responsible Integrated Management System May Support Food Traceability. *International Journal of Decision Support System Technology*, *8*(2), 1–17. doi:10.4018/IJDSST.2016040101

Glykas, M., & George, J. (2017). Quality and Process Management Systems in the UAE Maritime Industry. *International Journal of Productivity Management and Assessment Technologies*, *5*(1), 20–39. doi:10.4018/IJPMAT.2017010102

Glykas, M., Valiris, G., Kokkinaki, A., & Koutsoukou, Z. (2018). Banking Business Process Management Implementation. *International Journal of Productivity Management and Assessment Technologies*, *6*(1), 50–69. doi:10.4018/IJPMAT.2018010104

Gomes, J., & Romão, M. (2017). The Balanced Scorecard: Keeping Updated and Aligned with Today's Business Trends. *International Journal of Productivity Management and Assessment Technologies*, *5*(2), 1–15. doi:10.4018/IJPMAT.2017070101

Gomes, J., & Romão, M. (2017). Aligning Information Systems and Technology with Benefit Management and Balanced Scorecard. In S. De Haes & W. Van Grembergen (Eds.), *Strategic IT Governance and Alignment in Business Settings* (pp. 112–131). Hershey, PA: IGI Global. doi:10.4018/978-1-5225-0861-8.ch005

Grefen, P., & Turetken, O. (2017). Advanced Business Process Management in Networked E-Business Scenarios. *International Journal of E-Business Research*, *13*(4), 70–104. doi:10.4018/IJEBR.2017100105

Haider, A., & Saetang, S. (2017). Strategic IT Alignment in Service Sector. In S. Rozenes & Y. Cohen (Eds.), *Handbook of Research on Strategic Alliances and Value Co-Creation in the Service Industry* (pp. 231–258). Hershey, PA: IGI Global. doi:10.4018/978-1-5225-2084-9.ch012

Haider, A., & Tang, S. S. (2016). Maximising Value Through IT and Business Alignment: A Case of IT Governance Institutionalisation at a Thai Bank. *International Journal of Technology Diffusion*, *7*(3), 33–58. doi:10.4018/IJTD.2016070104

Hajilari, A. B., Ghadaksaz, M., & Fasghandis, G. S. (2017). Assessing Organizational Readiness for Implementing ERP System Using Fuzzy Expert System Approach. *International Journal of Enterprise Information Systems*, *13*(1), 67–85. doi:10.4018/IJEIS.2017010105

Haldorai, A., Ramu, A., & Murugan, S. (2018). Social Aware Cognitive Radio Networks: Effectiveness of Social Networks as a Strategic Tool for Organizational Business Management. In H. Bansal, G. Shrivastava, G. Nguyen, & L. Stanciu (Eds.), *Social Network Analytics for Contemporary Business Organizations* (pp. 188–202). Hershey, PA: IGI Global. doi:10.4018/978-1-5225-5097-6.ch010

Hall, O. P. Jr. (2017). Social Media Driven Management Education. *International Journal of Knowledge-Based Organizations*, *7*(2), 43–59. doi:10.4018/IJKBO.2017040104

Hanifah, H., Halim, H. A., Ahmad, N. H., & Vafaei-Zadeh, A. (2017). Innovation Culture as a Mediator Between Specific Human Capital and Innovation Performance Among Bumiputera SMEs in Malaysia. In N. Ahmad, T. Ramayah, H. Halim, & S. Rahman (Eds.), *Handbook of Research on Small and Medium Enterprises in Developing Countries* (pp. 261–279). Hershey, PA: IGI Global. doi:10.4018/978-1-5225-2165-5.ch012

Hartlieb, S., & Silvius, G. (2017). Handling Uncertainty in Project Management and Business Development: Similarities and Differences. In Y. Raydugin (Ed.), *Handbook of Research on Leveraging Risk and Uncertainties for Effective Project Management* (pp. 337–362). Hershey, PA: IGI Global. doi:10.4018/978-1-5225-1790-0.ch016

Hass, K. B. (2017). Living on the Edge: Managing Project Complexity. In Y. Raydugin (Ed.), *Handbook of Research on Leveraging Risk and Uncertainties for Effective Project Management* (pp. 177–201). Hershey, PA: IGI Global. doi:10.4018/978-1-5225-1790-0.ch009

Hassan, A., & Privitera, D. S. (2016). Google AdSense as a Mobile Technology in Education. In J. Holland (Ed.), *Wearable Technology and Mobile Innovations for Next-Generation Education* (pp. 200–223). Hershey, PA: IGI Global. doi:10.4018/978-1-5225-0069-8.ch011

Hassan, A., & Rahimi, R. (2016). Consuming "Innovation" in Tourism: Augmented Reality as an Innovation Tool in Digital Tourism Marketing. In N. Pappas & I. Bregoli (Eds.), *Global Dynamics in Travel, Tourism, and Hospitality* (pp. 130–147). Hershey, PA: IGI Global. doi:10.4018/978-1-5225-0201-2.ch008

Hawking, P., & Carmine Sellitto, C. (2017). Developing an Effective Strategy for Organizational Business Intelligence. In M. Tavana (Ed.), *Enterprise Information Systems and the Digitalization of Business Functions* (pp. 222–237). Hershey, PA: IGI Global. doi:10.4018/978-1-5225-2382-6.ch010

Hawking, P., & Sellitto, C. (2017). A Fast-Moving Consumer Goods Company and Business Intelligence Strategy Development. *International Journal of Enterprise Information Systems*, *13*(2), 22–33. doi:10.4018/IJEIS.2017040102

Hawking, P., & Sellitto, C. (2017). Business Intelligence Strategy: Two Case Studies. *International Journal of Business Intelligence Research*, *8*(2), 17–30. doi:10.4018/IJBIR.2017070102

Haynes, J. D., Arockiasamy, S., Al Rashdi, M., & Al Rashdi, S. (2016). Business and E Business Strategies for Coopetition and Thematic Management as a Sustained Basis for Ethics and Social Responsibility in Emerging Markets. In M. Al-Shammari & H. Masri (Eds.), *Ethical and Social Perspectives on Global Business Interaction in Emerging Markets* (pp. 25–39). Hershey, PA: IGI Global. doi:10.4018/978-1-4666-9864-2.ch002

Hee, W. J., Jalleh, G., Lai, H., & Lin, C. (2017). E-Commerce and IT Projects: Evaluation and Management Issues in Australian and Taiwanese Hospitals. *International Journal of Public Health Management and Ethics*, *2*(1), 69–90. doi:10.4018/IJPHME.2017010104

Hernandez, A. A. (2018). Exploring the Factors to Green IT Adoption of SMEs in the Philippines. *Journal of Cases on Information Technology*, *20*(2), 49–66. doi:10.4018/JCIT.2018040104

Hernandez, A. A., & Ona, S. E. (2016). Green IT Adoption: Lessons from the Philippines Business Process Outsourcing Industry. *International Journal of Social Ecology and Sustainable Development*, *7*(1), 1–34. doi:10.4018/IJSESD.2016010101

Hollman, A., Bickford, S., & Hollman, T. (2017). Cyber InSecurity: A Post-Mortem Attempt to Assess Cyber Problems from IT and Business Management Perspectives. *Journal of Cases on Information Technology*, *19*(3), 42–70. doi:10.4018/JCIT.2017070104

Igbinakhase, I. (2017). Responsible and Sustainable Management Practices in Developing and Developed Business Environments. In Z. Fields (Ed.), *Collective Creativity for Responsible and Sustainable Business Practice* (pp. 180–207). Hershey, PA: IGI Global. doi:10.4018/978-1-5225-1823-5.ch010

Ilahi, L., Ghannouchi, S. A., & Martinho, R. (2016). A Business Process Management Approach to Home Healthcare Processes: On the Gap between Intention and Reality. In M. Cruz-Cunha, I. Miranda, R. Martinho, & R. Rijo (Eds.), *Encyclopedia of E-Health and Telemedicine* (pp. 439–457). Hershey, PA: IGI Global. doi:10.4018/978-1-4666-9978-6.ch035

Iwata, J. J., & Hoskins, R. G. (2017). Managing Indigenous Knowledge in Tanzania: A Business Perspective. In P. Jain & N. Mnjama (Eds.), *Managing Knowledge Resources and Records in Modern Organizations* (pp. 198–214). Hershey, PA: IGI Global. doi:10.4018/978-1-5225-1965-2.ch012

Jabeen, F., Ahmad, S. Z., & Alkaabi, S. (2016). The Internationalization Decision-Making of United Arab Emirates Family Businesses. In N. Zakaria, A. Abdul-Talib, & N. Osman (Eds.), *Handbook of Research on Impacts of International Business and Political Affairs on the Global Economy* (pp. 1–22). Hershey, PA: IGI Global. doi:10.4018/978-1-4666-9806-2.ch001

Jain, P. (2017). Ethical and Legal Issues in Knowledge Management Life-Cycle in Business. In P. Jain & N. Mnjama (Eds.), *Managing Knowledge Resources and Records in Modern Organizations* (pp. 82–101). Hershey, PA: IGI Global. doi:10.4018/978-1-5225-1965-2.ch006

Jamali, D., Abdallah, H., & Matar, F. (2016). Opportunities and Challenges for CSR Mainstreaming in Business Schools. *International Journal of Technology and Educational Marketing*, *6*(2), 1–29. doi:10.4018/IJTEM.2016070101

James, S., & Hauli, E. (2017). Holistic Management Education at Tanzanian Rural Development Planning Institute. In N. Baporikar (Ed.), *Management Education for Global Leadership* (pp. 112–136). Hershey, PA: IGI Global. doi:10.4018/978-1-5225-1013-0.ch006

Janošková, M., Csikósová, A., & Čulková, K. (2018). Measurement of Company Performance as Part of Its Strategic Management. In R. Leon (Ed.), *Managerial Strategies for Business Sustainability During Turbulent Times* (pp. 309–335). Hershey, PA: IGI Global. doi:10.4018/978-1-5225-2716-9.ch017

Jean-Vasile, A., & Alecu, A. (2017). Theoretical and Practical Approaches in Understanding the Influences of Cost-Productivity-Profit Trinomial in Contemporary Enterprises. In A. Jean Vasile & D. Nicolò (Eds.), *Sustainable Entrepreneurship and Investments in the Green Economy* (pp. 28–62). Hershey, PA: IGI Global. doi:10.4018/978-1-5225-2075-7.ch002

Jha, D. G. (2016). Preparing for Information Technology Driven Changes. In S. Tiwari & L. Nafees (Eds.), *Innovative Management Education Pedagogies for Preparing Next-Generation Leaders* (pp. 258–274). Hershey, PA: IGI Global. doi:10.4018/978-1-4666-9691-4.ch015

Joia, L. A., & Correia, J. C. (2018). CIO Competencies From the IT Professional Perspective: Insights From Brazil. *Journal of Global Information Management, 26*(2), 74–103. doi:10.4018/JGIM.2018040104

Juma, A., & Mzera, N. (2017). Knowledge Management and Records Management and Competitive Advantage in Business. In P. Jain & N. Mnjama (Eds.), *Managing Knowledge Resources and Records in Modern Organizations* (pp. 15–28). Hershey, PA: IGI Global. doi:10.4018/978-1-5225-1965-2.ch002

K., I., & A, V. (2018). Monitoring and Auditing in the Cloud. In K. Munir (Ed.), *Cloud Computing Technologies for Green Enterprises* (pp. 318-350). Hershey, PA: IGI Global. doi:10.4018/978-1-5225-3038-1.ch013

Kabra, G., Ghosh, V., & Ramesh, A. (2018). Enterprise Integrated Business Process Management and Business Intelligence Framework for Business Process Sustainability. In A. Paul, D. Bhattacharyya, & S. Anand (Eds.), *Green Initiatives for Business Sustainability and Value Creation* (pp. 228–238). Hershey, PA: IGI Global. doi:10.4018/978-1-5225-2662-9.ch010

Kaoud, M. (2017). Investigation of Customer Knowledge Management: A Case Study Research. *International Journal of Service Science, Management, Engineering, and Technology, 8*(2), 12–22. doi:10.4018/IJSSMET.2017040102

Kara, M. E., & Fırat, S. Ü. (2016). Sustainability, Risk, and Business Intelligence in Supply Chains. In M. Erdoğdu, T. Arun, & I. Ahmad (Eds.), *Handbook of Research on Green Economic Development Initiatives and Strategies* (pp. 501–538). Hershey, PA: IGI Global. doi:10.4018/978-1-5225-0440-5.ch022

Katuu, S. (2018). A Comparative Assessment of Enterprise Content Management Maturity Models. In N. Gwangwava & M. Mutingi (Eds.), *E-Manufacturing and E-Service Strategies in Contemporary Organizations* (pp. 93–118). Hershey, PA: IGI Global. doi:10.4018/978-1-5225-3628-4.ch005

Khan, M. A. (2016). MNEs Management Strategies in Developing Countries: Establishing the Context. In M. Khan (Ed.), *Multinational Enterprise Management Strategies in Developing Countries* (pp. 1–33). Hershey, PA: IGI Global. doi:10.4018/978-1-5225-0276-0.ch001

Khan, M. A. (2016). Operational Approaches in Organizational Structure: A Case for MNEs in Developing Countries. In M. Khan (Ed.), *Multinational Enterprise Management Strategies in Developing Countries* (pp. 129–151). Hershey, PA: IGI Global. doi:10.4018/978-1-5225-0276-0.ch007

Kinnunen, S., Ylä-Kujala, A., Marttonen-Arola, S., Kärri, T., & Baglee, D. (2018). Internet of Things in Asset Management: Insights from Industrial Professionals and Academia. *International Journal of Service Science, Management, Engineering, and Technology*, *9*(2), 104–119. doi:10.4018/IJSSMET.2018040105

Klein, A. Z., Sabino de Freitas, A., Machado, L., Freitas, J. C. Jr, Graziola, P. G. Jr, & Schlemmer, E. (2017). Virtual Worlds Applications for Management Education. In L. Tomei (Ed.), *Exploring the New Era of Technology-Infused Education* (pp. 279–299). Hershey, PA: IGI Global. doi:10.4018/978-1-5225-1709-2.ch017

Kożuch, B., & Jabłoński, A. (2017). Adopting the Concept of Business Models in Public Management. In M. Lewandowski & B. Kożuch (Eds.), *Public Sector Entrepreneurship and the Integration of Innovative Business Models* (pp. 10–46). Hershey, PA: IGI Global. doi:10.4018/978-1-5225-2215-7.ch002

Kumar, J., Adhikary, A., & Jha, A. (2017). Small Active Investors' Perceptions and Preferences Towards Tax Saving Mutual Fund Schemes in Eastern India: An Empirical Note. *International Journal of Asian Business and Information Management*, *8*(2), 35–45. doi:10.4018/IJABIM.2017040103

Lassoued, Y., Bouzguenda, L., & Mahmoud, T. (2016). Context-Aware Business Process Versions Management. *International Journal of e-Collaboration*, *12*(3), 7–33. doi:10.4018/IJeC.2016070102

Lavassani, K. M., & Movahedi, B. (2017). Applications Driven Information Systems: Beyond Networks toward Business Ecosystems. *International Journal of Innovation in the Digital Economy*, *8*(1), 61–75. doi:10.4018/IJIDE.2017010104

Lazzareschi, V. H., & Brito, M. S. (2017). Strategic Information Management: Proposal of Business Project Model. In G. Jamil, A. Soares, & C. Pessoa (Eds.), *Handbook of Research on Information Management for Effective Logistics and Supply Chains* (pp. 59–88). Hershey, PA: IGI Global. doi:10.4018/978-1-5225-0973-8.ch004

Lederer, M., Kurz, M., & Lazarov, P. (2017). Usage and Suitability of Methods for Strategic Business Process Initiatives: A Multi Case Study Research. *International Journal of Productivity Management and Assessment Technologies*, *5*(1), 40–51. doi:10.4018/IJPMAT.2017010103

Lee, I. (2017). A Social Enterprise Business Model and a Case Study of Pacific Community Ventures (PCV). In V. Potocan, M. Üngan, & Z. Nedelko (Eds.), *Handbook of Research on Managerial Solutions in Non-Profit Organizations* (pp. 182–204). Hershey, PA: IGI Global. doi:10.4018/978-1-5225-0731-4.ch009

Lee, L. J., & Leu, J. (2016). Exploring the Effectiveness of IT Application and Value Method in the Innovation Performance of Enterprise. *International Journal of Enterprise Information Systems*, *12*(2), 47–65. doi:10.4018/IJEIS.2016040104

Lee, Y. (2016). Alignment Effect of Entrepreneurial Orientation and Marketing Orientation on Firm Performance. *International Journal of Customer Relationship Marketing and Management*, *7*(4), 58–69. doi:10.4018/IJCRMM.2016100104

Leon, L. A., Seal, K. C., Przasnyski, Z. H., & Wiedenman, I. (2017). Skills and Competencies Required for Jobs in Business Analytics: A Content Analysis of Job Advertisements Using Text Mining. *International Journal of Business Intelligence Research*, *8*(1), 1–25. doi:10.4018/IJBIR.2017010101

Leu, J., Lee, L. J., & Krischke, A. (2016). Value Engineering-Based Method for Implementing the ISO14001 System in the Green Supply Chains. *International Journal of Strategic Decision Sciences*, *7*(4), 1–20. doi:10.4018/IJSDS.2016100101

Levy, C. L., & Elias, N. I. (2017). SOHO Users' Perceptions of Reliability and Continuity of Cloud-Based Services. In M. Moore (Ed.), *Cybersecurity Breaches and Issues Surrounding Online Threat Protection* (pp. 248–287). Hershey, PA: IGI Global. doi:10.4018/978-1-5225-1941-6.ch011

Levy, M. (2018). Change Management Serving Knowledge Management and Organizational Development: Reflections and Review. In N. Baporikar (Ed.), *Global Practices in Knowledge Management for Societal and Organizational Development* (pp. 256–270). Hershey, PA: IGI Global. doi:10.4018/978-1-5225-3009-1.ch012

Lewandowski, M. (2017). Public Organizations and Business Model Innovation: The Role of Public Service Design. In M. Lewandowski & B. Kożuch (Eds.), *Public Sector Entrepreneurship and the Integration of Innovative Business Models* (pp. 47–72). Hershey, PA: IGI Global. doi:10.4018/978-1-5225-2215-7.ch003

Lhannaoui, H., Kabbaj, M. I., & Bakkoury, Z. (2017). A Survey of Risk-Aware Business Process Modelling. *International Journal of Risk and Contingency Management, 6*(3), 14–26. doi:10.4018/IJRCM.2017070102

Li, J., Sun, W., Jiang, W., Yang, H., & Zhang, L. (2017). How the Nature of Exogenous Shocks and Crises Impact Company Performance?: The Effects of Industry Characteristics. *International Journal of Risk and Contingency Management, 6*(4), 40–55. doi:10.4018/IJRCM.2017100103

Lu, C., & Liu, S. (2016). Cultural Tourism O2O Business Model Innovation-A Case Study of CTrip. *Journal of Electronic Commerce in Organizations, 14*(2), 16–31. doi:10.4018/JECO.2016040102

Machen, B., Hosseini, M. R., Wood, A., & Bakhshi, J. (2016). An Investigation into using SAP-PS as a Multidimensional Project Control System (MPCS). *International Journal of Enterprise Information Systems, 12*(2), 66–81. doi:10.4018/IJEIS.2016040105

Malega, P. (2017). Small and Medium Enterprises in the Slovak Republic: Status and Competitiveness of SMEs in the Global Markets and Possibilities of Optimization. In M. Vemić (Ed.), *Optimal Management Strategies in Small and Medium Enterprises* (pp. 102–124). Hershey, PA: IGI Global. doi:10.4018/978-1-5225-1949-2.ch006

Malewska, K. M. (2017). Intuition in Decision-Making on the Example of a Non-Profit Organization. In V. Potocan, M. Ünğan, & Z. Nedelko (Eds.), *Handbook of Research on Managerial Solutions in Non-Profit Organizations* (pp. 378–399). Hershey, PA: IGI Global. doi:10.4018/978-1-5225-0731-4.ch018

Maroofi, F. (2017). Entrepreneurial Orientation and Organizational Learning Ability Analysis for Innovation and Firm Performance. In N. Baporikar (Ed.), *Innovation and Shifting Perspectives in Management Education* (pp. 144–165). Hershey, PA: IGI Global. doi:10.4018/978-1-5225-1019-2.ch007

Martins, P. V., & Zacarias, M. (2017). A Web-based Tool for Business Process Improvement. *International Journal of Web Portals, 9*(2), 68–84. doi:10.4018/IJWP.2017070104

Matthies, B., & Coners, A. (2017). Exploring the Conceptual Nature of e-Business Projects. *Journal of Electronic Commerce in Organizations, 15*(3), 33–63. doi:10.4018/JECO.2017070103

McKee, J. (2018). Architecture as a Tool to Solve Business Planning Problems. In M. Khosrow-Pour, D.B.A. (Ed.), Encyclopedia of Information Science and Technology, Fourth Edition (pp. 573-586). Hershey, PA: IGI Global. doi:10.4018/978-1-5225-2255-3.ch050

McMurray, A. J., Cross, J., & Caponecchia, C. (2018). The Risk Management Profession in Australia: Business Continuity Plan Practices. In N. Bajgoric (Ed.), *Always-On Enterprise Information Systems for Modern Organizations* (pp. 112–129). Hershey, PA: IGI Global. doi:10.4018/978-1-5225-3704-5.ch006

Meddah, I. H., & Belkadi, K. (2018). Mining Patterns Using Business Process Management. In R. Hamou (Ed.), *Handbook of Research on Biomimicry in Information Retrieval and Knowledge Management* (pp. 78–89). Hershey, PA: IGI Global. doi:10.4018/978-1-5225-3004-6.ch005

Mendes, L. (2017). TQM and Knowledge Management: An Integrated Approach Towards Tacit Knowledge Management. In D. Jaziri-Bouagina & G. Jamil (Eds.), *Handbook of Research on Tacit Knowledge Management for Organizational Success* (pp. 236–263). Hershey, PA: IGI Global. doi:10.4018/978-1-5225-2394-9.ch009

Mnjama, N. M. (2017). Preservation of Recorded Information in Public and Private Sector Organizations. In P. Jain & N. Mnjama (Eds.), *Managing Knowledge Resources and Records in Modern Organizations* (pp. 149–167). Hershey, PA: IGI Global. doi:10.4018/978-1-5225-1965-2.ch009

Mokoqama, M., & Fields, Z. (2017). Principles of Responsible Management Education (PRME): Call for Responsible Management Education. In Z. Fields (Ed.), *Collective Creativity for Responsible and Sustainable Business Practice* (pp. 229–241). Hershey, PA: IGI Global. doi:10.4018/978-1-5225-1823-5.ch012

Muniapan, B. (2017). Philosophy and Management: The Relevance of Vedanta in Management. In P. Ordóñez de Pablos (Ed.), *Managerial Strategies and Solutions for Business Success in Asia* (pp. 124–139). Hershey, PA: IGI Global. doi:10.4018/978-1-5225-1886-0.ch007

Muniapan, B., Gregory, M. L., & Ling, L. A. (2016). Marketing Education in Sarawak: Looking at It from the Employers' Viewpoint. In B. Smith & A. Porath (Eds.), *Global Perspectives on Contemporary Marketing Education* (pp. 112–130). Hershey, PA: IGI Global. doi:10.4018/978-1-4666-9784-3.ch008

Murad, S. E., & Dowaji, S. (2017). Using Value-Based Approach for Managing Cloud-Based Services. In A. Turuk, B. Sahoo, & S. Addya (Eds.), *Resource Management and Efficiency in Cloud Computing Environments* (pp. 33–60). Hershey, PA: IGI Global. doi:10.4018/978-1-5225-1721-4.ch002

Mutahar, A. M., Daud, N. M., Thurasamy, R., Isaac, O., & Abdulsalam, R. (2018). The Mediating of Perceived Usefulness and Perceived Ease of Use: The Case of Mobile Banking in Yemen. *International Journal of Technology Diffusion*, *9*(2), 21–40. doi:10.4018/IJTD.2018040102

Naidoo, V. (2017). E-Learning and Management Education at African Universities. In N. Baporikar (Ed.), *Management Education for Global Leadership* (pp. 181–201). Hershey, PA: IGI Global. doi:10.4018/978-1-5225-1013-0.ch009

Naidoo, V., & Igbinakhase, I. (2018). Opportunities and Challenges of Knowledge Retention in SMEs. In N. Baporikar (Ed.), *Knowledge Integration Strategies for Entrepreneurship and Sustainability* (pp. 70–94). Hershey, PA: IGI Global. doi:10.4018/978-1-5225-5115-7.ch004

Nayak, S., & Prabhu, N. (2017). Paradigm Shift in Management Education: Need for a Cross Functional Perspective. In N. Baporikar (Ed.), *Management Education for Global Leadership* (pp. 241–255). Hershey, PA: IGI Global. doi:10.4018/978-1-5225-1013-0.ch012

Ndede-Amadi, A. A. (2016). Student Interest in the IS Specialization as Predictor of the Success Potential of New Information Systems Programmes within the Schools of Business in Kenyan Public Universities. *International Journal of Information Systems and Social Change*, *7*(2), 63–79. doi:10.4018/IJISSC.2016040104

Nedelko, Z., & Potocan, V. (2016). Management Practices for Processes Optimization: Case of Slovenia. In G. Alor-Hernández, C. Sánchez-Ramírez, & J. García-Alcaraz (Eds.), *Handbook of Research on Managerial Strategies for Achieving Optimal Performance in Industrial Processes* (pp. 545–561). Hershey, PA: IGI Global. doi:10.4018/978-1-5225-0130-5.ch025

Nedelko, Z., & Potocan, V. (2017). Management Solutions in Non-Profit Organizations: Case of Slovenia. In V. Potocan, M. Üngan, & Z. Nedelko (Eds.), *Handbook of Research on Managerial Solutions in Non-Profit Organizations* (pp. 1–22). Hershey, PA: IGI Global. doi:10.4018/978-1-5225-0731-4.ch001

Nedelko, Z., & Potocan, V. (2017). Priority of Management Tools Utilization among Managers: International Comparison. In V. Wang (Ed.), *Encyclopedia of Strategic Leadership and Management* (pp. 1083–1094). Hershey, PA: IGI Global. doi:10.4018/978-1-5225-1049-9.ch075

Nedelko, Z., Raudeliūnienė, J., & Črešnar, R. (2018). Knowledge Dynamics in Supply Chain Management. In N. Baporikar (Ed.), *Knowledge Integration Strategies for Entrepreneurship and Sustainability* (pp. 150–166). Hershey, PA: IGI Global. doi:10.4018/978-1-5225-5115-7.ch008

Nguyen, H. T., & Hipsher, S. A. (2018). Innovation and Creativity Used by Private Sector Firms in a Resources-Constrained Environment. In S. Hipsher (Ed.), *Examining the Private Sector's Role in Wealth Creation and Poverty Reduction* (pp. 219–238). Hershey, PA: IGI Global. doi:10.4018/978-1-5225-3117-3.ch010

Nycz, M., & Pólkowski, Z. (2016). Business Intelligence as a Modern IT Supporting Management of Local Government Units in Poland. *International Journal of Knowledge and Systems Science*, *7*(4), 1–18. doi:10.4018/IJKSS.2016100101

Obaji, N. O., Senin, A. A., & Olugu, M. U. (2016). Supportive Government Policy as a Mechanism for Business Incubation Performance in Nigeria. *International Journal of Information Systems and Social Change*, *7*(4), 52–66. doi:10.4018/IJISSC.2016100103

Obicci, P. A. (2017). Risk Sharing in a Partnership. In *Risk Management Strategies in Public-Private Partnerships* (pp. 115–152). Hershey, PA: IGI Global. doi:10.4018/978-1-5225-2503-5.ch004

Obidallah, W. J., & Raahemi, B. (2017). Managing Changes in Service Oriented Virtual Organizations: A Structural and Procedural Framework to Facilitate the Process of Change. *Journal of Electronic Commerce in Organizations*, *15*(1), 59–83. doi:10.4018/JECO.2017010104

Ojasalo, J., & Ojasalo, K. (2016). Service Logic Business Model Canvas for Lean Development of SMEs and Start-Ups. In N. Baporikar (Ed.), *Handbook of Research on Entrepreneurship in the Contemporary Knowledge-Based Global Economy* (pp. 217–243). Hershey, PA: IGI Global. doi:10.4018/978-1-4666-8798-1.ch010

Ojo, O. (2017). Impact of Innovation on the Entrepreneurial Success in Selected Business Enterprises in South-West Nigeria. *International Journal of Innovation in the Digital Economy*, *8*(2), 29–38. doi:10.4018/IJIDE.2017040103

Okdinawati, L., Simatupang, T. M., & Sunitiyoso, Y. (2017). Multi-Agent Reinforcement Learning for Value Co-Creation of Collaborative Transportation Management (CTM). *International Journal of Information Systems and Supply Chain Management*, *10*(3), 84–95. doi:10.4018/IJISSCM.2017070105

Ortner, E., Mevius, M., Wiedmann, P., & Kurz, F. (2016). Design of Interactional Decision Support Applications for E-Participation in Smart Cities. *International Journal of Electronic Government Research*, *12*(2), 18–38. doi:10.4018/IJEGR.2016040102

Pal, K. (2018). Building High Quality Big Data-Based Applications in Supply Chains. In A. Kumar & S. Saurav (Eds.), *Supply Chain Management Strategies and Risk Assessment in Retail Environments* (pp. 1–24). Hershey, PA: IGI Global. doi:10.4018/978-1-5225-3056-5.ch001

Palos-Sanchez, P. R., & Correia, M. B. (2018). Perspectives of the Adoption of Cloud Computing in the Tourism Sector. In J. Rodrigues, C. Ramos, P. Cardoso, & C. Henriques (Eds.), *Handbook of Research on Technological Developments for Cultural Heritage and eTourism Applications* (pp. 377–400). Hershey, PA: IGI Global. doi:10.4018/978-1-5225-2927-9.ch018

Parry, V. K., & Lind, M. L. (2016). Alignment of Business Strategy and Information Technology Considering Information Technology Governance, Project Portfolio Control, and Risk Management. *International Journal of Information Technology Project Management*, *7*(4), 21–37. doi:10.4018/IJITPM.2016100102

Pashkova, N., Trujillo-Barrera, A., Apostolakis, G., Van Dijk, G., Drakos, P. D., & Baourakis, G. (2016). Business Management Models of Microfinance Institutions (MFIs) in Africa: A Study into Their Enabling Environments. *International Journal of Food and Beverage Manufacturing and Business Models*, *1*(2), 63–82. doi:10.4018/IJFBMBM.2016070105

Patiño, B. E. (2017). New Generation Management by Convergence and Individual Identity: A Systemic and Human-Oriented Approach. In N. Baporikar (Ed.), *Innovation and Shifting Perspectives in Management Education* (pp. 119–143). Hershey, PA: IGI Global. doi:10.4018/978-1-5225-1019-2.ch006

Pawliczek, A., & Rössler, M. (2017). Knowledge of Management Tools and Systems in SMEs: Knowledge Transfer in Management. In A. Bencsik (Ed.), *Knowledge Management Initiatives and Strategies in Small and Medium Enterprises* (pp. 180–203). Hershey, PA: IGI Global. doi:10.4018/978-1-5225-1642-2.ch009

Pejic-Bach, M., Omazic, M. A., Aleksic, A., & Zoroja, J. (2018). Knowledge-Based Decision Making: A Multi-Case Analysis. In R. Leon (Ed.), *Managerial Strategies for Business Sustainability During Turbulent Times* (pp. 160–184). Hershey, PA: IGI Global. doi:10.4018/978-1-5225-2716-9.ch009

Perano, M., Hysa, X., & Calabrese, M. (2018). Strategic Planning, Cultural Context, and Business Continuity Management: Business Cases in the City of Shkoder. In A. Presenza & L. Sheehan (Eds.), *Geopolitics and Strategic Management in the Global Economy* (pp. 57–77). Hershey, PA: IGI Global. doi:10.4018/978-1-5225-2673-5.ch004

Pereira, R., Mira da Silva, M., & Lapão, L. V. (2017). IT Governance Maturity Patterns in Portuguese Healthcare. In S. De Haes & W. Van Grembergen (Eds.), *Strategic IT Governance and Alignment in Business Settings* (pp. 24–52). Hershey, PA: IGI Global. doi:10.4018/978-1-5225-0861-8.ch002

Perez-Uribe, R., & Ocampo-Guzman, D. (2016). Conflict within Colombian Family Owned SMEs: An Explosive Blend between Feelings and Business. In J. Saiz-Álvarez (Ed.), *Handbook of Research on Social Entrepreneurship and Solidarity Economics* (pp. 329–354). Hershey, PA: IGI Global. doi:10.4018/978-1-5225-0097-1.ch017

Pérez-Uribe, R. I., Torres, D. A., Jurado, S. P., & Prada, D. M. (2018). Cloud Tools for the Development of Project Management in SMEs. In R. Perez-Uribe, C. Salcedo-Perez, & D. Ocampo-Guzman (Eds.), *Handbook of Research on Intrapreneurship and Organizational Sustainability in SMEs* (pp. 95–120). Hershey, PA: IGI Global. doi:10.4018/978-1-5225-3543-0.ch005

Petrisor, I., & Cozmiuc, D. (2017). Global Supply Chain Management Organization at Siemens in the Advent of Industry 4.0. In L. Saglietto & C. Cezanne (Eds.), *Global Intermediation and Logistics Service Providers* (pp. 123–142). Hershey, PA: IGI Global. doi:10.4018/978-1-5225-2133-4.ch007

Pierce, J. M., Velliaris, D. M., & Edwards, J. (2017). A Living Case Study: A Journey Not a Destination. In N. Silton (Ed.), *Exploring the Benefits of Creativity in Education, Media, and the Arts* (pp. 158–178). Hershey, PA: IGI Global. doi:10.4018/978-1-5225-0504-4.ch008

Radosavljevic, M., & Andjelkovic, A. (2017). Multi-Criteria Decision Making Approach for Choosing Business Process for the Improvement: Upgrading of the Six Sigma Methodology. In J. Stanković, P. Delias, S. Marinković, & S. Rochhia (Eds.), *Tools and Techniques for Economic Decision Analysis* (pp. 225–247). Hershey, PA: IGI Global. doi:10.4018/978-1-5225-0959-2.ch011

Radovic, V. M. (2017). Corporate Sustainability and Responsibility and Disaster Risk Reduction: A Serbian Overview. In M. Camilleri (Ed.), *CSR 2.0 and the New Era of Corporate Citizenship* (pp. 147–164). Hershey, PA: IGI Global. doi:10.4018/978-1-5225-1842-6.ch008

Raghunath, K. M., Devi, S. L., & Patro, C. S. (2018). Impact of Risk Assessment Models on Risk Factors: A Holistic Outlook. In K. Strang, M. Korstanje, & N. Vajjhala (Eds.), *Research, Practices, and Innovations in Global Risk and Contingency Management* (pp. 134–153). Hershey, PA: IGI Global. doi:10.4018/978-1-5225-4754-9.ch008

Raman, A., & Goyal, D. P. (2017). Extending IMPLEMENT Framework for Enterprise Information Systems Implementation to Information System Innovation. In M. Tavana (Ed.), *Enterprise Information Systems and the Digitalization of Business Functions* (pp. 137–177). Hershey, PA: IGI Global. doi:10.4018/978-1-5225-2382-6.ch007

Rao, Y., & Zhang, Y. (2017). The Construction and Development of Academic Library Digital Special Subject Databases. In L. Ruan, Q. Zhu, & Y. Ye (Eds.), *Academic Library Development and Administration in China* (pp. 163–183). Hershey, PA: IGI Global. doi:10.4018/978-1-5225-0550-1.ch010

Ravasan, A. Z., Mohammadi, M. M., & Hamidi, H. (2018). An Investigation Into the Critical Success Factors of Implementing Information Technology Service Management Frameworks. In K. Jakobs (Ed.), *Corporate and Global Standardization Initiatives in Contemporary Society* (pp. 200–218). Hershey, PA: IGI Global. doi:10.4018/978-1-5225-5320-5.ch009

Renna, P., Izzo, C., & Romaniello, T. (2016). The Business Process Management Systems to Support Continuous Improvements. In W. Nuninger & J. Châtelet (Eds.), *Handbook of Research on Quality Assurance and Value Management in Higher Education* (pp. 237–256). Hershey, PA: IGI Global. doi:10.4018/978-1-5225-0024-7.ch009

Rezaie, S., Mirabedini, S. J., & Abtahi, A. (2018). Designing a Model for Implementation of Business Intelligence in the Banking Industry. *International Journal of Enterprise Information Systems, 14*(1), 77–103. doi:10.4018/IJEIS.2018010105

Riccò, R. (2016). Diversity Management: Bringing Equality, Equity, and Inclusion in the Workplace. In J. Prescott (Ed.), *Handbook of Research on Race, Gender, and the Fight for Equality* (pp. 335–359). Hershey, PA: IGI Global. doi:10.4018/978-1-5225-0047-6.ch015

Romano, L., Grimaldi, R., & Colasuonno, F. S. (2017). Demand Management as a Success Factor in Project Portfolio Management. In L. Romano (Ed.), *Project Portfolio Management Strategies for Effective Organizational Operations* (pp. 202–219). Hershey, PA: IGI Global. doi:10.4018/978-1-5225-2151-8.ch008

Rostek, K. B. (2016). Risk Management: Role and Importance in Business Organization. In D. Jakóbczak (Ed.), *Analyzing Risk through Probabilistic Modeling in Operations Research* (pp. 149–178). Hershey, PA: IGI Global. doi:10.4018/978-1-4666-9458-3.ch007

Rouhani, S., & Savoji, S. R. (2016). A Success Assessment Model for BI Tools Implementation: An Empirical Study of Banking Industry. *International Journal of Business Intelligence Research, 7*(1), 25–44. doi:10.4018/IJBIR.2016010103

Ruan, Z. (2016). A Corpus-Based Functional Analysis of Complex Nominal Groups in Written Business Discourse: The Case of "Business". *International Journal of Computer-Assisted Language Learning and Teaching*, *6*(2), 74–90. doi:10.4018/IJCALLT.2016040105

Ruhi, U. (2018). Towards an Interdisciplinary Socio-Technical Definition of Virtual Communities. In M. Khosrow-Pour, D.B.A. (Ed.), Encyclopedia of Information Science and Technology, Fourth Edition (pp. 4278-4295). Hershey, PA: IGI Global. doi:10.4018/978-1-5225-2255-3.ch371

Ryan, J., Doster, B., Daily, S., & Lewis, C. (2016). A Case Study Perspective for Balanced Perioperative Workflow Achievement through Data-Driven Process Improvement. *International Journal of Healthcare Information Systems and Informatics*, *11*(3), 19–41. doi:10.4018/IJHISI.2016070102

Safari, M. R., & Jiang, Q. (2018). The Theory and Practice of IT Governance Maturity and Strategies Alignment: Evidence From Banking Industry. *Journal of Global Information Management*, *26*(2), 127–146. doi:10.4018/JGIM.2018040106

Sahoo, J., Pati, B., & Mohanty, B. (2017). Knowledge Management as an Academic Discipline: An Assessment. In B. Gunjal (Ed.), *Managing Knowledge and Scholarly Assets in Academic Libraries* (pp. 99–126). Hershey, PA: IGI Global. doi:10.4018/978-1-5225-1741-2.ch005

Saini, D. (2017). Relevance of Teaching Values and Ethics in Management Education. In N. Baporikar (Ed.), *Management Education for Global Leadership* (pp. 90–111). Hershey, PA: IGI Global. doi:10.4018/978-1-5225-1013-0.ch005

Sambhanthan, A. (2017). Assessing and Benchmarking Sustainability in Organisations: An Integrated Conceptual Model. *International Journal of Systems and Service-Oriented Engineering*, *7*(4), 22–43. doi:10.4018/IJSSOE.2017100102

Sambhanthan, A., & Potdar, V. (2017). A Study of the Parameters Impacting Sustainability in Information Technology Organizations. *International Journal of Knowledge-Based Organizations*, *7*(3), 27–39. doi:10.4018/IJKBO.2017070103

Sánchez-Fernández, M. D., & Manríquez, M. R. (2018). The Entrepreneurial Spirit Based on Social Values: The Digital Generation. In P. Isaias & L. Carvalho (Eds.), *User Innovation and the Entrepreneurship Phenomenon in the Digital Economy* (pp. 173–193). Hershey, PA: IGI Global. doi:10.4018/978-1-5225-2826-5.ch009

Sanchez-Ruiz, L., & Blanco, B. (2017). Process Management for SMEs: Barriers, Enablers, and Benefits. In M. Vemić (Ed.), *Optimal Management Strategies in Small and Medium Enterprises* (pp. 293–319). Hershey, PA: IGI Global. doi:10.4018/978-1-5225-1949-2.ch014

Sanz, L. F., Gómez-Pérez, J., & Castillo-Martinez, A. (2018). Analysis of the European ICT Competence Frameworks. In V. Ahuja & S. Rathore (Eds.), *Multidisciplinary Perspectives on Human Capital and Information Technology Professionals* (pp. 225–245). Hershey, PA: IGI Global. doi:10.4018/978-1-5225-5297-0.ch012

Sarvepalli, A., & Godin, J. (2017). Business Process Management in the Classroom. *Journal of Cases on Information Technology, 19*(2), 17–28. doi:10.4018/JCIT.2017040102

Satpathy, B., & Muniapan, B. (2016). Ancient Wisdom for Transformational Leadership and Its Insights from the Bhagavad-Gita. In U. Aung & P. Ordoñez de Pablos (Eds.), *Managerial Strategies and Practice in the Asian Business Sector* (pp. 1–10). Hershey, PA: IGI Global. doi:10.4018/978-1-4666-9758-4.ch001

Saygili, E. E., Ozturkoglu, Y., & Kocakulah, M. C. (2017). End Users' Perceptions of Critical Success Factors in ERP Applications. *International Journal of Enterprise Information Systems, 13*(4), 58–75. doi:10.4018/IJEIS.2017100104

Saygili, E. E., & Saygili, A. T. (2017). Contemporary Issues in Enterprise Information Systems: A Critical Review of CSFs in ERP Implementations. In M. Tavana (Ed.), *Enterprise Information Systems and the Digitalization of Business Functions* (pp. 120–136). Hershey, PA: IGI Global. doi:10.4018/978-1-5225-2382-6.ch006

Seidenstricker, S., & Antonino, A. (2018). Business Model Innovation-Oriented Technology Management for Emergent Technologies. In M. Khosrow-Pour, D.B.A. (Ed.), Encyclopedia of Information Science and Technology, Fourth Edition (pp. 4560-4569). Hershey, PA: IGI Global. doi:10.4018/978-1-5225-2255-3.ch396

Senaratne, S., & Gunarathne, A. D. (2017). Excellence Perspective for Management Education from a Global Accountants' Hub in Asia. In N. Baporikar (Ed.), *Management Education for Global Leadership* (pp. 158–180). Hershey, PA: IGI Global. doi:10.4018/978-1-5225-1013-0.ch008

Sensuse, D. I., & Cahyaningsih, E. (2018). Knowledge Management Models: A Summative Review. *International Journal of Information Systems in the Service Sector, 10*(1), 71–100. doi:10.4018/IJISSS.2018010105

Sensuse, D. I., Wibowo, W. C., & Cahyaningsih, E. (2016). Indonesian Government Knowledge Management Model: A Theoretical Model. *Information Resources Management Journal, 29*(1), 91–108. doi:10.4018/irmj.2016010106

Seth, M., Goyal, D., & Kiran, R. (2017). Diminution of Impediments in Implementation of Supply Chain Management Information System for Enhancing its Effectiveness in Indian Automobile Industry. *Journal of Global Information Management, 25*(3), 1–20. doi:10.4018/JGIM.2017070101

Seyal, A. H., & Rahman, M. N. (2017). Investigating Impact of Inter-Organizational Factors in Measuring ERP Systems Success: Bruneian Perspectives. In M. Tavana (Ed.), *Enterprise Information Systems and the Digitalization of Business Functions* (pp. 178–204). Hershey, PA: IGI Global. doi:10.4018/978-1-5225-2382-6.ch008

Shaikh, A. A., & Karjaluoto, H. (2016). On Some Misconceptions Concerning Digital Banking and Alternative Delivery Channels. *International Journal of E-Business Research, 12*(3), 1–16. doi:10.4018/IJEBR.2016070101

Shams, S. M. (2016). Stakeholder Relationship Management in Online Business and Competitive Value Propositions: Evidence from the Sports Industry. *International Journal of Online Marketing, 6*(2), 1–17. doi:10.4018/IJOM.2016040101

Shamsuzzoha, A. (2016). Management of Risk and Resilience within Collaborative Business Network. In R. Addo-Tenkorang, J. Kantola, P. Helo, & A. Shamsuzzoha (Eds.), *Supply Chain Strategies and the Engineer-to-Order Approach* (pp. 143–159). Hershey, PA: IGI Global. doi:10.4018/978-1-5225-0021-6.ch008

Shaqrah, A. A. (2018). Analyzing Business Intelligence Systems Based on 7s Model of McKinsey. *International Journal of Business Intelligence Research, 9*(1), 53–63. doi:10.4018/IJBIR.2018010104

Sharma, A. J. (2017). Enhancing Sustainability through Experiential Learning in Management Education. In N. Baporikar (Ed.), *Management Education for Global Leadership* (pp. 256–274). Hershey, PA: IGI Global. doi:10.4018/978-1-5225-1013-0.ch013

Shetty, K. P. (2017). Responsible Global Leadership: Ethical Challenges in Management Education. In N. Baporikar (Ed.), *Innovation and Shifting Perspectives in Management Education* (pp. 194–223). Hershey, PA: IGI Global. doi:10.4018/978-1-5225-1019-2.ch009

Sinthupundaja, J., & Kohda, Y. (2017). Effects of Corporate Social Responsibility and Creating Shared Value on Sustainability. *International Journal of Sustainable Entrepreneurship and Corporate Social Responsibility*, *2*(1), 27–38. doi:10.4018/IJSECSR.2017010103

Škarica, I., & Hrgović, A. V. (2018). Implementation of Total Quality Management Principles in Public Health Institutes in the Republic of Croatia. *International Journal of Productivity Management and Assessment Technologies*, *6*(1), 1–16. doi:10.4018/IJPMAT.2018010101

Smuts, H., Kotzé, P., Van der Merwe, A., & Loock, M. (2017). Framework for Managing Shared Knowledge in an Information Systems Outsourcing Context. *International Journal of Knowledge Management*, *13*(4), 1–30. doi:10.4018/IJKM.2017100101

Soares, E. R., & Zaidan, F. H. (2016). Information Architecture and Business Modeling in Modern Organizations of Information Technology: Professional Career Plan in Organizations IT. In G. Jamil, J. Poças Rascão, F. Ribeiro, & A. Malheiro da Silva (Eds.), *Handbook of Research on Information Architecture and Management in Modern Organizations* (pp. 439–457). Hershey, PA: IGI Global. doi:10.4018/978-1-4666-8637-3.ch020

Sousa, M. J., Cruz, R., Dias, I., & Caracol, C. (2017). Information Management Systems in the Supply Chain. In G. Jamil, A. Soares, & C. Pessoa (Eds.), *Handbook of Research on Information Management for Effective Logistics and Supply Chains* (pp. 469–485). Hershey, PA: IGI Global. doi:10.4018/978-1-5225-0973-8.ch025

Spremic, M., Turulja, L., & Bajgoric, N. (2018). Two Approaches in Assessing Business Continuity Management Attitudes in the Organizational Context. In N. Bajgoric (Ed.), *Always-On Enterprise Information Systems for Modern Organizations* (pp. 159–183). Hershey, PA: IGI Global. doi:10.4018/978-1-5225-3704-5.ch008

Steenkamp, A. L. (2018). Some Insights in Computer Science and Information Technology. In *Examining the Changing Role of Supervision in Doctoral Research Projects: Emerging Research and Opportunities* (pp. 113–133). Hershey, PA: IGI Global. doi:10.4018/978-1-5225-2610-0.ch005

Studdard, N., Dawson, M., Burton, S. L., Jackson, N., Leonard, B., Quisenberry, W., & Rahim, E. (2016). Nurturing Social Entrepreneurship and Building Social Entrepreneurial Self-Efficacy: Focusing on Primary and Secondary Schooling to Develop Future Social Entrepreneurs. In Z. Fields (Ed.), *Incorporating Business Models and Strategies into Social Entrepreneurship* (pp. 154–175). Hershey, PA: IGI Global. doi:10.4018/978-1-4666-8748-6.ch010

Sun, Z. (2016). A Framework for Developing Management Intelligent Systems. *International Journal of Systems and Service-Oriented Engineering*, *6*(1), 37–53. doi:10.4018/IJSSOE.2016010103

Swami, B., & Mphele, G. T. (2016). Problems Preventing Growth of Small Entrepreneurs: A Case Study of a Few Small Entrepreneurs in Botswana Sub-Urban Areas. In N. Baporikar (Ed.), *Handbook of Research on Entrepreneurship in the Contemporary Knowledge-Based Global Economy* (pp. 479–508). Hershey, PA: IGI Global. doi:10.4018/978-1-4666-8798-1.ch020

Tabach, A., & Croteau, A. (2017). Configurations of Information Technology Governance Practices and Business Unit Performance. *International Journal of IT/Business Alignment and Governance*, *8*(2), 1–27. doi:10.4018/IJITBAG.2017070101

Talaue, G. M., & Iqbal, T. (2017). Assessment of e-Business Mode of Selected Private Universities in the Philippines and Pakistan. *International Journal of Online Marketing*, *7*(4), 63–77. doi:10.4018/IJOM.2017100105

Tam, G. C. (2017). Project Manager Sustainability Competence. In *Managerial Strategies and Green Solutions for Project Sustainability* (pp. 178–207). Hershey, PA: IGI Global. doi:10.4018/978-1-5225-2371-0.ch008

Tambo, T. (2018). Fashion Retail Innovation: About Context, Antecedents, and Outcome in Technological Change Projects. In I. Management Association (Ed.), Fashion and Textiles: Breakthroughs in Research and Practice (pp. 233-260). Hershey, PA: IGI Global. doi:10.4018/978-1-5225-3432-7.ch010

Tambo, T., & Mikkelsen, O. E. (2016). Fashion Supply Chain Optimization: Linking Make-to-Order Purchasing and B2B E-Commerce. In S. Joshi & R. Joshi (Eds.), *Designing and Implementing Global Supply Chain Management* (pp. 1–21). Hershey, PA: IGI Global. doi:10.4018/978-1-4666-9720-1.ch001

Tandon, K. (2016). Innovative Andragogy: The Paradigm Shift to Heutagogy. In S. Tiwari & L. Nafees (Eds.), *Innovative Management Education Pedagogies for Preparing Next-Generation Leaders* (pp. 238–257). Hershey, PA: IGI Global. doi:10.4018/978-1-4666-9691-4.ch014

Tantau, A. D., & Frăţilă, L. C. (2018). Information and Management System for Renewable Energy Business. In *Entrepreneurship and Business Development in the Renewable Energy Sector* (pp. 200–244). Hershey, PA: IGI Global. doi:10.4018/978-1-5225-3625-3.ch006

Teixeira, N., Pardal, P. N., & Rafael, B. G. (2018). Internationalization, Financial Performance, and Organizational Challenges: A Success Case in Portugal. In L. Carvalho (Ed.), *Handbook of Research on Entrepreneurial Ecosystems and Social Dynamics in a Globalized World* (pp. 379–423). Hershey, PA: IGI Global. doi:10.4018/978-1-5225-3525-6.ch017

Trad, A., & Kalpić, D. (2016). The E-Business Transformation Framework for E-Commerce Architecture-Modeling Projects. In I. Lee (Ed.), *Encyclopedia of E-Commerce Development, Implementation, and Management* (pp. 733–753). Hershey, PA: IGI Global. doi:10.4018/978-1-4666-9787-4.ch052

Trad, A., & Kalpić, D. (2016). The E-Business Transformation Framework for E-Commerce Control and Monitoring Pattern. In I. Lee (Ed.), *Encyclopedia of E-Commerce Development, Implementation, and Management* (pp. 754–777). Hershey, PA: IGI Global. doi:10.4018/978-1-4666-9787-4.ch053

Trad, A., & Kalpić, D. (2018). The Business Transformation Framework, Agile Project and Change Management. In M. Khosrow-Pour, D.B.A. (Ed.), Encyclopedia of Information Science and Technology, Fourth Edition (pp. 620-635). Hershey, PA: IGI Global. doi:10.4018/978-1-5225-2255-3.ch054

Trad, A., & Kalpić, D. (2018). The Business Transformation and Enterprise Architecture Framework: The Financial Engineering E-Risk Management and E-Law Integration. In B. Sergi, F. Fidanoski, M. Ziolo, & V. Naumovski (Eds.), *Regaining Global Stability After the Financial Crisis* (pp. 46–65). Hershey, PA: IGI Global. doi:10.4018/978-1-5225-4026-7.ch003

Turulja, L., & Bajgoric, N. (2018). Business Continuity and Information Systems: A Systematic Literature Review. In N. Bajgoric (Ed.), *Always-On Enterprise Information Systems for Modern Organizations* (pp. 60–87). Hershey, PA: IGI Global. doi:10.4018/978-1-5225-3704-5.ch004

van Wessel, R. M., de Vries, H. J., & Ribbers, P. M. (2016). Business Benefits through Company IT Standardization. In K. Jakobs (Ed.), *Effective Standardization Management in Corporate Settings* (pp. 34–53). Hershey, PA: IGI Global. doi:10.4018/978-1-4666-9737-9.ch003

Vargas-Hernández, J. G. (2017). Professional Integrity in Business Management Education. In N. Baporikar (Ed.), *Management Education for Global Leadership* (pp. 70–89). Hershey, PA: IGI Global. doi:10.4018/978-1-5225-1013-0.ch004

Vasista, T. G., & AlAbdullatif, A. M. (2017). Role of Electronic Customer Relationship Management in Demand Chain Management: A Predictive Analytic Approach. *International Journal of Information Systems and Supply Chain Management, 10*(1), 53–67. doi:10.4018/IJISSCM.2017010104

Vergidis, K. (2016). Rediscovering Business Processes: Definitions, Patterns, and Modelling Approaches. In P. Papajorgji, F. Pinet, A. Guimarães, & J. Papathanasiou (Eds.), *Automated Enterprise Systems for Maximizing Business Performance* (pp. 97–122). Hershey, PA: IGI Global. doi:10.4018/978-1-4666-8841-4.ch007

Vieru, D., & Bourdeau, S. (2017). Survival in the Digital Era: A Digital Competence-Based Multi-Case Study in the Canadian SME Clothing Industry. *International Journal of Social and Organizational Dynamics in IT, 6*(1), 17–34. doi:10.4018/IJSODIT.2017010102

Vijayan, G., & Kamarulzaman, N. H. (2017). An Introduction to Sustainable Supply Chain Management and Business Implications. In M. Khan, M. Hussain, & M. Ajmal (Eds.), *Green Supply Chain Management for Sustainable Business Practice* (pp. 27–50). Hershey, PA: IGI Global. doi:10.4018/978-1-5225-0635-5.ch002

Vlachvei, A., & Notta, O. (2017). Firm Competitiveness: Theories, Evidence, and Measurement. In A. Vlachvei, O. Notta, K. Karantininis, & N. Tsounis (Eds.), *Factors Affecting Firm Competitiveness and Performance in the Modern Business World* (pp. 1–42). Hershey, PA: IGI Global. doi:10.4018/978-1-5225-0843-4.ch001

von Rosing, M., Fullington, N., & Walker, J. (2016). Using the Business Ontology and Enterprise Standards to Transform Three Leading Organizations. *International Journal of Conceptual Structures and Smart Applications, 4*(1), 71–99. doi:10.4018/IJCSSA.2016010104

von Rosing, M., & von Scheel, H. (2016). Using the Business Ontology to Develop Enterprise Standards. *International Journal of Conceptual Structures and Smart Applications, 4*(1), 48–70. doi:10.4018/IJCSSA.2016010103

Walczak, S. (2016). Artificial Neural Networks and other AI Applications for Business Management Decision Support. *International Journal of Sociotechnology and Knowledge Development, 8*(4), 1–20. doi:10.4018/IJSKD.2016100101

Wamba, S. F., Akter, S., Kang, H., Bhattacharya, M., & Upal, M. (2016). The Primer of Social Media Analytics. *Journal of Organizational and End User Computing, 28*(2), 1–12. doi:10.4018/JOEUC.2016040101

Wang, C., Schofield, M., Li, X., & Ou, X. (2017). Do Chinese Students in Public and Private Higher Education Institutes Perform at Different Level in One of the Leadership Skills: Critical Thinking?: An Exploratory Comparison. In V. Wang (Ed.), *Encyclopedia of Strategic Leadership and Management* (pp. 160–181). Hershey, PA: IGI Global. doi:10.4018/978-1-5225-1049-9.ch013

Wang, F., Raisinghani, M. S., Mora, M., & Wang, X. (2016). Strategic E-Business Management through a Balanced Scored Card Approach. In I. Lee (Ed.), *Encyclopedia of E-Commerce Development, Implementation, and Management* (pp. 361–386). Hershey, PA: IGI Global. doi:10.4018/978-1-4666-9787-4.ch027

Wang, J. (2017). Multi-Agent based Production Management Decision System Modelling for the Textile Enterprise. *Journal of Global Information Management, 25*(4), 1–15. doi:10.4018/JGIM.2017100101

Wiedemann, A., & Gewald, H. (2017). Examining Cross-Domain Alignment: The Correlation of Business Strategy, IT Management, and IT Business Value. *International Journal of IT/Business Alignment and Governance, 8*(1), 17–31. doi:10.4018/IJITBAG.2017010102

Wolf, R., & Thiel, M. (2018). Advancing Global Business Ethics in China: Reducing Poverty Through Human and Social Welfare. In S. Hipsher (Ed.), *Examining the Private Sector's Role in Wealth Creation and Poverty Reduction* (pp. 67–84). Hershey, PA: IGI Global. doi:10.4018/978-1-5225-3117-3.ch004

Wu, J., Ding, F., Xu, M., Mo, Z., & Jin, A. (2016). Investigating the Determinants of Decision-Making on Adoption of Public Cloud Computing in E-government. *Journal of Global Information Management, 24*(3), 71–89. doi:10.4018/JGIM.2016070104

Xu, L., & de Vrieze, P. (2016). Building Situational Applications for Virtual Enterprises. In I. Lee (Ed.), *Encyclopedia of E-Commerce Development, Implementation, and Management* (pp. 715–724). Hershey, PA: IGI Global. doi:10.4018/978-1-4666-9787-4.ch050

Yablonsky, S. (2018). Innovation Platforms: Data and Analytics Platforms. In *Multi-Sided Platforms (MSPs) and Sharing Strategies in the Digital Economy: Emerging Research and Opportunities* (pp. 72–95). Hershey, PA: IGI Global. doi:10.4018/978-1-5225-5457-8.ch003

Yusoff, A., Ahmad, N. H., & Halim, H. A. (2017). Agropreneurship among Gen Y in Malaysia: The Role of Academic Institutions. In N. Ahmad, T. Ramayah, H. Halim, & S. Rahman (Eds.), *Handbook of Research on Small and Medium Enterprises in Developing Countries* (pp. 23–47). Hershey, PA: IGI Global. doi:10.4018/978-1-5225-2165-5.ch002

Zanin, F., Comuzzi, E., & Costantini, A. (2018). The Effect of Business Strategy and Stock Market Listing on the Use of Risk Assessment Tools. In *Management Control Systems in Complex Settings: Emerging Research and Opportunities* (pp. 145–168). Hershey, PA: IGI Global. doi:10.4018/978-1-5225-3987-2.ch007

Zgheib, P. W. (2017). Corporate Innovation and Intrapreneurship in the Middle East. In P. Zgheib (Ed.), *Entrepreneurship and Business Innovation in the Middle East* (pp. 37–56). Hershey, PA: IGI Global. doi:10.4018/978-1-5225-2066-5.ch003

About the Contributors

Ilkben Akansel, Dr., gained her Assoc. Prof. Dr. title in 2017 in Economics Thought. She graduated from two different B.A., firstly in economics department; secondly in business administration, her M. Sc. was in economics too. She decided to gain her Ph.D. in another field, public relations. She was appointed as an Assist. Prof. Dr. in Business and Administration department in University of Artvin Faculty of Economics and Administrative Sciences. She decided to make her Assoc. Prof. Dr. proficiency exam in economics field. She was appointed as Assoc. Prof. Dr. in University of Bartin, Faculty of Economics and Administrative Sciences in Economics department. She has several international publications. She has been published many articles with some international indexes. Her areas of specialization are Institutional Economics, Political Economics, Public Relations. Her graduations are University of Gazi (Ankara, Turkey), Anadolu University of Business Administration (Eskişehir, Turkey), University of Ankara (Ankara, Turkey).

* * *

H. Isil Alkan is Assistant Professor in Department of Economics of Faculty of Economics and Administrative Sciences, Ondokuz Mayıs University. She holds B.A. from Economics (Gazi University), M.A. from Agricultural Economics (Ondokuz Mayıs University) and Ph. D. from Economics (Gazi University). She has teaching and research experience in the area of Economy Policy, Agricultural Economics and Gender Economics. She has several manuscripts, conference papers and book chapters in the stated fields. She is the author of the book; Female Labour in Agriculture Sector (Gazi Bookstore, 2018).

Tugba Aydin Halisoglu is Assistant Professor at Artvin Coruh University, Department of Political Science and Public Administration. She obtained her BA and MA degrees in Public Administration at Akdeniz University and PhD in Political

Theory at Luiss Guido Carli University. Her academic interests are in the fields of nationalism, migration, citizenship, European Union and Central Asian relations.

Ilke Civelekoglu, University of Virginia, PhD, is a full-time associate professor at Istanbul Ticaret University. She specializes in international and comparative political economy. She published several book chapters and various articles in journals, such as Turkish Studies, International Development, and Uluslararasi Iliskiler Dergisi.

Derya Guler Aydin received a master's degree in Economics from Hacettepe University, and the Ph.D. degree in Economics from Hacettepe University, Ankara, Turkey in 2002 and 2008, respectively. She conducted postdoctoral research at Sheffield University in 2011. She is currently working as an Associate Professor at the Department of Economics, Hacettepe University. Her research interests include History of Economic Analysis, Methodology of Science, Institutional Economics and Feminist Economics.

Ikbal Maulana is a researcher in the Research Center for Science, Technology and Innovation Policy and Management, Indonesian Institute of Sciences (P2KMI – LIPI). His research interests include sociology of knowledge, sociology of technology, philosophy of technology and media studies. Recently, due to what happen in Indonesian politics and society, he focuses his research on the impact of social media on politics, social transformation, as well as individual transformation.

Kubra Onder was born in Ankara. She graduated from Gazi University, Faculty of Economics and Administrative Sciences, Department of Economics. She has a master's degree from the same university and a PhD degree from Süleyman Demirel University. She started working as a specialist and manager in the Ministry of National Defense. She has worked as an assistant professor at Burdur Mehmet Akif Ersoy University from February 2015 until April 2019. She is currently working as an Associate Professor at the Department of Economics, Mehmet Akif Ersoy University. Her research interests inculude micro economy, industrial economics, time series, and panel data analysis.

Itir Ozer-Imer received a master's degree in Economics from Hacettepe University, and the Ph.D. degree in Economics from Hacettepe University, Ankara, Turkey in 2001 and 2007, respectively. She has conducted postdoctoral research at George Mason University, School of Public Policy from February 2011 until February 2012. She is currently working as an Associate Professor at the Department of International Relations, Hacettepe University. Her research interests include international political economy, economic development, international trade and finance, and economic integration.

Başak Özoral received her Ph.D. from the McGill University in 2011. Her research focuses on political economy, modernization in the Middle East, economy and culture in the Middle East and globalization. She taught at Qatar University and American University in Dubai for five years. She teaches courses on the Middle East, political economy, and research methods, and she regularly co-authors papers with graduate students at Istanbul Commerce University.

Muhammet Sahin was born in Van. He graduated from Suleyman Demirel University, Faculty of Economics and Administrative Sciences, Department of Finance. He has a master's degree and a PhD degree from the same university. He started working as an officer The Ministry of Finance. In 2009, he started to work as an assistant professor at Gumushane University. He has been working as a Dr. lecturer.

Pınar Yardımcı was hired as the lecturer in public finance and economics by the Silifke-Tasucu Vocational School at The University of Selcuk in 1992. She received her MS in Economics from the University of Cukurova in 1997 and PhD in Economics from the University of Selcuk in 2006. She is currently associate professor of international economics and Head of Foreign Trade Department in the Silifke-Tasucu Vocational School at The University of Selcuk. She is the author of International Economic Institutions (2014, Detay Publishing) and studies about economic development and international economics.

Gloria Zúñiga y Postigo, is an Associate Professor of Philosophy at Ashford University in the United States. She heads the business ethics program, and oversees the curriculum design and management of the online course offerings in business ethics. Her areas of expertise fall in the interdisciplinary area known as philosophy, politics, and economics. She is particularly interested in examinations of social phenomena (known in philosophy as social ontology, or the philosophy of society). This includes the description of the various domains of the human social world, including that objects that constitute them and the relations among them), and the dynamics among the different kinds of value phenomena in social reality. Dr. Zúñiga y Postigo's work is influenced by the Austro-German philosophical tradition, including thinkers such as Brentano, Meinong, Ehrenfels, Husserl, Reinach, and Stein. She also draws from the contributions of the Austrian School of Economics, especially Menger and Hayek. Dr. Zúñiga y Postigo's current research pertains to business ethics, and affective phenomena, especially empathy in the tradition of Edith Stein. Her interests is in neuroethics, neurophenomenology, and evolutionary economics has also shed light on examination of Hayek's Sensory Order, especially the role of intersubjectivity in the mechanics of choice. She also explores the geography of different understandings of responsibility, from corporate social responsibility, social capital, to the framework of commutative and distribute justice in Catholic social thought.

Index

19th century 2, 28, 30, 86, 92, 196

A

Akerlof 33, 185
artifact 227, 237-241, 243-244, 254
asymmetric information 28, 30, 33-34, 47, 101

B

behavioral economics 2, 176-177, 179, 185, 188-190

C

Carl Menger 213-214
Celeb 202, 208
complexity science 84-86, 89-92, 97, 101-102, 106, 113, 125
conspicious consumption 8
Constabulary 200, 208
consumer 9, 11, 32, 48-53, 57-61, 64, 180, 183-184, 238, 244
consumer behaviors 60
consumer culture 48, 50, 52-53, 57-60, 64
consumer society 9, 52, 64
consumerism 49-52, 55, 57, 60, 64
consumerism in the Gulf 55
critical theory 66, 69, 74-75, 77-78, 80-81
Cultural Capital 64
cultural identity 55, 60

D

developing countries 28, 52, 96, 98, 234-236, 242, 245-250, 252-254
discrimination 3, 7, 10, 12, 14-16, 18-19, 26, 31, 36
Dubai 48-50, 53-60, 64

E

economic nationalism 92, 127, 129, 131, 141
economic objects 212, 227, 231
economic value 42, 212, 214-215, 217-219, 222-224, 228, 231
epistemic 219-220, 231
ethics 148, 213-214
EU 102-104, 106-108, 113, 127-129, 132-136, 139-141, 145, 170
European Union 84-85, 99, 102, 108, 127-128, 134, 139-141
experimental economics 176-177, 187-189
externality 32, 38, 42-43, 47

F

feminist economics 1-13, 15-17, 19-21, 26

G

gender 2-10, 13-22, 26, 132
global economic institutions 97
global economic system 84

globalization 15, 18, 37, 39, 49-50, 52-54, 56-58, 60-61, 85, 92, 95, 97-98, 100-101, 107, 113, 131, 166-167, 170-171
governance 161, 170-172, 234, 248, 254
government intervention 27, 29-30, 33, 42, 92

H

heteredox economics 26
homo economicus 16, 146, 152, 154, 176-179, 187, 189-190
Horizontal Segregation 14, 26
HUMAN UNDERSTANDING 70

I

idle class 14, 18
Incomplete Competition Market 47
innovation 84-85, 91-98, 100-113, 126, 244-246, 250-252
innovation system 85, 93-98, 101, 103-109, 111-113, 126, 252
institution 4, 6-7, 10, 13-14, 169, 251
institutional economics 1-4, 6-8, 10, 13-14, 16-22, 26, 91
Irregular Migration 127, 129, 132-133, 136, 139, 145

J

John Searle 219

K

Kahneman 179, 181-184, 187, 189
Kant 87, 146-154, 222-223
knowledge 47, 51, 66-71, 73-76, 78, 80, 84-86, 89, 91, 93-95, 97-101, 103-105, 108, 112-114, 125-126, 147-149, 152, 154, 176-178, 185-186, 213-214, 224, 231, 236-239, 241-243, 245-247, 249-250, 253-254
knowledge-based economy 84-85, 93-95, 100, 103, 113, 125

M

mainstream economics 1-3, 18-19, 66, 69, 91, 154, 176-178, 181, 185-186, 190
market 7, 14-20, 27-43, 47, 50-53, 77, 92-93, 97, 99-104, 128, 139-140, 152, 162, 166-170, 172, 179, 190, 197-202, 205-206, 226, 235-236, 239, 242, 244, 247-250, 252-254
market failure 27-30, 32, 35, 38, 41-43, 47, 100, 102, 252
Mersin RIS Plus project 84, 107, 109, 111-114
migration 112, 127-129, 132-133, 135-137, 139-140, 145
money 9, 11-13, 40, 113, 165, 198-199, 212, 215, 217, 226-227, 231, 240, 242, 253

N

narh 196-197, 199-202, 204-206, 209
narh prices 196, 199, 201-202, 205
Narh system 201, 204-205
nationalism 92, 127-131, 141, 145, 246
neoclassical economics 1-2, 7, 15, 17, 19, 47, 176-179, 181, 189-190, 248
neuroeconomics 176-177, 188-189
noumenon 146, 149-153

O

ontology 171, 212-215, 217-218, 222, 225, 227, 231
ontology of economics 213, 217-218
Ottomans 201

P

Paul Anthony Samuelson 47
phenomenon 2, 5, 31, 34, 48, 50, 52, 68, 149, 152-154, 169-170, 227-228
philosophy 1-2, 8, 10, 21, 29, 66-68, 70, 75-76, 84-86, 89, 148, 205, 212-215, 219, 224, 228, 231
Positive Economics 146, 152, 154

positivism 67-74, 78-80
primordial approach 127, 129, 131-132
Profiteering 198-199, 201, 209
public goods 27-30, 35-43, 47

R

rationalism 67, 74, 148
rationality 17-19, 28, 30, 47, 78, 89, 93, 153, 176-181, 183-184, 189-190
refugees 127, 134-135, 139-141
regional development 84-85, 92-93, 95, 97-99, 102, 105, 107-108, 110, 168
regional innovation systems 85, 95, 102, 113

S

Scale Economics 47
segregation 3, 12, 14, 18, 26
sense of belonging 127-129, 131-132, 136-137, 140-141
social objects 215-217, 222, 227, 231
social ontology 215
socio-technical system 243-246, 250, 254
spontaneous orders 231
state 4, 10, 28-29, 71, 93, 101, 129-130, 133, 135, 138, 141, 162-172, 197-198, 200, 202, 205, 209, 236, 252
subjective 68, 76, 141, 150, 163, 178, 212, 218-220, 222, 231-232
subjectivity 68, 212, 214-215, 218
Syria 127-128
Systems Theory 86-88, 126

T

technological capability 234-236, 242, 245-247, 249, 254
technology development 102, 235, 239-243, 245, 250-251, 253
Thaler 179, 181, 183-184, 189-190
the Ottoman Archives 196-197, 201, 209
the UAE 48-49, 54-58, 60-61, 64
The United Arab Emirates (UAE) 64
Tversky 181-184, 189

U

urban actors 162-163, 172
urban development 161-164, 166, 168-169, 172

V

Veblen 1-3, 5-22, 51, 87
Vertical Segregation 14, 26

Ensure Quality Research is Introduced to the Academic Community

Become an IGI Global Reviewer for Authored Book Projects

The overall success of an authored book project is dependent on quality and timely reviews.

In this competitive age of scholarly publishing, constructive and timely feedback significantly expedites the turnaround time of manuscripts from submission to acceptance, allowing the publication and discovery of forward-thinking research at a much more expeditious rate. Several IGI Global authored book projects are currently seeking highly-qualified experts in the field to fill vacancies on their respective editorial review boards:

Applications and Inquiries may be sent to:
development@igi-global.com

Applicants must have a doctorate (or an equivalent degree) as well as publishing and reviewing experience. Reviewers are asked to complete the open-ended evaluation questions with as much detail as possible in a timely, collegial, and constructive manner. All reviewers' tenures run for one-year terms on the editorial review boards and are expected to complete at least three reviews per term. Upon successful completion of this term, reviewers can be considered for an additional term.

If you have a colleague that may be interested in this opportunity, we encourage you to share this information with them.

www.ingramcontent.com/pod-product-compliance
Lightning Source LLC
LaVergne TN
LVHW081344300926
849161LV00008B/2062